Fortunate One

To Brad Westbrook,

A great friend and Ally.

Keep the faith,

Guy [signature] Nov 5 2021

Fortunate One

From Nantucket to
the White House:
A Memoir

GARY HOLMES

ACADEMY
PRESS

For permission requests, write to the below address:

PYP Academy Press
141 Weston Street, #155
Hartford, CT, 06141

The opinions expressed by the author are not necessarily those held by PYP Academy Press.

Ordering Information: Quantity sales and special discounts are available on quantity purchases by corporations, associations, and others. For details, contact the author at: garyholmes76@gmail.com.

Edited by: Chloë Siennah
Cover design by: Nelly Murariu
Typeset by: Medlar Publishing Solutions Pvt Ltd., India

Printed in the United States of America.
ISBN: 978-1-955985-06-2 (hardcover)
ISBN: 978-1-955985-05-5 (paperback)
ISBN: 978-1-955985-07-9 (ebook)

Library of Congress Control Number: 2021917554

First edition, October 2021.

The information contained within this book is strictly for informational purposes. The material may include information, products, or services by third parties. As such, the Author and Publisher do not assume responsibility or liability for any third-party material or opinions. The publisher is not responsible for websites (or their content) that are not owned by the publisher. Readers are advised to do their own due diligence when it comes to making decisions.

The mission of the Publish Your Purpose Academy Press is to discover and publish authors who are striving to make a difference in the world. We give underrepresented voices power and a stage to share their stories, speak their truth, and impact their communities. Do you have a book idea you would like us to consider publishing? Please visit PublishYourPurposePress.com for more information.

 PYP Academy Press
141 Weston Street, #155
Hartford, CT, 06141

*This memoir is dedicated to
my parents and the values they tried to instill in me*

Contents

Introduction

've been a little hesitant to tell people I was writing this memoir because whenever I did, they'd inevitably ask why, as in, who are *you* to write an autobiography? Trust me, it's a question I've posed to myself. I'm not famous, don't have a tragic childhood to resolve therapeutically through the written word, and have no commercial venture to advance through the promotion of a "personal brand."

I could fall back on the cliché that everybody has a story to tell, but if you've ever listened to a golfer recount his most recent round, you know that not every story is equally compelling. It will be up to you, Dear Reader, to determine whether my story was worth telling, but here are my goals: to recapture a world that no longer exists and to evoke what it was like to be born in the '50s, grow up in the '60s, attend college in the '70s, and start a career in the '80s. I know this isn't exactly the same as Laura Ingalls Wilder recounting her experiences in that little house on the prairie, but the social and technological changes that have occurred since the 1950s are almost as dramatic as the ones she lived through.

To some extent, my story parallels that of millions of other baby boomers born in the mid-1950s. I'm probably not the only seven year old who ate orange-flavored aspirin when he couldn't find candy in the house or walked unescorted to school while dodging potentially pedophilic kidnappers and speeding 18-wheelers. I want readers my age to nod in recognition and say, "Yeah, that happened to me too," and I hope that later generations will marvel that we ever survived childhood or managed to launch ourselves into adulthood.

But just as every index finger is fundamentally the same while every fingerprint is different, the story that follows is undeniably, uniquely my own. I entered the world on Nantucket Island, grew up in a declining industrial city, almost failed college, worked as a small-town reporter, and eventually landed in the White House. Along the way, I lived in a haunted house; had not one, but two lesbian girlfriends in high school; wrote newspaper stories about a Manhattan scientist who disappeared one morning from a remote, iced-in island; sparred with the owner of the *Washington Post*; chatted up a couple of U.S. Presidents; and helped prepare the debate remarks that almost torpedoed the re-election campaign for one of them.

It's taken me two years to write this book, but in truth, it's been 60 years in the making. As long as I can remember, I've felt the autobiographical impulse. In the *second grade*, at the tender age of eight, I made my first attempt at a memoir, scribbling out three paragraphs before abandoning the effort to do my arithmetic assignment instead. Ever since, I've been cataloguing my life—a project that sometimes verged on hoarding. I kept every letter and postcard that arrived in my mailbox, stored many important school papers, and maintained boxes of junior and senior high school yearbooks, datebooks, calendars, and relevant newspaper clippings. My mother saved my report cards and my correspondence from vacations and college. Starting in my mid-20s, I religiously kept a daily diary. Holding onto memories, both through physical materials and, more mystically, in the inscrutable regions of the hippocampus, neocortex, and amygdala, has been a life-long obsession.

I reviewed all this documentation before I started writing, reading every letter and diary entry through November 1988. The experience mostly confirmed my existing memories, although in some cases I had been wrong about chronology or had remembered events out of sequence. In other cases, I was reminded of people who had completely vanished from my active memory. Who exactly was that college classmate who sent me those three letters in the summer of 1975? Had I really shared so many cocktails and dinners with those former colleagues in Washington, D.C.? Some of these rediscoveries I folded into this narrative; the rest I just re-deposited into my already overstuffed memory bank.

Excavating these memories was sometimes a delight, sometimes painful, and often just plain embarrassing, curing me of a misconception that life was better then than it is now. I wish I could send a message back in time and advise the earlier version of myself to lighten up, not fret about the future so much, and not get aggravated so easily. I would tell the younger Gary: You can't control your destiny, but don't worry, you're lucky. You won't win the lottery, but you *will* win the lottery of life.

In some respects, it was easier to write 100,000 words of memories than it was to come up with the two words that formed the title. My college friend, Jim Robinson, who plays such a crucial role in this story, initially suggested "Fortune Son," which would have been perfect, except I didn't want people thinking they were getting John Fogarty's life story. In the end, he helped me settle on "Fortunate One."

A political progressive might take one look at my life and dismiss it as "privileged." A person of faith might look at the same set of facts and say I was "blessed." Whatever term you want to use, I certainly concede that good fortune smiled on me from the day I was born. Being white, male, and straight provided me with advantages, but to be born in America to nurturing, hard-working, married parents was the biggest break of all. As if that wasn't enough, I grew up free from financial anxiety because the small business my parents created prospered during a prosperous era. Although I skirted close to physical injury many times, I always escaped with mere scars or skinned knees. I had robust health, access to good education, and exposure to friends who stimulated me intellectually and socially. Importantly, the women I dated were perceptive enough to see that I was ultimately not right for them, so I was available when the right one did enter my life.

I can make the case that the children of 1950s America were the luckiest generation in history. The advances in medicine alone—the vaccines, antibiotics, and new surgical procedures—made sure that a record number of us reached adulthood. I had pneumonia in the fourth grade, something that merits a mere half sentence in this story; if I'd been born 20 years earlier, I might not have lived long enough to write anything. We were lucky to be born into the richest, most dominant national economy the world had ever seen, which created huge opportunities for us to leap ahead of our parents economically, a gift that has not always been available to our own children.

More specifically, I'd argue that the boys born in 1954 were the luckiest of a lucky generation: old enough to experience the Beatles but just young enough to avoid getting drafted; old enough to benefit from the sexual revolution and co-ed dorms, but young enough not to come to maturity worrying about AIDS and STDs; old enough to feel safe and secure at school or walking down the street, but young enough to avoid the social conformities of the 1950s; old enough to assume college was a given for any smart kid, but young enough to miss the crippling anxiety of getting into the "right" school or assuming massive debt.

Even with all this happy talk about good fortune, I'm no Pollyanna about the bumps along the way, and I've tried to be as truthful as possible without going out of my way to settle scores. My goal is not to embarrass people, so in a few cases I have changed names, particularly those of some former bosses and colleagues in Washington. I haven't said anything libelous or even unfair; they were nice enough to hire me, so I don't want to make them feel betrayed, even 35 years later. To avoid cumbersome circumlocutions like "my new boss, who I'll call John," readers can assume that if I provide a given name and surname, it's real. If I only mention a first name, it's been changed.

Some "real" names I'd like to thank for being early readers and editors are three of my oldest school friends, Jim Robinson, Philip Tasho, and Liz Prevett, who confirmed many of my memories, called out awkward writing, and generally kept me from making self-inflicted mistakes. I also had close editing help from a former colleague, Tim Clifford, who tragically died of ALS before I finished the drafting. My wife, Meg Ricci, also read an early draft. Finally, I had the assistance of a professional editor, Chloë Siennah. I didn't always take their advice, so they are blameless for any offenses made against the historical record or prevailing political and social orthodoxies.

This volume ends when I'm 34 years old, which is chronologically the midpoint of my life—so far at least. It also marks the conclusion of my searching period. During these first three decades, I was trying to figure out who I wanted to be. By the time I reach the last pages of the final chapter, I am more or less fully formed. And upon reflection I've realized that most of the major lucky breaks of my life—the moments when my path could have veered significantly in another direction—occurred during this first half of my life. Good fortune has continued to bless me since then, but the only remaining "hinge" moment of almost unbelievably good luck left to describe is the birth of my son. He truly has been a "fortunate son," but that's for another book.

CHAPTER 1

Birth

On the day of my birth—13 months into the Eisenhower presidency and six months before Elvis released his first hit record—my very pregnant mother woke up feeling so odd that she stayed home instead of driving out to milk the cows. Only 21 years old, she and my 22-year-old father owned a small dairy about five miles out of town on the flat and then-deserted south shore of Nantucket Island. Yes, in those days, Nantucket had a dairy farmer, and that farmer was my father.

Early in her pregnancy, my mother asked her doctor when she should go to the hospital. His answer? "You'll know." This was in the benighted days before "What to Expect" books, Lamaze classes, and sonograms, but he was right. As the day of March 5th, 1954 wore on, she did, in fact, know that the time had come.

Returning from his milking duties at noon, my father discovered what he surely must have suspected when he left a few hours earlier—that his young wife was in the early stages of labor. My mother, not knowing when she'd eat again, prepared a robust lunch that they ate together, and then, after one last cigarette to calm her nerves, asked to be driven to the hospital.

Her destination—the original Nantucket Cottage Hospital—was neither a cottage nor a hospital as we'd understand the terms today. Imagine your grandmother's house, but outfitted with a few hospital beds and some medical equipment. That's what this was, a rudimentary medical facility created in 1912 out of a pair of weathered two-story 18th century houses. Connecting these former dwellings was a passageway that served as entrance, lobby, business center, and reception area. Turn right from the front door and you'd end up in the nurses' residence; turn left and you'd enter the medical care part of the facility.

My mother had been born in this very building two decades earlier—delivered in fact by the same physician, Dr. Ernest Menges, who met her there later that afternoon. Not much about birth rituals had changed since my mother's own birth, especially the role of fathers. In keeping with the iron law of mid-century obstetrics, my father's participation in the birthing

The original Nantucket Cottage Hospital,
photo courtesy of the Nantucket Historical Association.

process consisted solely of depositing his wife at the front desk. With that task successfully accomplished, there was nothing else for him to do but drive back to the farm for the afternoon milking and pensively await the phone call announcing whether he'd become the proud father of a girl or a boy.

The hospital staff directed my mother from the front desk to a small room across the hall where she herself had been born. This chamber was used by two types of patients: women in labor and terminal patients who were not expected to live long; functioning, in other words, as Nantucket's version of the circle of life.

The only people in attendance for my birth were Dr. Menges and two nurses, one of whom was my father's maiden lady aunt, Edith Holmes, the hospital's gentle, capable, and cheerful head of nursing. Mothers and best friends did not come rushing over with temple massages and heating pads to provide moral support. And if a midwife had arrived, she would have been treated like a witch doctor and driven into the street.

I'm told that the birth itself—at 7:15pm—was unremarkable, consisting mostly of contractions, cooling compresses, and at the end, a whiff of gas to numb the pain and induce outright unconsciousness. Soon after the deed was done, I was whisked away to the nursery while my mother slowly regained consciousness. She was then walked to a small, three-bed women's ward on the second floor and wasn't allowed to see me until the following morning. The umbilical cord was definitely not put in cold storage for future use.

The bill for the delivery—there was no insurance—came to $150.

No one arrived at the hospital the next day with a camera to capture my first gurgles and I escaped the nursery only sporadically for tightly regulated bottle feedings. Even my father was denied a glance of his firstborn until the next day's visiting hours and not a moment sooner.

My parents named me Gary, although until the last minute, I was going to be Glenn. My mother was looking for a given name that theoretically couldn't be shortened into a nickname. My uncle had the perfectly respectable birth name of James and she believed a grown man should not have the misfortune of being stuck with a diminutive like "Jimmy" all his life. She switched at the last minute, reasoning there is no cutesy moniker for Gary either. Alas, there is almost no name, no matter how short or monosyllabic, that cannot be made into a nickname, and various friends would later call me "Gare." My wife takes it a step further, sometimes calling me "Ga" when she's feeling particularly affectionate. (For what it's worth, my brother-in-law calls his best friend "Glenny," so there's no winning this game.)

Despite being completely healthy, I didn't leave the hospital for a week—after which I was driven home by my father, cradled in my mother's arms as she sat in the car's front seat, completely unprotected by not-yet-invented seat belts or infant car seats. Modern mothers who are familiar with being dumped onto the street after one night in the maternity wing might be interested to know that 1950s best practices required the mother to remain in the hospital for at least seven days to recover from the rigors of labor. In this regard, she was luckier than my grandmother, who, having given birth in the 1930s, was sentenced to two whole weeks of hospital bed rest. She later claimed those were the two most boring weeks of her life.

Naturally, there were no televisions or radios—never mind internet devices—to amuse young mothers as they lay in the women's ward, but my mother considered herself relatively fortunate because she occupied the bed nearest the window and could look out to West Chester Street to see who was arriving and leaving the hospital.

A few days after I was born, I had company in the nursery. Another young mother had also delivered a baby boy. This small detail never came up until three decades later, when I heard that Nantucket had just recorded its first murder since the Civil War. My mother casually informed me that the perpetrator and I had been born practically at the same time and had even shared space in the nursery. She remembered being in the women's ward with his mother.

It turned out that my first roommate, a hardened townie, had been in and out of trouble with the law for most of his life. Arrested for receiving stolen property at 17; arrested again for fighting with a police officer at 24. Now, at age 29, he had shot a long-time adversary in the stomach, becoming the protagonist in a case that drew national attention thanks to the mystery novel headlines: "A Murder on Nantucket." Eventually he was convicted of premeditated murder, had the sentence reduced to manslaughter, and was retried and convicted a second time before being sentenced to 14–20 years in Walpole state prison.

For most people, this story was a curiosity. But what I couldn't stop thinking about were the vagaries of fate. The two of us slept next to each other right out of the womb and never saw each other again. His family had stayed put on Nantucket with its insular and sometimes grievance-filled culture; mine had moved away, where I'd had all the advantages of an upwardly mobile household. What if the nurses had mixed us up in our bassinets? Would I have turned out to be a murderer? How is it, I wondered, that two babies lying side by side in the same nursery, born to two local working class mothers from similar backgrounds and with similar prospects, could end up in such different places?

Not for the first time, I observed that life is just one roll of the dice after another.

CHAPTER 2

Early Nantucket

My parents, the dairy farmers, had been high school sweethearts—two out of 22 graduates of the Nantucket High School class of 1950.

My mother, an island native with a genealogical line stretching back to Nantucket's founding father, Tristram Coffin, had been born Jean Harris and her family could boast of a whaling captain ancestor from the 1840s (Captain Samuel Harris of the whaler *Phoebe*—we still have his Captain's logs). Her more recent progenitors, though, were humble and landlocked islanders who simply did their work, went to church, and tried not to stand out.

Her father, Arthur Harris, was a carpenter and property caretaker. He and my great-grandfather, Lester Harris, built and maintained homes for the genteel WASPs who then constituted the island's summer population. Every Sunday in the long off-season, he would load the family into their station wagon and check the unoccupied houses for which he was responsible. Then, they would park at one of the island's many beaches and watch the waves roll in. This was not a routine that an active child like my mother would find terribly stimulating.

A phlegmatic bear-like man who ambled through life on bad knees caused by too much roof work, my grandfather would later express surprise that the Harrises had produced such an energetic daughter. "She could wear out a beaver," he'd marvel later in life. Friends, sports, school activities—my mother woke up each morning eager to accomplish something and stayed on the go all day until her head hit the pillow.

My father almost matched her in energy and determination. The fifth of six children (and thusly named Quentin), he was a classic scamp—the mischievous one in an old Yankee household that valued order and good behavior. The impishness hadn't gone over well with his stern parents and he always self-identified as the black sheep of the family. His case wasn't helped when he was held back in the second grade. It pained me greatly—it really did hurt my heart—when, even in his 80s, he would later refer to himself as the "dumb one" in the family, which he certainly was not. No one in that family was "dumb." Nowadays, he would likely be diagnosed with attention deficit disorder, but at that time there was no coddling of boys who didn't fall immediately into line.

His parents may not have appreciated his devilishness, but my mother certainly did when the two of them crossed paths one summer as young teens in the mid-1940s.

This is how they met. My paternal grandfather, Carl Holmes, had graduated from the Massachusetts Marine Academy in the early 1920s, and spent a few years at sea before settling down as a telephone company technician in the mid-sized industrial city of Brockton, Massachusetts. But his dream had always been to grow flowers. To that end, he built a few greenhouses and created a flower business out of the family home in Brockton.

My grandfather was surprisingly notional for a sober-minded old Yankee. He had visited Nantucket in the late 1930s and impulsively decided that was the life for him. He bought some abandoned island farmland a few years later, figuring the climate would be ideal for cultivating gladiolus. He wasn't wrong about that, and for several years during and after the war, the Holmes family would pack up and move to the island during the summer to labor in the flower fields.

It was inevitable on that tightly interwoven island that a local girl and a summer boy would eventually come across one another. When she was 13, my mother and a friend were making a bit of pocket change at the local bowling alley by resetting pins (there were no automatic pin-setting machines in those days, or rigidly enforced child labor laws, for that matter) when a towheaded eighth-grader walked in and started flirting with them. Being the wise guy that he was, he wouldn't divulge his name, so they called him "Butch." Somehow, over the course of the summer, my mother managed to wrangle not only his name but his home address. She then initiated a correspondence during the school year, and when he returned the following summer, they just picked up where they left off. It certainly didn't hurt that he was now a foot taller than when he'd left in September.

Two years after V-J Day, my grandfather took the plunge, selling the Brockton house, complete with greenhouses and a small floral business called Holmes Greenhouses, to my Aunt Jean and Uncle Jimmy and moving the family to the island year-round. He became a full-time flower farmer and my grandmother turned their house on Fair Street into a small bed and breakfast. My father and his brother, Wayne, joined my mother in the Nantucket High School Class of 1950. Soon thereafter, my parents' casual summer flirting ripened into traditional high school dating.

There was nothing glamorous or high society about Nantucket in those days. Located 30 miles to sea off Cape Cod and accessible primarily via a three-hour ferry ride from Woods Hole, the island's tourist season lasted only from the end of the school year in late June through Labor Day. There were a handful of big airy hotels, some cozy guest houses, and a few seasonal restaurants. The island bustled in the summer but it wasn't frantic like it is today. The "summer people" contributed enough money during those ten weeks to keep the island afloat for the rest of the year. But even with a small fishing economy, no one was getting rich.

For high school students surrounded by the same handful of kids they'd known since first grade, they might as well have been growing up in an isolated town in Texas or Alaska. The broad expanses of wild, low-growth bushes and shrubs that now seem so romantic to off-islanders and naturalists were

My parents at their senior high school dance.

vaguely oppressive to teenagers who wanted more out of life. No wonder half of them couldn't wait to get the hell off that rock and see what the outside world had to offer.

And yet it wasn't a bad place to grow up. At their intimate class reunions, my parents and their classmates would start telling stories and always end up laughing through the night. In a way, they had it easier than the generations that came after them. Born in the Depression with only radio and their own imaginations to amuse themselves, their expectations were low.

One way to experience the outside world was through athletics. My father played football, basketball, and baseball, and my mother was on the girls' basketball team. For away games, they'd take the afternoon ferry to Woods Hole, drive to their opponents' town and play the game or games, then stay overnight in the spare bedrooms of the opposing players, returning to Nantucket the next morning. Because the school trusted them not to get into serious trouble, they'd be lightly supervised and get up to a lot of relatively benign hijinks.

With only 22 graduates, the Class of 1950 could not afford traditional photo-based yearbooks, but they did cobble together a mimeographed collection of memories. As a kid, I could not get enough of flipping through those already-weathering pages. I learned that my father's nickname was "Squint," which is better than Paul Conway, who was known all his life as "Coot." And although Gardner Ceely wrote in the class book that his favorite amusement was "making love," it was my father who was named "Class Sheik."

At graduation, more boys in their class headed to the military than to college. My father, who had graduated from the island's small vocational program, did neither. He spent two semesters at the University of Massachusetts' agricultural school, where he studied animal husbandry so he could learn how to make a living from cows. For her part, my mother attended a business school in Boston where she trained to be a bookkeeper.

Back from their brief educational sojourns, they married in the fall of 1951 in Nantucket's First Congregational Church. She was 19 and he was 20. My father shaved once a week and neither of them were even old enough to drink. They were so young that my father needed to get written approval from his parents to wed. (No such approval was needed for young brides, however, since it was then understood that they matured faster and were more aware of what they were signing up for.) Regardless, teenagers in the 1950s couldn't *wait* to grow up and assume adult responsibilities. None of that "I'm going to be young until I die" nonsense for them.

The modest punch-and-cookies wedding reception in the church parlor was a prelude to the main event—a party for the young guests at a friend's house, during which, according to tradition, the high-spirited pranksters among them would try to uncover the secret location that the bride and groom had been offered for their bridal chamber. This cat-and-mouse game almost always had the same outcome and sure enough, at some point during the night, a small crowd of friends assembled in the street outside my parents' formerly private room and catcalled encouragement and unsolicited advice until they were shooed away.

Upon returning from the week-long bus tour of Maine and New Hampshire that constituted their honeymoon, my parents moved into a small apartment on the second floor of my great-grandparents' house and settled into their new life as dairy farmers. By this time, my grandfather, tired of the cost of shipping flowers off-island, had given up his dream of island horticulture and moved back to the mainland. He sold the farmland to my father. My parents, who bought a small herd of cows, built a barn and a chicken coop and started producing milk and eggs. My mother managed the egg business while my father delivered milk to the homes of their local customers.

The cows became like family, each with their own names and unique personalities, but my mother developed a lifelong aversion to chickens, who she said were "stupid" and would peck to death any of their number who showed signs of injury or blood. Stupid or not, the eggs made more money than the milk ever did.

I wouldn't exactly say that our family was poor since we all ate regularly and had a place to lay our heads, but there was no money to spare. My mother cried the first Christmas after I was born because they could only afford a single small toy, but her fears were unwarranted because I was more than happy playing with the box it came in.

My mother took numerous black and white baby pictures with her Kodak, and in almost every snapshot I am delighted with life. There I am, blonde as can be, laughing as my legs stick out between the spindly slats in my crib—a photo that would today occasion a visit from Child Services. In another, I'm pictured with my already-balding 24-year-old father as we proudly show off our matching bow ties. In a third, I'm flashing a wide-mouthed grin as I sit on my mother's lap while my unsmiling grandparents and outright taciturn great-grandparents stand stiffly behind us in front of a tinsel-covered Christmas tree.

Life was a low-key affair, with a lot of downtime in the long off-season. My parents socialized with other young couples and played canasta, went

My parents and me during our first Christmas together.

With my Nantucket grandparents, Arthur and Francis Harris.

dancing, or drove to the beach after work to cast for fish that would end up on their dinner plates. On Sunday nights, they shared the Sabbath meals with my grandparents and great-grandparents. My father joined the Masons, where my great-grandfather was a long-standing Senior Warden.

It was around this time that the local dentist decided that my father's decaying teeth were too much trouble to salvage and extracted every last tooth in his mouth. He removed half of them before I was born and the rest of them shortly thereafter. I can only assume that this barbarism was considered a dental best practice in the mid-20th century, just as lobotomies were used to treat mental illness, because my father submitted without even asking for a second opinion. For the next 60 years, he had a full set of upper and lower dentures, which he'd occasionally pop out to astonish and amuse wide-eyed five year olds.

Oral healthcare aside, this was a generally happy time for the three of us. And yet my father's bovine dream wasn't working out any better than my grandfather's gladiolus business had. In debt and unable to compete with bigger mainland dairies, he decided to cut his losses after only four years and pursue his fortune on the mainland.

But before departing, we had to wait for my sister to be born. The circumstances of her birth were somewhat different than mine: my mother went into labor after dinner and was taken to the hospital at midnight, where she was once again directed into the small birthing room. The night nurse called Dr. Menges, but he was either out with another patient or too sound asleep to be awakened. These attempts to summon the doctor went on too long for anyone's comfort and eventually the nurses dosed my mother with enough gas to render her unconscious. When she came to, the doctor was there and so was my newborn sister; my mother never knew for sure who really delivered the baby.

My sister is named Thalia after my father's oldest sister. In Greek mythology, this is the name of a goddess, a muse, and a nymph. Why my very serious grandparents landed on such a surprisingly exotic name for their first child remains a mystery. Maybe they were more fanciful than they seemed.

Two weeks after Thalia's birth, our young family boarded a small airplane that bucked and bounced in a legendarily turbulent flight all the way to New Bedford, which was then the closest airport on the mainland. Meanwhile, the cows were loaded onto the Woods Hole ferry. The kids and cattle were all headed in the same direction: to the new farm my grandfather had purchased in East Bridgewater, Massachusetts, the next town over from Brockton. It was time for the next phase of our lives to begin.

CHAPTER 3

East Bridgewater

Fleeing from Nantucket in the winter of 1956, my father and mother were only 25 and 24 years old respectively, but already weighed down by a two-year-old child, a newborn baby, and the accumulated debt from a failed agricultural business. They didn't despair, though. This was the '50s, after all, and the future welcomed bright, ambitious go-getters with open arms.

After moving to East Bridgewater from Nantucket four years earlier, my grandparents had immediately planted gladiolus in the fields and erected a couple of greenhouses for year-round plants. They also built a barn that housed the cows we'd brought over from the island. My father, quickly discovering that selling milk wholesale is not nearly as lucrative as retail, soon disposed of the cows and departed from the business entirely. This resulted in the new barn being used as an expensive shed for my grandfather's tractor. (My father's interest in the dairy business never waned, though. He was still subscribing to the *Jersey Journal*, a trade magazine for dairy cows, when he died more than half a century later.)

The barn and greenhouses were charmingly rustic but the house really stood out. An old, imposing white colonial, well set back from the road,

Pappy and Grandma Holmes's house and farm in East Bridgewater, MA.

My sister and me in my grandparents' living room.

Learning to milk cows in my grandparents' barn.

it must have been a grand dwelling in the early 19th century. My grand-parents occupied demure twin beds in the downstairs front room, and my parents slept upstairs, with Thalia and me nestled in an adjoining alcove. On the other side of the staircase was a rudimentary sitting room where I occasionally sat on a braided rug to watch *The Howdy Doody Show* on our used Admiral TV, the one with a 12-inch screen built into a wooden cabinet with a three-foot high speaker.

Family legend has it that we shared the premises with an uninvited guest from a different dimension. It's true, I lived in a haunted house. This is not a claim I make lightly, but my parents and grandparents were the most no-nonsense people on Earth and if these plainspoken Yankees said a house was haunted, that house was goddamn-well haunted.

The strongest testimony comes from my mother, who saw a translucent figure gliding across the dining room and through a wall early one morning. For me, this evidence is dispositive because my mother is not someone prone to flights of fancy, but there were other more mysterious stories that quickly became family lore. One snowy evening, my grandparents came home to find the house completely empty, save for the dinner that was somehow already cooking on the stove, with no footprints in the snow leading up to the house. There were tales of walking noises coming from the second floor, a spinning wheel that rotated for no obvious reason, and numerous articles of clothing and luggage that would disappear one day only to reappear the next.

Speculation about the source of the haunting quickly zeroed in on a family that had inhabited the house a century earlier and tragically lost their children to illnesses. My grandparents began to refer to our interdimensional visitor as "Aunt Gussie." The grieving mother's real life name was Augusta, and because my grandmother adamantly refused to believe the house was haunted by a male ghost who could be watching her change clothes or take a bath, it was decided that this bereaved woman was our restless spirit.

My grandparents consulted with paranormal experts, who reinforced the theory that Aunt Gussie haunted the house in sorrow for her own lost children. In fact, it was thought that the repopulation of the house with new toddlers might have triggered her reappearance. And wouldn't you know it? These poltergeist activities largely disappeared after my sister and I moved with my parents to our own house a couple of years later, only to start back up again in the 1980s when a new family bought and renovated the home.

I personally never encountered any ghosts, and my relationship to the supernatural ends there. But the house definitely gave me the creeps when I was old enough to comprehend the many eerie stories. Just knowing that children had died there unnerved me. The downstairs had a distinct Victorian era gloom, even on the sunniest of days, but it wasn't overtly scary. It was the upstairs (where we had once slept!) that was downright spooky.

Behind the two front rooms loomed a large, unfinished attic that functioned as an ungoverned storage space. Lift the latch of the rough wooden door at the back of either room and you'd be in a different world—dusty, airless, dimly lit, with trunks of old clothes and broken furniture. When my sister and I were slightly older, we would thrill-scare ourselves by exploring this space. No particular item was inherently frightening, but the accumulation of formerly useful possessions now assigned to a kind of silent purgatory was unsettling, especially in a house that already possessed an other-wordly entity. Who knew what went on behind those doors?

My parents and grandparents treated these hauntings as something between a joke and an oddity and never let them interfere with the important business of getting on with life. Once ensconced in the East Bridgewater house, my father found a job in the warehouse of Star Market, a local supermarket chain, and my mother became a bookkeeper at Potvin Shoe, a baby shoe factory in Brockton. These were working class jobs, but the pay was decent enough to allow my parents to pay off their farm debt and save for a down payment on a house.

Meanwhile, even as they managed their own flower business, my grandparents became our babysitters. The house was not childproofed at all and the grounds included cows, tractors, dangerous tools (pitchforks, axes, saws, etc.), acres of unsupervised open land, and poisonous fertilizer. Somehow we escaped unscathed.

One day, six decades later, I looked at a photo of my grandparents during the years they were babysitting us, did a quick calculation and realized, *Holy cow, they were younger then than I am now.* How could this be possible? They were old, in clear contrast to my youthful, mid-60s self. My grandmother looks particularly worn down by life, unsmiling and dowdy in her house dress and clunky shoes (the idea that she would ever wear slacks—or God forbid, shorts—was preposterous). My grandfather seems a little livelier, even with his white fringe of hair circling his bald head. He remained physically vigorous and in complete control of his marbles well into his late 90s—but 30 years earlier, he'd already had the bearing of old age. Maybe it was all those years working the gladiolus fields, but more likely, he'd felt that when he hit 60 it was time to start acting his age.

Even after we moved to our own house, my grandparents still babysat my sister and me because my parents worked full-time, which meant my mother had to ferry us back and forth to the farm every day, with all of us merrily singing "She'll be Comin' Round the Mountain When She Comes" over and over again. In these years, I developed the opinion that my grandmother was severe and humorless, while my genial, easy-going grandfather—called "Pappy" by all my cousins—was a softie. It wasn't until my uncles and aunts were well into their 70s and 80s that they set the record straight. It turns out that when they were growing up, my grandmother had been a warm, loving, maternal figure, while my grandfather was a demanding disciplinarian and taskmaster. Apparently, over time, he had mellowed and she had hardened.

Our days on the farm consisted of a lot of morning television—*Romper Room*, *Captain Kangaroo*, Groucho Marx's *You Bet Your Life*, and *I Love Lucy* reruns. If the afternoon programming hadn't featured soap operas and talk shows, we might never have turned the set off. After lunch, I sometimes learned a little bit about nature. Stretching back from the new greenhouses to a forest several hundred yards away, were acres and acres of open land, divided into three fields by ancient stone walls that could have been built by Robert Frost himself. There was a gentle brook at the edge of the forest that was home to tiny tadpoles and sometimes, if we were lucky, we might catch a glimpse of a white-tailed deer.

My mother bought a movie camera about this time, and many of our home movies document this seemingly idyllic time in our life: my sister and I trying to work a hula hoop, my first attempt to milk a cow, backyard baseball games with cousins and uncles. It couldn't look more like the 1950s if Eisenhower himself were there practicing his golf swing.

On special nights when my parents had other plans, my grandparents would load us and several days' worth of gladiolus cuttings into a van, and drive to Boston, where they'd sell them at the city's wholesale flower market. It's cheaper now to import cut flowers from South America or Israel than it is to grow them locally, but for two decades, this is how my grandparents supported themselves.

One thing I didn't get from my grandparents was a lot of doting. Altogether, they had 13 grandchildren—so the two of us were nothing to get excited about. And besides, they had a living to make. There was no time for pats on the head, spontaneous hugs, or teachable moments. As long as we didn't run into the street or fall out of the hay loft, we were on our own. And that was just fine with me. My parents were affectionate enough and I didn't need another generation pawing me all the time. Even at an early age, I was learning to be a proper WASP.

Our days of being babysat ended when I entered first grade and my sister enrolled in nursery school. The East Bridgewater house remained the anchor for the extended Holmes family for another two decades, though. It's where we gathered for family reunions and the place where I encountered my out-of-state cousins. For years, we dutifully returned every Christmas Eve to open one present with my grandparents before rushing home to prepare for the real deal the next morning.

Shortly after we entered the 21st century, I drove by the old place to see what it looked like. The house itself remains imposing, but the huge side lawn and fallow fields are gone. All those open acres were sold to a developer who built a road straight down the west boundary of the property and erected about 20 generic houses behind the old homestead. I suppose those houses will eventually attain their own lived-in, individual charm, but at the moment, I was disheartened that the seemingly endless fields that once powered my childhood imagination had become so relentlessly suburban.

CHAPTER 4

Brockton

My first clear memory is from 1958, arriving at four years old to the house in Brockton that would be my home for the next 18 years.

Here's what I remember: a brand new "ranch" house, that single-story starter home of choice for so many post-war families; a small living room with a picture window, a fireplace, and a brick-red rug. Rooms adorned with knockoffs of classic Danish modern furniture purchased from Sears. Two easy chairs and a couch with pale wood framing and pegged legs that kept the business parts of these pieces elevated a foot or more above the floor, and plastic protecting the green burlap-covered seats and backs. This was the kind of furniture that would eventually grace the Museum of Modern Art, and would have gone perfectly with martinis and Miles Davis—if anyone in the family favored them. Which we didn't. At least not then.

The rest of the house was equally modest: three small bedrooms, a single cramped bathroom, and a kitchen divided by a low wall into a food preparation space and a small dining alcove. The cellar, with its cinder block walls and cement floor, was unfinished, perpetually chilly, and a little damp, but adequate as a home for the washer, dryer, and, eventually, a ping pong table and then, when we were really flush, a pool table.

The house had big, broad, yellow shingles. No special shade of yellow, just the same yellow you'd find on an art class color spectrum. The square windows had aluminum frames and flimsy glass panels that slid open sideways to let in the warm summer air.

Our one-car garage sheltered a vehicle for a few years, but eventually became the repository for so many tools, hoses, trash cans, lawnmowers, and other equipment that we eventually parked all our cars, starting with our olive green 1962 Ford Falcon, in the driveway. That vehicle didn't have any seat belts either, so if Thalia and I were sitting in the front seat when my mother hit the brakes, we'd slide forward onto the floor or occasionally bounce off the unpadded glove compartment.

Life in that house was "fine." That's to say, it was what it was. As a Manhattan apartment, it would be spacious. As a 21st century suburban home, it would seem criminally claustrophobic. But none of us gave it too much thought. My parents worked like crazy, and my sister and I spent a lot of time outside. In fact, we were hardly home anyway except to eat, sleep, and watch television.

Aside from electricity, indoor plumbing, and central heating, we had few extra amenities from civilized, modern life. No air conditioning, of course, so on humid summer nights we suffocated like the inmates of a Florida prison camp. No television remotes, either. If we wanted to change the channel or increase the volume, Thalia or I had to get off the floor and turn one of the knobs. No microwaves, icemakers, or dishwashers.

We lacked a garbage disposal too, so we dealt with household waste by depositing organic material—eggshells, uneaten toast ends, meat gristle, etc.—in a plastic, triangle-shaped dish that rested in a corner of the kitchen sink. Some poor soul then had to take it outside at the end of the day and transfer it into the metal garbage can kept hidden behind a small picket fence stockade. Today, someone who did this would be applauded for a commitment to organic composting, but in 1960, the garbage merely sat in that container rotting, stinking, and growing maggots until Thursday, when the garbage man delivered it to the piggery on the East Side of town, which

With my sister and our family dog, Mike, in the back entrance to our post-war ranch house.

smelled to high heaven whenever we drove by and thanked God we lived on the West Side.

We *did* have a telephone attached to the wall in the kitchen, with a long cord dangling halfway to the floor. We didn't own that phone; it was rented from AT&T, as was every additional phone we installed. We didn't stay on the phone for long, either. Any call outside the Brockton city limits was "long distance," which meant expensive. The quickest way to shut us kids up was to yell, "Quiet, I'm on a LONG DISTANCE call!" Our "exchange" was JUniper, because the 58 in our number—587-4280—corresponded to the letters JU on the dial. This meant we gave out our number as Juniper 7-4280. If you dialed 0, an operator could look up a phone number for free, place a collect call, or, in an emergency, break into a "busy" line to deliver a message. When the phone rang, we always answered it even though we didn't know who it was. Or maybe *especially* because we didn't know who it was. There were no answering machines or caller IDs (and blissfully, no mass market cold calling) so through a combination of curiosity, courtesy, and habit, we could not fathom allowing a ringing telephone to go deliberately unanswered.

No one spent any more time in the stripped-down bathroom than was absolutely necessary. It had a standard toilet, sink, and bathtub into which we once innocently placed a portable jacuzzi that succeeded in creating so many soap bubbles that we had to drain the water and start the bath again. The medicine cabinet had only a few over-the-counter medications, including Flintstones vitamins and orange-flavored baby aspirin that I sometimes sampled when we were short of candy. In the event of a cut or scrape, we had access to Iodine, which, when applied, hurt worse than the injury itself, and Mercurochrome, which went on painlessly, but was later banned because its base was, you know, mercury.

We paid for everything through three monetary mechanisms: store credit, cash, or check. And there were two main ways to get cash. You could either go to the bank and withdraw money, or you could go to the supermarket and write out a check for more than the value of your purchases, following which the cashier would hand you the difference in cash. We didn't have to show an ID, which hardly anyone except FBI agents had anyway.

During this period, our milk arrived via the milkman, who left the bottles in a metal box in our garage a couple times a week. The newspaper—the Brockton Enterprise—was deposited on our doorstep every afternoon between five and six p.m. by entrepreneurial 14 year olds. And if an enterprising Avon Lady or magazine salesman knocked, someone would open the door and listen respectfully instead of cowering in the bedroom pretending not to be home.

I slept on the bottom tier of a metal bunk bed in a small bedroom that also had a bureau, a monstrously heavy oak desk built by my Nantucket grandfather, and a flimsy bookcase. From the very beginning, I collected and reread my books, and these shelves displayed my first library. My sister and I were considered lucky because we didn't have to share a room with a sibling.

The mortgage on this dwelling came to $99 a month, which seems like a bargain except that my father was making $90 per week. Somehow, my mother kept us fed on a food budget of $20 per week, which included a lot of hamburger.

None of this seemed strange and we absolutely didn't feel deprived of anything. We were grateful to live in America and felt sorry for the poor Europeans who lacked our abundance.

Our years followed a few seasonal rhythms. In the winter, it always snowed up to our short little knees and sometimes to our shoulders. We sledded down the hill at the end of the adjacent street, Malvern Road (which is no longer possible since the city salts and sands this road immediately after every storm); during the holidays we went into Boston to see the decorated Christmas windows at Jordan Marsh and Filenes. If we got colds, my mother would rub Vicks Vape-O-Rub on our chests and cover the ointment with Kleenex. In the spring, we celebrated Easter with baskets overflowing with jellybeans and chocolate eggs, just like the church service later that morning overflowed with congregants. In the summer, we went fishing at the ponds in Field's Park, and for two weeks in July we thrilled to the Brockton Fair, with its dizzying carnival rides, rigged midway games, fireworks, and freak shows that, for 25 cents, invited you to stare at a morbidly obese woman, a grotesquely hairy "Monkey Man," or "Sylvia, the girl with the world's largest feet." In the fall, and with no guilty conscience about the environmental impact, we raked and burned every last leaf that fell in our yard. And since my parents worked round-the-clock in the summer, fall was also the season for increasingly elaborate family road trips—vacations to a different place of wonder every year: to the New York City World's Fair, Washington D.C., or Pennsylvania Dutch Country.

My Brockton years can be broken down into two clearly distinct periods—before and after I hit adolescence, which arrived somewhere around 1966 or 1967. As it happened, my transition from child to teen more or less corresponded to an important inflection point for both our family, the town of Brockton, and American culture as a whole.

We didn't know it when we bought the Brockton house (for $13,900), but our city was nearing the end of a century-long run of relative prosperity and industrial importance. The sixth-largest metropolis in Massachusetts, with a population hovering around 75,000 souls, Brockton was The Shoe City, and entered the 1960s as the leading manufacturer of footwear in the country. The elegant Victorian and Elizabethan-esque mansions that graced West Elm and Moraine Street testified to the city's relative prosperity.

Brockton in 1958 was no paradise, but it was a thriving factory city of immigrants. The Swedes on the South Side were fully assimilated, with only their last names to remind us they'd ever come over on the boat. More recent immigrants from Eastern Europe—Lithuanians, Poles, Czechs—congregated on the North Side. The substantial Greek population congregated in the center of the city, where they had a recently erected Orthodox church to serve them. The Jews were on the more prosperous West Side, and the Irish were scattered everywhere, especially in the hundreds of new tract homes built in previously open fields by the Campanelli Brothers, who enticed them down from South Boston. There wasn't a designated Italian neighborhood, but Rocky Marciano, the former heavy-weight boxing champion of the world and Brockton's most famous son, was only one generation removed from the old country and still called center-city Dover Street home. At the time, I marveled at the city's apparent diversity, though today I realize the city was remarkably white, with only a handful of Black folks living downtown and almost no Latino or Asian families at all.

Regardless of ethnicity or family tree, all white Brocktonians spoke with the classic nasal-heavy, dropped-R Boston accent that is frequently but inaccurately imitated by outsiders for humorous effect. We were like fish who don't realize they are swimming in water, though. I had no idea that I didn't sound like a TV broadcaster until a family trip at age 14, when my father walked into a car rental agency in Las Vegas and said he wanted to "rent a cah." To my complete bewilderment, the clerks almost fell to the floor with laughter.

Our new hometown had a Main Street that boasted a bustling commercial center, with three separate family-owned department stores, including Edgar's, which introduced one of the nation's first in-store Santas in the 1890s. The city also had three downtown movie theaters—The Brockton, The Center, and The Colonial—all heavily redolent of buttered popcorn with soft drink-sticky floors. The Colonial had both a balcony and a red velvet curtain upon which the opening credits of the feature presentation were projected for four or five seconds before the curtains parted. Downtown seemed to offer just about everything. Red Sox tickets could be picked up at the tobacco shops, there were thriving book, shoe, and jewelry stores, and hundreds of other local specialty businesses in that mile-long commercial strip. At night, teenagers from all the neighboring towns cruised up and down Main Street in their parents' cars like it was an urban "American Graffiti."

And downtown was not just for shopping. The city's imposing, fortress-like high school sat on a hill only one block off of Main Street. Massive Catholic and Protestant churches weren't far away, and neither was the Romanesque Revival-style City Hall, the Plymouth County Courthouse, the YMCA, the YWCA, or the public library. It was exciting to go downtown.

Most of this had vanished at the beginning of the '70s. The buildings were still there but the vitality was non-existent. By the time I graduated from high school—from the city's new, futuristic educational campus set in a distant residential neighborhood—downtown was a shell of its former self and the city as a whole was a dead man walking.

The economic trends that hit Brockton in the 1960s were not unique to us. Almost every city in New England suffered a similar collapse, but to those of us living in that particular city, it was shocking and disorienting. First, like dinner party guests who suddenly realize the host has fallen asleep and then get up en masse to leave, all the shoe companies decided they could maximize their profits if they relocated their operations to the low-wage American south. Just like that, hundreds, maybe even thousands, of jobs disappeared. The downtown housing stock, always a bit iffy, became outright slummy. And the federal government did us no favors when they built low-income housing projects just a short walk from City Hall.

Simultaneous to the evaporation of the factories came the appearance of Westgate Mall. Even when thriving, the downtown business district had begun to self-strangulate through a lack of parking. What was the point of enticing customers downtown if they were going to circle block after block in growing aggravation until they finally found a parking space far from their destination? How thrilled I was, even at age ten, when a whole new shopping experience—with tons of parking!—arose in the vacant fields near the Route 24 highway exit. It was only about a mile from our house, which meant I could easily walk to this commercial nirvana anytime I wanted. No kid thought twice about walking a mile to get where he wanted to go, and no parent worried what might happen along the way.

The mall initially felt like a fever dream to my ten-year-old self. I marveled at the range of stores, although in retrospect, I realize that its anchor tenants—Woolworths and Bradlees—were a little low rent, as were the restaurants—Friendly's, Papa Gino's Pizzeria, and the department store lunch counters. But what did we know? Think of the convenience! The developers even thought to include a free-standing chapel, which we snarkily dubbed "Our Lady of the Mall." And perhaps most importantly, the General Cinema Corporation built two modern movie auditoriums adjacent to the main shopping complex, and starting with *Mary Poppins*, these theaters began to educate me in the ways of the world.

Paradoxically, even as Brockton itself began to hit the skids, our family began an upward trajectory. My father had graduated out of the Star Market warehouse into a job setting up supermarket florist departments, but he hustled other work on the side: he refereed youth basketball, plowed snow, and always kept a lookout for something better. My mother, an early participant in the "gig economy," took in extra bookkeeping work, which she did at night. Then one summer afternoon, my Uncle Jimmy mentioned to my father how hard it was to find someone to handle the service work on his new swimming pool. A lightbulb went off as he sensed a business opportunity.

And that is how my ever-enterprising father, who had no experience with swimming pools, but knew how to work with his hands, started servicing pools at nights and on the weekends. Soon, he quit the supermarket to do this full-time. This was an auspicious moment because the post-war economy continued to boom and the mass production revolution that spawned ranch houses, fast food franchises, motel chains, frozen dinners, and so many other areas of consumption had also hit the swimming pool business.

*My father with his truck, mid-trajectory during his climb
as a successful Brockton businessman.*

As manufacturers developed inexpensive ways to produce in-ground pools, families no longer needed to be mansion-rich to afford their own backyard paradise.

Thus it happened that my parents were present at the birth of the swimming pool revolution. At first, my father just cleaned and serviced pools. Later, he purchased a house on the south side of the city and converted the downstairs into a storefront from which he and my mother sold pool supplies, chemicals, equipment, and toys. Soon after, they expanded further into the actual sale and installation of in-ground pools, which was even more lucrative than retail sales. At their peak, the business sold three, sometimes four pools a week and had multiple crews of brawny college kids doing the installations. Some of these pools landed in the handful of Brockton neighborhoods that were holding on to their faded glory, but most ended up in the bigger yards of the city's leafy surrounding towns.

It wasn't until I was well out of college and had my class consciousness raised by reading Tom Wolfe that I understood what had happened to our family. In practically the blink of an eye, we had risen from the working class to the upper-middle class. Through their own hard work, initiative, and willingness to take a risk—and the sheer luck of being at the right place at the right time—my father, the failed farmer and one-time warehouse worker who never went to college, and my mother, the former shoe factory bookkeeper, became small business owners with a store and a couple dozen seasonal employees. No wonder we were Republicans.

The rise in the family fortunes resulted in a modest lifestyle upgrade. Nothing showy of course, because we were still New England Yankees. My parents didn't upgrade their friends, which constituted the same group of tradesmen, former co-workers, and friends-of-friends they picked up along the way. The biggest change to our life was something that was absent: anxiety about money. My parents never stressed about family finances or forced us to confront the cost of everything we desired. Thalia and I knew instinctively not to be greedy and didn't really request much anyway, so when we wanted something, we usually got it—skates, portable TVs for our rooms, record players, and the other modest luxuries of a mid-'60s childhood.

We didn't move to a better neighborhood, and we didn't tear down and rebuild our house. We *did* add a large, comfortable family room to the back of the house, which provided much needed breathing room to what had become a cramped space for teenagers. That new wing of the house had its hidden luxury touches: a cedar closet and a second bathroom, attached to which was a sauna. Even today, that seems like a slightly decadent choice but at the time, in-home saunas, like everything else Scandinavian (except the socialist politics), seemed like the wave of the future.

At this point, the living room's cheap, '50s-era Sears furniture became a distant memory, replaced by two plush, orange-y velvet armchairs and a more traditional yellow divan. All the rooms got wall-to-wall carpeting. The cheap linoleum countertops and pressed wood cabinets in the kitchen received an upgrade. Workers arrived to tear off the big clunky house shingles and replace them with white vinyl siding, while the flimsy aluminum sliding windows became heavy, horizontal crank-outs, which my mother described as "the Cadillac of windows." And we finally got the dishwasher, microwave, garbage disposal, and color TV with a remote. My bunk bed went to the Salvation

Army, and I gained a new, spacious double bed. Since I was slight in stature, and given how small the room was, this was an unnecessary extravagance, but it did, very occasionally, come in handy later, especially during college vacations.

Because we were in the pool business, we had our own pool. This really changed things. We fenced in the backyard, which now became the focus of our social life, with pool parties, barbecues, late night swims, and invigorating plunges after a hot sauna. And yet, after about five or six years, we found ourselves growing a little jaded with pool pleasures. The night of my high school graduation was the best and last pool party.

Perhaps nothing better symbolized our advanced standard of living than our vacations. In the second grade, our fall vacation consisted of a long weekend in a cabin in New Hampshire; in the tenth grade, we all flew to Hawaii, Los Angeles, and Las Vegas so my parents could attend a pool convention and Thalia and I could visit Disneyland. And yet of all the phenomena I encountered on that trip, nothing impressed me like Las Vegas, with the slot machines in the airport, the garish neon, and the casino shows where we sat at tiny tables and watched Paul Anka sing and Frank Gorshen ("The Riddler" from *Batman*) perform impressions.

Anyone expecting a transition at this point to a story about how our family became undone by personal dysfunction or hubristic economic overreach will be disappointed. We didn't live in John Updike's world. There was very little drinking, no psychosis, no religious fanaticism, and whatever risks we took were fairly sensible ones. We were the personification of the petite bourgeoisie. Once my parents achieved an appropriate level of financial success, we plateaued and were satisfied with life. Later, in the 1990s, the "big box" revolution of superstores would flatten small businesses like independent pool stores, but by this time my sister and I were well out of college, the retirement plans were funded, and my parents had downsized their business aspirations. In at the right time, out at the right time.

CHAPTER 5

Rochelle Street

Brockton's Rochelle Street, where I lived for 18 years and grew into adulthood, was the quintessentially safe 1960's suburban neighborhood: a dead-end road; only four houses; and a handful of placid, nearly somnolent neighbors.

We lived in the middle of three brand new, identical—and I mean carbon copy—ranch houses, each a mystery behind closed doors. On one side of us were the Doanes, a mid-60s couple with a collie dog named Why (sometimes called Whysie), a big fenced-in backyard garden, and two older daughters. One of the daughters—Ginger, who, unlike *Gilligan's* Ginger Grant, had naturally red hair—still lived at home. She was a very well-put-together professional working gal, whose morning departure was virtually the only sign of life in that house. We barely knew anything else about them.

On the other side of us lived the Hershes, a 50-something pair with two sons in high school and college. They were more neighborly. A heart attack survivor, Mr. Hersh no longer trusted himself to drive because the stress could be bad for his pulmonary system, and his wife carted him around everywhere, including to and from his job at the local VA hospital. He once lamented to my parents that he would never be able to work with his hands like my father because he was Jewish, and his culture frowned upon physical labor. During my senior year of high school, they hired me to cut their grass and gave me a $100 check as a graduation present, which is more than any of my blood relatives did.

Despite the Hershes' geniality, they were from a different generation than my parents and we weren't buddy-buddy. There was one time, however, right after we installed our pool and were still in that first blush of inviting every living person we knew to come over for a swim, that they arrived for a dip. Mr. Hersh reposed on a chaise lounge because immersion in cold water might precipitate a coronary. But Mrs. Hersh was game. She dove off the diving board and didn't realize the straps of her one-piece suit had come undone when she splashed down. She glided the length of the pool underwater and surfaced in the shallow end bare-chested, right in front of my father and our slack-jawed guests. Oops.

From the front door, our street seemed suburban, with bike-riding, tree-climbing, baseball-playing, woods-exploring, free-range kids, but we

27 Rochelle Street after the vinyl siding was installed.

were just a tiny refuge in a more densely populated city. Our street had only recently been carved out of a patch of undeveloped woods and because the full development of the area remained at least a decade in the future, I had the good luck to be living among various adventure terrains.

These were the days when a mother would send kids to run wild after breakfast and expect them back for lunch and not before. Then, after peanut butter sandwiches, out they'd go again until she rang the bell for dinner. So I wandered the neighborhood most days, sometimes to play with my sister and our nearby friends, but sometimes just to explore. And we had a lot to explore: woods, vacant lots, and a boulder-filled pit. Does this sound like the place in which you'd want little kids to run loose? Well, we all survived.

Although I'm not sure how we made it. The boulder pit, which looked like something out of the Flintstones, was particularly treacherous. How those huge rocks landed there I cannot imagine, but we blithely played cavemen, leaping from boulder to boulder, completely unconcerned that we might slip and crack our heads. And because they were piled on top of each other, there were nooks and crannies to hide in. This almost ended disastrously for me one day when I was about ten years old and all alone in the rock pit. With exploration on my mind and half hoping to find an undiscovered cave, I took it upon myself to crawl under the most enormous boulder of them all. For a long moment I was stuck, unable to move forward or backward in a dark crevice where no one could hear my cries for help. Eventually, I managed to wriggle myself free, but the experience scared me so much that I never tried anything like it again.

The bottom of the street featured yet another vacant lot, this one boasting a number of trees that were excellent for climbing—an activity then considered "good for developing balance" rather than an excellent way to break your neck. This land was purportedly owned by a never-seen "Old Man Ward," who was said to live in the adjacent house. If there really was a Mr. Ward, he didn't seem to care much about personal liability, turning a blind eye whenever I climbed his trees. One oak allowed me to ascend higher than the top of a telephone pole, and two others were so close to each other that I could climb up one tree, jump from the branches of one to the next, and climb down the other. I also liked to dangle upside down from the lower limbs, hoping that girls from my elementary school class would ride by on their bikes and admire my athletic prowess—a never-achieved feat.

In the years before Lyme disease, the woods behind our house were reasonably safe. This was not a full-fledged forest, but big enough so that when you stood in the middle you couldn't see anything but trees on all sides and could imagine yourself as an explorer like Daniel Boone or Davy Crockett. A path ran directly from our backyard over the fallen trunk of a dead tree and up a steep, canopied hill that we could run up and down and pretend to be escaping from villains. A handful of other paths branched off of this main avenue, leading to rocky outcroppings that could pass as forts. Bats (no rabies, I assume) inhabited these trees and during summer twilight, they would swoop down to hunt insects in our backyard. We amused ourselves by tossing up acorns and watching these tiny mammals dive for dinner until, realizing they'd been fooled, they pulled away at the last minute.

There was another vacant lot at the dead-end part of our street. The main attraction in this weed-strewn area was not the heap of rusting metal or tower of rotting lumber, but a large pile of grass-covered dirt. This is where we played "army," shooting at each other with the plastic rifles and toy guns we'd received for Christmas before dramatically rolling down the mound and clutching our stomachs when we'd been "killed."

On the other side of this particular lot stood a gray, three-decker apartment building, and one day, two young boys, Tommy and Marky Landry, emerged to play with us. When I was nine and they were seven and five, they became my occasional playmates. Over time, I noticed an interesting and all-purpose adjective that they used a lot: "fuckin'." I had no idea what it meant, but eventually adopted it myself. I have to hand it to my mother; she didn't faint when she heard the word escape my lips. She just said it wasn't a nice thing to say and gently steered me away from those Landry boys, who, fortunately, moved to another town anyway.

I don't want to make it sound like I was a solitary child living only in my imagination. This was the '60s, after all, and little boomers clotted every neighborhood. My chief companion was my sister, a full participant in any game or physical activity we could manage. Despite being two years younger, we were the same height. She was the one who inherited my parents' athleticism and we competed as equals.

Right around the corner of our street were two more houses with kids. The Perdikis family lived at the corner of Rochelle and Malvern in a two-story house built before the war. Compared to our ranch, it was spacious, with a big dining room that no one ever went into. They were Greek, which I only mention because ethnic identity was front and center in the neighborhood, except for people like us who had no obvious ethnicity. Mrs. Perdikis—Libby (given name "Liberty")—resembled a suburban Jackie Onassis. Mr. Perdikis—Chris (given name "Christos")—was a bit dour, perhaps because he had been a POW in Germany during World War II, which, true to generational norm, he never mentioned. They had two sons. Jimmy was my age and we spent *a lot* of time together as kids. His brother Johnny also tagged along for group play.

Across the street from the Perdikises were the Kovners: Michael, Gary, and Emily. They lived in a newly built split level and were Jewish. That family demonstrated more emotion than the rest of the neighborhood combined. One day, when Michael locked himself out of the house, he decided to gain entry by using a rock to break the windowpane next to the door handle, and then reach in to unlock the door. (And sure, maybe the rest of us were standing around on the lawn egging him on.) Almost immediately after he finally found the will to smash the glass, his grandparents arrived. They weren't like my adoring grandparents on Nantucket or even my taciturn Pappy and Gramma Holmes in East Bridgewater. They didn't even live in that house but as soon as they stepped out of the car, they loudly berated Michael in front of us, exclaiming, "Don't you have the goddamn brains you were born with?" That sent us scattering.

The six of us—the two Holmeses, the two Perdikises and the two Kovner boys—were a small gang, knocking on each other's doors to see if anyone could come out and engage in what is now known as "unstructured play." In the winter, we built snow forts with our mitten-covered hands and started high-spirited snowball fights. We occasionally feuded with each other over petty slights—disputes that our parents were either unaware of or indifferent to. We burned off a lot of energy because we had the run of the entire neighborhood. And as we grew a little older, our play evolved from imaginary games to sports. Our street, a dirt road when we moved in, finally got paved, but still had no traffic—so it became an asphalt playground for softball, whiffle ball, basketball, street hockey, touch football, and anything else we could think of. This sense of neighborliness lasted until high school, when Jimmy and I ended up having a different schedule than the rest of the group. And then we were strangers again.

I don't mean to sugarcoat my childhood or turn it into some kind of Tom Sawyer fantasy. I was bored a lot. We only had one screen—the television—and there was nothing worth watching until primetime. I might play cards with my sister ("War" and cribbage) or pick up a book to read. What I did *not* do was complain about nothing to do, which would inevitably result in an assigned chore that was worse than any tedium I might fall into.

Thalia and me with the Kovner boys in a "piggyback fight."

Ironically, for all the loose parenting that would have landed my parents in jail in the 21st century, the danger, when it came, wasn't from swinging from treetop to treetop or leaping from boulder to boulder. It was much more mundane.

One day when I was 12, we found a discarded golf club and decided to build a two-hole miniature golf course in the vacant lot across the street. We only had one golf ball, so we took turns pretending to be golfers. When it was Gary Kovner's turn, he *had* to be a wise guy and wound up dramatically, as if he was teeing off on a fairway. I was standing behind him and the resulting backswing hit me smack in my left eyebrow. Half an inch lower and it would have smashed the eyeball itself. I ran home wailing and was rushed to the emergency room, where I got nine stitches and a tetanus shot. (Childhood being what it was, a few years before this, I had been taken to the same hospital to treat the same eye periphery after falling victim to a ricocheting metal spatula at a backyard barbeque. So I grew up with two scars at the edge of my eye socket, having narrowly escaped being blinded in that eye twice!)

On another occasion when I was about nine, we were riding our bikes—without helmets, naturally—up and down the gentle incline on Rochelle Street, trying to generate as much speed as possible. At the end of one of those runs, I hit the brakes in a patch of sand, which caused me to skid out of Rochelle Street and onto Malvern Road, where I plowed into the side of a passing car. A half-second sooner and it would have been the car plowing into *me*. My bike was mangled but I was fortunate enough to emerge without a single wound. The driver, an elderly woman, ended up in worse shape than I did because of the fright the whole incident had given her.

Remarkably, despite ranging over our un-childproofed neighborhood for more than a dozen years, those two lacerations around my left eye were the extent of my childhood injuries. I experienced no broken bones, blunt force traumas, or organ damage. In fact, I was never admitted for an overnight stay in the hospital for any reason until I was over 60. I really was a fortunate one.

CHAPTER 6

Ellis Brett, Part One

'm sure the wooden, two-story Ellis Brett elementary school had been a state-of-the-art educational facility back in 1895, but it was an anachronism when I started first grade in 1960. It consisted of 12 airy classrooms, with a wide-open, all-purpose area in the middle of each floor that functioned as a performance space, temporary nursing station, or visiting library as needed. Each classroom had a high ceiling, lots of windows, and an exterior door leading out to an iron fire escape. Although we never sheltered under our desks to prepare for a nuclear attack, we did regularly scamper outside for fire drills—and a good thing, too, because the building, dry as a pile of Arizona mesquite, might have burst into flames at the drop of a match.

I lived only half a mile away, so I walked myself to school. Every morning, I stopped at the Perdikis house to pick up Jimmy, after which we continued on together. No one thought it strange to see two six year olds strolling down Pleasant Street (aka Route 27), which, with its whizzing cars and lumbering trucks, was one of Brockton's major thoroughfares. There were no flashing lights to warn drivers about school crossing either. Why bother?

When we got to Belair Street, we met our school custodian and crossing guard, Mr. Kundis, who made sure we got to the other side of the street without being flattened.

The second day of school turned out to be one of the most crucial days of my life. Recognizing an imbalance between the two new first-grade classes (mine had 42 students and the other had 38), our principal entered the classroom to announce that since Freddie Tedesco and I were the last two students to register, we were being moved to the other first grade class. That was the domain of Miss Marsha Lindsay, a pretty teacher in her mid-20s. This is where I met my two best friends, who would shape my childhood, influence my adulthood, and remain the center of my social life through high school and beyond.

Miss Lindsay's room was set up with about 20 miniature two-person desks, one of which I was assigned to share with Philip Tasho, a dark-haired Albanian-American boy who served as the best man at my wedding nearly three decades later. We didn't get off to the smoothest start, though. One day, he grabbed a crayon and scribbled all over the side of my desk, then tried to pin the blame on me. Not made for a life of crime, he cracked under

Ellis Brett School.

Miss Lindsay's close questioning, confessed to the whole thing, and ended up weeping during lunch break as he erased all traces of his transgression.

He had his revenge mid-year though, when we changed desk partners and he was assigned to sit with the class's six-year-old heartthrob, Jaye Jantamaso, who, in a room full of Debbies and Susans, was adorable in the sweet, endearing way that baby chipmunks are adorable. On the walk home that bitter day, it was my turn to weep at the unfairness of the universe, which would allow the undeserving Philip Tasho to share a desk with my elementary school crush.

The Jaye Jantamaso fiasco aside, I generally liked first grade, and not just because I could freebase the white paste that Miss Lindsay handed out for craft projects. I liked almost everything about my six years at Ellis Brett, as decrepit as the physical structure was. I was reasonably bright and eager to please, and teachers took to me. The school provided old-fashioned 3-Rs education, with kids arranged in neat rows and teachers standing in front of chalk-stained blackboards (which were actually olive green). This kind of instruction suited me, but there were a few kids, mostly over-energized boys, who couldn't really adapt. They ran around when they should have been sitting still and we considered them naughty. In second grade, our teacher's frustration with one hyper boy reached a boiling point, and she tied him to his desk chair. Somehow she wasn't fired or sued, but this was a never-to-be-repeated punishment. Deemed to have behavioral problems stemming from his parents' divorce, this same kid emerged later from a private session with the school psychologist in a rage, sputtering that the "asshole" asked too many questions about his mother, and vowing he'd "kick him in the nuts" if he ever did that again. I didn't exactly know what that meant, but by this time, I'd learned not to repeat expressions said in that tone of voice.

The days and years at Ellis Brett were full of rhythms and rituals. In the mornings, we arrived at the school a few minutes early and ran around in the expansive playground. When the bell rang, we formed lines by class and gender before being escorted to our classrooms—the boys through the boys' bathroom in the basement and the girls through the girls' bathrooms. Once ensconced in our classroom, the first thing on the agenda was the Pledge of Allegiance, guided by one honored child who would lead the class as we stood to face the flag with our hands over our hearts. We then sang "My Country 'Tis of Thee," followed by an opening prayer. In deference to the many Jewish students in our school, we recited a passage from the Old Testament, which is how I came to memorize both the 23rd and 100th Psalms. This practice lasted until 1963, when school prayer was outlawed by the Supreme Court. All the adults seemed to agree it was a damn shame that some atheist crank could deny the rest of us this moment of grace.

My third grade teacher, the crotchety Miss Hazel Bond, was particularly incensed. She'd been teaching elementary school since the presidency of Calvin Coolidge and could have given my grandmother lessons in how to dress like an old lady. I am now half a decade older than she was then, but with that prune face she seemed so ancient to me as a child that I wouldn't have been surprised to hear she'd had a pterodactyl as a pet. Politically, she might as well have been a member of the John Birch Society, based on the running commentary she provided about contemporary society. She railed against the Court and asserted that we would continue to pray in defiance of the entire federal government. Needless to say, that didn't last long.

At lunchtime, those of us who walked to school returned home, once again braving the dangers of Pleasant Street traffic. We then returned an hour later with full bellies for yet another death-defying trek to school. The unfortunate young souls who had to take the bus to school ate their lunch at their desks and burned off energy in the playground when they were done. When it snowed and the usual mid-day round trip was deemed too dangerous, the entire class brought lunches to school and we all ate at our desks together. Those were always fun days, despite the classroom's lingering sour-milk and damp-wool smell. To my delight, I got to make use of my barn-themed lunchbox, which carried a thermos of cold chocolate milk where the hayloft would have been.

The sorting between the "smart" and "slow" kids started right out of the gate. For reading, math, and music, we were divided into four different groups according to ability. Not having been to kindergarten and lacking prior instruction in any academic subject, I was assigned to the second reading group. Within a month, I had learned so quickly that I was moved up with the "smarter" kids in the first group. Reading came easily and I quickly learned its value. One day at home, I picked up a TV Guide and a lightbulb went off: I knew so many of the words that I could figure out what would be on TV!

Our report cards covered over a dozen areas, ranging from social development to academic performance. There were three grades: G for "good," AV for "average," and U for "unsatisfactory." Each subject had three to six sub-categories of achievement, where the teacher could mark an N for "needs improvement." My grades were decent but when I found my old report cards stashed away in my mother's desk a few years ago, I discovered they weren't nearly as good as I remembered. I didn't get any U's, to be sure, but I never swept the board with G's as my memory had led me to believe.

I always got G's in deportment and was reprimanded only once, in the third grade, by Miss Bond, who terrorized all the boys in our class. She would call malefactors to the front of the room, grab their chins in her bony fingers

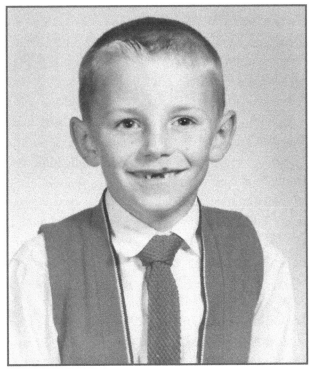

My second grade picture.

and berate them for their many sins. If she was really upset, she'd use her knuckles to hit up, up, up from beneath the chin, slamming her victim's teeth together. Usually she directed her ire at the usual group of overactive misbehavers who had been starting trouble since the first grade, but one day I entered her line of fire. She was a demon about "school property," and I had accidentally dropped one of my books on the ground which scuffed the cover and slightly tore one of the inside pages. She seized my chin in her pincers and accused me of being careless and negligent.

As someone whose life-long ambition is never to be reprimanded for anything, I arrived home for lunch agitated and distraught, nearly weeping when I recounted this injustice to my mother. Humiliated in front of the entire class, and for what? An honest accident and some very minor wear and tear to a replaceable book?

Back at school after lunch, I was summoned to the principal's office and told to bring my book. To my astonishment, there sat my mother, who had apparently marched down to the school to find out what on Earth was happening in that classroom. The principal, Mrs. Evelyn McCarthy, a very professional 50-something educator with eyeglasses that hung from her neck in a beaded string, asked to see the damaged item in question, and then used about an inch of scotch tape to repair the slightly torn page. She gently explained to me, although not in these exact words, "Look, you have to understand... Miss Bond is, well, *old* and you can't take everything she says seriously, okay?" Oh, okay. I took comfort in knowing that even adults could see Miss Bond was an old bat. But my most important takeaway from this incident was that my mother absolutely, unequivocally had my back. She would never take my side if I was truly in the wrong, but knowing you have that kind of unspoken support from a parent when you *are* in the right is crucial for any child.

I spent six years with the same group of kids. This gave me plenty of time to figure out who my friends were. After hanging out on the playground with a fellow student during recess, our mothers would arrange playdates at each other's houses. "Playdate" was not a word then, but it's appropriate in this context because it really felt like adult dating in many ways. Two of us would get together to test our chemistry, and if any existed, there would be a second visit, and then a third, and then we were formally friends. I did my share of playing the field, but it became apparent that I was particularly sympatico with my former first grade desk-mate, Philip Tasho, and another student, Richie Martel. We became a loose trio until the day Richie died 30 years later, after which Philip and I eulogized him at his memorial service. Since we were on the same wavelength in terms of humor, interests, and world view, Phillip and Richie became my quiet-play friends. In the fourth grade, for example, Richie and I had a long debate about whether Barry Goldwater could legally become President, because he was born in Arizona before it was a state and was therefore not an American-born citizen, as required by the U.S. Constitution. Kind of an odd conversation for two ten year olds, right? But it wasn't all political-nerdery. Richie was also the one who introduced me to DC comic books, *The Man From U.N.C.L.E.*, and Bill Cosby.

I had an on-and-off relationship with a third kid, which in retrospect was pretty out of character for me. Billy Hallisey lived on Wheeler Avenue, one road over from Rochelle Street. The youngest of three boys in a rough-around-the-edges Irish Catholic family and a little impertinent, he did not care for rules, eventually developing an Elvis-like sneer. His very kind mother said she was glad we were friends because I was a "good influence" on him. Even though Wheeler Ave was within shouting distance of where I lived, that neighborhood was significantly less cloistered than mine, with older, tougher, and more mature kids. Since those other hoodlums-in-training were bad news, I was supposed to help keep Billy on the straight and narrow through my upright example.

I'm not really sure why Billy and I started hanging out together. Proximity played its part, as did the "opposites attract" principle. We were more like frenemies (another concept that didn't exist then) than buddies. In the third grade, after having given up all hope of attracting the attention of Jaye Jantomaso, we were rivals for the affection of a different girl, Kathy Flanagan, who lived down the road at the other end of Wheeler Avenue. She had about eight brothers and sisters, which was notable, but not yet "Ripley's Believe It Or Not" strange. Her father was a gym teacher, and Billy and I must have been obnoxious about our rivalry, because he summoned us to the house, where he informed us that his ten-year-old was too young to be exclusive to anyone and that we should cool it. (I even remember the date—May 15th, 1963—because it was the day that the astronaut Gordon Cooper spent 34 hours circling the earth.) We did cool it, my ardor ebbed, and I almost never thought about her again. One day in junior high school, when we were no longer friendly, Billy and I happened to fall into a conversation about old times and he asked if I'd seen Kathy Flanagan recently. He said her face was covered with pimples and implied that we were both better off not to have fallen into her clutches. It surprised me that he would even bring up that remote episode from our shared past. Maybe he was more sentimental than I realized.

Billy also gave me a lesson in religious prejudice. It turns out he wasn't a fan of the Reformation and started riffing on different faiths, stoutly maintaining that Catholics were God's favorite people. He didn't precisely use the expression "one true Church" but that was the gist, and he began ridiculing me for being Protestant. This went on for weeks and he even came up with a ranking of best religions. Catholics were on top, of course. The Jews were second best because Jesus had been Jewish. Protestants were third best, and the hapless Greek Orthodox were fourth. I was defenseless against this onslaught, having given no thought to the relative merits of the various religions. I knew people went to different churches but assumed it was like attending different elementary schools—the same experience but in different buildings. When I told my mother about this theological attack, she said to ignore it—that Billy's priest would be unhappy if he knew he was saying these things. I accepted her claim at the time, though now I'm pretty sure the idea of Catholic superiority had been gestated at the church itself, if not by a priest then by a nun. Regardless, I held a very serious grudge against Catholics for a long time afterwards, one that didn't fully disappear until I married one myself.

I also have Billy to thank for teaching me the mechanics of human reproduction near the end of sixth grade. And it's a good thing he did, because no one else was going to, although I did start finding "your body is changing" books that had been strategically and casually left around the house where I could happen upon them. Billy didn't get everything right, which is to be expected from a kid who literally learned everything he knew on a street corner from those Wheeler Avenue knuckleheads. He maintained, for example, that women bled from their nipples every month and put pads in their bras to absorb the blood. That didn't make sense, but then neither did the actual baby-making part. I'd always known that babies emerged from a woman's belly, but had assumed it involved some kind of spontaneous generation in which a strong wish by the mother launched a pregnancy.

If I'd had half a brain, I would have noticed that men and women didn't share the same anatomy and deduced there was a reason for that. But I was clueless and didn't know enough to even wonder about that kind of stuff. There was no sexualized advertising, dirty jokes on sitcoms, internet porn, or cinematic sex scenes to pique my curiosity, so I was happily living in my own innocent bubble. My reaction to Billy's news was a fairly common one: "I'm NEVER doing *that*!" Still, even if I was appalled, I felt relieved to be out of the dark about this whole other world that, in my naïveté, I'd never even suspected existed. The scales almost immediately fell from my eyes. For several years now, my classmates had been making jokes that went completely over my head, and I finally realized they were related to this thing.

Soon after this, Billy and I broke up for good. And then, in the summer after 10th grade, my mother informed me there'd been a car accident that killed two kids in my class and put Billy in a coma. He died a few months later. I didn't grieve, exactly, because we hadn't been friends for a long time, and even when we were hanging around together, we never shared the true sympathy and affection that comes from real friendship. But I was sad, and I did feel guilty that I'd let down his mother's hopes that I'd be a good influence on him. Several years later, I confessed these feelings to my girlfriend, who told me to let it go. She said she'd known Billy in high school and he'd been a bully and a creep. Forget it, there was nothing I could have done to change him, and I should get over my savior complex and move on.

She was right, of course. We couldn't have remained friends unless we'd both fundamentally changed our personalities. He'd been barreling into adulthood with his fast friends while I was content reading comic books. Still, 16-year-old Billy died the same year as my 91-year-old great-grandfather, and that didn't seem quite fair.

CHAPTER 7

Ellis Brett, Part Two

The Ellis Brett School, named after a former Brockton grandee whose accomplishments were long lost to history even by the 1960s, was a deeply matriarchal institution with a dozen female teachers, a female principal, a female secretary, and just one adult male onsite—Mr. Kundis, the janitor, visible only during his crossing guard duties. As for security, there wasn't any. The school was completely accessible to everyone. Visitors who entered the front door could stride unchallenged to any classroom; if they wanted to visit the principal, they had to climb the tall, broad staircase that greeted you at the front door, and then walk to the very rear of the second floor. In other words, her office was as far away from the main entrance as possible.

Aside from the classrooms and the principal's office, the building's only other rooms were the janitor's lair and the bathrooms, both located in the cellar. Consequently, if we needed to use the toilet, we would raise our hands and ask, "Can I go to the basement?" The boys' room consisted of a dozen urinals lined up at the front, a half dozen stalls to the side, a couple of sinks, and a "bubbler" (known to the rest of the world as a water fountain). I have no idea what the girls' room looked like since I would have more willingly walked into the school's furnace than entered that space.

This is what else the school did not have: air conditioning, a wheelchair ramp, an elevator, a public address system, a video system, a school nurse, a cafeteria, a gym, a library, or an art room. In one nod to modernity, the teachers wheeled televisions into our classes for space launches and the occasional student programming on Channel 2, the "educational channel" (now known as WGBH, the PBS affiliate).

Even though anyone could walk in off the street, I felt safer in school than any other place, with the exception of my own home. And why not? Who would enter that school with malicious intent? There was nothing to steal, and after all, the "crazy" people of Massachusetts were supposedly locked away in an extensive system of state mental hospitals.

I'd like to say that grade schoolers were healthier in the 1960s than they are now, but I'm not sure that's accurate. We just had different kinds of illnesses. No one got smallpox, thankfully, because we all had to be vaccinated—boys on their left forearms and girls on their thighs, so the scar wouldn't show when they wore sleeveless blouses and ball gowns in the future. Other infectious diseases were relatively common and it was thought that chicken pox, which swept my class in the first grade, and measles, which hit us in the second, were rites of passage. Not to diminish the seriousness of these diseases, but our attitude towards them was very different then—if 400–500 Americans died per year of measles (as was the case in 1962), well, that was nothing compared to car crashes and heart attacks!

On the other hand, no one had asthma or allergies. If a mother brought in a batch of whole wheat cookies topped with a dairy-laden peanut butter frosting, we would have descended on them like a pack of wolves instead of politely asking if eating one would send us into anaphylactic shock. It's amazing we weren't sick more often, considering our sketchy nutrition. In between meals, I survived on Coca Cola, potato chips, and 'Nilla Wafer cookies, with the occasional Pop Tart when I needed some fruit. And candy! So many varieties and so little time. How I loved our local brands—Waleco Coconut Bars, Sky Bars, Christmas ribbon candy—as well as other since-forgotten national products like NECCO Wafers, Smarties, Mini Rolls, and Rolos.

Our addiction to comics books and penny candy supported two competing "variety" stores—Matta's and Mrs. Fosters—both run by cranky geriatrics who didn't seem to like the kids whose nickels and dimes kept them afloat.

Ellis Brett had a good reputation for academics. Kids seemed to actually be learning things, although I never witnessed a heart-warming example of a particular teacher changing a student's life. I don't think we were making that big of an impression on them either, to be fair. When I was in college and on duty in my parents' pool store, my fifth grade teacher, Barbara Reagan, walked in to buy some chlorine. I reintroduced myself but she didn't even pretend to remember me. I'd have felt bad, but when I tried to prompt her memory by referring to the more accomplished members of the class, she couldn't recall any of them either.

My teachers ranged in age from 25 to 65, and despite having more than 40 students each and no aides, they somehow managed to keep us straight, usually remembering the names of our siblings too. They all maintained their authority in class. Some yelled, some cajoled, some charmed, but regardless of their particular method, I never saw an out-of-control classroom. We were still living in a culture of self-discipline, and it was expected that parents and teachers would conspire to reinforce good behavior. Parents modeled it themselves and threatened divine retribution if their kids embarrassed them at school, and most of us came from two-parent homes whose folks usually had time and energy to keep us in line.

A great deal of emphasis was put on learning things—as in facts. We didn't "learn how to learn," we were just told bits of knowledge and taught to remember them. This kind of "rote" learning is deeply unpopular in education circles now, but it worked well enough for me. I didn't particularly enjoy memorizing the multiplication table, but it's come in handy more than once. I also memorized vocabulary words, the various species of birds, the order of the planets, the names of the Greek Gods, and the colorful customs that went with various foreign countries. I learned to write with cursive script, which, I was shocked to learn 40 years later, is no longer taught in schools, so that millennials today only know how to print, and print rather illegibly at that.

Most importantly, school was where I learned to read. My parents read to us only sporadically—home reading wasn't emphasized as much as it is now—and we owned just a handful of children's books. So I was completely illiterate at age six. I never even cracked the cover of *Dr. Suess* or *Winnie the Pooh* until I was a father myself. But although my mother was not into kiddie literature, she was a steady reader, maintaining a collection of three or four shelves of paperback best-sellers, like *To Kill a Mockingbird* and *Advise and Consent*.

When my mother noticed that I enjoyed reading, she started buying books for me too. On trips to the Brockton Public Market, she'd sometimes allow me to pick out one little hardback Disney book that sold for a quarter. Once, she even bought me a fancy illustrated collection of classic Disney stories that featured the novelizations of half a dozen movies ranging from *Snow White* to *Sleeping Beauty*. I read these over and over again until the book fell apart. I soon developed a life-long interest in history, so in the third grade, she bought me a Young Reader volume of brief presidential biographies from Washington to JFK. The sanitized series made every president, even the worst (I see you, James Buchanan), seem heroic. I became so obsessed with presidents that I memorized all their names in sequence—a parlor trick I am still capable of performing. I favored Lincoln, and stuffed my bookshelf with "Honest Abe" biographies. After visiting the Hall of Presidents at the New York World's Fair, my parents bought me an LP of an actor reading famous Lincoln speeches, which I listened to until I knew those addresses by heart.

At Ellis Brett, we also learned the love of country. The Pledge of Allegiance and the patriotic songs that launched the day were only the start of the pro-America pedagogy. Brockton is in Plymouth County and not far from Plymouth Rock, so we heard a lot about the Pilgrims, which segued into the American Revolution, the Western expansion, and the rest of the American saga. It's hard now to evoke the country's optimism for the future. Although the Vietnam War was underway, the protests hadn't started yet and most of us in school believed in American exceptionalism. Some of our fathers had been in World War II and saved civilization. And weren't our astronauts just the latest in a long string of American heroes (explorers, pioneers, inventors, Congressional giants, military leaders, scientists, and business tycoons) who demonstrated how great America was? Woke academics now claim that this version of American history sugarcoats our country's various sins, but that's not completely fair. I learned from my teachers to be indignant about the evils of slavery, and only the most amoral of us could have come away from our history lessons without thinking there was something wrong about how we stole all that Native American land.

Even my geography lessons reinforced a conception of national superiority. In addition to studying Eskimos and igloos, the Dutch dikes, the Panama Canal, the pyramids, and the Bedouins with their desert living, I also learned about impoverishment around the world, where no one had our supermarkets or central heating. In the fourth grade, before we turned to the chapter on China, our teacher made a clarifying announcement that we wouldn't be studying the culture of Red China, but free China instead. This puzzled me at the time, but I now understand she meant we would be studying Taiwan. Red or Free China made no difference to me, I was still appalled at their backwardness.

Most of the country had an extreme aversion to Communism. In school, my teachers didn't directly propagandize us, but they didn't need to. It was in the air. We all knew from television and general social discourse that the Russians and the Chinese wanted to take over the world. Until 1964, our bête noire was Nikita Khrushchev, the chief Russian bad guy, now largely forgotten but known then to every American as our sworn enemy. Yet not everything seeped down to us. The Cuban missile crisis nearly ended the world when I was in the third grade, and I never heard a thing about it until seven or eight years later in a high school history class, to which my reaction was, "Are you kidding me?! *That* happened when I was alive?"

The Kennedy assassination was the great traumatic national event of my early childhood. No boomer can pass up a chance to tell his experience, so here's mine. On Friday, November 22nd, 1963, I was in the fourth grade, leaving school at 3:00pm for the weekend, when another kid ran up to me and announced, "Kennedy's been shot!" When I got home, my mother was watching television, a completely unprecedented activity for her. I followed some of the reporting, but wasn't glued to the television over the next three days. I was mostly outside playing, as usual, while the adults were huddled inside watching the funeral. But as shocking as the assassination itself was, I was even more aghast to hear on the radio the following Sunday, just as we were pulling into our driveway after a mournful church service, that Lee Harvey Oswald had also been shot. At that point, even to my young self, it seemed like the wheels were coming off the country.

The Kennedy assassination cast a pall over the rest of my childhood. In Massachusetts, where the Kennedy family dominated our consciousness like the Royal Family does in Britain, the mythology was inescapable. It was like living in a house where the eldest son had died tragically and no one could bring themselves to remove the black crepe from his high school graduation picture. In a way, the Kennedy assassination was the point where I began to lose my innocence—not because of the murder itself, because even then I knew that random, terrible things happened—but because of the way the national news and the public in general started calling JFK "one of the greatest presidents of all time." Just because he'd been killed? Why did that make him as important as George Washington or my hero Abe Lincoln, the Great Emancipator himself? As I grew older and prematurely cynical, it started becoming clear to me that society salved complicated feelings with simple-minded, sentimental stories and that the media always leapt at the opportunity to oblige that desire.

But national tragedy or not, life moved on at Ellis Brett. As winter approached, we learned Christmas carols, and because there were so many Jewish kids in our class, we also sang "Dreidel, Dreidel, Dreidel," the only Hanukkah song that we knew. On Valentine's Day, we deposited little heart-themed cards in the boxes of the kids we liked, emphasizing the Darwinian aspect of elementary school, since some of us received a nice collection of cards and others only a handful. (I got enough not to be embarrassed, but never any special cards from the girls I had crushes on.) In late spring, we had our school fair, which, with its bike parade, games, face painting, knick-knack tables, and pony rides, I loved even more than Christmas morning. At Halloween, we had our annual costume parade, taking a break from our studies to march around the block in front of our parents dressed as ghosts, witches, hobos, or baseball players.

Our class was strictly divided by gender. The boys rarely mixed with the girls during recess; they skipped rope and played hopscotch while we played tag and climbed on the jungle gym. The girls wore dresses with slips that we'd sometimes catch a forbidden glance of, and the boys wore long trousers. We were occasionally prone to fads. In the fourth grade, all the boys wanted to wear Madras plaid shirts, and then in the fifth grade, long sleeved velour pull-overs. I was always a follower when it came to fashion. The one time I tried to be a trend-setter, I picked out fire-engine-red rubbers and proudly donned them on the next rainy day, only to discover to my embarrassment that only girls wore them. My mother probably knew this would happen, as instead of giving me grief when I said I didn't want to wear them anymore, she just quietly passed them on to my sister.

Ellis Brett was probably the most egalitarian institution I was ever a part of. Hardly any of our parents had been to college, and none of them were professionals or particularly well-off. No one came from a big house or had significantly nicer clothes than anyone else (although when I look at class photos now, I suspect that some of the girls from bigger families wore hand-me-down dresses). The class also lacked a social hierarchy, because there were no overpowering personalities among us. Jaye Jantamaso might have been the most popular girl, but she didn't wield her popularity as a weapon. Among the boys, no one stepped forward as the alpha male. And although we were divided into groups depending on academic ability, there was no obvious genius to lord his or her intellect over the others.

But this conformity had its downside if you didn't fit the mold. Within each grade there was usually an outcast or scapegoat who was bullied or shunned, almost as if the larger group could only cohere in opposition to a perceived alien. In our class, it was a girl named Adrien, who joined us in the third grade and immediately grated on the wrong kids—the "bad boy" troublemakers who didn't exactly have an excess of empathy to begin with. She was thin with chalky, white skin and chapped lips. Her hair had never been cut, so she had long braids, of which she seemed excessively proud. She lived far enough away to take the bus, but her parents drove her to and from school every day like she was a princess. Her parents were very distinctive too. They were Greek-Americans who seemed vaguely continental. Her father, tall and good-looking with a 1930's movie star mustache, was a professional artist who supported himself with an art store. Unfortunately, in addition to coming from a sightly nonconforming family, Adrien also had an affected way of speaking and lacked the innate social skill of relating to the other girls. She was just "off" enough to be accused of having "cooties."

What really shocks me now is that no adult stepped in to stop her ostracism. Her parents witnessed the bullying, because the boys were brazen enough to yell "cooties!" at her when she got into the car after school. The teachers must have been aware too, but the harassment never stopped. I'd like to say there was a happy ending to Adrien's story, but there wasn't. In a junior high talent show, she appeared on stage as a go-go dancer and lip-synced to "These Boots Are Made For Walking," further cementing her reputation for weirdness. In senior year, she sat at my table during English class and remained a little strange, still not picking up on social cues, talking mostly about herself and her supposedly extraordinary fluency in the French language. And then 30 years later, I learned that she could be seen wandering aimlessly in Brockton, practically homeless.

Ellis Brett is where I developed a love/hate relationship with the practice of putting words on paper. My fifth grade teacher, Mrs. Reagan, focused on writing and insisted on at least one book report per month. She even had a chart on the wall with gold stars next to our names indicating how many reports we had turned in. Some of the overachieving girls—curse them— produced so many reports that their stars went clear across the chart. I could barely do the minimum, struggling to think of something to say about any book other than, "It was interesting." Worse, every Friday she had us watch and take notes on a televised science program and then write a summary of it over the weekend. How tortured I was every Sunday after church as I struggled to write these reports. And yet it was in the fifth grade when I started to write short stories on my own—little tales of boys' mild adventures that I never showed anyone because I was discriminating enough to know that they weren't very good.

My fifth grade class. I am last on the right in the second row. In the top row, Richie Martel stands second from the left and Philip Tasho is second from the right.

Fifth grade is also where I made a major faux pas in attempting to demonstrate how smart I was. In a discussion about tiny countries, I piped up that the smallest country of all—the place where the Pope lived—was "Vacation City." A nonplussed Mrs. Reagan finally deduced that I was talking about the Vatican. This goof went over the heads of everyone in the class except for my friend Richie Martel, who, as a Catholic, found this delightfully ridiculous and never let me forget it. For the rest of his life, when he wanted to bring me down a peg, he'd just say: "Maybe you should tell them that in Vacation City."

As we advanced through the years, our teachers decided we could handle more specialized areas of knowledge. My sixth grade teacher, the jolly but somewhat spacey Mrs. Spradlin, had us research whether UFOs were real. Later, she decided we needed to learn about "the dangers of drugs" and told us an alarming story about a college dance she attended where some boys had boldly offered her illegal substances on the steps of the gym. Once again, I was in such a bubble that I assumed she was talking about pharmaceuticals. And the problem with drugs was what? She never mentioned any substances by name or explained why someone would want to do drugs in the first place, so I was completely mystified when she assigned a report on their dangers. I never did the assignment and she never insisted on it, so my more adult life lessons would have to wait until junior high.

And junior high was right on the horizon, though I hated to leave Ellis Brett. I was finally at the top of the food chain by virtue of being a sixth grader. I'd also been selected for the prestigious position of school safety guard, whose responsibilities consisted of somewhat officiously keeping the younger kids in line as they crossed the street or spent too much time drinking from the water bubbler. What a shame to go from being a big shot to the most menial being in creation—a junior high school seventh grader.

But it was more than a loss of status that I mourned when I left Ellis Brett. My six years at the school were then literally half my life, and while I was there I really thought those days would last forever. As early as seventh grade, my friends Philip, Rich (no longer "Richie"), and I started on a lifetime of reminiscing about our shared experiences with the lovely Miss Lindsay, the mean Miss Bond, and the eccentric Mrs. Spradlin. And yet for all my nostalgia, when I walked out of that building in June 1966—no graduation ceremony, thank you very much—I never went back. I always intended to return for a visit, but it never happened. 15 years later, it was converted into an apartment complex with 23 one- and two-bedroom units. I've always fantasized about posing as a potential renter to get a look at the inside, but so far that hasn't happened either.

And here's the other thing that I can't really explain. I spent six years with the same group of kids. We had shared our most formative years together. If you showed me a class photo from any of those years, I could identify each one of them by name and tell a related anecdote. But once we left Ellis Brett, I barely saw any of them again except for Philip and Rich and one or two others. If I passed my former classmates in the hall, we usually wouldn't even acknowledge each other. What was there to say? "Hey, remember Goldie, our goldfish in the first grade?" It wasn't until Facebook that I reconnected with any of them. Given that all my high school friends had fled the city after college, I was surprised to learn how many Ellis Bretters had stayed in the Brockton area.

I did have one more interaction with my first grade crush, Jaye Jantomaso, however. My father occasionally serviced her family's pool and once, in the eighth grade, I accompanied him on the job. Jaye was home and the two of us ran off together and snuck around the back of the house to spy on our fathers, like we were first graders again. She even confided to me that all this excitement made her feel like she had to go to the bathroom, which seemed like a remarkably intimate thing to say. By this time, she was already going to the Cardinal Spellman School on the other side of town, so there was no chance we would see each other again, and we didn't. But about 15 years later, when I was 30 years old and working in Washington, my sister had a professional interaction with her; when Thalia mentioned my name, Jaye said, "Oh yes, he was my first boyfriend." What?!?! Since when???? I wish someone had told me when it would have meant something! To be honest, though, I think she was just flirting or flattering me long distance. She still had the full reservoir of charm that made her the most popular girl in the first grade, after all.

CHAPTER 8

Family Life

Until junior high school, my family meant everything to me. Most of what I observed and believed was filtered through a family perspective. If my parents were for it, I was too.

Except for the oddity that both my parents worked, we had the standard family unit with one mother, one father, and two kids. In this respect, we were like everyone else, or so it seemed. Sociologists would later identify these years as the last hurrah of the nuclear family, but you didn't need a census chart to know that the two parent/two kid model reigned supreme. All you had to do was look around. The concept of the single parent did not even exist—there were just "divorcees" and their faithless ex-spouses. The only time I was ever exposed to an unmarried parent was on TV, where a number of men—widowed dads and single uncles—tried, with mixed success, to lead their alternative families. And the concept of gay parenting was even more inconceivable—how would that even work?

According to the media, radical changes were happening in the out-side world, but definitely not in our house. Well into the late 1960s, we still behaved, dressed, and entertained ourselves as if Eisenhower were still president. I presented as a somewhat skinny but completely average kid dressed in sturdy Sears & Roebuck clothing. My beautiful blonde hair was, for several years, shorn off by my mother into a harsh buzz cut and when it grew back I looked very Aryan.

I was a normal height and in very good health, except for December 1964, when I came down with pneumonia and was out of school for a month. I even escaped the epidemic of tonsillitis that swept American kids in the '50s and '60s. My sister was not so lucky. One sore throat and she was whisked to Brockton Hospital where she was left frightened and alone overnight. When my mother was finally allowed to see her during visiting hours the next day, she found her somewhat traumatized and clad in a blood-stained hospital gown.

In keeping with the times, my folks were serious but not obsessive about child-rearing. There was no such thing as "me time," only family time, and I never heard them complain about how stressful, exhausting, and soul-sucking parenting was. They brought my sister and me along on their vacations, attended our sporting and school events, and made it obvious that we were their priority. My mother once made the off-hand remark that she would never consider sending us to boarding school (as was the case with several of my cousins) because she wanted to enjoy her kids. I was to learn over the years that not every mother "enjoyed" her children.

On the other hand, this family-first ethos did not translate into the excessive togetherness that consumes many upper middle class families today. There was a clear distinction between the adults' and the kids' worlds and the adults didn't monitor the kids every waking hour.

The four of us almost always ate dinner together, however. My father treated these meals as important opportunities to instruct me on proper dining etiquette, leading to fraught moments, especially if I misused the silverware, buttered the bread the wrong way, or reached for the food without offering it to someone else first. My father himself had been indoctrinated that a gentleman allows everyone else to go first, and it was a deep, intense part of his self-image that he absolutely had to be the last one to sit down for dinner, the last in line at a buffet, and the last to eat a forkful of anything. He couldn't insist that I follow suit, because only one person could be last and that had to be him, but he could try to make me internalize the general principle of self-abnegation.

Regrettably, I was a notoriously picky eater and half of what I did eat came under protest. If it didn't taste like much, that's what I liked. Fortunately for my palette, most 1960s cuisine was bland. Pasta meant spaghetti from a box, tuna emerged from a can instead of a fish market, vegetables arrived frozen, and lettuce was always iceberg. Water, when we thought to drink it, flowed from the kitchen faucet—certainly not bottled from an underground spring in another state. Store-bought ice cream was vanilla, sometimes chocolate, or on the rarest of occasions, strawberry. I couldn't stomach eggs, onions, peppers, ham, fish (except fried clams, which was my favorite meal) or anything that smelled weird. When my parents prepared tripe, which is pickled cow's stomach, I thought I was going to pass out. And because it consisted of cheese and tomatoes, both of which were on my "not gonna eat" list, I didn't even like pizza until I was a teenager. When I ate a sandwich I would consume it up to the top crust, which I would leave on my plate.

My mother didn't make it a major issue, recognizing my food fussiness for the phase that it was. I could choke down string beans, potatoes, and a few cuts of meat, so she could at least serve me the blessed trinity of protein, starch, and vegetable. Sometimes we'd have pancakes for dinner, although for some crazy reason I refused the maple syrup. The most ethnic our food got was Prince spaghetti—but unlike lucky Anthony from the commercial who went home to a lovingly simmered meat sauce, our spaghetti was topped with layers of browned hamburger and jarred tomato sauce, just as my grandmother had prepared it in 1940s Nantucket.

Saturday was the one night of the week that we never shared a meal. This was my parents' sacrosanct "friends night." From the day they married until my father died 65 years later, they almost always went out or entertained on Saturday nights. They were the most relentlessly sociable people I've ever known and regularly saw a remarkably wide assortment of other couples at house parties, social clubs, restaurants, and other mysterious places where adults gathered to laugh, trade mildly humorous barbs, dance, or play cards. At the raucous New Year's Eve parties at our house, my sister and I watched with mouths agape as they played Twister and other party games.

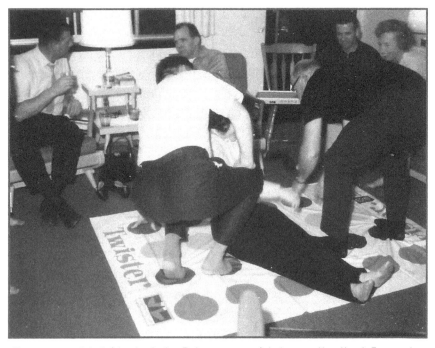

My parents and their friends playing Twister at one of their many New Year's Eve parties.

The polar opposite of Saturday night was the next day, the Lord's Day. In puritanical 1960s Massachusetts, Sunday remained a rigorously enforced day of rest. All commercial establishments shut down and the idea of spending Sabbath morning playing organized youth sports was unimaginable. You couldn't even operate a jukebox on Sunday. And to emphasize the singularity of the day, our meals were all out of order: Sunday breakfast was fried dough; the night before, my mother would create a yeasty concoction that would rise overnight and turn into something resembling pizza dough. The next morning, she would grab pieces from this inflated mound and fry them in a cast iron pan until both sides were hard and black. We'd eat these with butter before heading for church and Sunday school, after which we'd come home, change our clothes, and have a special roast dinner at 1:00pm. The evening meal, if there was one, was half a sandwich or a small snack.

Sunday was family day, but "family" meant more than just the four of us on Rochelle Street. Some combination of the extended family of grandparents, aunts, uncles, and cousins came together on Sunday afternoons. More often than not, we had Sunday dinner with my father's people, especially my grandparents, my Uncle Carl and his family, or my Aunt Jean and her family. The traditional afternoon meal was followed by lethargic, desultory conversation and general hanging around while the kids tried to amuse themselves, usually in front of the television. Sometimes, though, we would rouse ourselves to put on a "show," which consisted of us lip-synching to popular records like "Alvin and the Chipmunks."

In the summer, we'd sometimes go over to my Aunt Jean's house for a Sunday cookout because they had a pool. All the mothers religiously believed that swimming after a meal would cause stomach cramps followed by drowning, so after consuming our hamburgers and hotdogs, we'd have to kill an hour before returning to the water.

My mother's family wasn't local, but it's not as though we ignored them. Each summer, starting in the second grade, I spent two weeks with my grandparents in Nantucket. I was terribly homesick that first year when my mother left me behind for the return boat, but my sister kept me company the following year, and until I got a full-time summer job eight years later, these two weeks with Grandma and Grampa Harris were a regular routine.

These visits provided the perfect excuse to be as lazy as possible. Mornings were for desultory television viewing; reruns of syndicated shows like *I Love Lucy* and *The Andy Griffith Show* already seemed like they belonged to an earlier generation, but they were better than the alternative, which was physical activity. One summer, I insisted that we get back from whatever afternoon outing we had planned by 3:30pm so that I could catch the new episodes of the horror soap opera *Dark Shadows*. After lunch, we'd go to the beach, and if my correspondence home was any indication, no one seemed too concerned if we got sunburned, not even when I wrote that I was so burned I couldn't raise my arm above my head. In fact, the opposite was true: in her return letters, my mother encouraged me to "get good and brown."

On the weekends, we'd drive out to my grandparents' summer cottage at Madaket, on the western part of the island, where we'd swim in the surf, play with my younger cousins, Sally and Peggy, and go fishing in my grandfather's boat. And every weekend like clockwork, my sister caught more fish than I did.

My letters home included complaints about my grandparents' beagle Cindy, updates on my sleeping and eating habits (I was doing a lot of each), reports of Sunday night band concerts and Fourth of July fireworks, gossip about my Aunt Sara's many sisters, accountings of my spending, and lists of the books I had read (when I was 16, I read *The Andromeda Strain*, *The Love Machine*, and *The Peter Principle*. The previous summer I had polished off *Gone With The Wind*.) Here's the text of a typical letter that I wrote when I was ten:

> *Tuesday 9:00*
> *Dear Mom and Dad,*
>
> *Boy did I get sunburned on Sunday. My back is killing me. Sunday, Thalia caught a bass and a blue. It was chilly so we didn't go to the beach. Cindy is worse than Mike [ed. note: Mike was our dog at home]. I mean it. She has torn a pillow since we've been here. I'm sorry this isn't such good writing. I'd like to hear from you more often even if it is only one or two dollars. Sally and Peggy are getting used to me. Well, I cant think of anything else to say.*
>
> *Your loving son,*
> *Gary*

During this period, I idolized my father and adored my mother, and was proud of how young and active they were. When I entered first grade, they were still in their 20s, and to me, more vibrant than the stodgy parents of my less fortunate classmates. I always wanted to spend more time with them, particularly my father (who was frequently working), and I resented it when he'd pay attention to my cousins or his friends' children. A kid at heart, he would have made a wonderful camp counselor, and when he was with my sister and me it felt more like having a big brother around than a father. He'd wrestle with us, play catch in the backyard, chase us around, and otherwise make us feel we were the center of his world.

With so many orphans on TV and in the movies, I worried constantly that my parents would die abruptly, and that Thalia and I would have to live with relatives. When I had my first existential crisis about death, my father comforted me with the reassurance that he'd be waiting for me in heaven when I died. "When I see you floating up to join us, I'll tell my friends, 'Here comes my boy.'" That actually did make me feel better.

He was a surprisingly advanced thinker considering his background. Or maybe it was just a natural empathy that made him sensitive to social unfairness. Once, when I was about seven and he had me pinned during a wrestling match, I called him a "black monster"—he quickly halted the roughhousing to lecture me on not using the word "black" in a negative context because it might hurt the feelings of Black people. I also heard him refer to Boston's anti-busing leader Louise Day Hicks as a "bigot," which didn't sound good at all. Once, after Grandma Holmes muttered snide remarks about the presence of Black actors on television, he pulled my sister and me aside to let us know that he disagreed with his mother's comments and that everyone should have an equal chance. That was before the Black Power movement, the Great Society expansion of government, and the various revolutionary crusades of the late 1960s, which deeply divided the country and pushed him into a more traditionally conservative box. He remained supportive of basic civil rights and fairness, but didn't like being lectured that he was part of the problem.

You'd think that my desire to spend time with my dad would have translated into tagging along on his pool jobs, but these occasional father-son bonding attempts weren't a success. I quickly grew bored watching him vacuum the pool or fix a water filter. One spring day when I was about ten, my father was getting a customer's pool ready for the summer and I absentmindedly walked out on a diving board that hadn't yet been bolted down and subsequently plunged myself into the freezing water. That was the end of the "take your son to work" field trips. That particular pool customer cynically suggested to my father that I had deliberately caused this ruckus to get out of working with him that day—an idea that he rejected with disgust. I was lucky that my parents took things in stride, because I made more than my fair share of goofball mistakes. When I was skating at the local pond, for instance, and ruined the leather boot of my skates by placing them too close to the fire we were warming ourselves around, my mother didn't berate me for being so careless because she could already see how remorseful I was.

A thoroughly modern mom, my mother wore Bermuda shorts and blouses in the summer and slacks and turtlenecks in the winter. A bit of a former tomboy, she neither carried a pocketbook nor wore a dress around the house. She didn't wear makeup either. During my whole childhood, I never saw her or my sister primping in front of the mirror or applying cosmetics. She made sure we had a HiFi record player in our new Brockton house and bought a handful of classic Broadway cast albums and musical soundtracks for us to listen to. Every summer, we went to see a musical in a theatre-in-the-round tent at the South Shore Music Circus. I've never been able to listen to any song from *Oklahoma* without being immediately transported back to my seven-year-old self. Not understanding its double entendres, I'd exuberantly sing "I'm Just a Girl Who Can't Say No" to anyone who would listen. To this day, my wife mocks my enthusiasm for classic Broadway, joking that I know a little too much about Rogers & Hammerstein for a straight guy.

My one objection to my mother's lifestyle was that she smoked, which affronted my delicate sense of smell. My sister and I campaigned so vigorously against it that she quit cold turkey on November 22nd, 1964, the first anniversary of the JFK assassination. I had been especially disgusted by the combined odors of coffee and cigarettes, and consequently have never taken even a sip of coffee. Smoking *so* revolted me that I also never tried marijuana, which of course required inhaling smoke. In high school and college, I was such an antismoking loudmouth about both tobacco and marijuana that if my friends smoked, they knew better than to do it around me. And even after that, I wouldn't date any women who smoked either. (It's hard now to remember just how pervasive smoking was in the 1960s. People used to smoke in airplanes, hospitals, restaurants, college classrooms—you name it. Ugh!)

My parents were not big believers in child enrichment activities, but beginning in the second grade, they did enroll me in various athletic programs at the local YMCA—a tall, imposing building in downtown Brockton. They must have thought I needed more structured exercise to address the undisciplined hanging around I did in our neighborhood. Sadly, either they didn't show me how to check in, or more likely, I didn't pay attention to their instructions, but on my first day I climbed the stairs to the second floor check-in desk and found myself in a room full of strangers without knowing what to do. I was crying so pitifully that the Y's manager came out of his office to see what the problem was. He very kindly demonstrated that all I had to do was present my card at the front desk and then proceed to the locker room. Since then, I've had a mild phobia about entering strange buildings without explicit instructions on where to go. And not surprisingly, I suppose, when I joined the YMCA in Washington 30 years later, I had flashbacks and near-panic attacks every time I used the facility.

Once I figured out its entrance policies, the Y became a somewhat important part of my life. I learned how to swim in their pool, although I cowered in front of the 20-something swimming instructor, a stocky guy who thought it hilarious to toss boys into the pool without warning. The other kids seemed to like it, but I trembled at the prospect. As a light-shooting guard, I played a lot of basketball in their gyms, not only as a member of the Y, but later, through our city-wide church basketball league. But my greatest achievement was not an athletic one. Our county-wide junior Olympics had one non-physical contest—a checkers tournament—and in the second grade, I finished first in Brockton and third in Plymouth County, beating out even fifth and sixth graders. Alas, I peaked too soon and never again won an organized, medal-awarded skill contest anywhere else.

My home entertainment was very anodyne and homogenized. American society at the time was a monoculture perpetuated by three TV networks, a handful of movie studios, the major book publishers, and a few national magazines. My busy parents rarely engaged with popular culture except for taking us to a few Doris Day movies at the drive-in, so my sister and I were on our own. But we were in safe hands with any screen we sat in front of. The occasional James Bond movie aside, every mass market product we consumed upheld traditional morality. On television, we mostly watched sitcoms. This included family shows that featured a lot of kids (*Leave it to Beaver*, *The Patty*

Duke Show) and those that had dumb premises (friendly witches, genies, talking cars, etc.) We also watched a few Westerns and World War II dramas, which provided a skewed look at history. In college, I was shocked to learn that the period from D-Day to V-E Day took only ten months. After shows like *Combat* and *Hogan's Heroes*, which lasted years and years, I had assumed that the war in Europe was a much more prolonged effort.

As is the case with many of my generation, I can point to the day when I began to culturally split from my family: February 9th, 1964, the night The Beatles appeared on *The Ed Sullivan Show*. This is a cliché as true for me as it was for millions of other baby boomers. I had barely heard of them until that afternoon, when we showed up for a family-to-family visit at the home of my parents' friends the Cowles, but their two daughters were squirming with excitement over this new group. We watched, they squealed, I became a fan. The first record I ever owned was an American version of the "Please Please Me" album that my mother purchased at the Coats Field department store in downtown Brockton. I still own it and still think it's great.

Although my mother had bought me a Beatles record, she couldn't understand their appeal at all. At age 32, it's not like she was an old fogey, but she was on the other side of a very deep generation gap. My father was actively hostile to The Beatles, with their too-long hair and insouciance. Like many other adults, he saw them as threats to the established order. If kids could start demanding a culture of their own, completely divorced from their parents' established traditions, where would it end?

Despite parental opposition, I plunged deep into Beatlemania, attending their first two movies (*A Hard Day's Night* and *Help*) multiple times and collecting Beatles trading cards. I'd spin their records in the living room while singing along and rocking out on a badminton racket, all the while keeping the door ajar in case a talent scout drove by, heard my sweet vocals, and decided to sign me on as a backup singer.

The Beatles became the thin wedge that began to separate me from my parents. Until then, everyone in the house had listened to the same records;

now suddenly, I owned LPs that no one else wanted to hear. The disconnect this set in motion would have happened anyway, since teenagers eventually do establish their own identity, but I was hitting adolescence at the peak of the counterculture, when kids' and parents' sensibilities were further apart than any time before or since. I turned 13 in 1967, just a few months before "The Summer of Love," and was 14 during Woodstock, when most adults wanted nothing to do with any part of youth culture. This was very different from my son's childhood, when my wife and I enjoyed the music and comedy CDs that he'd discovered, and he continued to listen to ours (including The Beatles).

I never became an alienated or angsty teenager, but about this time I did begin to perceive that I was a bit unlike the rest of the family. It wasn't just the music—there was a difference in temperament too. My parents had been athletic and good with practical things, where I was analytical and possibly thinking too much. I couldn't tinker with a car or fix an appliance to save my life. My parents, with their dozens of close friends, were extreme extroverts, and although I had some close pals, I was shy around strangers and would be just as happy to spend time by myself. I loved taking off on my bike to explore Brockton or sitting in my room listening to Bill Cosby comedy albums or just lying on my bed daydreaming. And of course there was all that reading: comic books, baseball magazines, biographies of famous Americans, adventure stories by Robert Louis Stevenson, *Nancy Drew* books I'd discovered at my grandparents' house, humor journals like *Mad*, and mainstream magazines like *Reader's Digest* and *Time*.

I was no child prodigy or spaced-out kid, and far from the smartest one in my class, so I was surprised to learn that my Nantucket grandfather and uncle—both practical-minded carpenters—had nicknamed me "the absent-minded professor." What I had done to earn that title, I don't know, but more than once my mother cautioned me not to call attention to things I learned in school because it looked like I was flaunting my intelligence.

Absent-minded professor or not, I was lucky that my parents didn't insist on raising a mini-me. By the time I entered junior high school, I had shown zero aptitude for any practical trade, and it was obvious that I was on a college track. This meant I'd be on a different path than they had followed.

Attending college wasn't something they insisted on, but it was pretty clear that I was expected to work hard and become the best version of whatever I was supposed to be. When I headed off to junior high school and started to evolve into that new version of myself, I began to worry about a much wider community than my little bubble at home. I was slowly breaking out of the family cocoon.

CHAPTER 9

West is Best

I never thought much about social distinctions until I went to junior high school. On television, I learned about the fabulously rich, desperately poor, enormously famous, and wretchedly miserable, but everyone seemed pretty average within my own orbit. Not until the seventh grade did I learn that there exist many gradations within the world of average.

In the mid-1960s, the first level of stratification started with which junior high school you attended. The city had recently constructed four of them that corresponded to the quadrants of the compass: north, south, east, and west. Theoretically equal in layout and resources, each featured a two-story, gray, polished brick building with all the modern educational conveniences that Ellis Brett had lacked. But as the Supreme Court had previously observed in another context, there is no such thing as separate but equal. The city's affluent neighborhoods were located on the West Side, so West Junior High prided itself as the rich school with the smartest students. The school was predominantly white; my class had just five Black students, one Hispanic, and a kid who identified as Cape Verdean Portuguese and was mildly put off when I thought he was African American. Our unofficial motto stated:

"West is Best." As for the East Side, the poorest part of town, literally on the wrong side of the railroad tracks that bisected the city and home to our housing projects, our mocking motto for them was "East is Least."

Within West Junior High, I discovered numerous other status gradations, the most blatantly obvious of which was academic tracking. The school grouped us into four levels of academic instruction: Advanced, Honors, Standard, and Basic. My friends and I heartlessly translated these levels as Very Smart, Pretty Smart, Average, and Dumb. This was not fair, because the Basic students were neither unintelligent nor destined for careers in fast food sales, but we were just beginning to learn the art of putting down others to mitigate our own insecurities.

As it turned out, no alumni from Ellis Brett made it into the Advanced classes, which were largely reserved for the kids who'd attended Goddard, Brockton's one magnet school for elementary school geniuses. The kids in those classes—especially a remarkable cohort of accomplished, charismatic, funny, overconfident girls—were definitely a different order of student from the rest of us. They had known each other for years and were mostly the offspring of doctors, lawyers, and other professionals. According to popular culture, most junior high schools are under the thumb of brutish athletes, rich kids, and beauty queens, but at West, the dominant social group consisted of academically high-achieving girls. They were constantly lauded as a hybrid between Shirley MacLaine and Margaret Chase Smith, and I couldn't help but feel like a second class citizen in my own school.

Even within my less elevated Honors classes, I struggled to integrate into a whole new peer group. Nine or ten elementary schools funneled their graduates into West Junior High, and walking the corridors was like being dropped into a particularly anxiety-ridden carnival midway of early teen angst. I was so preoccupied with my own insecurities that I didn't realize everyone else was going through the same thing. To say that the seventh grade is an awkward age is putting it mildly. Half the girls were a foot taller than the boys; some of the boys had bad acne, braces, or the faint traces of early pubescent facial hair; and no one was comfortable in his or her skin. The one safe space was lunch, which I ate with my old Ellis Brett friends Philip Tasho, Rich Martel, and Jimmy Perdickis, in a wide, low-ceilinged room that always

West Junior High School.

smelled of Sloppy Joes regardless of that day's menu. Always fussy about my food, I couldn't stomach the cafeteria's chicken ala king, stringy pizza, or dried pork chops, and survived almost solely on mother's peanut butter sandwiches ("NO JELLY, please!") for three years.

Although not yet the viper pit it became in the Instagram era, junior high school in the 1960s did have its own set of norms. According to one firm social custom, boys couldn't wear white socks. There were a couple of misfits who innocently broke these rules and became objects of derision. One girl with a deeper social conscience than I tried to convince me of the injustice of this convention. These fashion offenders, she argued, were the sons of tradesmen who wore white socks with their work boots, so there was no reason for their homes to have dark socks. Maybe, maybe not, but you can rest assured that for the rest of my life I always dressed with appropriate situational footwear and hose.

Gym offered another opportunity for humiliation. After our exertions, all the boys were expected to get naked in front of each other, stripping off the gym clothes and unnecessary jock straps that we'd carried to school in our gym bags, and take a nice, hygienic, communal shower to wash away the buckets of sweat we had theoretically worked up playing dodgeball or whatever. Having been told repeatedly by my father not to accidentally expose myself to my babysitters, I was an intensely modest child, and I hated this; I'd never even seen a fully naked person before and now I was expected to prance around like I was in a nudist colony? Worse, we were all in various stages of development, or non-development in many cases. One day after showers, I observed a couple of pre-adolescent seventh graders as smooth and white as a pair of flounders, staring at a taller, fully developed classmate as he toweled off. "What are you looking at?" the bigger guy growled, "Looking for something to eat?" Off they slinked.

I mostly escaped social disgrace by rendering myself invisible, although I did have one nemesis who tried to make life difficult: Robert Joyce, who sat behind me in most of my alphabetically arranged classes. He was even shorter and runtier than I, but with half a dozen older siblings, far worldlier. He pegged me pretty quickly as an easy target. Naïvely thinking we were friends, I answered truthfully when he asked if I "liked" any girls in our class. Yes, I admitted. Patricia Fox, a very cute classmate, seemed really nice. He was scornful, claiming she was "flat as a board" because she hadn't filled out yet (although he was equally undeveloped, so who was *he* to complain?) He proceeded to tell everyone that I had a crush on her, which had the other girls in the class tittering. After that, I was too embarrassed to ever talk to her, so to this day I have never exchanged two words with the girl who, in high school, morphed into the popular, amply proportioned Patty Fox. Robert also tried to embarrass me by nicknaming me "El Boner," falsely claiming that I displayed a noticeable erection one day. Whenever there was a quiet moment in class after this, he would lean over and in a soft mocking tone whisper either "flat as a board" or "El Boner." I was not sorry when he transferred to Catholic school in the ninth grade.

The school believed that boys should learn to be men and girls should grow up to be women. Boys went to Shop Class, where it took us an entire year to build end tables for our mothers. Girls attended Home Economics, where they learned a little about cooking and very little about economics. The one class that really should have been segregated by gender—Health—was co-ed, which meant there would be no in-depth discussions about what was happening to our bodies. There was no one to tell us, for example, that our sweat glands were now producing a pungent aroma, which is why some of our classrooms subsequently smelled like locker rooms (actually, worse than locker rooms, because the second we excreted a drop of perspiration in gym, it was into those showers again). And there was no sex education at all. If someone had tried to demonstrate how to cover a banana with a condom, which was known to me then as a "safe," there would have been a parental riot.

It was okay to stand out only if your achievements seemed effortless. If you were a natural athlete, instinctive fashion plate, or obvious brainiac, great, but trying too hard was a bad look. One subcategory of kids who did stand out because they clearly didn't give a damn about anything were the greasers. "Greaser" was already an outdated expression that, in the 1950s, had applied to working class rebels who slicked their hair back and wore leather jackets. But in junior high, Philip, Rich, and I characterized a greaser as any guy who: 1) disdained authority, and 2) smoked. These kids were not an organized group, just semi-alienated individuals who seemed to think school was beneath contempt. They ranged from Ronald Caputo, a surly and scary first generation American who wore work clothes to school and was said to have been sent "up the river," (i.e. to reform school, whatever that was) to another kid named Chad, who had a nicer wardrobe, but hair that swept down across his forehead to his disdainful eyes. What they all shared was a hard stare that implied they'd be happy to beat you up with minimal provocation.

Another group of kids who stood out were the developmentally disabled. Most had what I now recognize as Down Syndrome, and they were all housed in one classroom—the unfortunately numbered Room 113—which was across the hall from my seventh-grade homeroom, at the end of the school's most distant corridor. These kids never left that room as far as I could tell, and they disturbed me because they aroused feelings of pity and revulsion that I didn't know how to handle.

I'm not really sure how much actual learning was going on in junior high school. These years were a bridge between the childlike wonder of elementary school and the more serious curiosity of high school. For three years, junior high functioned as a holding pen for molting teenagers. With our evolving brains occupied with trying to figure out where we and our bodies fit into society, there was little cognitive energy left over for academics. The amount of learning we absorbed in three years could have probably been crammed into one year by a well-constructed home schooling program.

That's not to say I didn't enjoy a few of my classes. My favorite class in seventh grade was English, where we learned about Ernest Hemingway, free-form poetry, and diagramming sentences. Our teacher, Miss Long, young and earnest but with no ear lobes at all, believed we could appreciate poetry by analyzing the lyrics of popular songs. She asked us to write a paper to be read aloud to the class, applying what we learned about rhyme schemes and literary themes to a "meaningful" song, perhaps not understanding that seventh graders were not only at various levels of physical development but musical as well. She was expecting deep thoughts on "Eleanor Rigby," "The Sounds of Silence," and "Strawberry Fields Forever." Unfortunately, my early Beatles fixation had temporarily gone on hiatus and I'd regressed to less sophisticated music. I did my essay on "Snoopy and the Red Baron" by The Royal Guardsmen, not because I loved the song, but because its lyrics had been printed in *Parade* magazine. But even that wasn't the worst selection. A girl named Linda had analyzed "A Spoonful of Sugar" from Mary Poppins, which caused Miss Long to remark that she'd been hoping for something less juvenile. I thought that was a bit harsh. I mean, what did she expect? We were six months out of elementary school.

My poor musical taste aside, I did have one personal triumph that year. The school held weekly assemblies in our vast auditorium, and each class was expected to supply content. When it was Miss Long's turn, I volunteered to write a play illustrating the development of vocabulary through wax museum figures. My idea was to make them come to life at night and debate among themselves who contributed more to the English language: a Viking, a pioneer, a pilgrim, etc. And yes, the producers of the movie *Night at the Museum* do owe me a royalty for copyright infringement, since my play has basically the same premise as their movie. My dialogue was less than scintillating, though. I had a go-go dancer say to an astronaut:

"You think we use stupid expressions? At least we don't go around yelling 'Mayday' in June." Also, from a caveman: "Me help start whole language by finding bright, hot thing and calling it fire." Neil Simon had nothing to worry about.

If my son had written that play in the 2000s, my wife and I would have been at the school with a couple of iPhones, and the video would have been posted on social media that afternoon, after which we would have enrolled him in a special after-school creative writing class. Back then, it never occurred to anyone—least of all me—that a parent would attend a school assembly or think there was anything special about writing a play that was produced for the whole school. When I got home that night, they asked how it went. I said, "Good," and that was that.

The adjustment to junior high school was difficult in the beginning, but eventually it began to work out. I wasn't a star, but I wasn't a reject either. When my classmates signed my end-of-year yearbooks, at least half of them wrote "To a good kid," which was generic but could have been worse. I had a small part in the eighth grade school play and was the prop manager for the ninth grade school musical. My friend Rich Martel had been recruited as an editor of the school yearbook, and he got me a spot on the yearbook staff so he'd have a friend to help him. Two years in a row, I shared my locker with Mike Gordon (the second time at *his* request), our class's best athlete who would go on to play a few games as catcher for the Chicago Cubs. I wasn't a loser if I was locker friends with Mike Gordon, right?

Crucially, I started to make friends with girls. One was Eleanor Eastman, a foster child living with a fundamentalist minister who led his flock at the Olivet Memorial Church, a lovely, modern, airy structure on Torrey Street. She would call me on the phone or find ways to come over to my house, where she also tried to befriend my mother, going so far as to send her letters in the summer. I didn't understand the concept of foster care then. All I knew was that Eleanor rarely saw her birth mother, who suffered from an unspecified set of problems, and never mentioned a birth father. When I finally met her foster father, he gave me a cold, wary stare. He didn't know whether I was trouble but he did know that, as a Congregationalist, I was barely one step above an outright pagan.

In the eighth grade, Eleanor convinced me to attend a special youth weekend at her church. Before I left the house the first morning, my father pulled me aside and warned, "Don't believe everything they say," the subtext being, "It's okay to be religious but don't take it too seriously, especially if they start speaking in tongues." Regrettably, no one spoke in tongues. Instead, there were about 50 other seemingly normal kids. We engaged in two days of activities and contests, like basketball and board games. One of the contests was "Name That Scripture." The youth leader would call out a bible verse, which was followed immediately by kids popping up and giving the citation—like *Jeopardy!* contestants answering the easy ten dollar questions. The culmination of the weekend was a barn-burning sermon by Eleanor's foster father about God's saving grace, etc., etc. This concluding peroration featured an invitation for all the youth who felt called by God's love to come to the front altar and commit their lives to Jesus. Two-thirds of the kids hopped up right away and walked to the front, some with tears streaming down their cheeks. Then slowly, one by one, the other stragglers went up too. Eventually, I was the only kid still sitting in the pews. As loath as I was to stand out, I was not going to claim sacred feelings I did not have, so my father's fears about me joining a cult were unfounded.

I went to my first co-ed party around this time. Michael Kovner, who lived down the street, celebrated his birthday by inviting a group of friends from Hebrew school, plus a couple of stray gentiles like me, to a party in his basement. I didn't know any of the girls, but just being in their presence as the Turtles' "Happy Together" spun on the record player was intoxicating and arousing in a way I couldn't identify. My throat tightened and felt like someone had reached through my mouth and pressed his thumbs against the pulsing blood vessels in the soft tissue. Soon after, I acquired my own '45 singles—"Kind of a Drag" by the Buckinghams and "Silence is Golden" by the Tremeloes—as a party gift at Michael's Bar Mitzvah and started buying them for myself at 59 cents. The great thing about singles was that you could curate your own musical line-up by stacking them on top of each other in the record player, after which they would drop down one after another and play automatically. Of course, I always imagined that the perfect mix of songs would impress the girls.

In eighth grade, the city received federal funding to expand its program for gifted students into junior high school. The program was pretentiously branded "Ceilings Unlimited" (C.U.), which, if you think about it, means exactly the opposite of what it tries to convey, since an unlimited number of ceilings would be a barrier to educational growth and exploration. The gifted kids selected for this program had one designated space of their own and didn't move from class to class like the rest of us. There, they'd receive more challenging instruction than they could get from even the Advanced classes. My friend Rich Martel was one of the few kids to make the leap from Honors into C.U., which meant he and I would never again be in a class together. His presence in this special program became our running joke; later in college he would confide to me that a concept in his philosophy class was so hard that "not even someone from C.U. could figure it out."

The creation of C.U., which sucked in everyone who had been in the school's Advanced classes, opened up opportunities for the rest of us to move up the academic food chain. For some reason, I was moved into the Advanced science class in eighth grade, a level that stuck through high school and eventually culminated in A.P. Biology. This would have significant consequences because I would—wrongly—come to believe that I had a special talent in science, and I'd go on to enter college as a biology major.

In truth, my strongest academic subjects, by far, were history and English. In my eighth grade history class, I enjoyed sparring about politics with my young, idealistic, left-leaning teacher Miss Salanikis, although the fun went out of that when first, Martin Luther King, and then, Bobby Kennedy, were assassinated. And ninth grade political science came pretty easy to me, because I already knew how the national, state, and city governments worked. I even knew the names of all our city councilors and most of the members of the U.S. Senate.

But my favorite class in all of junior high school was ninth grade English, led by a recent Boston University graduate named Linda Michelin. An educator who seemed to genuinely care about us as people, she was a good teacher who made literature engaging. Even learning new vocabulary words was fun; once a week we had a 10-minute test to prove we'd absorbed new words by using them in a paragraph, and I relished the chance to write amusing sentences that were sometimes rewarded with red-penciled smiley faces when she handed back my submission.

I was known in that class as "Holmespeare" because of my unconventional interpretations of the play *Julius Caesar*. As I gained confidence in the class, I became a little bit of a wise guy with a lot of contrary opinions. When the time came for her to sign my ninth grade yearbook, Miss Michelin would write: "Holmespeare, Best of luck with unrhymed poetry. *Julie Baby* (that was my pet name for the play), when Nixon destroys the nation, I'll be sure to write to you and ask your opinion as I always do. Just don't disagree with me. After all, 'Wilt thou lift up Mt. Olympus?' "

I was not the smartest person in the class or Miss Michelin's favorite, though. That would be Theresa Carr, who called herself T.C. As junior high school was drawing to a close, I wrote her a fan letter about some point she had made in class. She answered with alacrity ("alacrity" was one of the vocabulary words Miss Michelin introduced us to, by the way). Soon we were handing each other letters every couple of days. She wasn't particularly pretty and I wasn't exactly smitten, but I was fascinated by the offbeat way she thought.

T.C.'s letters had a mock-formal tone and were filled with philosophizing about religion and social issues, requests for me to grow my hair long, and stories about her best friend Pat Kurkul, another girl in our class whom she had nicknamed "Weird," as in, "I asked Weird to come over to my house today but she was busy." (It's a small irony that long after T.C. became a distant memory, Pat would go on to be one of my lifelong friends. We were so close that she and her future wife would be two out of a handful of friends invited to my very tiny wedding 20 years later.) She would admonish me to write longer letters, outline her plans to become a famous author (the title of her book was going to be "The Easy Life of a Teacher"), provide descriptions of her family activities, and lecture me at such length that it began to look like she was padding the content to fill five or six pages of lined notebook paper.

This was 1969 and the country was in a turmoil that was just beginning to reach Brockton. T.C. would later deny it, but I still have it in writing that she supported Nixon over Humphrey in 1968. I assume this was because her parents were passionate Republicans (the kind who would have watched *Fox News* if it had been around). But if her politics were still unexamined, she was already searching far and wide for a new religion. Raised a Catholic, she had rejected that faith and claimed to be both an atheist and a Buddhist who also dabbled in Taoism, Confucianism, and Zoroastrianism.

She and Pat played on the school's softball team and I attended a couple of games where I heckled "Hey, Buddhist" from the stands when she batted. My sister, arguably already the best female athlete in the school despite being a mere seventh grader, was also on the team, so there was no secret in our house about my interests. That became even more obvious when letters from T.C. started arriving in the mailbox during summer vacation. I had signed my first letter as "Anonymous," so she jokingly wrote back "Dear Anomalous," because that had been another one of Miss Michelin's vocabulary words. She was one of the many who referred to me as "Holmespeare," although this time in the third person as in "Is Holmespeare planning to attend the awards ceremony on Thursday?"

Halfway through the summer, she somewhat plaintively wrote, "Can't you think of anything we can argue about? We've sort of run religion down to the ground." Intellectual argumentation was a strange thing upon which to base a teenage romance, but that's how I got my first girlfriend. It was never exactly clear when she officially became my girlfriend because we weren't physical with each other yet, but by the end of summer, we were implicitly recognized by our friends and each other as a couple.

At that point, I could look back on junior high school with satisfaction at having successfully navigated the transition from boyhood to adolescence. I wasn't at my full height yet, but I was no longer a shrimp either and all my body parts were fully coordinated. We didn't have a phony graduation ceremony to send us on to the next level, but we did have a fun little pizza party in our home rooms. And unlike three years earlier when I'd been anxious about moving into junior high, I found myself very much looking forward to high school.

CHAPTER 10

High School Days, Part One

Whoen I became a high school sophomore in the fall of 1969, the post-War culture that dominated America for two decades still ruled our blue collar city. The youth rebellion, with its long hair, grungy clothing, sexual liberation, contempt for authority, and rejection of bourgeois values, had been largely kept at bay. What I knew about the counterculture had been gleaned primarily from TV screens, mainstream news magazines, the music industry, and movies like *Easy Rider*—in other words, from the entertainment industrial complex that hippies supposedly despised—not from real life.

The Brockton High School halls through which we ventured seemed like a museum for the year 1949, or even 1929. A three-story, high-ceilinged early 20th century pile of brick with wide hallways and wooden desks bolted to the floors of nearly identical classrooms, it had been designed to project authority and a respect for tradition. Unfortunately, the dusty display cases of oxidizing championship trophies that celebrated the triumphs of earlier generations were meaningless to us and might as well have been consigned to a mortuary.

But if the facility itself promoted the quintessential Bobby Soxer high school experience, it was obvious from day one that this was not what we were going to get. After our troops returned from World War II and launched the baby boom, Brockton's city planners had been slow to address the implications for the local schools. The first boomers hit tenth grade around 1960 and totally overwhelmed the high school within a few short years. Lacking the space to house everyone, the school committee resorted to "double sessions" that split up the grades. Juniors and seniors attended in the morning, and sophomores went in the afternoon. Though it solved our space problem, this functional but utilitarian approach to education deprived us of many of the bells and whistles that contribute to school spirit: the after-school clubs, pep rallies, and sense of a cohesive, we're-all-in-this-together experience that traditionally defines high school for most people.

My average day in tenth grade went something like this: wake at 9:00am (frequently in an empty house, or sometimes with my mother tsk-tsking that I was sleeping so late); consume cereal for breakfast while watching *Jeopardy!* or soap operas; eat a sandwich for lunch two hours later; walk or cadge a ride to school downtown; gather in the school's crowded auditorium with a thousand other rambunctious sophomores at noon; migrate to homeroom for attendance-taking and the Pledge of Allegiance after the upperclassmen had left the building; head off to academic classes at 12:45pm, which proceeded without breaks until 5:06pm; walk or get a ride home; finish homework after dinner; unwind in front of the TV until midnight.

Even with the '70s knocking on the door, we still dressed like the dutiful children of the '50s. Just two years earlier, boys had been required to wear neckties to school every day, and even our somewhat looser dress code still called for neat collared shirts, pressed pants and leather shoes. The girls, of course, needed to attend in dresses or skirts. I was still so under the sway of the mid-'60s look that, in order to appear more grown up, I would occasionally accent my outfit with one of my many fat polyester ties, thus projecting the image of a contented middle manager at an insurance company. The only time we could break the dress code was the school's annual "Jeans Day," during which we could contribute a dollar to charity and parade around in what I still called "dungarees." That felt as transgressive as wearing our Halloween costumes to school back at Ellis Brett.

After sophomore year, the school largely gave up trying to maintain a *Happy Days* dress code. By the time we graduated, girls could wear pants or short skirts, boys could sport T-shirts and work boots and anyone could wear jeans. This meant a lot of diversity. In a single classroom you could have the *Bye Bye Birdie* Ann-Margaret sitting next to Hanoi Jane Fonda, or Tab Hunter alongside Bob Dylan.

But the fight over clothes was nothing compared to arguments over hair. It's hard now to comprehend that hair was once such a bitterly contested subject. Well into the middle of the 1960s, the ideal American man looked like an astronaut, sporting either a Brylcreemed pompadour or a crew cut. That began to change with The Beatles, whose unruly mop-tops broke the tyranny of neatness. After that, hair quickly became political, and dinner tables everywhere became battlegrounds. If you rejected the crew cut, you were supposedly giving the finger to everything associated with the military and corporate America, something that most parents interpreted as a challenge to their own authority.

I was hardly a revolutionary, but I was tired of presenting as a square. My mother had stopped giving me crew cuts midway through elementary school, but I still would have fit in at a military academy with the way I dressed. I wanted to grow my hair out at least a little bit and don some dungarees, more for comfort than to make any kind of statement. But my mother adamantly opposed any offspring of hers wearing denim, which she associated with farming and considered disrespectful, so jeans stayed out of my wardrobe until college. The most I was able to get away with was a rumpled, third-hand, green corduroy sports coat that I picked up in the used clothes section of our local Army Navy store, a fashion statement that parents loathed but didn't forbid. Man, I thought that jacket was cool.

Although I was always the dutiful son and didn't make a big stink about it, clothes and hair remained a lingering family issue, with mild resentment on both sides. One Thanksgiving, my older cousin Paul showed up from Amherst College with shoulder-length tresses that literally scandalized the rest of us who had never seen hair like that close up. Not even his status as the favorite cousin could overcome the dismay that befell every adult that day. When my Uncle Carl expressed astonishment at Paul's hair, my father gestured to me and said sourly, "Well, Gary's isn't much better." That was ridiculous, given that barely one follicle touched the top of my ears. But I think that was his way of signaling to me, "Don't even think about it, buddy."

My sophomore year was one of the most tumultuous periods in American history, with massive anti-war demonstrations across college campuses that culminated in the Kent State shootings. Black Power surged. Seemingly out of nowhere came complaints about pollution and the subsequent launch of the first Earth Day, where environmentalists confidently predicted that factories and their sun-reflecting particulates would cause a global freeze by the year 2000. Just as suddenly, women started protesting about "male chauvinism," denouncing both *Playboy* magazine and suburbia, while demanding more avenues to self-fulfillment. There were a lot of new opinions to digest all at once.

I started playing soccer in the 10th grade to prove I wasn't just a book nerd.

Meanwhile, I had three posters on the wall of my bedroom: a close-up of the actor Omar Sharif from *Dr. Zhivago*, a glow-in-the-dark drawing of the Maharishi Mahesh Yogi, and a poster with portraits of the first 34 U.S. presidents. Clearly my head was residing in a number of different spaces. And while I absolutely abjured any scent for myself, which would have been pretentious or "phony," I sometimes came home smelling of incense or the patchouli oil that my female friends doused themselves with.

Since I didn't need to be at school until noon, I could follow all this turmoil on *The Dick Cavett Show*, the highbrow alternative to Johnny Carson. It had become an open forum for politicians, celebrities, and intellectuals to debate the issues of the day, and I soaked it all up into the early hours of the morning. I also read *Time* magazine, which provided the establishment's perspective on the social upheaval, and the *Boston Phoenix*, an underground newspaper that was the local voice of the left. Even though I was a conservative, I was interested in the ferment.

Eventually, Brockton High buckled to late-'60s turmoil. Some upperclassmen, unhappy with what they considered censorship in the *Brocktonia*, the school-sanctioned student newspaper, created an alternative paper called *A.P.A.T.H.Y.*, which was an acronym for "A Polite Answer to Hypocrisy's Yeoman." Then our student government was exposed as a joke. Just two years earlier, school rules had dictated that the President and Treasurer be a boy, and that girls fill the roles of Vice President and Secretary. Those gender-based rules were now gone, but the administration was still on guard against Bolshevism. When it came time to have the traditional assembly at which the candidates for class offices would make their campaign speeches, the administration excluded one presidential candidate from the ballot—the long-haired, radicalized Michael Murphy. That didn't stop him from rushing the stage halfway through the presidential speeches, grabbing the microphone, and declaring that our rights were being denied. This only lasted about 15 seconds before he was hustled off by the school's burliest vice principal, never to surface again as a figure of notoriety. Hardly anyone took school government seriously after that, and we ended up electing the goofball Lester Zembrowski as class president, primarily because he amused us by screwing up his election speech so badly.

Later that year, the city cancelled high school one day because students from all the local colleges—Stonehill, Massasoit Junior College, and Bridgewater State—had converged on downtown Brockton for an anti-war protest about a block from our classrooms, and the authorities decided it wasn't a good idea to add 4,000 high school kids to the mix. This was secretly thrilling in the way that an approaching tornado makes your heart race, but at this point I began to wonder if society really would dissolve.

Political passions eventually drove a major wedge between me and my free-thinking girlfriend T.C. (who we will now refer to as Theresa, since she dropped the nickname around this time), but that was all in the future. As 15 year olds in the fall of 1969, we were still in the exquisitely sweet process of getting to know one another. We spent hours on the phone together and I soon became well-acquainted with her house, her parents, her two younger sisters, and the family's pair of always-shedding German shepherds. Her mother Zola once introduced me as "practically a son," a designation I neither sought nor encouraged.

Although having a girlfriend had its obvious benefits, the real long-term advantage of the relationship was that we were able to pool our social resources and develop a large group of friends. I'd made no lasting friendships at West Junior High, but now Theresa was introducing me to her friends and in turn, I was integrating them with mine; before you knew it there were about a dozen of us hanging out together.

At the center of this amorphous group was Theresa and her still-best friend Pat, and me and my best friend Philip. It wasn't exactly double dating, but we were a tight foursome for about a year, especially when I turned 16-and-a-half and got my driver's license. We celebrated at Wah Sun in downtown Brockton, which was both the first time I consumed Chinese food, and the first time I ate in an adult restaurant with just my friends. Thanks to my driver's license, the four of us were exploring the world together: the pizza place, the drive-in, or the beach. And the next thing you know, we were cruising up the Southeast Expressway to Boston and Cambridge for concerts, movies, cafés, and the other sophisticated things we imagined young adults were doing. 40 years later when my own son got his license, it was unimaginable that I'd have let him drive our car into the center of a major city, especially one that still had a "Combat Zone," which was then Boston's red light district and porn hub. But in 1970, there I was, not even 17 years old, trying to navigate the tangled streets of Boston without even the help of a GPS.

I look back on this period with a great deal of fondness. It was so much fun and the four of us were all experiencing it at the same time—a new school, with new friends, new ideas, and a whole new start. But there was one embarrassing-in-retrospect element to it. I was very shy about the romantic aspects of dating, and my relationship with Theresa was chaste for a long time. If she'd been wearing a chador, she couldn't have been better protected than she was sitting alone with me in a car. She made her displeasure with this unnaturally platonic arrangement known to her friends, who in turn counseled me to get with the program. (The idea that she could have flirted or done something other than sit passively and wait for me to make the first move seems not to have occurred to anybody.) One cold afternoon, after we'd all been into Boston to see the Saturday matinee of *Hair*, another friend, Nancy Piesco, took a moment from dropping me off at home to light a fire under me; as her father's car idled in front of my house, she warned that Theresa was so starved for affection there was no telling what harmful thing she might do to herself if she didn't get some physical response from me. Talk about pressure. Eventually, we shared some teenage embraces on the living room couch during a New Year's Eve babysitting assignment and everything was fine. Until it stopped being fine.

The heart of our conflict wasn't politics as narrowly defined. We didn't argue over political candidates or even about the Vietnam War itself. The problem was that we had a different understanding of authenticity. I had been heavily influenced by *Mad* magazine, which satirized pretentiousness and artificiality, and also by *The Catcher in the Rye*, with its disdain for phoniness of all kinds. As I hit high school, I was becoming skeptical about behavior that I suspected my other, less authentic classmates manufactured for effect. One time, I innocently made what I thought was an obvious observation, that people create self-images and present facades to the world; she read me the riot act, lamenting that I was too cynical, and how could I live in this world if I really thought people were like that? What it boiled down to was that we had a *Sense and Sensibility* conflict. I was analytical, detached, and skeptical, whereas she wanted to grab new ideas about meaning and being and embody them immediately.

She was more than the usual tangle of contradictions. On the one hand, she was conspicuously playful. At her instigation, she and her friends sometimes used baby talk, as in "Wednesday is a poopy day." They also adopted *Winnie the Pooh* nicknames like Piglet and Tigger, which made me gag, especially since I was convinced she didn't really understand A.A. Milne's gentle subversive humor. For all her forced playfulness, she just didn't have the mirth gene. She never told jokes, which she found vaguely aggressive and was quick to take offense to on social or political grounds. She saw the world in black and white and couldn't appreciate the grays and complexities in between, where humor, wit, irony, and even wisdom lie.

As time went on, we increasingly rubbed each other raw. She was in an English class called "Writers of the Mod Generation." My phoniness antenna was already up with that title, but what really annoyed me was that the teacher, a gaunt, bearded 23-year-old Harvard graduate named Mark Pendergrast, instructed the class to call him Mark instead of Mr. Pendergrast. He'd be denied tenure two years later and eventually go on to be a well-known freelance writer with books about Coca Cola, coffee, the city of Atlanta, and repressed memory, but for a brief moment he was a student sensation. Theresa and all her friends very quickly fell in love with him and it was "Mark said this" and "Mark said that." Soon, I was referring to him sarcastically as "Marky Maypo" after the cartoon baby in the oatmeal ad. I'm not proud of this juvenile response, but it bugged me that these girls were putting on airs through their prideful over-familiarity with a teacher *and* making it clear I wasn't part of that cool crowd.

Another time, several of us were in Nancy's downstairs playroom listening to Elton John's recently released debut album. When the song "Take Me to the Pilot" came on, one of the other guys, a drummer in the school band, became increasingly frenzied as he played "air drums" with invisible drumsticks. My attitude was basically "oh, brother" and I made a snarky remark to

Theresa on the ride home about his overly demonstrative display, to which she angrily replied that when the spirit moves you, it's natural that you'd lose control in the ecstasy of the moment. Well, maybe, but I wondered whether he managed to control himself when he was listening at home alone without an audience.

These petty arguments are hardly worth remembering, but they illustrate which side the two of us fell in the culture divide of the late 1960s. I was not just politically but personally conservative, convinced that most of the counterculture was a fraud and a put-on. I loved the era's music but not the self-indulgence, and nothing made me gag more than media commentary that our generation was the most educated, generous, forward-looking, spiritual, and unmaterialistic generation in history. The expression "OK, boomer" did not exist back then, but if it had, I would have said it a dozen times a day.

Unfortunately, I see only now that I was pretty rigid and unforgiving of people who took themselves too seriously. We were just teenagers stumbling around in the dark, trying to figure out who we were, and I should have taken that into account. If an awkward classmate referred to herself as a "poetess," a better person than I would have rolled with it instead of snickering. And sometimes I was just plain wrong. When Theresa subscribed to a new magazine called *Intellectual Digest*, I thought that was an act of unbelievable pretentiousness, but when I got around to reading it myself, I found the content surprisingly interesting.

By the time we got to junior year, Theresa and many of her friends had abandoned female grooming norms, including shaving her legs and underarms. I guess this was something Simone de Beauvoir did? Not that it mattered much; she had once worn tight-fitting short dresses but now she increasingly showed up in jeans, army shirts, and other full-body cover-ups. She also stopped washing her hair daily, prompting an acquaintance who shared her politics but not her fashion sense to remark uncharitably, "Here comes the girl with the Wesson Oil hair."

To express their existential despair, she and her friends created the PhD.S.C.—The PhD Suicide Club. The premise was that they would all earn PhD's and then, in a protest against materialism, commit mass suicide—a goal thankfully forgotten before they earned even their first diploma. She also started superficially cutting her wrists, leaving non-lethal but visible scars. I now understand that teenage cutting is a cry for help, but at the time I wrote it off as weirdness for its own sake.

When it started, our relationship had been built on intellectual friction and debating our different perspectives, but that became untenable when one of us completely rejected the very premise of the '60s, and the other eagerly embraced it. Simple momentum and our shared circle of friends kept us together for over two years, but as we neared the end of junior year, she had transferred much of her emotional attention to her female friends and developed an obvious but unspoken infatuation with Carol Romans, another girl in our group.

The end came one summer night when about 20 of us were just hanging around another girl's house and I walked into a room and saw her smoking a joint with our hostess's older brother. I was an anti-drug zealot, but what really made me mad is that she was inhaling so deeply that she'd clearly been sneaking around behind my back long enough to be good at it. I drove her home in angry silence that night, and she never called me again and I never called her either. That fall, I sat next to her in A.P. Biology and we each did our best to pretend that the other was invisible.

In senior year, she embarked on a very public romantic relationship with Cynthia Cook, another smart and iconoclastic figure at our school. This was scandalous in 1972. As far as I could tell, even though some of their distant acquaintances were disgusted, they had the support and acceptance of their closer friends. For my part, I was more bemused than anything that the girl who, two years earlier, had been complaining so loudly that I hadn't been forward enough with her physically had now emerged as the school's leading lesbian.

Cynthia would go on to attend a prestigious college and eventually marry, but for Theresa there was no turning back. When she went off to UMass, she became a full-time activist and had some kind of breakdown that required intervention from a school psychologist. After graduation, she identified as a Marxist; I was told that the Communist party gave her more grief for being a lesbian than she ever got in high school. She became a union carpenter in New Haven and occasionally worked for the cause in Cuba. She got injured on the job and then started splitting her time between Key West and Connecticut. In later years, she developed facial hair, and rather than resort to electrolysis or conventional treatments, she boldly grew a remarkably long Ho Chi Minh beard.

All the statements in the preceding paragraph came from information I sporadically picked up second- and third-hand in the 40 years after we graduated from high school. In the mid-1980s, someone who'd attended UMass with her told me she had talked about her high school friends "all the time" in college. This woman said Theresa kept a photo of me kicking a soccer ball in her dorm room and that she'd even confided the story about my prolonged shyness in kissing her. It turns out even radical lesbians engage in girl talk.

Then in 2015, I heard she'd died of cancer only a year earlier. A Google search located an obituary with the headline, "Oft-Jailed Activist Receives Final Release." The photo confirmed the beard and the obituary said that after a long period of atheism, she'd "embraced Tibetan Buddhism near the end of the 20th century." I ruefully smiled at the idea that she'd come full circle to where she'd been in the ninth grade. Another obituary said she was a "self-described Marxist-Leninist lesbian feminist" who had worked with many groups, including the New Haven Committee Against Repression, the Committee in Solidarity with the People of El Salvador (CISPES), Spinsters Opposed to Nuclear Genocide (SONG), the Women's Pentagon Action, and the Coalition to Stop Trident.

The irony is that we had both evolved into even more extreme versions of ourselves than we ever could have imagined back in high school. I never really thought she'd turn into an actual communist, even if I'd joked about it at the time, and I'm sure she never imagined that Ronald Reagan would be President and that I'd work in his White House. But there was another outcome she might not have anticipated—my approach to life. I still find much of humanity ridiculous, but have worked to be more accepting and forgiving; not knowing what people are going through, I'm more willing to give them a break. I'm sure she'd still find me unbearably insufferable. And while it's true I'll always be a skeptic, I do try to leaven it with a heavy dose of empathy, which is something that we all need, myself included.

CHAPTER 11

High School Days, Part Two

I'll say this for Brockton—the city fathers were not totally somnambulant in the mid-1960s. Facing a future of crumbling shoe factories, shuttered downtown stores, and middle-class flight, they rolled the dice. In 1965, the City Council authorized $8 million to build a high school, gambling that a brand new state-of-the-art building would make the city attractive to families and arrest the urban trends that afflicted other industrial cities in the American Northeast.

With a body of 5,000, Brockton could have easily built two schools, but opted instead for the classic 1960s Great Society solution—throwing money at the problem. Rather than settling for a couple of modest institutions, they shot the moon on a mega-school that would put the city on the map for something other than being Rocky Marciano's hometown. We'd be the biggest high school east of the Mississippi! We'd also be the school of the future—a tricked-out, high-tech marvel that would make the rest of the state envy our foresight, wisdom, and good fortune. It was fitting that the new facility had one of the few planetariums in Massachusetts, because we were definitely reaching for the stars.

When it opened in the fall of 1970, students would no longer converge on that mausoleum downtown. The new facility, grandiloquently called a campus, was situated in a former dairy pasture at the edge of town. There it sat, surrounded by acres of parking lots, multiple sports fields, several tennis courts, a skating rink, and the cherry on the top: a 10,000-seat football stadium named for Rocky himself. This would-be temple of learning was a masterpiece of modernist architecture, consisting of eight three-story, interlocking cement boxes that featured rectangular, gray concrete exterior planes separated by narrow black windows stretching from the ground to its many flat roofs. It looked more like the IBM corporate headquarters than a school.

The facility, said to be as big as an aircraft carrier, consisted of: 1) four general academic buildings—the Red, Green, Yellow, and Azure houses (Why "azure" and not blue? Never explained)—each of which had its own cafeteria and an "Instructional Resource Center," a pretentious name for "library;" 2) a central science center that connected the four houses; 3) a huge fine arts building, with music rooms, art studios, and a 1,600-seat auditorium facing

Brockton High looked more like an IBM headquarters than a high school.

a stage rivaling anything on Broadway, all of which anchored one end of the complex; and 4) a physical education building, with various gyms, work-out rooms, and an Olympic-sized swimming pool, which anchored the other end.

Although daunted by the building, which was sometimes hard to navigate, we were still excited to be part of an educational experiment to see if bigger really could be better. Surprisingly, being a very small fish in a very big pond was liberating, at least for me. It was easy to get lost in the crowd but also possible to find your own kind. A side benefit of such a massive population was that no clique or social group could dominate. The school's jocks, cheerleaders, rich kids, and teen beauties were so vastly outnumbered by average shmoos that they couldn't wield the social weapons that would have been available to them at a smaller school. This meant that niche groups thrived. Even our small lesbian community, some out, some not, generally escaped social opprobrium because no one could enforce traditional conformity. (Although, to be fair, no gay boy dared risk public exposure, so this was not exactly a diversity paradise.)

Having four huge cafeterias helped enormously in leveling the social scene. If you wanted to avoid an obnoxious group, you just ate lunch somewhere else. My friends and I congregated in the Yellow cafeteria, and since the school followed a complicated six-day, alphabet-based schedule (running from A Day to F Day), no day of the week was exactly the same and you never knew who would show up for lunch. We were all so casual and open that if someone arrived with a new acquaintance he or she would be welcome at our table.

Unfortunately, despite the dazzling physical plant, Brockton High School could not rescue Brockton. At its core, Brockton was still a working class city, and the new high school was designed for more exalted aspirations. Most importantly, the planners overlooked the critical element of teaching. A school is much more than a building. If your goal is to raise a student body into a higher station in life, you need an outstanding faculty and visionary leadership, something we sorely lacked. What we got was old wine being poured into new wineskins.

With so many kids, the personal touch was definitely lacking. When my European history teacher wanted to move me into her advanced class, taught later in the day at the same time my English class met, my guidance counselor could not have been less interested. The only way I could be moved to that later period, he said, was to enroll in an English class that met at the same time as my history class. And the only one available was an advanced English class, which wasn't a bad idea either, since I was then twiddling my thumbs in a watered-down "Honors" English. But he was a guidance bureaucrat, not a guidance counselor, and did nothing to help me out. What I should have done was march into that English teacher's classroom and tell him I deserved to be in his advanced class, but I was much too reserved to advocate for myself and instead languished in sullen silence.

This was far from the greatest educational tragedy at Brockton High, but that indifference makes me wonder what would happen to a kid who was really struggling. Would anyone go to bat for him or her? Or was that asking too much? After all, who could map out the best educational plan for any individual student when there were 5,000 of us to look after?

Because I was shut out of advanced social studies classes, I continued to get put into lousy ones. For U.S. history I had Alice Hogan, a former gym teacher whose pedagogy came perilously close to reading out of the textbook; she taught nothing I hadn't already learned in eighth grade history, or maybe even in the third. She had a chip on her shoulder, thinking the world was sneering at her kind; her brothers were police officers and she wouldn't let us say the word "cop," claiming it was a slur. She also distrusted intellectual enthusiasm. For my midterm essay, I chose the trendy topic of "revolution." I'm pretty sure that in all her years of teaching, she never received another essay that included extensive quotes from Edmund Burke's *Reflections on the Revolution in France.* She grudgingly gave me an A, but refused to hand the paper back, strongly implying that I had plagiarized someone's college essay and didn't want me passing it off to another shyster who would try to dupe a less discerning social studies teacher than she.

Some of my English teachers were bad too. Wanting to learn how to write fiction, I took two creative writing classes in which the students mostly sat around their tables shooting the breeze. One of these teachers was the still-popular Mark Pendergrast. Despite my "Marky Maypo" cracks from a year earlier, I actually did like him personally. He complimented my short story about a sadistic carny who terrorizes riders at an amusement park and he laughed at a satirical soap opera script that Philip and I had written. But he had no advice on how to improve them and didn't push me to write more.

There was plenty of creativity in that school trying to break free. In another English class during my junior year, Philip sat at a table with two kids—Stanley Lloyd and Steve Oliveri—who were enthusiastic members of "Teens Encounter Christ" or T.E.C., a very sincere, slightly hip youth spirituality movement. Enamored by the recently released *Jesus Christ Superstar*, Steve wrote a short play called *JC*, which consisted of contemporary set pieces interspersed with tracks from the album. As an Albanian, Philip looked ethnic enough to be cast as the Messiah stand-in. As a friend of the table, I managed to get drafted as part of the fickle mob that exalted, then turned on our protagonist. We presented it in the school's "Little Theatre," making it available for other kids to attend during study periods. It was a massive hit—all eight performances that day were standing room only. But *JC* was a one-time thing and they wouldn't let us do more. The school administrators didn't foster other independent projects like that, finding them disruptive and not very educational.

I did have some outstanding classes, but they were rare. Senior year, I took a semester on American literature with Mr. O'Brien, who was as young as Mark Pendergrast but his opposite in almost every way. He was a UMass graduate rather than a Harvard one, and instead of shaggy and bearded like Mr. Pendergast, he was painfully clean-cut and intense. Mr. O'Brien was very professional, certainly not over-familiar with his students, and most importantly, he was intellectually demanding. His class was nearly as challenging as the introductory American Literature course I took in college two years later. Philip, Pat, and I all loved the class because Mr. O'Brien respected our ability to learn. The only downside was that he was hilariously prone to immature emotional outbursts, like the time a classmate asked if a particular author would be on the final exam, and he reacted by berating us for caring about our grades and not learning for learning's sake. Another day he stalked out of the room ten minutes into class, leaving us alone all period because he thought we hadn't adequately prepared for the day. He was seriously unamused the afternoon Pat bounced into class on a giant bouncy ball.

107

On another occasion, he jealously blurted out that Philip, Pat, and I were more invested in the fish we were dissecting in A.P. Biology than we were about Henry David Thoreau.

Which brings me to A.P. Bio, the capstone of my Brockton High academic career. More than half a dozen of us arranged to take the course as seniors and we were able to establish a distinctive class culture that was both jokey and enthusiastic about the subject at hand. It was the kind of class where, if we were hungry on a field trip, someone would start humming a fast food jingle and everyone on the bus would spontaneously break into song ("You deserve a break today, so get up and come away to McDonald's"). Our teacher, Lois Souza, was easy-going, and despite probably thinking we were full of ourselves, let us follow our enthusiasms. That's how we ended up dissecting that fish, an oversized skate we found on the beach during one of our field trips. At the end of the year, I had enjoyed the class so much that I decided I wanted to be a doctor, which is how I ended up entering college as a biology major.

High school is about a lot more than academics, though, and I became a zealous joiner of clubs and groups. I took an after-school course in scuba diving with the aforementioned Miss Souza and joined the scuba diving club. This culminated in a diving trip to Antigua that ended up with more adults than kids. In fact, there were only two of us from Brockton High—me and Mary Killoran, another A.P. Bio classmate. Half the group were Miss Souza's friends or business associates and they treated it as an adult vacation. I had my first alcoholic beverages on this trip—Tom Collinses—and we made jokes about "demon gin" the rest of the trip. I didn't sneak these cocktails either; they were bought for me at the pool bar by my boozy fellow divers, who thought a sweet, sugary drink was the best way to launch my drinking career. And this was on a school-sponsored trip with two teachers looking on approvingly! That was the '70s for you.

To do something athletic and prove to my parents that I wasn't just a book nerd, I joined the soccer team. I had literally never touched a soccer ball when I tried out for the tenth grade squad, which was made up of two types—guys like me who weren't good enough for more established sports, and the highly skilled sons of immigrants who had been playing since they were tots. It was in our post-practice showers that I learned about circumcision, or rather, uncircumcision, which I'd never seen before at West Junior High, where everyone looked the same. I played for three years, and even managed to become a starter since the sport was so new to the athletic program that there weren't enough experienced players to fill out the squad. The team was a strange amalgam of personality types and we never really gelled. Aside from Charlie Sedell, who was a friend of mine separate from soccer, I would merely nod to any member of the team when I saw them out of uniform. But there were a few strange bonding rituals. On our bus ride to play New Bedford, for instance, the highest-testosterone players of the group saw a sign for the *Moby-Dick* museum and became convulsed with laughter, repeating the same tired joke about "Moby's dick" over and over for the rest of the trip. There was also an occasion when two seniors launched into a naked, 10-minute towel-snapping battle in the middle of the locker room to the general amusement of the rest of us. Homoerotic much?

By the time I was a senior, I could tell that Brockton was rapidly changing demographically because the best soccer players were now Spanish-speaking Latino freshmen. They were undoubtedly beginning to dominate the sport, and in the future, there would be no more inexperienced white boys like me deciding on a whim to show up for tryouts and learn the game from scratch.

Having bombed my junior high French classes, I decided to start fresh with Russian, mostly because my friend Philip was taking it too. Together, we joined the Russian club. The club didn't do much that was actually Russian-focused, but we did arrange a trip to Boston Garden to see James Taylor for four dollars a seat plus the shared cost of a bus. James was outstanding, but his opening act was even better. A woman we had never heard of came out and started singing "I Feel the Earth Move Under My Feet," then a song called "It's Too Late," and for some reason she also sang Aretha Franklin's "Natural Woman." It was later, with the release of the album "Tapestry," that I realized we'd seen one of Carole King's first concerts.

I was also on the yearbook staff and even elected deputy editor during junior year. But our terrible advisor, Mr. Keane, didn't like me or my high-spirited friends, which he had already expressed through the C he gave me in his journalism class (please note: despite this ridiculous grade, I did become a real-life reporter after college). When the returning staff showed up to begin work as seniors, we discovered Mr. Keane had unilaterally appointed the yearbook's two editors: his own daughter and another kid completely unknown to the staff. He seemed to be provoking us to quit, and during one confrontation, Philip called him a "fat slob," which was accurate but, well, impolitic. When said slob tried to give Philip detention, we had a big staff/advisor sit-down with the school's assistant principal, Mr. Ryan, who informed us that, no, there was no such thing as detention for after-school activities. Mr. Ryan probably didn't like Mr. Keane any more than we did, since he was obviously a tub of lazy mediocrity. We considered this a moral victory, but a half-dozen of us ended up quitting anyway.

The whole concept of after-school activities and rah-rah school spirit eventually became risible to us. To avoid study period in the cafeteria, we convinced Miss Souza to give us a pass to do "independent study" in an empty lab. This room evolved into a common gathering place for all our friends. Looking around the lab one day at the fashion choice we had all adopted, Carol said we should call ourselves "The Sweater Club." To join, you needed to have five sweaters and one of them had to be blue, a bar so low that it was its own joke. Pat was acclaimed president and Rich Martel produced a "Welcome to the Sweater Club" brochure, complete with sheep-inspired art, that, with its extensive application forms, was actually a parody of the college admission process that we were all suffering through. In an act of mild subversion, we submitted fake meeting information to the morning announcements, which were regularly read over the PA. No one questioned what a Sweater Club was or why there were announcements about it. The school was just too big for the administrators to have a handle on every organization. As a final spoof, we wrote a satirical report of our imagined activities (e.g., a fictional trip to Garland Knitting Mill, a local sweater factory) for the local newspaper's special graduation issue. We thought that was the funniest thing we'd ever heard of.

These were the very mild hijinks of a tiny and virtually anonymous slice of the school's population, but apparently not everyone was enjoying Brockton High School as much as we were. Junior year saw a wave of disruptive bomb threats, each of which resulted in the immediate evacuation of the school. This meant herding 5,000 kids into the Rocky Marciano football stadium until the bomb-sniffing dogs determined it was a false alarm. The first time was fun, as the bored crowd amused itself with school cheers. The next five or six times were a drag, especially as the weather got colder. I don't know if anyone was ever caught, but the evacuations eventually ceased and were never repeated.

More alarming, we experienced a number of racial brawls when I was a senior. The school couldn't have had more than a couple hundred Black students, which is not surprising considering that the U.S. Census for 1970 says that the "negro" population of the city was only 2.5 percent (by 2020 it was 60 percent Black and 20 percent white). I'd heard rumors about kids being jumped in the stairwells by opposite-race antagonists, but one day as I walked across the glassed-in bridge to the Phys Ed building, I witnessed a vicious fight on the street below, mostly between an equal number of white and Black girls. (The local newspaper was all over this and reported that the racial hostility was caused by white girls dating Black guys.) That confrontation was eventually broken up by a few teachers, but not before a Black girl managed to knock a white girl to the ground and drag her by her long hair across the concrete sidewalk. The well-meaning faculty, especially the younger, idealistic teachers, tried to quiet things down through a series of "talk-ins," but I think the subsequent police presence likely had a more profound impact on keeping the peace.

In the end, though, what I remember most about high school was my friends. Somewhat to my surprise, the group that Theresa and I had assembled over two years held together and even expanded after the two of us split up. She had pointedly told Pat that "you don't need to hang out with them anymore, you know," meaning this was her chance to eject us boys out of her life. But none of the girls opted for female solidarity and life went on as usual, except that when Philip, Pat, and I planned an outing, Pat's friend, Carol, tended to fill out the fourth spot that Theresa had previously occupied.

With Philip and Pat, my two best friends from high school.

We prided ourselves on being "normal," with no drama. Normal, a term popularized by Rich Martel, didn't mean conformist. At a time when some of our classmates were floridly taking on new identities, normal meant no pretenses or enthusiasms that weren't authentically earned. We liked people who were funny, ironic, honest, somewhat detached, and most of all, nice (but not boring nice—we were teenagers, not social workers, and it wasn't our job to rehabilitate the incurably dull).

Normal, for example, meant rejecting the prom as a vestige of a square world that had ceased to exist. The idea of spending good money to rent a powder blue tuxedo, eat bad food, and go through the preposterous ritual of buying your date a corsage was absurd. Among all our friends, only Rich attended, and Philip and I spent prom night at his house happily watching *The Mary Tyler Moore Show*. Similarly, although I did buy a class ring (for $26, I got a big chunky thing with a veneer of gold and a red quartz faux gem that theoretically resembled a ruby), I never wore it, realizing that it was a déclassé combination of corn and pretentiousness.

It was a fairly literary group and I tried to keep up, brandishing my Scribner paperback copies of Fitzgerald and Hemingway, with their colorful covers painted in the style of Van Gogh, Manet, and Degas—covers so evocative that when I now glimpse them on my bookshelf I'm pulled through a portal to the early 1970s, when I first consumed them as a raw, unsophisticated reader. Once, when I mused out loud that the lifestyle in *The Sun Also Rises* seemed romantic, Carol scoffed, "Romantic? One's an alcoholic, one's a nymphomaniac, and one's impotent." "Wait," I protested, "who's impotent?" I had missed all the signs that the protagonist, Jake Barnes, had been grievously injured in World War I, and made some lame arguments like, "How could he be impotent if he still has to shave?" Obviously I had a lot to learn about sex, male biology, and how to read a novel.

The one attribute shared by most of my friends was that we were about to become first-generation college students. Our fathers tended to be classic working stiffs. Mine had a pool business, Philip's owned a bar in Boston, Rich's was an inspector for the electric company, Pat's drove a bread truck, Judi's worked in the Grossman's hardware store warehouse, Elizabeth's was a house painter, Nancy's owned a sporting goods store, Carol's was a city health inspector, and Stanley's was estranged from the family and sometimes out of work.

But so what? I didn't have any class consciousness. The late 1960s were remarkably egalitarian thanks to a booming economy that enabled working class families to own respectable homes that weren't all that different from those of the professional middle class. Our house had a pool, but it was still just a ranch house with a new family room tacked on. Some of my friends lived with economic anxiety, but even they expected—somehow—to access the college system and ultimately rise in the world.

The biggest exception to this working class hero angle was Jane Prince, the daughter of a judge who was one year ahead of us in school. I had known her only slightly as a volunteer manager of the soccer team, and then slightly better as a member of the Russian Club. One day, when Philip and I were walking down her street and saw her sitting on her front steps, I jokingly remarked, "How ghetto!" It was Philip's contention that sitting on the stoop was "ghetto" behavior, an assertion now so politically incorrect that I hesitate to repeat it here. In any event, she laughed, and we fell into a conversation that has never really stopped and soon she became a beloved friend to the two of us and a quasi-maybe-girlfriend of Rich's. When she went off to college at the University of New Hampshire, a few of us visited her on campus and got our first exposure to college life.

Our group spent a lot of time hanging out at each other's houses, listening to music and kidding around. Remarkably, there was no drinking or drug use (at least not when I was around). We rejected the expression "high on life" as the grossest, corniest, nerdiest phrase that could ever be uttered outside a bible camp, but it does describe what we were, at least when we were together. Not that drugs didn't seem to be everywhere. One summer, at the Brockton Fair during a performance by The Carpenters (!!!), a girl standing next to us suddenly fell to the ground and started writhing and screaming that her mind was on fire. After the EMTs carted her away, the girls in our group debated whether the cause was "bad drugs" or a "bad trip." I understood the distinction but found either prospect equally scary.

We also went on a lot of road trips. My parents had been eager to buy me a car and you could fill the whole tank for five bucks. We didn't think twice about squeezing in six people (sometimes seven, which was not a big deal since we didn't have seatbelts, anyway) before heading out to buy blueberry muffins at the Pewter Pot in the Braintree Mall or grab one of the café tables at Ken's deli on Boston's Boylston Street, which we considered the absolute height of sophistication. I had a recurring joke that other pedestrians trembled at our approach, viewing us as a "marauding band of teenage thugs," the joke being the preposterousness of anyone recoiling from us for anything other than aesthetic reasons. Six was also the perfect amount for a drive-in movie or a trip to Cape Cod. And there was nothing as exhilarating as waiting for the next Top 40 hit to come on the radio so we could all sing along. We knew all the lyrics to both "American Pie" and Harry Chapin's "Taxi."

Music was central to our shared sensibility. We all liked the same Top 40 hits. I was amazed and moved when The Beatles premiered "Hey Jude" on *The Smothers Brothers Show*, an eight-minute video that was the climax of the 1960s counterculture movement. We attended a lot of concerts in Boston, mostly at the ancient Boston Garden. I'd been there with my parents to see the Ice Capades and the Celtics, but now I mostly associate that musty old place with the rock bands we watched there: Chicago, Santana, and Three Dog Night. "Watch out for the marijuana," our mothers would warn. "If you smell anything sickly sweet, stay away and don't breathe it in."

As we approached the end of the school year, we all got into college. Most of the girls in our group were headed for the cheaper state schools and universities, while the boys would be attending more prestigious private colleges, which did not cost more than the median family's annual income back then. This gender disparity might have been a coincidence, but at least a couple of the girls had parents who refused to send daughters to expensive colleges. Again, that was a 1970s mindset that was clearly unfair and resented by the girls in our group, but not as uncommon as you'd think.

Something else happened in the month before graduation. Pat and I were spending a lot of time together and without any planning on either of our parts, we were suddenly dating. In retrospect, this was not a smart move. She was one of my best friends and we were headed off to college in a few months. Why jeopardize a friendship? Yet it was sweet to have a girlfriend again, even though none of our friends could really figure out what was going on.

We graduated on a warm Sunday afternoon in June, all 1,000 of us fidgeting at our seats on the football field as we awaited our names to be called. The next day, Philip, Rich, and I left to spend a week on Nantucket at my grandparents' cottage. We'd been friends since first grade and wanted to mark the milestone together. We had a blast exploring the island and trying to cook our own meals. One night, Eunice Oxenford, a girl Rich knew from Ceilings Unlimited who was working at an exclusive island hotel as a maid, came over for dinner. When the four of us ended up playing Risk, she smiled at us guys patronizingly, not caring whether or not she lost Yakutsk and Mongolia, even as the three boys battled loudly for domination. That night taught me more about the differences between boys and girls than a year's subscription to *Ms.* magazine could ever hope to. Even mild-mannered boys like us would still end up competing over a map-based game to try to impress a girl who couldn't have cared less about the outcome.

The summer before college was a wonderful little chapter for all of us, but when it was over, we were dispersed, first to colleges all around the country and then to careers that were definitely not in Brockton. Remarkably, none of us settled back in our hometown after graduation. We established new lives in big cities like Boston, New York, or Washington, or small towns in New Hampshire or Connecticut and even the occasional suburb. None of us hated Brockton and desperately had to get out; we just had bigger aspirations.

Still, if I could have one night to live over again, it might well be from one of those summer days back in the Shoe City. I envision a dozen of us splashing in the pool, laughing and singing "We're So Sorry Uncle Albert," "Maggie May," "Joy to the World," or anything from Neil Young's "After the Goldrush." We'd be completely carefree, drinking cold Cokes and devouring pizza slices without concern about our weight, and every joke would seem hilarious. We'd been lucky to find each other in that massive high school. No one at Brockton High would tell stories about us after we were gone, but that was alright, because we'd all remember each other (though some more fondly or clearly than others). And forever forward, whenever two or more of us were gathered, someone would invariably ask, "Remember when…?"

CHAPTER 12

Off to College

I did not like leaving the security of Brockton High School at all. After coasting in my classes and being cocooned within my cozy group of friends, I hadn't fully grasped the academic, psychological, or social rigors of college.

I never affirmatively decided what I'd do after high school, and as usual, just sleepwalked into my future. Given that only half my cousins received a degree, college wasn't something preordained in our family, either. But after getting placed in the "first group" in elementary school, I simply assumed I'd end up in the same boat as the other smart kids—whatever that was. Sometime in junior high school, I intuited from watching *G.E. College Bowl* that there was something called college and that there was an unspoken assumption within the family that this was to be the destiny of both me and my sister.

Our family had no strategic plan on how to get me into the "best" college or even knew you could game the system. We were like country rubes in a fancy restaurant who didn't know how to order from the menu. I was lucky that way. My parents had moved up the economic ladder so fast they hadn't yet absorbed the expectations of the upper-middle-classes and never hectored me about getting good grades or pushed me to participate in school activities that would look good on my transcript.

As a result, I never felt the crippling college anxiety that afflicts kids as young as middle schoolers today. My parents and their friends didn't measure their status according to the school their child attended, and their attitude was that whatever worked out, worked out. Any liberal arts college or state school I attended would provide more education than my parents had gotten, and they were remarkably hands-off about the whole process.

Fortunately, I always did well on standardized tests, which, fairly or not, created opportunities. I never took an SAT prep course but still obtained solid scores. When the results leaked out via the gossip mill, I noted with uncharitable satisfaction that I outperformed quite a few peers from Brockton High's elite "Ceilings Unlimited" program. In another unbelievably lucky break, my parents' swimming pool business prospered at just the right time, enabling me to attend college without worrying about tuition. Unlike many of my friends, I wouldn't need to navigate loans and scholarships or be limited to places the family could afford. They didn't even create a designated college fund; when the $3,600 annual invoice for tuition, room, and board arrived, they just paid it out of their swimming pool profits, with the understanding that I'd use my summer earnings to carry any additional personal expenses. And when my sister started attending Northeastern two years later, they whipped out the checkbook for her too.

Heading into high school, I didn't know the names of any colleges other than Harvard and Yale, so I went to the bookstore, bought a three-inch-thick almanac of institutions of higher education and researched every school in Maine, New Hampshire, and Vermont. I assumed upper New England would be far enough away from home to achieve some distance, but close enough to get back for vacations and emergencies. Aside from a few "safety" state schools, I only applied to three colleges.

I was too intimidated to do any on-campus interviews, but to have any reasonable chance of getting into Dartmouth, I couldn't avoid an alumni interview in my hometown. I showed up at a nice house on the West Side of Brockton, wearing a brownish plaid sports jacket with a boring tie and waited silently on a couch with the other nervous applicants before being ushered into the den, where I faced sincere questions from three nice Dartmouth men. All I remember is telling them I had read *The Peter Principle*, (which posited that employees rise through organizations until they reach their level of incompetence). I was even able to explain it cogently. But what a strange book to be reading as a senior in high school, right? I didn't get the sense these guys were very impressed.

My other targets were Middlebury in Vermont and Colby in Maine. My guidance counsellor, previously so unhelpful in getting me into advanced classes, told me to forget about Middlebury. Last year, they'd rejected his favorite student, who'd ranked number two in the BHS class of 1971. The school's administrators had vainly pulled out all the stops to get her in, so obviously I, who wasn't even in the National Honor Society, had no chance.

When April 15th rolled around, I got rejected from Dartmouth, accepted at Colby, and put on the waiting list at Middlebury. I planned to go to Colby, but one August morning, a Middlebury dean called to say they'd be happy to have me if I wanted to start in the February term. Somehow, I had the idea that this was the better, more prestigious option and said yes. And then, just weeks later, I got ANOTHER call from Middlebury saying I could start in the fall like everyone else. I thought about calling my guidance counselor with the news, but was pretty sure he had forgotten my name by then (assuming he ever knew it without looking at my file).

I scrambled to get ready, which wasn't as hard as it would be today, because I only had to pack fall clothes, a lamp, and a clock radio. I didn't even have a winter coat. The week before I left, I stopped at a gas station and the attendant was the captain of my high school soccer team, Tasho Hatsiopolis, one of the nicer guys on the squad. When I told him my higher education plans, he said, "Middleboro? Is that a community college?" It was a good reminder that not everyone was as impressed as I was by where I was headed.

The emotional transition in leaving home was hard. Always prone to homesickness, this would be the biggest leap yet. That drive from Brockton to Middlebury, with my parents and I silently contemplating the end of that period

119

of our lives, was stomach-churning. We had lunch at Rosie's, a family-style restaurant about five miles south of town. It's still open, but I've never eaten there since because the memory of that sad anxiousness is still so intense.

Arriving on campus, I discovered I'd be living in a converted study lounge, complete with a stove, a sink, and a refrigerator. This was a nice space for two guys, but I wondered why it was so urgent to admit me in the fall if they didn't have a regular room available. Did they need our tuition check? It didn't take long to unpack and when we were done, I couldn't wait for my parents to leave. Why prolong the moment? All their forced, cheerful mingling with the other parents was unbearable. So, once my bed was made and my clothes were in my bureau, they made their way out. I was surprised that my mother was crying as we hugged goodbye at the car. She and my father, in separate correspondence, later apologized for this lapse from the stiff upper lip and hastened to reassure me that everything was perfectly fine and I shouldn't worry about that momentary show of emotion.

Back in the room, I surveyed my new reality. My roommate was Harry Blackmun (definitely not the Supreme Court Justice), the son of an Episcopalian minister from one of the rich Boston suburbs. He'd once attended school in England and retained the faintest trace of a British drawl. An enthusiast of J.R.R. Tolkien, he taped up a long, horizontal poster that outlined the *Lord of the Rings* saga, which I had never heard of. Also down the hall were an assortment of potheads, jocks, extroverts, and introverted guys like me who were not very socially developed.

On day two of freshman weekend, we all piled into buses, drove into the Green Mountains, and spent the day at Breadloaf, the site of the college's well-known summer writer's workshop. We hiked, engaged in contests of strength (tug of war) and skill (wood chopping, the College President's specialty), listened to rah-rah speeches, had a barbeque, and went to a dance in a charming old barn. During the hike, I fell in with four ebullient girls, including a girl named Ann, with whom I was immediately smitten. But after an hour, and afraid that I was imposing myself, I peeled off before they could get "tired" of me. Later, during the dance, Ann came over and sat next to me, but I was too paralyzed to ask her to dance and she eventually walked away. True, I did have a girlfriend back in Brockton, which provided an excuse for not chasing after new girls, but honestly I was just too shy to socialize like a regular guy.

But it wasn't just at dances that I was struggling to find friends. I was living in Allen Hall, a small co-ed dorm on the edge of campus. These were still in the days when freshmen were still called freshmen, not "first years," and the majority of dorms were still single sex. Allen was the only freshman co-ed dorm, and with 60 of us living in near isolation, it was almost an experiment in teen behaviorism. Battell, the girls-only freshman dorm, still had 11:00pm parietals for the month of September, but we had girls living free and easy just down the corridor. Almost immediately I heard that one girl (who had gone to private school in New York City, of course) already had a guy sleeping over, to the distress of her roommate. Apparently these two were also taking loud showers in the girls' bathroom, which no one in the corridor was too happy about. Wow, so the stories about the libertine life of college were true!

I didn't have first-hand knowledge of these goings-on because I didn't dare venture down that wing for a long time. It was a chicken and egg situation: because I didn't know any of the girls, I didn't want to wander down the corridor like a gawking tourist in a foreign country, but without entering the space I couldn't easily meet them. Remarkably, my shyness was actually getting worse as I got older. I thought I'd grow in confidence as I matured, but it was really the other way around.

For the first several weeks of school, I dutifully walked over to the dining hall with the guys who lived on my floor, but never found a way to insert myself meaningfully into the conversation. No one else shared my sense of humor or worldview and a lot of my observations were met with some variation of the "Uh, okay…" response; only I had thought it had been eye-rollingly hilarious that during Convocation, our President had actually quoted from "The Desiderata," which was then being falsely attributed to an ancient Sanskrit monk, something that I intuitively knew was a scam: "…And whatever your labors and aspirations, in the noisy confusion of life, keep peace in your soul. With all its sham, drudgery and broken dreams, it is still a beautiful world. Be cheerful. Strive to be happy." Ugh. Save it for Hallmark.

I came to think that Middlebury was one of the most beautiful places in the world.

More than one high school friend wrote ironically to ask if I'd been to any "pot parties," because the media had stoked the fears of our parents that marijuana would melt our brains, damage our chromosomes, or serve as a gateway to heroin addiction. No, I could answer honestly, then and in subsequent FBI background checks, I stayed away from pot parties. Occasionally, when I was with friends-of-friends, someone would break out a joint and I'd just wave it away. A bigger concern of mine was the other kind of smoking—tobacco, which I still detested. Like the rest of America, Middlebury was a place where people smoked almost everywhere—in the dorms, in classrooms, and in the dining halls. Professors and students smoked in class; even the athletes smoked! Fortunately, the college at least segregated roommates by smoking/non-smoking so I could breathe fresh air in my dorm room.

Some of the guys in my hall started hanging around the college's six fraternities for more testosterone-fueled companionship, but that wasn't for me. In my four years at college, I only set foot in a frat once: after being invited to tag along with a group going to watch stag films that winter. A middle-aged man who clearly enjoyed the whoops, hollers, and exclamations of "Can you believe that?" ran the film projector, displaying the soundless images on the white walls of the frat's social room. This was the first time I saw real pornography and on our icy walk back to the dorm I wanted to discuss the business end of the industry—how much the performers got paid, the distribution model, etc. With everyone else lost in their own thoughts, some a little embarrassed, no one engaged in that particular conservational gambit.

By the end of the fall, I had come to appreciate that Middlebury College was one of the most beautiful places in the world, especially when the trees blazed orange. We were nestled in the middle of Vermont's Champlain Valley, with the pumpkin-colored Green Mountains looming over us only a few miles to the east and the snow-covered Adirondacks laid out far away in the west. Fall was literally golden. The buildings surrounding the quad dated back to the 19th century and the additional structures radiating out were architecturally consistent and built with marble, granite, gray bricks, and flagstone. But the beauty of the surroundings couldn't compensate for my feelings of loneliness and I felt guilty for not appreciating it more.

Part of the experience of being in college in the 1970s was being fully immersed in the campus bubble and out of touch with the rest of the world. Obviously, there was no internet, and the only outside communication was the payphone down the hall. We could receive one good and one fuzzy TV signal from Burlington, but that didn't matter at first because neither Harry nor I had a TV anyway. We weren't allowed to have cars as freshmen, so I had to take a bus to go anywhere. I didn't even have a record player for the first six weeks.

I honestly don't remember how I kept myself up to date, but there was a very passionate presidential campaign underway and I felt confident in my grasp of current events. When Keith Block, our dorm's George-McGovern-for-President canvasser, knocked on my door to make sure I was registered to vote, he informed me that I was one of only four people in the dorm supporting Nixon. I was all in on Nixon's "peace with strength" strategy and I thought McGovern was a wooly headed, smarmy idealist. I probably picked up a lot of that at home, but to my credit, I did subscribe to *Time* magazine, read newspapers at the library, and occasionally watch the evening news on a shared TV in the dorm's common room. News didn't travel as fast as a tweet does today but somehow, it got through.

I made a lot of mistakes freshman year that were rooted in two contradictory impulses. I either overestimated my abilities and sought out challenges that were over my head, or undervalued my self-worth and didn't take even modest chances.

Having played soccer in high school, I joined the freshman soccer team, but discovered that most of the players—prep school kids or graduates of suburban public schools who'd been playing since junior high school or earlier—vastly outperformed me. So I sat quietly on the bench, not bonding with my more talented teammates, feeling inadequate, and using up time that could have been spent more productively studying or joining another activity for which I might have been better suited.

I also overestimated myself academically. After taking A.P. Biology in high school, I figured I could be a doctor. Foolishly, I skipped Intro to Biology and went straight to advanced courses like Invertebrate and Vertebrate Biology. And for no good reason, I also decided I should take a 300-level history course ("How English History Influenced English Literature") where I was the only freshman.

I was outright bad in all my science and math classes. A month into school, I got a 57 on a chemistry exam and the college sent my parents a note that I was failing, which set the stage for the rest of the year. The news was a little better in my liberal arts classes—I was at least mediocre. By that I mean B's and C's. Despite the so-so performance, these classes did provoke a lifetime of curiosity and self-learning. My political science class was taught by one of the most intimidating teachers on campus, Murray Dry, who, despite being about 30 years old, seemed to model himself on the imperious professor in *The Paper Chase*. Our first book in the class was Plato's *Republic*, which I first mistook for a novel because it featured a lot of guys standing around shooting the breeze about the good life. But although I was in over my head at the time, I find myself thinking of that class at least once a week now because the great political philosophers we studied—Machiavelli, Hobbes, Locke, Rousseau—still drive the conversation about how to build a just world.

Students were definitely not coddled in those days, and the college had a sink-or-swim philosophy. I did have an "advisor," a burly, hirsute art professor who could have counseled me on where to buy a cheap Andy Warhol in Soho, but had nothing to say about which biology courses I should take. I was periodically called to the dean's office to discuss my poor performance. When I assured them it was not due to excessive partying or psychological problems, they let me go. On my third visit, this time to the Dean of Students herself, Erica Wannacott asked if my high school had been "competitive." Not understanding academic euphemisms very well, I thought she was talking about athletic achievement or the school's general spirit of competitiveness. It was only halfway through my stammering response that I realized what she really meant was, "How badly does your high school suck?" and that I had probably just doomed a generation of future Brockton High School applicants to rejection letters.

Perhaps my biggest mistake was not cutting ties more with my Brockton past and throwing myself into Middlebury wholeheartedly. My high school friends and I spent an enormous amount of time writing letters to each other about how miserable we were. Rich sent me morose missives from Bowdoin complaining about how hard it was to find "normal" people to be friends with. Philip wasn't fitting in at Iowa's Grinnell College and Judi Herbert sent more than a dozen letters before Thanksgiving detailing her ups and downs at Fitchburg State. Instead of giving myself wholly to this new college experience, I was clinging to the past.

What really weighed on my mind is that I could feel my romantic relationship with Pat slipping away. If I'd had any sense, I would have had one of those "Let's just be friends" conversations before going to college, but we'd had a nice summer and I wanted to hold onto something comforting while I was away. Not being able to afford anything else, she was still living at home and attending nearby Bridgewater State College. When I arrived home at Thanksgiving, she broke up with me over the phone. I didn't talk to her again for six years.

I returned to Middlebury after Thanksgiving feeling that the world was conspiring against me because no one would confirm the obvious truth—that Pat had fallen in love with our other friend Carol, who was, admittedly, inscrutably beautiful. But then things started to get better. Judi Herbert hadn't been one of my closest high school friends, but in college she became, aside from Philip, my steadiest correspondent. Like many college girls at that time, she parted her long, brown hair in the middle and past her shoulders. Unlike many girls at the time, she had a warm, easy smile and seemed to care about and remember everything I told her.

She and Stanley Lloyd even came to visit me in October and we stayed up until 5:30am comparing notes about college and Brockton. She had been there at Pat's house when we telephonically broke up and then hopped on the phone immediately to console me. Our correspondence intensified. We saw each other at Christmas and then on New Year's Eve I moved out of the friend zone. So I had started the first semester of college with one hometown girlfriend and returned for the second semester with a different one. That's not how it usually works—the norm was to shed the "hometown honey" freshman year, not acquire one—but Judi was the one person in the world who seemed to understand me best.

Meanwhile at college, I was finally beginning to connect with my dorm-mates. One day, as I was quietly reading in my room, Harry and a female companion laughingly burst in. She pointed to me and said, "Who's that?" and then refused to believe I was his roommate because she'd never seen me in the dorm. This was Leslie Donovan, a gregarious and fun girl from Weston, Massachusetts, and for whatever reason, we quickly became friends. Suddenly, I had a reason to venture into the girls' part of the dorm and subsequently got myself acquainted with the other girls at her end of the hall.

There was another corridor of boys in the Allen basement that I barely knew since the guys on the second floor didn't mix much with the ones in the dungeon. But in a shared study on the first floor, I met Chris Ryer, then one of the few other Republicans in the dorm. We bonded over our shared academic struggles and our disdain for the excesses of freshman behavior (loud music at 3:00am, drunken yelling, fire extinguisher fights). I enjoyed

My hair got pretty shaggy in college.

his slightly sardonic sense of humor, which relied heavily on a steady rotation of quotes from the TV show *Columbo* and groan-inducing jokes: "Hey, why are they being so disrespectful to our state poet? There are signs on the side of the street that say 'Frost Heaves.'" He became my first college friend, as well as my first real guy friend—i.e. someone who cared about sports, girls, and physical activity.

127

With a growing cohort of dorm chums, I began to enjoy the college experience. I finally had people to yuck it up with at dinner. The drinking age was only 18, so we would occasionally go downtown to local hangouts like the Alibi, a classic basement dive bar down a sloping alley with live music, rough-hewn tables, and cheap drinks. Not one for the taste of beer, and barely consuming any alcohol at all, I would order what I mistakenly thought was a sophisticated drink—an apricot cordial!

Middlebury had a January term, four weeks during which students take just one class on a pass/fail basis. This was supposed to be a chance for students to experiment with subjects they don't usually take, but at least three-quarters of the courses were so easy (aka "guts") that students could spend most of the month skiing. Middlebury owned its own ski mountain— the Snow Bowl—and I used that month to take downhill lessons. It was exhilarating to be on the slopes on a sunny day, but I was quickly frustrated by my lack of progress, the expense, and most of all by watching ten year olds zoom past me like I was driving a go-cart at the Indy 500. I did very little skiing when second semester classes started and gave it up a couple of years after that.

Also that January, Chris and I learned how to play bridge and even found a few partners. Someone introduced us to Diplomacy, a board game about the origins of World War I that requires five or six people and takes all afternoon—a good way of killing a languorous snowy day. Our dorm had a kitchen and occasionally the girls would whip up a special feast, which is how I got introduced to spanakopita, moussaka, baklava, and other Greek delicacies I'd never even heard of.

I was lucky to make these friends; it's scandalously easy to feel isolated at a small place like Middlebury, where they just toss you into a dorm full of strangers and send you to classes where you're expected to have original-sounding opinions on Aristotle. That year, two other guys in my dorm—one with roommate problems and one with drug issues—had nervous breakdowns and had to be taken away for psychiatric treatment.

Eventually, I fell into a groove: to bed at midnight or 1:00am and up 15 minutes before my first morning class. I never ate breakfast at college, which was served only in a distant dining hall, so my first meal of the day was lunch, consumed at one of the Social Dining Units (SDUs), a mini-complex of three cozy dining halls, social spaces, and classrooms at my end of campus. The workload was heavy—an English class could cover a novel a week—and I spent a huge amount of time cloistered in library nooks and deserted study lounges. I had a hard time studying in the dorm, where Eric Clapton's "Layla" seemed to be playing nonstop.

I caught a lucky break that spring when the hated Nixon implemented a fully volunteer military. From 1940 to 1972, the prospect of the draft had hung over the head of every teenage boy. For generations, you could get out of it by joining the National Guard, or you could be deferred if you were a farmer (my father's way out), homosexual, married, or in college. But in the late '60s, the government had done away with student deferments and 18-year-old college students with lower lottery numbers could, for several years, be drafted into the army.

When they conducted the lottery on March 8th, 1973, many of us crowded into my resident advisor's room to watch it live on his TV. My birthday came up as number 24. That was so low that I certainly would have been drafted the year before, but 1973 became the first year since World War II without a call-up and I was off the hook. (By the way, I can't help but be cynical about this: the anti-war movement peaked in 1970 when the draft was also at its peak. Middlebury was a hotbed of anti-war activism and in 1970, just three years earlier, someone had even burned down the ROTC building. By the time I got to campus in 1972, with the draft basically over, the campus was politically inert. I couldn't help but feel it was the draft that most college students had objected to, not the war.)

Second semester of freshman year was my academic nadir. I received D's in Invertebrate Biology and Calculus and a C-minus in my advanced history class. If that C-minus had been another D, I'd have been on academic suspension, which would have meant taking a semester off. Somehow, I escaped opprobrium at home—I never discussed these lousy grades with my parents. I think they were more worried about my mental health than my academic achievement—a constant refrain in their letters that year had been, "Try to have some fun," and "Don't put so much pressure on yourself." Sound advice that I wish I had followed.

This was also the low point of my hair fashion. Finally free from my parents' rules about hair length, I didn't get one single haircut from September to June. My long, lank blonde hair, parted in the middle, fell straight to my shoulders in a style that Tom Petty would later popularize. It looked terrible and I voluntarily cut it as soon as I got home. It was the least I could do after all those D's.

CHAPTER 13

Surviving College

I didn't have a sophomore slump in college. I was already so far down that the only direction for me was up. So whatever the opposite of a sophomore slump is, that's what I had.

That doesn't mean my academic problems immediately abated, however. For at least one more semester, I stubbornly refused to be a "quitter" and powered ahead with my biology major, even though I was clearly a square peg in an amoeba-shaped hole. Sadly, I couldn't force myself to memorize anything that didn't fundamentally interest me. I liked absorbing the overall principles of biology, chemistry, and physics, but enough to learn all the muscles in a dissected cat? Not so much.

When the first semester resulted in another D and a C-minus and I had once again barely eluded academic probation, I decided that enough was finally enough. After I'd selected a new major in the liberal arts, those first three semesters became a bad memory. Within a few months, I would look back with incredulity that I had ever aspired to be a doctor.

Even with this change, I did not become a Rhodes Scholar—I never got an outright A until senior year. But I finally started receiving reliable B's and

131

could relax enough to enjoy my classes. Although I wasn't adept at writing papers or answering exam questions in a way that would impress professors, I was at least a sponge that absorbed new ideas and knowledge. And when I say "writing" papers, I mean that literally. It wasn't until the Christmas of 1973 that I got my first typewriter—a portable Olivetti electric that I carried around in a vinyl case. Up until that point, I hand wrote almost everything I turned in to my professors.

Despite chopping my shoulder-length hair at the end of freshman year, I was still pretty shaggy as a returning sophomore, sporting long sideburns and an alarming widow's peak that my listless locks only partially obscured. I was, however, the proud, ahead-of-the-curve owner of two pairs of "Earth Shoes"—a square-toed Scandinavian brand of footwear sold exclusively in Harvard Square in Cambridge that looked weird but supposedly had special health benefits because the heel's thinner sole made it "like walking uphill." One of the few times I was fashion forward!

My appearance was hardly unique. Our early '70s transition from well-scrubbed 18 year old high school seniors to hippie wannabes was nearly complete. Sitting in the middle of pastoral Vermont, we upper-middle-class Midd Kidds had rapidly adopted the rural strain of the counterculture, echoing the back-to-nature ethos of the idealized 1960s commune. Crunchy in the extreme, we flaunted flannel shirts and hiking boots. Some of the women wore long Earth Mother dresses and many of the manlier guys maintained unkempt beards. It was hard then to imagine then that so many of these classmates would go on to be investment bankers, lawyers, doctors, and other pillars of the establishment.

But it wasn't just that we *looked* countercultural. Many eager beaver high school standouts who showed up in 1972 began to embody the anti-establishment cynicism of the '60s. School spirit? What was that? We had a full array of intercollegiate sports but I don't remember a lot of rah-rah for the teams. Going on dates? Getting pinned? That was ancient history—prehistoric even. We did have one annual dress-up dance during Winter Carnival weekend but keg parties were much more common, and even more popular than that was sitting around a dorm room getting stoned. Ennui was in; enthusiasm was out.

Maybe it was the combined hangover effect of the Vietnam War, Watergate, the energy crisis, and the stagflation economy. Maybe it was prolonged exposure to the existentially despairing popular culture of the early '70s, such as the deeply misanthropic films *M.A.S.H.*, *Chinatown*, *Nashville*, and *Five Easy Pieces*. Regardless, we were jaded, nothing like the idealistic and eager-to-please generations that came before or after us. We weren't even the politically engaged campus of the 1960s. We had one die-hard socialist in the class—a guy who became a Bernie Sanders acolyte in Burlington a decade later—but he was almost as much of an oddity as I was as a Republican.

On the positive side, now that I was out of the hothouse environment of Allen Hall, my social life finally gelled. As sophomores, Chris Ryer and I became even tighter. Living two floors directly underneath him in Kelly Hall, I spent so much time in his room—where there was a couch, TV, and popcorn maker—that his roommate tried to ban me from the premises when it became clear I had become better friends with Chris than he was. Chris liked doing guy things and I happily followed his lead. We started a nightly game of three-on-three touch football in the back of the dorm, road bikes in

On a winter hike in the Adirondacks with Chris Ryer, who took this photo.

the Vermont countryside, and even hazarded camping trips. On one freezing hike in the Adirondacks, the bottle of wine I had foolishly carried five miles into the campsite froze and cracked. But the long shivering night was almost worth it the next morning when we picked our way among the black spruce and balsam firs to reach the summit and take photos of each other with dozens of other snowy peaks in the background.

Through Chris, I became acquainted with his high school friend, Jim Robinson. He'd lived on the other side of campus freshman year and previously been a stranger. Now that he and his roommate, Ron Witt, also lived in our dorm, we all started hanging out. In the 1980s, Jim would eventually get me two important jobs in Washington, D.C., so developing this friendship became another crucial hinge moment; this story would have been completely different if we hadn't hit it off.

Jim and I were sympatico across a wide area of interests. Most importantly, we were die-hard, distraught political conservatives at a time when the media and Democrats tortured our president over Watergate, and the Vietnam War approached its disastrous end. We were not ideologically identical, though; he was an ardent libertarian and a fan of Ayn Rand, who I thought was a bit of a moral monster, and I was a Burkean traditionalist, clinging to the values and traditions that had been developed over the centuries. But these were small, intra-conservative doctrinal distinctions at an overwhelmingly liberal institution like Middlebury. And even though Nixon was hardly a small-government conservative, he was the enemy of our enemies—the preening liberals who thought they knew better than the rest of us. His survival became our shared, doomed cause. If anyone on campus besides the two of us actually liked the guy, they kept it to themselves. We were in a two-man bunker. This wasn't fun at the time but it did teach me to accept that not everyone thought like I did and that you could engage people intellectually on political issues without getting overly emotional and storming out of the room.

We shared a similar world view and sense of humor that went beyond politics. Nothing bonded us like puncturing the pretentiousness, hypocrisy, and outright stupidity of the political, cultural, and academic establishments. The first time I made him laugh was when his roommate, Ron, expressed admiration for Cat Stevens' commitment to his music. He'd seen a video performance of "Moon Shadow" in which the future Yusuf Islam had demonstrated how deeply moved he was by his own song through tightly closed eyes and exaggerated facial contortions. Yeah, I replied, but I bet when he performs without a camera present it's like this: and then, with a bored, eye-rolling expression on my face, I sing-songed, "I'm being followed by a moon shadow, moon shadow, moon shadow." Only Jim seemed to think that was funny.

We also shared an unquenchable fascination with The Beatles, although he was a John guy and I was pro-Paul. Even beyond The Beatles, we had an overall similar musical taste, and I frequently succumbed to his enthusiasms. I had been dismissive of my girlfriend Judi's favorite performer, Joni Mitchell, but when Jim sat me down, played Joni's new "Court and Spark" album, and forced me to listen closely to the song "People's Parties," I had to concede the brilliance of the intricate, psychologically insightful lyrics. Only then did I become a committed Joni Mitchell fan. And I have to hand it to Judi for never asking why it took another guy friend to convince me to like Joni Mitchell.

Jim Robinson was the only other openly identifying conservative I knew at Middlebury.

A growing interest that I shared with no one at college—not with Jim, Chris, or anyone else—was classic movies. Until the 1960s, movies were as disposable as Kleenex and no one would have thought twice about rewatching something that came out decades earlier. But the new medium of television needed content, and old movies were a godsend. The growing popularity of Hollywood classics led to a new, hip institution: repertory cinema, independent urban theaters screening foreign films and the best of old Hollywood. Classic movies were also a cheap form of entertainment on college campuses.

Besides the *Wizard of Oz* and *Gone With The Wind*, the first old movie I ever saw was the Frank Capra rom-com, *It Happened One Night*, screened at Middlebury soon after freshman weekend. All of a sudden, I couldn't get enough of classic cinema and was diving deeply into the film theory that provided an intellectual justification for the art form. It also helped that my Brockton friends were film enthusiasts. Judi had developed a passion for Humphry Bogart, while Jane Prince keyed in on Jimmy Stewart and Kirk Douglas, and Rich Martel was gaga over Alfred Hitchcock. In those days before streaming services, CDs, or even VCRs, the only way to watch old movies was to go to a movie theater or catch one randomly on TV. By sophomore year, I was attending every movie screening at college that I could, even if I had to go by myself, which I frequently did.

At the end of the year, I decided to major in American Studies, which analyzes American culture through the lens of multiple disciplines, including literature, history, art, political science, economics, and religion. So did Jim, in a decision we reached independently but in dialogue with each other. Earlier, Leslie Donovan, Jim, and I had found ourselves in an introductory American Literature class taught by a tall, young Harvard Ph.D candidate named Phil Gura, who was on fire over the legacy of the American Puritans and the Transcendental movement. With his full beard, erect, lanky frame and Old-Man-in-the-Mountain countenance, he could have passed for a contemporary of Ralph Waldo Emerson or Henry David Thoreau.

Mr. Gura's enthusiasm captivated the three of us, and whether out of loneliness or an eagerness to mentor us on Cotton Mather, he would occasionally meet us at the Alibi or another downtown bar. He's the one who introduced us to the concept of American Studies. Jim and I bought into this academic discipline with the enthusiasm of acolytes. Figures as different as Emily Dickinson, Jonathan Edwards, Winslow Homer, and F. Scott Fitzgerald became as real to me as Archie Bunker or Mary Richards. Self-identified practical people sometimes ask what you can use a liberal arts education for, but as far as I'm concerned, I "used" my American Studies major almost every day of my career. Not only did I learn how to write and reason analytically, but knowing how Americans think and have always thought gave me a competitive advantage in my journalism, political, and public relations jobs.

It was about this time, though, that my increasing lack of self confidence in unfamiliar groups began to have a real-world impact. A key part of our educational experience was classroom participation, but I was often mute in our discussion sessions. I was completely different from my high school self, who had been talkative in class and sometimes even a leader. It was perhaps understandable that I'd been reticent to pipe up as a callow college freshman

This is the only decent photo that anyone took of me while I was in college.

from a mediocre high school, but even when I got my academic sea legs, I wasn't any better. Half my professors never knew my name and probably had no idea whether I was listening intently or daydreaming.

This confidence issue has been a perplexing problem all my life; even now, I won't speak up in any group where I don't already have a personal relationship with everyone in the room. This held me back in college but became an even bigger problem when I migrated to a profession that required meetings with strangers. And where did this feeling of inadequacy come from? I think shyness and introversion are immutable genetic traits and not learned behavior. I was encouraged and supported by parents and teachers, so a lack of emotional support couldn't have been the reason I became a wallflower. The only question is why it took until freshman year of college to realize I had a debilitating fear of looking stupid.

Still, I persisted, even in the face of self-doubt. It was a real gift at this time to have a drama-free relationship with Judi, who visited campus about once a semester, became friends with my friends, charmed my parents, and exchanged many loving letters about how much she missed me (24 missives during sophomore year alone—I counted—and I'm sure I sent as many back). She was a steady companion during school vacations, especially the summers, when it was bliss to have someone with whom to share the sultry nights and Brockton pizza.

During those hometown summers, she and I spent a lot of time with Philip Tasho and Jane Prince, just hanging out at each others' house. She read *New Yorker* magazine, which I thought was the height of sophistication, especially Pauline Kael's movie reviews, and as an English major at Fitchburg State College, where she was training to be an English teacher, she kept me on my literary toes. Since we all disdained the improper use of the English language, Philip and I made a joke out of it. The misuse of "hopefully" became "hopefully-wise," as in "hopefully-wise it won't rain today." The non-word "irregardless" became "irregardlessly-wise."

We tried hard to be unpretentious aesthetes, by differentiating what we liked for its own sake from what we liked because it made us look sophisticated. That wasn't easy, even given how intensely self-reflective we were, because the allure of the big city was palpable. Whenever possible, we'd drive into Boston or Cambridge and see old black and white films at the Brattle Theater, the Orson Welles Theatre, the Exeter Street Theatre, or the Park Square Theatre, of which only the Brattle still remains. We'd shop at the Harvard Coop for old movie posters or cheap impressionist prints, browse Cardullo's gourmet market across the street from Harvard to gaze at all the imported food, which we coveted but never actually bought, and wrap up the day at Café Pamplona, a spare, whitewashed, cellar-based coffee shop down a Cambridge side street that served small bowls of intense chocolate mousse that we'd eat with the world's tiniest spoons.

Decades later, after Judi had broken up with me, I once wondered out loud whether it had been smart to maintain a relationship with a hometown girlfriend when there had been so many beautiful girls right there on campus. Jim set me straight: I had been lucky, because single guys on the prowl spent an enormous amount of mental energy pursuing female companionship. With the girlfriend question off the table, I could keep my mind clear and focused on my academics and friendships. And of course—and this is the definitive, unimpeachable answer to any "maybe I should have" ponderings—if I'd had a different, college-based girlfriend, I might have married her. Or she might have distracted me from Jim and those jobs in Washington, D.C. And I might have never met my ultimate wife or fathered my son, a prospect that always makes me shudder.

By the end of sophomore year, my college experience had settled into a satisfaction level that was on par with my grades: it was a solid B. There is no question that many of my classmates absolutely loved the riotous good times of college. Many others became profoundly alienated, washing their hands of the experience and never looking back after graduation. Once I achieved my own equilibrium, I found myself halfway between those two poles; in love with both the idea of Middlebury and the physical place itself, while suspecting that I was letting the classic college experience pass me by. You could say I had the original Fear Of Missing Out.

I was fortunate to have good friends and interesting classes, but I didn't have many ecstatic, rip-roaringly fun moments. Maybe I was too sober-minded or just plain sober. The one time I did experiment with a little too much cheap white wine—in my room after second semester finals—Chris

139

and I and another friend, Sally Russell, ran outside to see the sunset behind the dorm; somehow I managed to collide smack into a tree, off of which I bounced before collapsing on the ground like a bad *Tom and Jerry* cartoon.

A better, more ethereal memory of that spring comes from the night I stepped out of the library during finals week and saw a crowd of students all silently facing north. A few weeks earlier, some friends and I had camped outside in the back of our dorm one night to watch a meteor shower in the clear, crisp Vermont sky. But this night was even better. The Aurora Borealis was in its full splendor—still the only time I've ever seen the Northern Lights. The yellow, blue, and green solar flares flickered in the sky for another 15 minutes. What a privilege it was to spend four years in a picturesque Vermont college, where, however imperfect, it was actually my job to learn, grow, and navigate my place in the world.

CHAPTER 14

Leaving College

My junior year of college was easily the best year at Middlebury, a brief buffer between the anxious semesters when I thought I might flunk out and the six-month nervous breakdown of senior year when I fretted daily about my post-graduate life. Nixon had resigned over the summer, so I didn't need to fight about Watergate anymore; the energy crisis had abated and you could buy gas again without waiting in endless lines; and I finally had roommates of my choosing.

Chris Ryer, Ron Witt, and I lived in a triple on the fifth floor of Gifford Hall, a stately stone fortress of a dorm built in 1940, and we delighted in our view of the Green Mountains from our dormer windows. Chris and I shared one of the side rooms, where above my bed, he built a wooden loft that was large enough for a double mattress. I guess his strategy was "If you build it, they will come," but they didn't. With Ron in the other side-chamber, this arrangement left us with a large, shared middle room that we filled with comfortable furniture, a television, a stereo, and a refrigerator. We also pooled the expense of a phone, got the *Boston Globe* delivered daily, and had two cars between us. I tacked up a poster of Wyeth's *Christina's World* over my desk and

Manet's *A Bar at the Folies-Bergère* over our armchair. The isolation of freshman and sophomore year was behind us and life finally felt normal.

Gifford, only recently co-ed, had been laid out as a men's dorm 35 years earlier. This was not an issue in the lower floors, which had two bathrooms that could be assigned to each of the then-recognized genders. But on the fifth floor, we only had one two-part bathroom. The first part had three showers, a couple of urinals, an open bathtub and some sinks, and the second had a long row of toilet stalls. Given that you never knew who might come in to brush their teeth, we all mastered the art of covering up before exiting the shower, and the guys mostly eschewed the urinals. But I never got used to sitting on the toilet with a woman in the adjoining one—especially if she wanted to chat, which Gillian, the senior who lived across the hall from us, always seemed to want to do.

Back then, the dorms were wide open 24 hours a day, which meant that anyone could waltz into the building at any time. One morning that fall, as I was waking up, I heard a knock on the door and Chris came into the bedroom to announce that my parents and their friends were waiting for me in the middle room. They had been in Vermont to look at foliage and thought it would be fun to surprise me by showing up unannounced. Ha, ha. I'm pretty sure this was my father's idea, because only he was amused to find me still in bed at 9:30am. My mother and their friends had the decency to be embarrassed by my embarrassment. And what if there had been a girl in the room? Okay, the chances of that happening were minuscule to nil, but still, it was presumptuous not to consider the possibility!

The open-dorm policy had another only-in-the-'70s consequence a few months later. Word flew up and down the hall that five or six grimy members of a mountain commune had decided to clean up in our bathroom. This I had to see. Pretending I had to brush my teeth, I walked in to discover an uncovered, mid-20s woman nonchalantly climbing out of the shower and a stark naked guy soaking in the tub. Now these were *real* hippies, not the ersatz ones that we pretended to be.

Jim was not in Vermont that fall, having decided to spend the first semester of junior year in the Washington Semester Program at American University. Chris and I drove down to see him during the 1974 Columbus

Day break. When we got out of the car, he breathlessly told us that earlier in the week, Wilbur Mills, the Chairman of the House Ways and Mills Committee, had been arrested for drunk driving with his mistress. I had no idea what he was talking about—these were the days when Washington could be agog for days about an inside-the-Beltway story to which the rest of the country was oblivious.

I loved everything about being in Washington that weekend. Jim took us to the very spot where Congressman Mills' girlfriend, Fanny Foxe, had just thrown herself into the Tidal Basin; to the steep and scary stone staircase in Georgetown that had featured so prominently in the recent movie *The Exorcist*; and to the gates of the White House, where I was amazed you could just peer through the bars and see TV correspondents filming their stand-up reports in the driveway. It all seemed thrilling and I desperately wanted to get back there full time.

I didn't rub elbows with anyone famous in Washington D.C., though. Ironically, I had to return to Vermont to stumble upon a legitimate political celebrity. Walking out of the mailroom one afternoon, Jim and I noticed a man in a suit standing by himself on the sidewalk. "That looks like Ronald Reagan," Jim said, and it was! It turned out that the former governor was taking Ron Junior on a college tour and Middlebury was the stop between Dartmouth and Yale. With his son being shown the campus highlights, Reagan was hanging out on his own, apparently with nothing to do. We approached and almost immediately, a small crowd surrounded and peppered him with questions. Reagan seemed to enjoy the give-and-take with the kids who challenged him on Vietnam, oil company profits, the cause of poverty in America, and then more Vietnam. He hadn't announced yet whether he would challenge Gerald Ford for the 1976 Republican nomination, but he was well-versed on a wide range of issues and none of the students could stump or rattle him. The next week, the town's local newspaper, *The Valley Voice*, ran a photo of Reagan, Jim, and me laughing about some quip—Jim with a leather choker around his neck and me clutching to my chest the copy of William F. Buckley's *National Review* that I had just retrieved from my mailbox.

Reagan was considered by the left to be a dumbbell or amiable dunce, but you had to wonder who was really out of touch. Two weeks later, I had an

the Valley Voice

battell building,

Vol. I, No. 45   Wednesday, April 23, 1975

Ex-Governor Ronald Reagan was a surprise visitor to the Middlebury College campus last week. He cheerfully denied that the possibility of Vermont instituting a presidential primary (since defeated) had anything to do with his presence in Vermont. New Hampshire was his next stop, though.

When Ronald Reagan visited the campus, Jim and I ended up on the front page of the local newspaper, grinning at some joke he'd just made.

early morning meeting with my American Studies advisor, Eleanor Ilgen, who informed me that Phnom Penh had just fallen to the Khmer Rouge. When she saw my stricken face she said, "I know. It's sad. But at least the killing will stop now." Mrs. Ilgen was a very kind and nurturing woman who knew a lot about the causes of the American Civil War, but she didn't know the first thing about the Cambodian civil war. After generations of communist atrocities and genocide (see: Stalin in the Ukraine, the Mao-generated famines in China, and the mass killings in North Vietnam and North Korea), it didn't take a crystal ball to know this wouldn't end well, although, to be fair, not even I anticipated the scale of the coming Cambodian Genocide. I left that meeting and walked to Jim's room and said, "you'll never believe what Eleanor Ilgen just said." From then on, "At least the killing will stop" became a life-long sardonic joke between the two of us about liberal naivete.

Politics aside, I was enjoying myself more but, foolishly, still not taking full advantage of the college experience. When the Student Activity Council sponsored appearances by B.B. King, Chick Corea, Leo Kotke, and the Alvin Ailey dance troupe, I didn't attend, either because I'd never heard of them or I was too lethargic. I rarely went to football or basketball games. And I wasn't a joiner. If I had to do it over, I would have found an extra-curricular activity to throw myself into—the radio station, the school newspaper, student government, an intramural team—but with schoolwork still weighing heavily on my mind and not wanting to miss precious hanging around time with my existing friends, I took the path of least resistance and kept my distance from new social experiences.

I did get involved in two tiny clubs, but not for social purposes. One involved my new fixation on classic movies. It turned out that Middlebury had an American Movie Club, which was run by a senior with the unique name of Dale Brilliant. It was a one-person "club" and because I helped her collect admission to screenings, she turned it over to me when I was a senior. The movies I planned for the next year were a huge hit. I could schedule *The Adventures of Robin Hood* or *All About Eve* at 7:00pm, 9:00pm, and 11:00pm and sell out all three shows. Even at 50 cents a head, we made good profits, and I was able to accumulate a sizable nest-egg and avoid bending the knee at the Student Activity Council to get a subsidy. Alas, in the middle of my Howard Hawks film festival, I got busted by a very angry member of that Council, who confronted me at the door for charging more than the 25-cent limit without their permission. Proving once again that the stakes are never too low for power-mad bureaucrats to assert their authority.

The second "club" I joined was a small conservative political group. Jim and I had been introduced to a classmate named Amanda who, although personally moderate, had formed a one-woman organization called Alternative View because she thought the campus needed a counterweight to its overwhelming liberal ethos. We became the group's only other members.

Alternative View sponsored only a few low-key events, but we scored big when former Nixon aide, Patrick Buchanan, then a conservative columnist, agreed to give a speech on campus. It turned out that our college President knew Buchanan from a group they both belonged to in Washington, and convinced him to accept our invitation. Even then, the hardline, scowling Pat Buchanan was not my favorite right-wing columnist—I much preferred the more erudite William Safire or George Will and I thought William F. Buckley was God. But I was excited to get him because he'd break through the liberal monopoly on campus.

In 2017, the Middlebury student body disgraced itself by staging a riot when Charles Murray tried to speak on campus, but in 1976, Jim and I were more worried about student indifference. We created deliberately provocative posters ("He advised Nixon to expand the bombing in Cambodia") to get a bigger turnout. We succeeded beyond our wildest dreams. The original venue—the auditorium where we normally screened movies—was overflowing, so 15 minutes before the start of the speech, we moved it to the college chapel, the largest space on campus.

The student body listened to Buchanan respectfully and asked a range of good questions. So I was surprised later in the week, when someone wrote a letter to the school newspaper bemoaning our collective shame of letting a fascist like Pat Buchanan speak at Middlebury and chastising the apathetic student body for not shouting him down. Thankfully, that kind of aggressive silencing of unpopular voices wouldn't be common on college campuses for another 40 years and Jim, Amanda, and I could congratulate ourselves on exposing our fellow classmates to a little diversity.

Once the speech was over, the college president had a small dinner at his house in Buchanan's honor. The guest list included a few favorite American Studies professors that Jim and I had selected. Buchanan told amusing stories about working for Nixon in the mid-1960s. Those rumors about Nixon not being able to hold his liquor were true. The professors, somewhat mystified by why they, with no background in politics, had been asked in the first place, sat primly with their even quieter wives and listened politely as Jim challenged Buchanan on a few points of conservative orthodoxy. The next day, one of them sourly observed to Jim and me that Buchanan had been "slick," which apparently meant that he'd marshalled his stories and arguments in the cogent way you'd expect from a columnist and former Presidential speechwriter. Would the same professors have sat mutely and apparently afraid to speak in front of a former speechwriter for JFK and then dismissed him as slick? Hardly.

There's a somewhat prurient coda to this story. Soon after she introduced us, our mutual friend, Sheara Friend, confided that Amanda wanted to lose her virginity sooner rather than later. Amanda was pretty frank about it one night when the two of us were alone in her room shooting the breeze about politics and life in general. "Hmmm," I thought, not doing much to advance that line of discussion. Later, at our five-year reunion, I asked Sheara if Amanda ever found anyone to do the deed. She started jumping around in her seat and gushed that during the summer after graduation, Amanda had an affair with our college President! Wow. I guess if you're going to lose your virginity, you might as well start at the top. And I couldn't help but wonder, in retrospect, about our President's then-surprising interest in getting Pat Buchanan to our event. Had he been trying to impress her by demonstrating he could get a big name to help her out?

Senior year, I lived by myself in a single in Forest Hall, an elegant, former women's dorm so named because it was financed by the Depression-era sale of a large Middlebury-owned forest in the Green Mountains to the National Park Service. It is theoretically the dream of every college student to live in a single room, but I have to admit, I missed the camaraderie of roommates. That option was closed to me, however, because Chris had decided to participate in the American University political science program in Washington and Jim needed his own space.

Aside from Chris and Jim, most of my best friends were women. Betsy Shreve, whose older sister, Anita Shreve, would later become a best-selling novelist, was from Duxbury, Massachusetts, and was in my room the night of October 21, 1975, when we watched the Red Sox win Game Six of the World Series. I'd thought we were the only ones watching, but when Carlton Fisk hit the game-winning home run off the left field foul pole, it seemed like the whole dorm erupted and people I barely knew rushed into my room to see what had happened. Just four days later, I was watching *The Mary Tyler Moore* show down the hall in my friend Sally Russell's room, when the "Chuckles the Clown" episode aired, causing me to collapse on the floor in laughter. Literally on the floor.

Leslie Donovan and I remained close, and she, Betsy, Jim, and I were a loose foursome, occasionally going into town for dinner. I also became friends with two American History majors—Sheara and her former room-mate, Cindy Regan—who shared my pain as we all wrote our theses.

As an American Studies major, I could choose any thesis topic related to American culture and I decided I wanted to research something on the movies. I appropriated my girlfriend's love for Humphrey Bogart and decided to look into his role as a film icon in the 1940s. Drawing heavily on Leslie Fiedler's *Love and Death in the American Novel*, I had a few interesting observations to make about how his hard-boiled persona exemplified the urbanization of America, why his cynicism resonated in post-war America, and why Bogart, with his refusal to conform to mainstream bourgeois social norms, was just another example of an American cultural rebel—similar to Natty Bumpo and Huck Finn—who sought to escape the civilizing clutches of the American woman.

If I had to do it over again, though, I would have examined how Bogart had become a cultural icon in the 1970s, rather than the 1940s. *Casablanca* had premiered in 1943, just 30 years before I saw it for the first time in 1973, but even then it seemed like an artifact of a lost civilization. Bogart's character Rick, a stand-in for pre-Pearl Harbor, isolationist America (the events of the movie are pointedly set in early December 1941), is at first cynical, claiming "I stick my neck out for no man." He becomes a self-sacrificing idealist when that cynicism crumbles in the face of Nazi bullying and an admission from his former lover, Ingrid Bergman, that she still loves him. Self-sacrificing idealism was decidedly not the ethos of my era, but the movie and Bogart himself were nevertheless hugely popular in the '60s and '70s. Throughout Harvard's final exam week, the Brattle Theatre played Bogart movies every night, and the students always rose and sang along—in French—when the *Casablanca* bar patrons sang "La Marseillaise." At Middlebury, it was almost the same thing. Every Bogart movie I screened sold out.

The most critically acclaimed movies of the late 1960s and early 1970s were cynical and nihilistic, yet here was Bogart, a classic American hero wrestling with his conscience and ultimately opting for idealism, seducing an entirely new generation of movie-goers. Despite our outward lassitude, I think that deep down, my generation secretly envied Bogart's strict moral code, his willingness to put others ahead of himself, and his compassion for the weaker and vulnerable.

I've been hard on my generation and perhaps even unfair. We didn't create the '60s—we had it thrust upon us. I think, for the most part, we were all just trying to make sense of changing social norms. When I leaf through my yearbook now, I see that the number of "normal" people in my class (the unpretentious, generous, and kind ones) considerably outnumbered the blowhards. Maybe it only seemed that the self-absorbed predominated because they drew so much attention to themselves.

Even in that apathetic age, there were a few shoots of idealism trying to break through at Middlebury, although I thought they were mostly wooly-headed. A classic example was the college's somewhat self-serving response to the energy crisis: the black-out dance. The popularity of the first Earth Day in 1970 had jump-started the environmental movement, and the sudden shortages of gasoline, heating oil, and electricity that shocked the economy in the early 1970s had given green activists the moral high ground to demand widespread cuts in energy use before we "ran out" of oil or "poisoned the earth." So how did the student body signal its virtuousness on this issue? By voluntarily blacking out the campus one night a year (i.e. no lights in our dorm rooms) and holding an electricity-free dance. For entertainment, the school hired a Jamaican steel band that required no electrical amplification. Of course, the band had to drive its gas-guzzling van up from New York

City and the dance itself could not safely be held in total darkness, so the real energy footprint of the blackout night was probably neutral at best. But the dance itself was actually a blast, even if the environmental impact was merely symbolic.

Greater sacrifices were asked of us by "Fast for Hunger" day. A group of students led by future CNN anchor, Frank Sesno, thought the best way to help alleviate world hunger was to ask the student body to forgo eating for a day so that the food we'd normally be consuming in the dining halls could be donated to the rest of the world. The college wouldn't actually be giving our food to local food banks, though. Instead, they'd calculate the money saved when students skipped out on meals that day and then cut a check for a world anti-hunger organization.

Okay, fine. Whatever. Maybe that was a nice gesture, even as I rolled my eyes at it. But the sermonizing and moral posturing really got under Jim's skin, which meant it got under mine too. It wasn't enough for the organizers that we skip meals in the dining halls. We weren't supposed to eat anything, anywhere, period. No pre-buying food ahead of time to munch quietly in your dorm room. No going downtown to eat a pizza or a sub. The point was to experience hunger and understand what it was like to go to bed on an empty stomach. Screw that! To Jim and me, there was no equivalence between the reality of actual starvation and skipping a couple of meals. The college couldn't forbid us from eating the food our parents had paid for, so it kept one dining hall open for dissenters. When Jim and I showed up for meals that day, we noticed that most of the school's Black student body also broke the food embargo. Without stereotyping, I think it's fair to say that many of them had a closer relationship to food insecurity than the rest of us and were no more interested in assuaging white liberal guilt than Jim and I were. Right on!

I guess these anecdotes make me sound cynical, but I just didn't have a lot of sympathy for empty, performative gestures, especially ones that had a coercive nature. I would have been more impressed if these activists had spent the day volunteering at a food bank instead of trying to shame a bunch of college kids into going hungry for a day.

These small ideological battles amused more than aggravated me. What really caused me angst was the prospect of graduating and leaping into an uncertain future. I kept a very sporadic journal during junior and senior year and many of the entries express growing anxiety about my prospects. At one point I wrote plaintively, "What am I to be?"

I had entertained the thought of being a writer and had even enrolled in a creative writing class, but, intimidated by the blank page and the other people in the class, I panicked, dropped the course, and enrolled in another literature class. I also submitted a short story to the Middlebury literary magazine, which was rejected. I didn't like the feeling of rejection and didn't try again, so my dreams of a literary career never materialized.

Middlebury's Career Services program didn't exist back in the 1970s. I didn't want to go to graduate school and I had no one to advise me on other careers. I don't remember any job fairs or offers to hook me up with alumni. Naturally, I hadn't had any summer internships since that concept didn't exist then. Nor did I take any aptitude tests. Indeed, what was I to be?

My college journal details a great deal of resentment among my peers about the grind we had been put through to reach graduation. We believed that students at the more prestigious Ivy League schools didn't have to work as hard as we did and that we didn't get the credit and recognition we deserved for our efforts. I have no idea whether these self-pitying feelings were justified, but I do remember being drained at the end of the year, especially from writing the short book that was my thesis. It was 100 pages long and each chapter had been rewritten at least once and sometimes twice. And I'll say this: Mrs. Ilgen wasn't an expert on geopolitics, but she was a good editor; she taught me more about writing than anyone else I later knew. She and my other thesis readers gave me a B+, which meant that I graduated cum laude despite my miserable grade point average. (Of course, with an unbroken string of A's over the last three years, Jim graduated summa cum laude and was elected into Phi Beta Kappa.)

As graduation came into sight, I briefly set aside my existential anxieties and began to enjoy the last sweet weeks of college, and even got a glimpse into the future of how we'd process knowledge. My very last paper, in Sociology, was an exercise that involved going to the basement of Voter Hall where, I was surprised to find, the college housed a massive computer; I had the machine compare data sets of teenagers who watched a lot of TV and those who went to the movies—an analysis that took a day and resulted in a multiple-page computer printout. When the data was analyzed, I concluded that teenagers who went to a lot of movies were considerably more socially active than those who watched TV. I finally, at the very end of college, got my first A+. It had taken almost four full years, but I had finally learned how to write a term paper.

Spring was unusually warm that year and about 20 of us celebrated with a carefree afternoon at nearby Lake Dunmore. In the photos from that afternoon, most of the guys are shirtless, so even though this was May, we must have been swimming. The next day, Chris, Jim, and I went to "The Quarry," a giant, spring-fed swimming hole in an old granite excavation site about a half hour drive from the college, where the more free-spirited members of the class were skinny-dipping. Chris and I modestly dove into the cold, clear quarry water in cut-off jeans, while Jim and most everyone else let it all hang

With Leslie Donovan, Betsy Shreve and Jim Robinson after we received our diplomas.

out. I was amazed that some of the women in our American Studies seminar could nonchalantly lie around and casually chat about their summer plans while they were so exposed.

Even after all the end-of-year celebrations, parties, and dinners, graduation day itself still seemed to rush upon me with little warning. My college days, which had been such a trial in the beginning, and then too often taken for granted, seemed irreplaceably precious. And just as my friends and I reached an emotional fever pitch in getting ready to say goodbye to each other, the outsiders descended. Parents, grandparents, uncles, aunts, siblings, all of them thrilled to celebrate with us but understandably a little oblivious to how their reappearance on campus had abruptly signaled the end. On a dime, we had to switch from thinking primarily about ourselves to playing host to our eager guests, rightfully excited to share the big moment. Meals had to be scheduled, smiling faces displayed, entertainment provided, and worst of all, dorm rooms emptied and packed into cars and trucks.

My parents and sister were there, of course, but also my Grandma Harris and Cousin Sally from Nantucket. My father, in particular, was in his element, so proud to see his son graduate. The commencement ceremony took place outside my dorm room, in the Forest Hall backyard—the first time the college had produced an outside graduation. The commencement address was delivered by Anne Morrow Lindberg, the widow of Charles Lindberg and a well-known writer in her own right, and the grandmother of Kristina Lindberg, a member of our class.

We lined up according to academic majors and marched between two long lines of professors, all attired in the regalia of their own alma maters. Those of us in American Studies sat in front of the Art majors so I was able to hear them complain that all the academic awards went to Science majors; they whined that it was easier to get all A's in disciplines where there were objective right and wrong answers, compared to majors like Art and Theatre where grades were *so* much more subjective. Apparently, jealousy and status-seeking never take a day off.

As it happened, one of those honorees was Betsy Shreve's boyfriend, Peter Gibb, also a friend of ours. When he stood on stage as the salutatorian, he looked shockingly haggard. When the ceremony ended and we sought each other out to take photos and hug goodbye, Betsy told us, gulping through sobs, that Peter's mother had died that morning back at home. She'd been ill for a while but I hadn't known she was that sick. Peter had learned the news before the ceremony started but kept it to himself so the rest of us, including Betsy, wouldn't feel sad when we got our diplomas.

On the drive home a few hours later, already a little gloomy because of the death of Peter's mother and the end of my college career, my mother informed me that they needed me to start my summer job at their pool store the very next day. That felt a little deflating after the emotion of the day, but they were short-staffed just as the season was heading into its busy time. And besides, what else was I going to do? I had no plans. Not for the next day, the next month, or the rest of my life.

CHAPTER 15

Working

For most of the Holmeses—and by this, I mean my immediate family, my uncles, aunts and cousins—work isn't just a way of earning money. It's a pre-capitalist virtue, maybe even a pre-Calvinist sacrament. We don't sacrifice burnt offerings to demonstrate our gratitude for life, we atone for our sins through the sweat of our brow. My parents were more impressed by toil than affluence. If the two were related, great; but nothing filled them with disgust like the sight of someone with money who hadn't worked for it. Given my privileged homelife, they didn't want me to grow up spoiled, so I started working years before any of my friends.

My first place of employment, at age 14, was their swimming pool store on Brockton's south side. My responsibilities there varied: cutting the grass, unloading delivery trucks, keeping the shelves stocked, and ringing up sales.

The building had a dank, airless cellar where we kept 100-pound sacks of pool chemicals—chlorine granules, diatomaceous earth for filters, alkalinity stabilizer, and PhPlus and PhMinus powder. Someone had to scoop these poisonous substances into five- and ten-pound plastic bottles that would be sold in the store and that someone was me. Of course, I never wore a mask or gloves. Maybe the chlorine killed all the germs because I rarely got sick.

At age 15, they assigned me to the work crew that installed in-ground swimming pools. This heavy physical labor involved a lot of toting and shoveling. I was about five foot six and 135 pounds, with even less musculature than I have now, so I don't know how much value I added.

Installing a pool usually took four or five days. On day one, a backhoe arrived to dig the hole in the ground. The next day, we assembled the wood walls that provide the sides of the pool. On day three, a dump truck would unload a huge pile of sand; we'd then have to shovel it into the pool hole and spread it around to create the contours of the floor, while simultaneously connecting the filter system and pipes. On the final day, we'd carefully insert the vinyl liner over the well-troweled sand—making sure there were no wrinkles on the floor—and begin to fill the pool with water. We'd also shovel dirt behind the walls and spread pea stone (little smooth pebbles) to provide a temporary ground cover that would last until the owners built a permanent deck around the pool.

This is how I learned to use the stick end of the shovel and since we usually worked shirtless, I developed a nice tan to boot. During my first year in the field, the business had just one crew of four guys, plus me and one pickup truck. We'd meet at the store at 7:00am, load the truck with shovels and rakes, and then drive to the job with half of us riding in the truck cab and the rest sitting on the floor of the exposed pickup bed, hoping that a sudden stop wouldn't fling us out into the road.

What I remember most about those two years working outside was the soundtrack of summer. We always had a radio blaring and the same Top 40 songs from WRKO would play over and over until they cycled out of rotation. Whenever I hear "Spinning Wheel" by Blood, Sweat & Tears, Kenny Rogers' "Ruby Don't Take Your Love to Town," "In the Year 2525" by Zagar and Evans, or "A Boy Named Sue" by Johnny Cash, I can't help but remember my calloused hands, the relative freedom of working in the fresh air, or the good natured camaraderie among the team.

The rest of the guys on the crew were college-age, bigger and stronger, and I'm sure they didn't relish having the boss's 15-year old son tagging along, but they treated me fine. Some of them, like Billy Tucker and Bruce Roscoe, worked for my parents for quite a few years and I developed a relationship with them not unlike the one I had with my older cousins, which means they mostly ignored me but occasionally took a benign interest in my ongoing development ("Hey I saw you driving your car last night. Was that your girlfriend sitting next to you?").

As the business grew, we had as many as three crews working at once and over the years, my parents probably hired about 100 different workers as seasonal help, which paid for a lot of tuition. They were good employees and the work site was generally fun with a great deal of joking and male bonding. They were definitely not choir boys, though. At least once a summer someone had a car crash, drunk driving citation, or soap-opera-level meltdown with a girlfriend—boys-will-be-boys exploits that my father took with a lot more equanimity than if it had been me.

Then there was the summer that the first of them got married. The stag party, to which I was obviously not invited, was a drunken debauch that culminated with the attendees herded into a small theater, where two Boston prostitutes conducted a striptease, after which they pulled the overly intoxicated groom and best man onto the stage, stripped them naked (except for their socks) and compelled them to perform sexual acts. When the groom and best man were exhausted from their labors, the rest of the guys threw five dollars and their names into a pot and the winner of this lottery took one of the women into a back room. Everyone had such a great time that when another member of their group of friends (this time not one of our employees) got married a year later, they organized the same schedule of events, although this time the groom and best men knew what was coming and didn't need to be coaxed onto the stage.

I'm still shocked by this, to be honest. Most of the guys on the crew, especially the groom, did not seem like the type to seek this out. I can only assume a combination of alcohol, testosterone, peer pressure, and undeveloped cerebral cortexes clouded their judgment. Or maybe they were just horny 22 year olds.

157

Working in the pool business was my summer occupation, but I also had winter responsibilities too. My father always had off-season jobs, and in the late 1960s, he won the bid to operate the skate rental concession at the new State rink, adjacent to the new Brockton High School. Damp and chilly, this was my winter workplace from age 16 to 20.

The business involved renting and sharpening skates and selling hockey equipment. Staffing became a family affair. My parents took some shifts, as did my sister and I. We only had to be open during the hours of public skating, so it wasn't a heavy schedule; during the cold months, I usually worked a couple of hours after school or at night, as well as one weekend shift.

This was a low-skill job, but I had to sharpen skates, which involved strapping the blade on a portable platform that moved back and forth against a stone grinder. Tiny fibers of metal flew off and clogged up my nose because we didn't use facemasks or vacuums to catch the metal. When I arrived at college and learned about black lung disease, I began to worry that I'd develop it eventually, but the subsequent four decades of anxiety proved a waste of energy since my pneumonic health remained unchanged over the years.

Even though this was a small operation, we did have a handful of employees, including Brockton High School's best hockey player, Mike MacDonald, a year younger than me. We worked together enough to become friendly, so I was glad to see him sophomore year of college when he stopped by the shop during winter break to chat about his first semester of Harvard, which he was attending on a hockey scholarship. Hmm. Having worked with him for a couple of years, I wouldn't have expected that out of all the students at Brockton High, *he* would be the one they'd want. But he was fitting in regardless—he'd even needed to buy a tuxedo because he attended so many black tie events! I was quite sure there wasn't a single tuxedo on the entire Middlebury campus and I could only stare in amazement at the idea that he was attending parties with women who wore their grandmothers' pearls and guys who inherited their summer jobs at the Nantucket Yacht Club.

After two summers of outdoor work building pools, my parents transferred me back into the retail store. I don't know whether they decided I wasn't pulling my weight with the manual labor or thought I'd be more useful in a job where I could exercise my brain, but for the next six summers, I was on a small team of indoor employees who sold everything that went with a pool—cleaning equipment, spare parts, toys, chemicals, filters, and witty signs.

I became particularly adept at pool chemistry. Customers would bring in glass jars of pool water—often sheepishly, because it reminded them of delivering urinalysis samples to their doctors—and I'd take it into a little room and conduct a variety of pH, chlorine, total alkalinity, and iron content tests to see what the problem was. Did you know that if there's iron in the water and you throw in chlorine, the water will oxidize and turn green? That was the kind of wisdom I'd dispense.

Most of our customers would pay in cash and a few with checks. Around 1970, we started accepting credit card transactions. We had a portable credit card imprinter into which we'd lay the card and a three-layer carbon paper receipt and yank a roller across to imprint the number on the receipt. If the transaction was more than $50, we either had to phone into a main BankAmericard or MasterCard call center to get it verified or look up the number on a monthly book of bad credit card numbers to confirm the card was still valid. No computers back then either, just paper slips that we'd mail in.

In 1972, the fall I left for college, my parents tore down their small house-based store and erected a much larger metal building that, with its glass front, somewhat resembled an automotive showroom. The retail area had two big spaces—the store itself, plus an adjoining room with a real in-ground swimming pool that displayed the very product that potential customers could install in their own backyards. The next spring, even though I was heading into final exams, I flew home from college in Vermont for two days to attend the grand opening. We sold "Buster Crabbe Pools," named after the Olympic gold-medal swimmer and star of the *Tarzan*, *Flash Gordon*, and *Buck Rogers* movies, and Buster Crabbe himself was there to give swimming lessons in the pool. He was 65 years old and still looked fantastic in a bathing suit, with his sun-leathered Hollywood good looks completely intact.

My parents with the former Olympian and movie star Buster Crabbe.

The grand opening, which included a nice photo in the local paper, was a huge success, with people coming from all over the area to see the semi-famous movie star. It established our store as the leading swimming pool establishment in the Brockton area. My parents had achieved what is known in the business world as "first mover advantage." They sold about 50–70 pools a year and made themselves the local experts on everything related to swimming pools. For the next 15 years, they had no real competition and when they sold the business, they were still on top.

But that was in the future. For the period under discussion here—through the summers in high school and college—the work was steady and not too arduous. I was required to clock in 40 hours a week, mostly during the day, sometimes at night, always on Saturday—and I came to enjoy a feeling of competence I never really experienced at any job since then. I also liked my co-workers, who usually included a male store manager (there were a few), and a series of younger female sales associates.

These younger women frequently became like favorite nieces to my parents, who took them on vacations, helped out financially, and provided emotional support. The female colleague I worked with the most—Sherry Thompson, a pretty and vivacious small-town girl from neighboring Stoughton—dated two different guys on the pool crew one summer; when forced to choose between them, she picked the pre-med Ivy League student who briefly became her fiancé, a status that evaporated when he returned to Princeton that fall. When she later married Enzo, a handsome Italian-American hairdresser from Boston, and subsequently had a baby daughter named Tennille (after Captain and Tennille), she asked my parents to be the godparents.

As my college graduation approached and I had no job prospects, my mother suggested that maybe I'd want to come into the business with them. It was not uncommon in the Buster Crabbe Pool universe for sons and daughters to become second-generation business partners. This supposedly secured the kids' financial future and allowed the parents to shed some responsibilities and look forward to early retirement.

That seemed like a bad idea. I didn't have a particular passion to be a small business owner, didn't want to be stuck in Brockton, and was afraid that I'd ruin my relationship with my parents. My father in particular had strong ideas about how to do things and I knew I'd resent being under his thumb all the time. And frankly, what was the point of all the studying and angst of getting that college education if I was just going to take over my parents' business? A few business courses at the local community college would have made more sense.

But what was the alternative? The go-go economy of the 1960s had sputtered to an end with the oil shocks and surge of inflation in the mid-1970s. I had no role models to advise me on professions that might interest me and was completely adrift. When I look back at my 22-year-old self, I want to shake him by the shoulders and say, "Take control of your life!" A year earlier, my friend Jane Prince and a college pal, facing similarly poor prospects, had loaded their belongings in a car and driven to Milwaukee. After a few months, they decided it was a dull town, so they moved north to Minneapolis, where they knew no one but somehow found jobs and apartments. Nothing so adventurous for me. I spent the summer immediately after graduation working at the pool store, the same as ever. Since I liked movies so much, I thought I'd find a film-related job and applied for positions as an assistant manager for a local cinema and a sales coordinator for a company that distributed movies to college campuses. Right up my alley, no? But I never made it past the first round of interviews.

I literally had zero prospects six months after graduation. Then my Grandma Holmes, who had been bedridden after suffering a stroke three years earlier, finally died shortly after Christmas. Judi accompanied me to the funeral a few days later—the first time she met my cousins, uncles, aunts and grandfather, whom she charmed tremendously. My Uncle Wayne attended, of course. After 15 years as a corporate lawyer, he'd moved back to Nantucket as a private attorney and at the funeral, informed my parents that the island's cable system, Nantucket Cablevision, wanted to spin off the local access channel to someone else.

This was in the very early days of cable TV and Nantucket, because it got lousy reception from the Boston and Providence TV stations, was one of the first places to get wired. To obtain a municipal cable franchise though, the investors (in this case a handful of Nantucket businessmen) needed to set aside a channel that provided news and covered local events, which they were tired of managing themselves. Even though I knew nothing about cable TV, running a small business, directing a news operation, managing people, or generating ad sales, my parents agreed with my uncle that this was a great opportunity for me. Who was I to disagree? If I didn't grab this, I might never get out of Brockton.

Everything moved fast after that. There was minimal haggling with the cable system over the finer points. They wanted more than $10,000 for the equipment and the "goodwill," and we agreed to throw in some extra money to support the business before the expected influx of summer ad revenue. We didn't scour the books to analyze the projected revenue or expenses too deeply, and we never even went to the island to look at the studio or meet the employees. Wayne handled all that, and only six weeks elapsed from the time he raised the idea at the funeral until I showed up on the island to take over. So yes, my father literally bought me my first job.

In early January, I moved Judi down to Charlottesville, Virginia so she could begin work on a master's degree in English at the University of Virginia. A month later, before I left for Nantucket, I took a train south for one last visit. It was a miserable ride because I came down with either the flu or food poisoning and threw up twice in the train's jostling bathroom. I never felt as sick as when I arrived, and went straight to bed in Judi's room. Feeling better 24 hours later, I made the rounds and tried to ingratiate myself with her new friends, including a medical student she talked about a lot. What none of us suspected, except maybe him, was that he would become her fiancé less than a year later.

When I got back to Brockton, I packed some clothes into my car and drove myself to the Steamship Authority terminal in Hyannis, Massachusetts and took the ferry over to Nantucket. It was the middle of February and the island was gray, damp, and cheerless. Wayne's wife, my Aunt Lee, was the co-owner of a downtown bicycle rental shop, Cook's Cycle, which offered an empty apartment above the bike storage space. That jaunty, nautical-themed room became my home until the start of summer, when the bike shop needed it back for their seasonal employees. The building was across the street from the Nantucket Yacht Club and when I looked out my window, I could see the club's empty slips and moorings in the harbor. This was not a residential area and at night, the bleak, empty streets showed no signs of life. When I was in bed with the lights off, it was completely silent except for the steady clanging of a metal lanyard banging against a bare flagpole. What, I wondered more than one dark night that winter, had I gotten myself into?

CHAPTER 16

Channel 3

T he Nantucket I remembered from visiting my grandparents in the mid-1960s was not the place I found in the winter of 1977, when I took command at Channel 3. Like Brockton, it was caught up in economic and social forces beyond its control, but the island's increasingly bright trajectory was almost the opposite of the ongoing immiseration of my hometown.

For decades, Nantucket had been a sedate, cash-poor, seaside outpost, living on the memory of its whaling era riches and supported by WASPy summer people who were happy to keep a low profile, quietly sip their gin and tonics at the yacht club, wear shabby clothes around town, and navigate the local waters in unpretentious wooden sailboats. In the summers of the 1960s, you could still drive to the end of Straight Wharf, then little more than a paved parking lot jutting out into the harbor. Once there, you'd buy an ice cream cone at the snack bar and sit in your car to gaze out at the boats hypnotically bobbing at their moorings. The big event of the week was the band concert on Sunday night, when we crowded around a temporary wooden platform erected on Main Street's cobblestones to listen to an ebullient woman in a man's white suit and narrow black necktie conduct a program borrowing heavily from the middlebrow Boston Pops repertoire. Those quaint, innocent, small-town pleasures had all vanished when I moved back.

The country's post-war economic boom created a much larger millionaire class with significantly more time and money to spend on recreation. This was the insight of a rich summer resident, Walter Beinecke, an heir to the S&H Green Stamp fortune and the controlling investor in the "Christmas Club" business. In the late 1960s, he started buying up the town's waterfront, biggest hotels, and fanciest restaurants. The ancient wharves, home first to whaling ships and later to commercial fishing boats, suddenly sprouted high-end retail stores, art galleries, and a world-class boat basin. It was a Disneyland version of a maritime village but it prevented the island from becoming a ticky-tacky tourist trap like Hyannis or Provincetown.

This strategy worked spectacularly well. Beinecke's savvy understanding of the new upper crust's aspirations, combined with the legitimate charm of Nantucket's historic pre-Civil War mansions and its remote, windswept natural beauty, quickly remade Nantucket into a major East Coast resort and playground for the rich, on par with the Hamptons, Hilton Head, and Palm Beach.

As the money poured into the island, so did a brigade of retirees, lawyers, doctors, artists, real estate agents, general contractors, bartenders, and hair stylists—people who had once enjoyed the island for its summer charms but had decided to make Nantucket their year-round home. From 1970 to 1980, the island's winter population grew by 50 percent, to more than 5,000 people.

Chief among the new blood that flooded into Nantucket during the 1970s was my Uncle Wayne, my father's younger brother. He had worked his way through Mercer University in Georgia after graduating as the "most likely to succeed" from Nantucket High School with my parents in the class of 1950. He had subsequently married my Aunt Lee, the daughter of Roy Sanguinetti, Nantucket's most prominent attorney. Wayne became a lawyer himself, initially slaving away on soulless corporate legal staffs in Pennsylvania and Ohio. After growing tired of the mainland rat race, he moved the family back to the island and took over his retiring father-in-law's legal practice at a time when there were only three lawyers on the island. Smart and sharp-elbowed, he became the attorney for many of the island's leading businesses and quickly established himself as one of the town's most dominant politicians, ultimately serving on almost every important town board.

Until I arrived on Nantucket, I didn't realize what an important and sometimes polarizing figure Wayne had become. Nor did I understand immediately why people would be wary that he had effectively gained operating control of one of the island's few news outlets. I quickly intuited that if I ran into people who didn't like him, which was frequently the case, I should emphasize that I was myself a native and that my parents were the more down-to-earth Quentin Holmes and Jean Harris—remember them? Or maybe I'd mention that I had Nantucket relatives on both sides of the family, including my grandfather Arthur Harris and my other uncle, Arthur "Brother" Harris. In a place like Nantucket where genealogies mattered, I was happy to play the "native" card when I needed to.

The business we had bought, known as Channel 3 because of its location on the cable line-up, was just a penny-ante operation. Nevertheless, we incorporated the business as the Nantucket Broadcasting Company and created an NBC logo because Wayne thought it would be great publicity if the real NBC sued us for copyright infringement, which alas, they never bothered to do. Located in the narrow basement of a former house on Federal Street, underneath an electronics store called "The Electric Mainsail," Channel 3's assets consisted of two video cameras, several monitors, and some aging transmission equipment. The "studio" was located at the far end of the cellar, with a curtain to cover up the stone foundation and a video set that accommodated a two-person plywood desk for newscasts. To be honest, we got ripped off. Cablevision should have paid us to take the operation off their hands, not the other way around.

Channel 3 had one full-time employee, Jason, a sullen tech guy a couple years older than me who was rightfully wary about my qualifications to run a TV station. Before I arrived, Wayne recruited two local women to be the TV news anchors—Lillian Waine, the 60-something wife of a local electrician and a homespun, amateur winter thespian and Nancy Burns, a late-20s, big blonde personality from the Boston suburbs who was socially connected to the arty and moneyed summer crowd.

The idea was that I would report and write the copy for a 15-minute Monday through Friday news broadcast at 5:30pm. I'd type the stories on my typewriter and hand them to Nancy and Lilian at 5:00pm for a quick read-through before going live. We'd try to break up the verbal narration with video segments recorded earlier in the day on three quarter inch tape—it was usually an interview I'd conducted but it could also be music from a kids' concert, a scene from a school play, or a birthday party from the nursing home. There was frequent tension on the set because Nancy aspired to be a polished, Leslie-Stahl-like newscaster and she chafed at Lilian's folksy, grand-motherly delivery, with its touches of Minnie Pearl.

After the news, we offered a series of 15-minute shows that Jason would produce: a man-in-the-street interview segment (*On the Street Where You Live* with Al Fee, whose day job was an assistant manager at the local First National supermarket), a program on local architecture, or a public affairs interview show that Wayne hosted. Jason would also be responsible for live broadcasting local high school football and basketball games (boys only, since the sponsoring booster club was only interested in one gender), as well as the annual town meeting and other important civic events.

Most of these shows were marginally supported by advertising, but to cover all the bills, we had to figure out how to squeeze more ad dollars out of the local merchants. Considering how much money was floating around town, this should have been easy, but I was from the "You don't want to buy an ad, do you?" school of salesmanship. For a while, Lilian tried to sell ads and then we hired other salespeople, but since there were no TV ratings, most of the local businesses didn't see the value. Some of them would throw us a few crumbs from their leftover marketing dollars as a civic goodwill gesture, not unlike their sponsorship of a local Little League team, but we never cracked the big ad budgets.

Despite having never previously written one line of news copy, I became a decent reporter. In the very early days, I got a lot of tips from Wayne, who knew all the town government gossip. In fact, thanks to him, I broke major news on our very first broadcast—that the disgruntled members of the police department were unionizing and joining the Teamsters. That was a classic small town news story, growing out of years of petty grievances, hurt feelings, and personal conflict. The selectman had recently recruited as their new police chief a well-credentialed but decidedly off-island law enforcement officer who ended a two century-long string of homegrown, good old boy top guns. The new guy was not popular with the dozen or so officers serving under him. They didn't like it that he and the captain wore professional-looking white shirts instead of the gray uniforms that were good enough for the rest of them. Nor did they like it that he was recruiting new officers from off-island. And there were conflicts over shift assignments and a general feeling of disrespect. There were also nasty rumors, almost certainly unsubstantiated, that his wife was seen alone at the Chicken Box, the town's ill-reputationed dive bar.

In a small town, the cops are celebrities, and the activities of the police department were a major focus of the island's attention in those days. With only

The new General Manager of Channel 3, outside his grandparents' house.

three national channels to watch on broadcast television, the police scanner was one of the island's most important sources of entertainment, especially on long winter nights. Everyone had an opinion on what the cops did. In the end, the anti-chief turmoil was like almost everything else I covered as a local reporter: there was the surface news and the more interesting story-behind-the-story. For example, three meter maids (all sisters, nicknamed "Charlie's Angels" because of their father's given name) were having affairs with three members of the force. Even though these were local women stepping out with local men married to local wives, somehow the outsider chief got blamed for letting his department become a little Peyton Place. But obviously none of this ever made it into print or on the air.

I tried to ingratiate myself with my new sources in the town building, the selectmen, the school committee, the police and fire departments, and the business community. Sometimes, I'd pick up some interesting historical tidbits. This is the kind of ancient anecdote you'd hear: the Chairman of the Planning Board was nicknamed "Hosey," which I thought was a play on the name José; but no, he got his nickname in the high school locker room because his male member was alleged to be as long as a hose.

Some sources became friends, particularly Madelyne Perry, the town clerk. Her son, slightly older than I was, had recently died in a car crash and she treated me as a surrogate son. She knew generations of island gossip and I'd hang out in her office to learn not only how the town actually worked, but also what children had been fathered by someone other than the men raising them, or which local officials had been enemies since birth. There's a game Nantucketers play: "Who are their people?" If I asked about a woman on the planning board, Madelyne would say, "Well, she was a Holdgate," and tell me who her parents and grandparents were and which of her multiple Holdgate brothers and sisters still lived on Nantucket and who they dated in high school. And I ate it up.

Despite making a few new acquaintances and having drop-in-any-time privileges at the homes of my grandparents and aunt and uncles, I was still quite lonely that first spring on Nantucket, living alone above the Cooks Cycle bike shop and eating Swanson fish sticks twice a week. And I was already beginning to feel the strain of trying to make Channel 3 into a profitable business.

Fortunately, I had something to look forward to. Judi and I had made plans to spend the summer together on Nantucket. When my grandparents decamped for the season to their cottage on the other end of the island, I moved into their house, having first made sure it would be okay for Judi to join me there. I had even found her a job as a clerk in a summer clothes shop. The plan had been for us to test out whether we enjoyed living together and to discuss plans to get married the following year or so.

So it was a very bitter disappointment when she called in early May and said she'd decided to stay in Virginia for the summer. A professor had advised her to continue her studies during the break. Getting her master's was important to her and she wanted to give it her best effort. I was hurt but somewhat mollified when she agreed to come north and stay with me for a few days.

The visit went fine, but it came as a shock to me on the second day when she emotionally described her turmoil back in Virginia. She felt in over her head in graduate school and uncertain about her future. How about if she quit altogether and we got married right away?

What? I panicked a bit. With a shaky job and no place to live once the summer ended, I was definitely not in a position to be married. For all I knew, I could be living in my childhood bedroom back in Brockton in six months. Plus, after four years of being instructed in how she wanted an equal relationship and her own career, something I completely bought into, I thought she'd resent me if she gave up her education to move to a remote island and become a store clerk. "Let's wait a year," I said. She'd have her degree then and I'd know more about my own prospects.

This was in the days when phone calls were expensive, so we continued our frequent correspondence. These were not my best letters, since I was still hurt about my lonely summer and unhappy with the pressure I felt in our failing family enterprise. But if you can't be honest with your long-time girlfriend, what's the point, right? At the end of the summer, I agitated for a September visit and even sent her a plane ticket, which she thought was presumptuous. But she did agree to come, signaling pretty clearly, but not clearly enough for me to understand the situation, that our relationship was on the line and that I needed to step up my game. But instead of pulling out all the stops to romance her, I acted like my regular self. And in my obtuseness, I thought the visit had been satisfactory since in a moment of passion she had uttered the magic words, "I love you."

Two weeks later, I got the Dear John letter. It was kind but still devastating. She'd realized during the visit that she no longer loved me in the way a woman should love her lover and that we had grown apart in those nine months. How could this be? She'd sworn up, down, left, and right for four years that she loved me more than life itself. The fact that this heartbreak—the oldest story ever told—had been experienced by uncountable men before me made it no less painful. There were many sad nights after this. We continued to correspond and any slim hope I had at reconciliation ended that Christmas when I saw her at her parents' house in Brockton and encountered an invisible wall, porous enough for voice penetration but impermeable to physical touch.

Somewhat cowardly, I had delayed sharing this bad news with my parents, who really did have a right to know since Judi was part of their life too. So I only had myself to blame that winter when my father called to ask what the heck was going on. My grandfather had been disturbed to read in the Brockton *Enterprise* that Miss Judith A. Herbert was engaged to someone else. My first reaction was, boy, that didn't take long. It had only been four or five months since she'd broken up with me. But more than anything, I was embarrassed that my parents had found out that way—and from my grandfather, of all people.

In the end, this break-up was probably the best thing for both of us. Even when things were going well for us, she had frequently been mad at me for kidding around about the wrong thing, making insensitive observations, voicing independent opinions of my own, being condescending, not intuiting when she needed unconditional emotional support, and scoffing at what I considered to be half-baked feminist pronouncements. In other words, I had assumed the privileges of a husband before closing the deal, and worse, took my position for granted at a time when there was a very viable alternative candidate lurking in the wings who would be 100 percent, unquestioningly supportive. She got her degree and went on to have an extremely happy marriage despite never pursuing a professional career. It took me ten years to meet my own spouse, and I, too, ended up in a terrific marriage. But that was all in the future. In the fall of 1977 and for many years later, it sure didn't feel like I'd gotten another lucky break.

Being on Nantucket that first year was a lot like freshman year of college. My girlfriend had broken up with me, I struggled to connect with my peers, and I was in over my head with the main thing I was supposed to be doing. From a distance of 40 years, I can now take some solace from the fact that none of the channel's multiple succeeding proprietors did better at squeezing a profit from an advertising-supported lineup of nightly news and public affairs programs. But at the time, I blamed myself for our business reverses.

We did try hard to make it work. We fired Jason, our unhappy cameraman and technical engineer, after another camera guy, Steve Gallagher, visited the island as a tourist from Buffalo, walked into Wayne's office and asked for a job. Great idea! We took him at his word that he knew what he was doing, and thankfully, he did.

We couldn't keep our operations in that cellar-based studio much longer. The dust and grainy particulates that fell from the ceiling weren't good for the equipment, it was dangerous to have only one exit, and it wasn't the space you'd want prospective advertisers to visit anyway. Because Wayne and my parents were wired in locally, we learned that the third floor of Pacific Club—an 18th century brick warehouse at the foot of Main Street that had evolved into a cribbage-playing hangout for old salts—was available for rent. Since the members of the Pacific House Board knew the Holmeses from way back and thought of Channel 3 as a quasi-public utility, they let us have the floor at below-market rent.

This space, at the top of two steep and ancient staircases, had once been home to the Nantucket District Court but had sat empty since the construction, more than a decade earlier, of a bigger courtroom in the new Town Building. Before we converted the floor into a TV studio, my Uncle Arthur, who did the renovation, needed to tear down the judge's bench and the rows of seats where generations of drunk drivers, petty thieves, bar-fight initiators, and Peeping Toms had awaited their fates. He was an excellent carpenter and left us with a spacious studio, a clean control room, an office, and a meeting room.

With a new studio and a motivated video team, we increased our professionalism. Channel 3 became a better resource for the community, with more talk, sports, political, and goofball programming. There was no shortage of arty or chatty townspeople who wanted to appear on TV or help behind the scenes. One local actress, Mara Cary, who had a short-lived kids' show, used to bring her toddler son, Donick, to the studio. 30 years later, I started to see the name Donick Cary in the credits for network TV shows (the head writer for David Letterman, the executive producer for *The Simpsons*, *Parks and Recreation*, and *New Girl*). And one of our interns, Jonathan Burkhart, became a network cameraman, movie producer, co-founder of the Nantucket Film Festival, and, I was startled to learn decades later, an inspiration for the musical *Rent*.

We also had an ongoing relationship with a local socialite named Abigail, who convinced one of her very rich friends to sponsor a ten episode series in which the two of them would interview famous summer visitors. The friend, Caroline, gave Abigail $500 to pay us for the airtime. Unfortunately, the two of them had an explosive fight after Abigail ended their interview with the real NBC's John Chancellor before Caroline had asked all her questions. We continued the series with Caroline alone. Abigail kept promising to hand over the money soon, but it turned out that although she swanned around at all the local summer charity galas, she actually lived in penury and never did pay us. Since that represented a week's worth of payroll, it hurt to have her basically steal from us, and I can't believe now that I was wimp enough to let her get away with it.

Even with our trouble finding advertisers, we did have one dependable revenue source. Every year on the last Sunday of June, the March of Dimes produced a 12-hour fundraising telethon at the Nantucket High School gym that aired over Channel 3, using our equipment and personnel. This was a very fun, very popular community talent show and with 12 hours to fill, anyone who wanted to get on TV now had their chance. We charged $5,000 for the airtime, which represented ten percent of our annual revenue. Every year, the March of Dimes grumbled at the price-gouging, but the Northeast Regional Chapter quickly paid up because Nantucket, with its deep-pocketed summer people, always turned out to be the country's most lucrative local event on a per capita basis, and the regional organizers wanted to keep the crown for hosting the best telethon.

When it became apparent that Channel 3 was turning into a long-term money pit, my parents became more involved in trying to find new ways to generate income. One day, my father got a call from a summer resident named Fred Gardner, a friend from the early 1950s, who now had his own advertising agency in New York City. Fred had the brainstorm that since the island's local advertising, sales, and consumer purchasing all formed a closed loop in the same captive market, Nantucket would be an ideal location for test-marketing new consumer products and commercials.

This was an interesting idea, so my parents, Nancy Burns, and I flew to New York and met Fred and his colleagues in their Madison Avenue offices. After listening to their pitch, we agreed to create a new company, Nantucket Marketing, Inc. that my father would fund. Nancy would be in charge of attracting business. We designed the letterhead and I wrote a pitch letter that we sent to all the big consumer companies. This was in the days before computer merges, and my poor mother had to retype each letter individually. We were thrilled to generate interest from a marketing executive at Procter & Gamble, who flew to Nantucket with his wife. When we met him at the Channel 3 offices, I realized that we didn't really have a business—we just had the simulacrum of a germ of a concept. This was in the days before PowerPoint and we just talked to him without making a formal presentation—we didn't even give him the demographics of the island to demonstrate why they should test his new products there. We were basically saying, "Hey, you should really think about using Nantucket as a test market and while you're at it, you should advertise on Channel 3." Not that it mattered, because I suspect that guy lacked any serious interest in our offer, anyway, and really just wanted an excuse to spend a couple of days on Nantucket with his wife.

When we realized this business was also a bust, my father wanted to get out of Channel 3 as soon as possible. And with Nantucket Marketing gone, Nancy quit the TV anchor gig, fed up with sharing the screen with Lillian and claiming, pretty acidly, that we just weren't serious about turning the station into something she wanted to be associated with. So I became a co-anchor with Lillian—I wrote the news, so I might as well deliver it too. All summer and fall, we tried to find buyers to take the business off our hands. This was a race against our declining bank balance, since my father swore he wouldn't put another cent into the business. He'd just close the doors if we ran out of money.

The process of selling the company proved awkward because word got back to the Channel 3 staff, and Steve, in particular, was furious that he and his wife had just moved to the island for a job that might disappear. Somehow, we kept it going. Occasionally, I didn't take a paycheck when there wasn't enough money in the checkbook to pay all of us. We had a few potential buyers, but it wasn't until early fall that a serious candidate surfaced—a rich New York lawyer with a teenage son interested in video and deeper pockets than we had.

Fortunately, just as my string was running out at Channel 3, one of the two reporters at the Nantucket *Inquirer and Mirror* quit, and the publisher asked if I'd be interested in the job. I jumped at the chance for a steady, reliable paycheck with limited management responsibilities. They wanted me to start right away, and because negotiations with the new buyer were dragging out, I secretly did both jobs until the sale closed two months later. Miraculously, once the deal was done, we got back most of the money we'd invested.

Over the years, I kept an eye on Channel 3's progress. The new owner kept things going for another three or four years and then sold it to someone else. It seemed that with each subsequent sale, the Channel's ambitions scaled back, until it eventually resurrected itself as a full-fledged non-profit, with a board of directors, a professional staff of five, and a focus on community programming that included lots of documentaries and live events (but no daily news show). Now called "Nantucket Community Television" and broadcasting on Channel 18, it finally seems to be fulfilling the mission of local origination broadcasting that the government had envisioned in the early 1970s.

My family owned Channel 3 for about 20 months, but it seemed more like 20 years. I learned a lot, but my primary lesson was personal: that I had a strong aversion to all kinds of risk and didn't have an entrepreneurial bone in my body. The question ahead of me now was whether journalism was my calling.

CHAPTER 17

Island Life

People fantasize of living on an island, imagining a romantic idyll, with self-actualizing possibilities rivaled only in isolated Scottish villages nestled in the moors. This is particularly true of Nantucket, with its breathtaking natural beauty, long stretches of lonely beaches, wide expanses of windswept grasslands, and miles of crisscrossing dirt roads that seemingly lead nowhere.

And to make it even more appealing, the town of Nantucket is a virtual museum of early 19th century architecture. As any reader of *Moby-Dick* knows, this was the whaling capital of the world from the late 18th to early 19th centuries. The mass slaughter of immense marine mammals brought astonishing riches to island captains and merchants. And then, poof! It was over as soon as refining petroleum into kerosene became cheaper and safer than sending ships around the world in search of oil-rich blubber. The Nantucket economy collapsed almost immediately, and with the island's population suddenly depleted, hardly anyone added to the housing stock for decades. That's why Nantucket is not burdened by the ranch houses, colonials, and split levels that predominate in the mainland suburbs. Thanks to a century of benign neglect and the creation of a powerful Historic District Commission in the

1960s, Nantucketers live almost exclusively in gray-shingled, white-trimmed saltbox farmhouses or Federal-era mansions.

Many summer visitors envied those of us who lived there year-round, but the day to day reality of island life was, for me, quite mundane. I had a full-time job and the standard personal and professional preoccupations of a recent college graduate. The idea of walking on the beach in November or ambling in the ancient pine forest in the spring didn't appeal to me. Now, of course, I wish I had gotten out and done more exploring. What a wasted opportunity.

Mostly I was trying to get by, earning less than $200 per week, which even in the 1970s wasn't much. This forced me into the large nomadic tribe of seasonal cottage-surfers who had affordable winter accommodations starting in September and then scrambled for someplace, any place else to live in June at the start of the high season. During the four years I lived in Nantucket, I moved five times, spending two summers in my grandparents' house and two winters in a small, two-bedroom cottage with bunk beds, poor insulation, and a propane heater. Everything I owned fit in my car. Eventually, I found a year-round studio apartment, which ended my peripatetic ways and gave me some peace of mind.

Nantucket was a classic in-bred small town, but what made it different from other little hives of insularity were the huge population fluctuations. In the dead of winter, there might be only 5,000 souls on the island, with just a handful of open restaurants and bars, little in the way of live entertainment besides the piano player at the Jared Coffin House, the only year-round hotel, and no movie theatres at all.

There's a tendency among communities to brag about their worst features, as if it takes character to survive in such a challenging environment. In Nantucket's case, the local boast, which I heard at least a hundred times, was that the island had the highest rate of alcoholism of any community in the country. This was almost certainly not true, and nobody ever cited a source. Still, it was undeniable that the booze flowed freely. Lillian Waine, our Channel 3 anchor, stated openly and often that she and her husband were in AA, which she called Nantucket's biggest social club. On a small island, no one is anonymous.

If the winters were dark, damp, and lonely, the summers were sunny, crowded, and boisterous. The population swelled to over 50,000 as the ferries unloaded a seemingly endless supply of fun-seeking mainlanders who filled up the hotels, guest houses, and summer rentals. With a steady stream of corporate jets delivering CEOs to their summer getaways, the Nantucket Memorial Airport became the third busiest airport in Massachusetts, after Boston's Logan and Hyannis. Cars clogged the once-deserted streets, and the restaurants and bars swiftly opened back up. Celebrities and socialites abounded; I once saw Frank Sinatra walking down Main Street; one night, at the Roadhouse (now called The Faregrounds), I witnessed a very drunk Jimmy Buffet hop on the stage between the sets of a local band to play some of his greatest hits; another night at the Roadhouse, the author, memoirist, and jazz pianist Frank Conroy was the musical entertainment, and another night, my friend Maureen, who'd accepted an invitation to a small get-together at my apartment, cancelled at the last minute after being invited to another party that Andy Warhol would be attending.

The recent reconstruction of the waterfront into a tourist mecca had not only changed the island's physical character, it also ended the island's conception of itself as an easy-going, staid community catering to people with good bloodlines and excellent bone structure. As the money flowed in, the season for separating tourists from their cash expanded dramatically. In the 1960s, there was only one major seasonal celebration—fireworks on the Fourth of July. By the 1970s, the first social event of the year was Daffodil Weekend, an April celebration of the million daffodil bulbs planted by the Nantucket Garden Club under the leadership of Mrs. Earle MacAusland, as Jean MacAusland always self-identified in the press. Mr. Earle MacAusland was the founder and publisher of *Gourmet* magazine, so the Garden Club was a high-status group. The climax of the weekend was a parade of daffodil-festooned antique cars from downtown to the village of Siasconset at the eastern end of the island, where celebrants would tailgate with candelabras, linen tablecloths, champagne, caviar, and other fine delicacies.

Memorial Day, once celebrated with a sweet parade of school children and veterans, morphed into Figawi weekend, a 200-strong sailboat procession from Hyannis to Nantucket, followed by two nights of drinking and carousing (the name Figawi smirkily comes from the question, "Where the fuck are we?" Ha, ha). Even Christmas became exploitable, as a once-intimate night of shopkeeper conviviality became "The Nantucket Christmas Stroll," an opportunity to fill up the island for one last weekend in December for a dress-up celebration of gaiety and lots of liquid Christmas cheer.

Even as the boom financed their Florida vacations, SUVs, and more comfortable lifestyles, many Nantucket natives resented the changes. Someone—maybe the Chamber of Commerce—had printed bumper stickers that read "It's Nicer on Nantucket." By the late 1970s, there was a much more popular bumper sticker: "It Used To Be Nicer on Nantucket."

The old-timers bemoaned the meddling ways of the many corporate retirees who sometimes found the island's small town ways not up to the standards of the multinational corporations where they'd once thrived. These locals also deeply resented environmental intruders who wanted to restrict growth or shut down beaches whenever the piping plovers nested. And they rolled their eyes at the arty newcomers and dropouts from bourgeois America who thought they could escape to the island for a fresh start.

But a handful of canny natives had made out like bandits, and they weren't complaining about the new prosperity at all, as tourism and the construction of vacation homes became the two dominant industries. After World War II, land in the deserted, remote areas of the island had been so worthless that some long-time owners simply abandoned their property and stopped paying their real estate taxes. According to the law, anyone could claim those abandoned properties simply by paying these back taxes. That's how some Nantucketers became rich—by acquiring acres of land for a few hundred dollars in the early 1960s and selling it decades later for tens or hundreds of thousands. But they weren't the only ones benefiting. Real estate agents, construction companies, and bar owners were all making more money than they ever dreamt of.

I wasn't unhappy on Nantucket after we disposed of Channel 3, but life seemed a little flat. I'd always been a bit solitary anyway and with almost nothing worth watching on television, I doubled down on my reading. I discovered the novels of Anthony Trollope, Anthony Burgess, and John Fowles. I read *War and Peace* one winter and *Anna Karenina* the next. I read books by conservative thinkers and started to build an intellectual background for my political leanings. I devoured histories and biographies.

Life was slower and less frantic in the 1970s. I didn't learn about the murder of John Lennon until 7:45am the next morning when I turned on the *Today* show and found the hosts in mourning. An event of that magnitude today would probably melt my iPhone, but back then, you could be blissfully unaware of major news for hours at a time.

I learned to cook for myself, if you can call it that: hamburgers and hotdogs, Birdseye frozen food, Campbell's "Hungry Man's" chunky soups, and pasta with Ragu tomato sauce. I bought both a crockpot and a pressure cooker. I found one go-to recipe in the *Joy of Cooking* that I used as my special dish for guests: turkey tetrazzini, an upscale version of chicken ala king that required a PINT of heavy cream. Man, those were the days.

With long distance calls so expensive, I spent an enormous amount of time writing letters and eagerly absorbing the replies. Not only was I still hearing from my high school buddies, but now I was corresponding with my college friends as well. With no internet or social media, letters were the only affordable way to stay in touch. My friends were almost all adrift too. A constant theme was money, or the lack thereof. They wanted to get apartments or travel, but with no income, forget it. I was the first person from either group of friends to have a professional job; in the end, most of them went to graduate school to jump start their careers. That wasn't for me. I was so burned out by exams and term papers that I couldn't bear the thought of getting another degree.

It was about this time that both my ex-girlfriend, Pat, and her former girlfriend, Carol, reconnected with me. Now that they were no longer together and I was no longer with Judi, they figured it was safe to reach out. Pat and I picked up right where we'd left off, excluding the romantic element. Carol and I had never been particularly close in high school, but we exchanged searching letters trying to understand why our group of once-close teenage friends had splintered. The irony was that Pat, Carol, and Judi, who had been so tightly bonded in high school that I considered them to be a female cabal, were no longer speaking to each other, but somehow managed to remain friends with me.

Much of the social life I had revolved around my relatives. I frequently had dinner at the home of my Uncle Wayne and Aunt Lee. Their former whaling captain's house was both huge and comfortable, with well-worn furnishings and wide, wooden-planked floors covered by faded oriental rugs. Lee held court around her rough-hewn kitchen table with a glass of Cutty Sark, and you never knew who else you'd find there. It could be her grandmother, the sassy, thrice-widowed "Lala" who told stories of old Nantucket bootleggers; her mother, the slightly spaced out "Lady Lu," who, like Lee, had attended Wellesley; or one of her golfing friends from the uber-exclusive Sankaty Golf Club. She usually had a jigsaw puzzle or half-finished board game in the works. One winter, we obsessively played the logic game Mastermind, which I almost always won and consequently enjoyed tremendously.

Wayne was arguably the most influential politician on the island through the sheer force of his personality, intelligence, and willingness to do the work. He cut a dapper (or, to some, peacocking) figure with his erect posture, straw hats in the summer, fedoras in the winter, and three piece suits year-round. Like all the local attorneys, he practiced a wide range of law, but with a specialty in aggressively representing wives during divorce cases. So there were a lot of ex-husbands who hated his guts. He didn't suffer fools lightly either, and people knew if he took a dim view of them, which was often. And yet, when the reckless playboy and future Congressman, Joseph Kennedy II, flipped his Jeep on the island's Polpis Road and paralyzed a female companion, it was Wayne who was summoned to the Kennedy Compound in Hyannisport to consult with Ted Kennedy and the clan on how to handle the case in the Nantucket District Court.

Wayne and Lee were friends with most of the island's younger professional couples, and they sometimes asked me to tag along when they went out for dinner with them. My role was to amuse them with my enthusiasm for conservative politics, Humphrey Bogart movies, and island gossip. I was guileless enough to think it was funny to tell the French waiter "I'll have the bunny" when ordering lapin à la moutarde (braised rabbit) at the extremely high-end

Chanticleer restaurant. At another dinner (definitely *not* at the Chanticleer) with my mother, aunt, and colleague, Nancy Ayotte, I was introduced to the notorious Long Island iced tea cocktail, which consisted of equal parts Coca Cola, vodka, tequila, light rum, triple sec, and gin. As someone who had only occasionally experimented with cheap white wine in college, this left me wobbly and giddy—until I drove everyone home, knocked over Nancy's mailbox while backing out of her driveway, and then went to bed, where I threw up in my sleep. So, yeah.

I also became closer to my grandparents, whom I had seen only a few times a year since becoming a teenager. Now I had dinner with them once a week, after which I helped my grandmother wash the dishes and then stayed for another hour while we watched TV together. My grandfather, who had recently retired from his job as a carpenter, was a gentle, soft-spoken man who had grown overweight despite the physical activity. My grandmother was good-hearted but opinionated, character traits that she passed on to my mother and then to me. Yet she also surprised me one night by revealing that she had only voted once for President—Eisenhower in 1956. Apparently she didn't feel confident in this important decision, which she felt should be left to the men.

I did have a few friends my own age, and they tended to be the other members of the Nantucket press corps. This was a small group—a couple of reporters for the *Inquirer and Mirror* (the weekly newspaper), the local bureau chief for the Hyannis-based daily, the *Cape Cod Times*, and whoever the Channel 3 reporter was at the time. We covered so many town meetings together that we all became pals, going out for drinks after Wednesday night Selectmen's meetings to chew over the town business that we'd just seen conducted.

That's how I met one of my best friends, Kate Stout, a writer from Kentucky. She had been named for Katharine Hepburn and like her namesake was tall, coltish, and always trousered. I met her one Monday morning in September 1977, when we were going in to cover the weekly District Court session. She was filling in for the vacationing regular *Cape Cod Times* reporter and as a grizzled six-month veteran, I showed her the ropes. She and her roommate, a gay playwright named Bobby, lived on Nantucket only in the off-season when they could afford the rent, and we hit it off right away. She called me "Sherlock" because of my last name, and "Clark" because I reminded her of Clark Kent. She had strong but good-humored opinions on literature (especially Virginia Woolf), island living, and the human species in general, and we remained good friends long after the last time either of us experienced a cold Nantucket winter.

I can't emphasize enough how close we local reporters were. In fact, if we hadn't been watching each other's backs, I might have missed one of my biggest news stories. One Saturday morning in September 1980, I started hearing rumors that Richard Nixon was going to visit Nantucket. I ran down to the police station, but they had obviously been sworn to secrecy by the Secret Service. After a fruitless morning of trying to get details, I gave up, assuming that Nixon would sneak into town and be whisked off to a private estate.

But later that afternoon, Nancy Ayotte, the local *Cape Cod Times* reporter, called from a payphone to say Nixon was on a yacht at Swain's Wharf and that I should get down there as soon as possible. Paying it forward, I called Kate, then holding down my old job as news director at Channel 3, and rushed to the waterfront. Sure enough, I found a big crowd at one of the docks waiting to see if Nixon was going to emerge in the flesh. He and his pals, Bebe Rebozo and Robert Abplanap, had cruised over from Martha's Vineyard on Abplanap's 115-foot yacht, "Star Mist," which could remain on the island only until dark because there were no available hotel rooms on the island for Nixon's Secret Service agents.

Nixon and Rebozo did eventually materialize, walking slowly down the dock and into the crowd. This was only six years after his scandal-driven resignation and Nixon was generally still reviled in polite society, so the excitement of the spectators surprised me. They even applauded. Even K. Dun Gifford, the well-known Kennedy aide who had helped spirit Mary Jo Kopechne's body off Martha's Vineyard before an autopsy could be conducted, made it a point to reach out his hand and warmly say, "Welcome to Nantucket, Mr. President."

What I didn't realize then is that people are always excited to see celebrities—even disgraced ones. Nixon worked the crowd like an experienced politician, shaking hands and offering benign conversational tidbits. At one point, he passed a tourist on a payphone who yelled that Nixon had to say hello to his wife because she didn't believe he was there. After asking the wife's name, Nixon took the receiver and said, "Hello, Betty? Who's this woman your husband's with?" Uproarious laughter. You'd have thought Bob Hope himself had delivered the punchline.

There was only one discordant note. A guy started yelling, "Where's Checkers? Where's Checkers?" This, of course, was a reference to Nixon's famous "Checkers Speech" in which he defended himself against allegations that he'd accepted gifts from wealthy donors—except for one gift, a pet dog named Checkers that his daughters just loved. Nixon seemed unfazed by the interruption and simply said to the heckler, in all apparent seriousness, "Checkers died in 1964. Cocker spaniels don't live long, you know."

Eventually Nixon and the gang reached the end of the wharf and approached a line of cars. Nancy and I asked Randy Norris, a Nantucket police sergeant, if we could come along in his vehicle. To my surprise, he said yes. Also to my surprise, the Pulitzer Prize-winning *Boston Globe* photographer, Stan Grossfeld, was already sitting in the front seat.

Eventually, we formed a five-car motorcade. Altogether there were eight secret service agents, two police sergeants, one state trooper, and us three reporters. Apparently the point of this excursion was to show Nixon a bit of the island, but since this had been thrown together at the last minute, there was no plan. After a while, Randy radioed ahead to the lead driver that he should head up Main Street so Nixon could see the whaling era mansions, and then drive out to the eastern end of the island, called Siasconset, for a view from the bluff.

As we slowly motored out on the 'Sconset Road, I realized that Bebe Rebozo had peeled off at some point and that Nixon was sitting by himself in the back of his car, which was being driven by two Secret Service agents. It's hard to imagine any other major politician being satisfied sitting alone, just staring out the window—at the very least they should have grabbed a local official as a tour guide—but that was Nixon the loner in a nutshell.

Nixon and me on the 'Sconset Bluff.

When we got out to Sankaty Light in Siasconset, everyone hopped out of their cars and started strolling down the 'Sconset Bluff. Thanks to years of erosion, most of this footpath no longer exists, but at the time, you could walk along a beautiful high bluff from Sankaty Lighthouse all the way to Siasconset Center. Nixon was particularly taken with the walk, later saying it reminded him of the California beaches he was more familiar with.

Eventually, Nixon noticed that Stan and I were taking pictures of each other, trying to photobomb ourselves into photos of him, and he motioned for us to approach and take actual posed pictures. So I took a picture of Stan and Nixon and he took a picture of me and Nixon. This also offered an opportunity for a chat. Everything that people always said about him was true—he mostly wanted to talk about sports. He was hopeful that the Houston Astros would make it into the playoffs that year so that Nolan Ryan would have a shot at a World Series appearance. He knew the Red Sox had a history of bad pitching. He was not optimistic about the Redskins' chance in the upcoming season. Stan then asked him about the upcoming 1980 presidential election and he correctly predicted that Reagan would beat Carter.

After the Bluff stroll, we all piled back into our cars and headed back into town. He strolled up and down Main Street, posing for more photos, making chit chat with tourists and generally causing a mini-sensation. Later that night, he had dinner at the island's fanciest restaurant, the Chanticleer (the very place where I had ordered "the bunny").

It was obvious that Nixon was an unnatural politician, repeatedly falling back on formulaic discussion topics. He seemed stiff, particularly in his get-up. To stroll the island, including the Siasconset Bluff, he was dressed in a blue-gray sports jacket, a maroon turtleneck, blue slacks and cordovan loafers, an outfit more suitable for "dress down Friday" at IBM than a weekend tour of Nantucket. And there was a visible stain on his crotch. What was that about?

At the end of his stroll, he told us he'd like to bring "Mrs. Nixon" back to Nantucket because he thought she'd enjoy the shopping, but after the dinner at the Chanticleer and a 10:00pm return trip to Martha's Vineyard, he never set foot on the island again.

In the days after Nixon's visit, I dutifully tracked down as many details as I could, but I wasn't exactly Woodward and Bernstein about it. For example, instead of directly calling the Chanticleer and asking about the meal, I relied on the second hand account of my friend Maureen (the same one who dumped me for Andy Warhol), who knew a waiter. He told her that Nixon ate pheasant pâté, Nantucket scallops, and a Grand Marnier soufflé, drank Chateau Margaux '59 at $180 per bottle and was happy to have Bebe Rebozo put the $900 meal on his credit card. Were those details accurate? No one contradicted them.

In my subsequent newspaper piece, I wrote that I couldn't tell whether the "Checkers" heckler was drunk or simply obnoxious. The next week, the heckler himself sent a "Letter to the Editor" claiming that we'd maligned him and that his heckling was justified because Nixon was a war criminal, etc., etc. The letter was accompanied by a drawing of a standing pig wearing a jacket and making Nixon's trademark "V for Victory" sign. The letter was signed by Richard Scarry. Yes, Richard Scarry, the children's author! We didn't print the sketch, which some thought was disrespectful. I thought it was funny and it's one of my great regrets that I never kept and framed that drawing.

About 20 years later while my family was vacationing on Nantucket, we attended a talk by Stan Grossfeld and the *Boston Globe* sportswriter Dan Shaughnessy. Stan showed moving photos of starving refugees, remarkable sports photos, and many other beautiful shots. There were even a few photos of Nantucket, including the picture of Stan and Nixon, which got a laugh. After the talk, I went up and reintroduced myself as the photographer of the one picture Stan had not taken himself. He claimed to remember me and made a big deal of telling my son that he was a "big fan" of mine. What a nice thing to say, although my son was probably too young to know what a compliment it was to be praised by Stan Grossfeld.

Since then, Nantucket has become a hangout for political celebrities. For several decades, Joe Biden had Thanksgiving dinner there every year. In the middle of his presidential campaign, John Kerry was infamously photographed windsurfing in Nantucket Harbor. In 2015, when Hillary Clinton attended a fundraiser at the home of a wealthy Nantucket donor, there was just the tiniest ho-hum mention of it in the *Inquirer and Mirror*. These days, it's hard to believe that any celebrity would generate the breathless front page coverage that we gave Nixon's visit in 1980. I kind of miss those more innocent days before we all became so jaded.

CHAPTER 18

The Inquirer and Mirror

When I worked at the Nantucket *Inquirer and Mirror* in the late 1970s and early 1980s, it was well on its way to becoming a gold mine—a remarkably homespun, do-it-yourself gold mine, but a gold mine all the same.

Local newspapers are now vestigial organs of the news industry, barely hanging on with tiny staffs and meager advertising. For most of the 20th century though, they were solid, reliable businesses, and their owners were pillars of their communities. But what made the *I&M* different from mainland weekly papers was the island's transformation into an upscale resort and the influx of the billionaires and mere millionaires—a dream target for advertisers.

Subscribing to the *Inky*, as it was also known, became a minor status symbol for thousands of summer residents. It was a way of demonstrating, if only to themselves, a connection to the island so strong that even during the cold, dreary winter, they needed to keep up with the local scene. Nantucket's official population in the late '70s had reached about 7,000 people. A newspaper in an ordinary town with that many residents would be extremely lucky to

191

have a circulation of 2,000. The *I&M* had a circulation of about 12–15,000, most of which we mailed off-island. In the summer, it was stuffed with so many ads from realtors, jewelers, restaurants, auctioneers, automobile dealers, and upscale antique stores that the paper numbered over 50 pages.

Martha's Vineyard, another charming place also rapidly metamorphosing into a luxe outpost overrun by celebrities and the newly rich, is Nantucket's irritating sister island. THEIR newspaper—the *Vineyard Gazette*—was owned by James "Scotty" Reston and his wife. Reston was a famous *New York Times* columnist and the very epitome of elite establishment journalism. The *Gazette*, managed by the Restons' son, Richard Reston, sported a beautiful, clean design and featured gorgeous, award-winning photography, a crusading editorial policy, a strict adherence to the A.P. Style of newspaper writing that governed journalism grammar, and a boastful public commitment to let-the-chips-fall-where-they-may reporting, of which I was skeptical.

That was not the *Inquirer and Mirror*. We had no editorial page or staff photographer. Our design was old-fashioned and cluttered, untouched by any professional graphic design consultant. We had no designated content sections either. If sports or society stories happened to be grouped in the same general area from time to time, that was good enough. And our ownership was about as far away from the snooty Restons as you could get. Or, as the acerbic Dick Mackay wrote in his book, *Nantucket! Nantucket! Nantucket!,* "[The *I&M* is] down to earth and accurate, in the sense that you can find out what is really going on in Nantucket by reading it. This is entirely preferable to the *Vineyard Gazette*, for instance, which is off-island owned and concerned with what the island OUGHT to be like."

Founded in 1821, the paper had been run for most of the 20th century by the Turner family, typical small-town proprietors, but in 1970 it was sold to a buying group led by the paper's general manager, Marie Giffin and her husband Tom. In a few years, the Giffins took full control and Marie became publisher.

Marie was not exactly a newspaper publisher out of central casting. Born in Illinois and educated in a music school to be a mezzo-soprano, she had married the son of the manager of Nantucket's steamship operations. When the Giffins moved to the island in the 1950s, she remained a commanding presence with a Beverly Sills vibe, despite largely giving up the music—except for the occasional rendition of "O Holy Night" at the office Christmas party. She raised a family and held a number of office jobs until landing at the *I&M* in the early 1960s. She quickly rose from receptionist to general manager and was in the right place at the right time when the paper came up for sale.

The *I&M* was a family affair—a classic mom-and-pop operation. Tom quit his aviation job and helped Marie manage the paper, operating behind the scenes, manning the darkroom, overseeing production and distribution, and writing "Flight Deck," a weekly column about goings-on at the Nantucket airport. When the Giffins became grandparents, Tom took cute pictures of the child, and Marie published them regularly in the paper. This was part of the charm of a cozy, small-town newspaper. Eventually the Giffins' daughter, Marianne, would take over as publisher and transform the *I&M* into an award-winning publication with an editorial page, sports section, and staff photographer.

Marie was not a heavy-handed, crusading publisher, but the paper's story selection and emphasis sometimes reflected her concerns, especially in her early days as publisher, when she supported land conservation efforts. It wasn't that hard to tell who she did and didn't like. She LOVED our congressman, Gerry Studds, and his every utterance received respectful coverage. She did not like our non-Nantucketer police chief or my Uncle Wayne, although she did not take that out on me.

Marie and I were not very close, but she made sure I always got my $20 a week raise on the anniversary of my hiring and she did stand up for me. One day, a liquor store owner arrived at the office in a rage because my account of the recent Selectmen's meeting had explicitly noted that he'd publicly lobbied against a competitor getting the same license he'd just been granted, using the same line of argument that had been used against him. Marie shrugged when he threatened to pull his advertising. She had hundreds of advertisers and this guy was a drop in the bucket. And besides, where else was he going to run his ads? On Channel 3? Be my guest.

Located a mile out of town in a former auto repair shop, the *I&M* headquarters had an unadorned, quasi-industrial feel, with no personal offices and lots of open space. (One area in which the *I&M* anticipated corporate trends was its use of "open space seating.") The enormous printing presses in the back room looked eager to chew up a wandering arm, so I kept a healthy distance on printing days. The presses were enormous because the paper itself was enormous, but not as big as it had once been. For years, when it was wide enough to cover the average kitchen table, it advertised itself as "The Biggest Newspaper in the World." When the paper switched from hot type printing to photo composition in the mid-1960s, it slimmed down a bit, but it was still 24 inches tall and 34 inches wide. Whenever I pick up an old copy today, I am amazed that my arms were ever able to spread wide enough to read it.

I sat at a heavy, battered metal desk that faced the front door. I wrote all my stories on a typewriter and handed the pages to Marie, who sat catty-corner behind me and also served as editor-in-chief. After her review, I'd bring it to a typesetter, who'd retype the whole story into a machine that produced a long strip of inch-wide hole-punched paper computer tape. This would be fed into a printer that would spit out a copy-ready version of the story formatted into a single column of glossy newsprint. Using an Exacto knife, we'd then trim off the excess paper and glue the story onto a mock-up of a newspaper page. Once the page was complete, we'd bring it to Tom in the darkroom and he'd produce a negative that could be given to the printers.

Putting together each page was always a puzzle since you'd have to fit news copy, photos, and ads into limited space. This was an imperfect science. The copy was not always glued on straight, leading to crooked columns, and occasionally, during the process of trying to arrange and then rearrange a page, loose paragraphs would get mixed up or accidentally dropped altogether. And yet, whenever I complained to friends that my beautiful prose had been butchered by lay-out goofs, they almost always said they didn't notice anything awry with the piece. Eventually, I stopped complaining, because if no one really cared if the paragraphs were out of order, why was I banging my head against the wall?

Most of my writing was done without a byline, which is just as well because some weeks I'd write the entire front page and having my name on so many stories would have looked ridiculous. When I first started, the *I&M* had another reporter, senior to me, named Suzy DeHeart, and we split most of the news reporting. When she was promoted to the new role of editor,

I shared the workload with an assortment of short-time colleagues, but sometimes I was the sole reporter for months at a time. Marie didn't seem very interested in recruiting people with journalism backgrounds—and certainly no one who had gone to journalism school—so each new reporter not only had to learn how town government worked, he or she also had to learn how to write news stories on the fly.

Given that there were only two (and for a short time, three) full-time reporters at the paper and dozens and dozens of ad-laden pages to fill, we relied heavily on outsiders for content. We didn't have a sports reporter, so the write-ups of high school sporting events fell to the coaches or, in the case of the major boys' sports, a paid stringer. The paper also paid for standing columns about the waterfront, airport, and social scene. I never read these because they were the most innocuous kind of gossip. It wasn't until later that I realized how important they were because they gave us an excuse to include a lot of local names in the paper—maybe the only time some of these people would be mentioned between their birth and death notices and high school graduations.

Even accounting for the nominally paid stringers and columnists, most of the paper's content was free to us. Island tourism supported dozens of art galleries, and each time one of them featured a new artist, they'd give us a photo of a painting and a long press release that we'd run verbatim. We'd publish press releases from the island's many performing arts organizations, the schools, the churches, the hospital, the island's varied charitable organizations, and the golf and yacht clubs. Parents touting their kids' births, graduations, weddings, and dean's list appearances made the cut as well. And we'd publish many, many letters to the editor, which took up lots of space. We also ran occasional essays from surprisingly decent amateur writers who wanted an outlet for their travel or food commentary. In other words, the *Inquirer and Mirror* of 1980 pioneered the business model for internet publishing in the 21st century—free or low-paid content coupled with hundreds of ads.

My week was pretty well circumscribed by the timing of town meetings and an unmovable publishing deadline on early Thursday afternoon. Monday morning was District Court, (trials for major crimes were held over until Superior Court, which met twice a year). On Monday and Tuesday night, there would usually be a meeting of the School Committee, Planning Board, or some other town board. On Wednesday morning, I'd meet with the police chief to get a rundown of the weekly crime report. The week climaxed with the Wednesday night Selectmen's meeting, where major town business was conducted.

All of this was relatively easy to handle. Someone proposed something, someone else opined on it, and then there was a vote. It happened and I wrote it up. I tried to find other interesting news by hanging around the Town Building—maybe someone was opening or closing a business or a senior citizen was getting an award for 50 years of service to a fraternal organization. People called in tips, too—the electric company might have a new plan for generating power that they wanted to publicize, or the Nantucket Historical Association might be launching a new publication. Sometimes, I'd try to generate human interest stories that required more imagination and work. Once, I was offered an interview with the then-former Governor Michael Dukakis, who turned out to be a lot more charming in person than he was on television.

I learned to always, always, ALWAYS have a pen in my pocket and a notebook close by, a habit I never lost. I also learned the importance of getting a good quote for a story and how to egg on interview subjects to say the thing I wanted them to say. And if they didn't, I could always pull a sentence from one paragraph and combine it with a sentence from another paragraph and hope I was capturing the essence of what they meant. Even though the *I&M* wasn't even the minor leagues of newspapering, the time I spent there was crucial to my future career in public relations because it helped me understand how reporters thought and what they needed. Critically, I learned what's a "story" and what's not.

Considering that Nantucket was just a small town, it received a disproportionate amount of national attention. There was the Nixon visit, of course, which generated national stories. Then in 1977, the island tried to secede from Massachusetts when redistricting eliminated our seat in the state's legislature—a movement that occasioned a high-profile visit from

196

New Hampshire's governor, who offered to take us in. And every time the harbor froze and kept the ferries from delivering food, a camera crew would fly in from somewhere to document our plight.

The biggest story I covered was also the most perplexing mystery in Nantucket history. One freezing morning in January 1980, a medical researcher from Columbia-Presbyterian Medical Center in Manhattan named Margaret Kilcoyne, who had arrived on the island two days before, bragging that she was going to win the Nobel Prize for her research into hypertension, disappeared from her vacation home on the eastern end of the island. It was not unusual for people to commit suicide in the winter, so we didn't really think twice about this, as sad as it was. Just the year before, the piano player at our local hotel bar had walked across the ice in Nantucket Harbor until he fell through and drowned. As a local newspaper, we didn't feel it was our job to highlight people's miseries, so we ran a four-paragraph story about the disappearance on page 11.

But the next Sunday, four people out walking their dogs found a neat pile of items in the woods: Kilcoyne's passport, wallet, bank book, and pair of sandals. What were those things doing there and how had they escaped notice when the area was searched a week earlier? The police conducted a second full-scale search and found one of her blouses rolled up and stuffed under a bush. But still no sign of a body.

The discovery of these items turned the case into a national mystery story. Prior to this, the operating assumption had been that a depressed Kilcoyne had woken up early one morning, walked a mile south to the Nobadeer beach, and plunged into the surf. But that pile of belongings was found a mile in the opposite direction. So the new premise had to be that she had woken up and walked a mile north, where she carefully arranged her most important personal things in a neat pile and then walked two miles south to the beach. Oh, and this walk would have been through dense scrub oak on a bitterly cold, windy morning. And to make it even more improbable, she had left her coat and boots in the house.

Again, Nantucket is an island, and there were no flights from the airport between the time she went to bed and the time she was reported missing. And with a frozen harbor, there would have been no boats off the island either, so she hadn't just hitchhiked away or secretly arranged for someone to spirit her away. So where was she? And that theory about her jumping into the surf began to seem a little dubious upon reflection. It was a lot more probable that the surf would have thrown a body back onto the beach than carrying it away, assuming she could have even worked up the fortitude to walk into the ocean on such a cold day.

The Nantucket media, myself included, realized we'd dropped the ball, and went all in on the story. When we started to piece it together, this is the general outline of what we learned: Margaret Kilcoyne, age 49, brilliant medical researcher in the field of hypertension, tall, vibrant, and maybe a little high-strung, was unmarried with few close friends except her brother, Leo. On the morning of Wednesday, January 23rd, she had left New York City and driven to Rye, New York, where she had gotten lost trying to find a hotel. She flagged down a young woman, who drove her to a Sheraton in Stamford, Connecticut. In gratitude, she took the woman out to dinner, where she ordered a $70 bottle of wine, drank a few sips, and gave the bottle to the waitress. She had completely dominated the conversation, talking relentlessly about how she was going to win the Nobel Prize for her research. She then offered jobs to both her new friend and the waitress.

She showed up on Nantucket the next morning and went shopping at the local Finast supermarket, buying $650 of food and $250 of alcohol. She airily informed the check-out clerk that she was planning to have a huge party to announce her medical breakthrough. Everyone who saw her that day said she seemed fine—very happy and upbeat.

Leo Kilcoyne drove from Worcester, Massachusetts to meet her the next day. That night, Leo and Margaret had dinner with two of her Nantucket friends, Richard and Grace Coffin (I later learned that she was bitterly estranged from the Coffins, so inviting them out of the blue for dinner was very unexpected). After the Coffins left at 10:30pm, Margaret went to bed, setting the alarm for 6:00am so she could go to morning mass. When Leo heard the alarm go off, her room was empty, her Volkswagen was in the driveway, and her winter coat and boots were still in the house.

Leo then called the police, who began an immediate search of the area. When they looked through the house, they found a cassette tape recording of a 90-minute, rambling, week-old conversation between Margaret and Leo. Leo told the police that the conversation had so alarmed him that he'd decided to meet her in Nantucket and find out what was going on. Among other things, she claimed she'd been communicating with Leo's dead wife, Julie, and that she, Margaret, had fundamentally altered her level of spirituality. "I have really passed into a new existence, transformed overnight, all systems go, and it is marvelous," she said.

The next two months were a bit of a circus, with the local police traveling to New York to check out her workplace and apartment; to Stamford, Connecticut to talk to the woman Margaret had met driving to Nantucket; and to the Boston suburbs, where a landlady claimed Margaret was holed up in a newly rented apartment. They felt stonewalled by Columbia-Presbyterian Medical Center, who wouldn't discuss her or her work in any detail. They also grew suspicious of Leo, who seemed awfully eager to end the investigation and left the island the day after she disappeared.

But eventually the tips and clues stopped surfacing, and there was nothing else for the police to do. They had to move on. The police chief never reconciled himself to the suicide theory, but I came to believe it was the most plausible despite the many weird details. After all, she had told another Nantucket acquaintance, Don Smith, that she would "jump off the Empire State Building" if God told her to do it. Maybe He had told her to walk into the surf.

Her research never earned her a posthumous Nobel Prize. When presented at a hypertension conference later that year, the results generated a yawn. Leo Kilcoyne had her declared officially dead in 1989, but the cold case periodically continues to haunt everyone associated with it. In 2016, former *I&M* reporter Jason Graziadei, who wasn't even born when Margaret Kilcoyne disappeared, wrote a long update about the case for *Nantucket Magazine*. Surprisingly, many people who looked for her still believe she's alive and hiding out somewhere. Because of this case, I've always wanted to write a detective novel about a woman who disappeared from an island, showing how someone could have faked her own disappearance. It's still rumbling around in the back of my head, and who knows, maybe I'll give it a shot sometime.

There have only been a handful of times when my personal and professional lives were both going great at the same time, and the year and a half after the Kilcoyne disappearance was strangely one of them. I had reached the point in my journalism career where people recognized my name, as in, "Oh, *you're* Gary Holmes. I really like your writing." That was a real ego boost.

I mailed a pitch letter to *Boston* magazine to see if they'd like to run the definitive account of the Kilcoyne story. They bit. I did some additional research and produced a very long account—my first draft was 36 pages. The piece, titled, "The Lady Vanishes," appeared in the November 1980 issue and they paid me $800 for my eight weeks of hard writing. I also got a separate check for $550 for a handful of black and white photos I shot one afternoon. I wondered whether I was freelancing in the wrong line of work.

I was becoming the go-to guy for freelance Nantucket journalism. WCVB, a Cape Cod radio station, proposed that I supply them a four-minute commentary about island life every other week, which they branded as "Nantucket Soundings." In those very analog days, I recorded these short segments on a cheap tape recorder, put the cassette in an envelope, and mailed it to the station, where they received it two days later. *Cape Cod* magazine asked me to write several feature stories about Nantucket oddities, which I did. The Associated Press realized they didn't have a stringer on Nantucket and recruited me to send them stories whenever something interesting happened. About a dozen times a year, I called the *Boston* bureau and dictated short pieces to a rewrite guy for 25 bucks each, but I never knew if any of them were ever sent out over the wire. Either way, I got paid. When Fodors, the travel publishers, wanted to publish a tourist guide for Nantucket, they asked me to write the Nantucket section. They paid me once for my work ($600), but not for any of the follow-up guides in which they used my work, especially not the ones where they irksomely put someone else's by-line on my writing.

I also started to write regular first-person essays in the *I&M* about island life. These became surprisingly popular. Using a deliberately wry voice that portrayed me as a bit of a naïf, I wrote about switching houses twice a year,

The Kilcoyne Disappearance

A lost woman. A new police chief. A Nantucket mystery.

Exclusive report by Gary Holmes

Shortly after noon on Saturday, January 26, 1980, the ferry *Uncatena* cruised to a point in Nantucket Sound off Cape Cod where land was no longer visible. Woods Hole was nearly two hours behind; an hour ahead lay Nantucket Island. For a short while, the boat was totally alone as it made its way through the frigid gray-green water.

Sitting by himself in the warmth of the passenger deck, Paul Hunter, a tall, heavyset man of forty-six, scanned the unbroken expanse of ocean through a dirty deckhouse window. "Jesus!" he later recalled thinking. "It's a long way out to sea."

Hunter was moving to Nantucket from Freeport, Maine, to be the island's new police chief. He had visited the island twice before on job interviews, but had flown over the twenty miles of water between the mainland and Nantucket, and until this moment, he had not appreciated the island's geographic isolation.

The island's location only underscored his own loneliness. His wife and two daughters — aged nine and ten— had remained in Freeport. His son was attending Worcester Polytechnic Institute, and his oldest daughter was working as a nurse in California. He would live alone on Nantucket until his wife sold or rented the Maine house.

Despite the separation, he looked forward to the change in jobs. He felt he had accomplished what he set out to do as Freeport's police chief—whip a sloppy department into shape—and was anxious to move back to his native Massachusetts, where he had spent two years as a state police dispatcher and fifteen years on the Natick police department. He was ready for a new challenge and thought

140 - November, 1980

Photographs © 1980 Gary Holmes

The Kilcoyne case attracted national attention and gave me a chance to publish a story in Boston Magazine.

201

island hitchhiking, celebrity sightings, the preppy life on Nantucket, my misadventures in sailing, the quest for the perfect tan, and other inconsequential topics. My most popular piece—"August is the Cruelest Month"—gave voice to the fatigue every islander felt at the end of the summer, and I had people stopping me on the street to thank me for writing it.

Rereading these pieces now, I cringe at the mannered, overly discursive prose, and wish I'd had an editor who could have taught me to be more concise. And yet they were well-received at the time, probably because they were so different from anything else in the paper. One August night, I went to cover a keynote speech at the Nantucket Boys and Girls Club annual fundraiser that was being delivered by Russell Baker, the *New York Times* humor columnist and island summer resident. Nancy Burns, the former Channel 3 co-anchor was there too, and when I said I was too shy to go up and talk to him, she brought me over and introduced me. After a couple of minutes of chit-chat, he brought the conversation to a close saying, "You have a nice touch. Keep on writing." Wow, Russell Baker knew my name *and* liked my writing?! That remains the biggest compliment anyone has ever given me for anything.

Perhaps the biggest perk of working at the *I&M* was the annual junket to the New England Press Association convention at the Sheraton Hotel on Boylston Street in Boston. I loved this weekend because I could have lunch and dinner at restaurants I'd always wanted to visit—all on the company tab, which Tom and Marie always paid, no questions asked. And it was fun to go to the seminars on journalism. One year, I even won an award for best feature photography for a picture of a local Santa.

It was an *I&M* tradition that on the first night of the convention, Tom and Marie would take us to the Top of the Hub—the tourist trappy restaurant with great views on the 52nd floor of the Prudential Tower. After that, we were on our own. In 1981, we'd staffed up and for a short time had three reporters: Jim Powers, a really smart local guy who'd recently dropped out of Yale, and Dale Scott, a Virginia-born refugee from Greenwich Village, an outright beauty, with thick, blonde hair, a lot of southern charm, and a cool Downtown aura. I had never considered dating her because she was way out of my league, but we had fun hanging around together in Boston, where for once, I was the one who knew the trendy hangouts. We had dinner at a funky

Armenian restaurant and then I took her to the Channel, Boston's hot new underground bar. One thing led to another and I didn't return to my hotel room until 7:00am the next day when I needed to change my clothes.

Back on Nantucket, it took us a while to sort out whether Boston was a one time, never-to-be-repeated encounter or a real thing, but we eventually became a serious couple. We professed our love for each other and ate dinner together three or four nights a week. She lived in the little village of Codfish Park at the eastern-most part of the island in the well-publicized "Solar House," owned by her Greenwich Village neighbor, Wade Greene. He was a former *New York Times* magazine editor who wanted to demonstrate that you didn't need fossil fuels to live comfortably. Considering how cold it was in that house at night, I'd say that was a failed experiment, although it did provide a newly-in-love couple with an extra reason to snuggle under the quilts. We decided to keep the relationship discreet, especially at work. Going public would have been a boost to my reputation because half the office ladies thought I was gay and the rest never imagined I could attract someone like her, but I didn't want them gossiping about us.

My previous girlfriend Judi had been an exacting English major with limited patience for my personal goofs, whereas Dale was more relaxed, at least at first. She called me "butt face" with a mischievous smile when she wanted to be endearing. With great aplomb, she drove an ancient white Mercedes, a white tank really, that she'd bought from a local handyman for a couple hundred dollars. Although we worked at a newspaper, words were not really the focus of her creativity. She was much more tactile and earthy, and eventually became an accomplished basket maker and weaver. She seemed solid and present, and when she wanted to turn that charm on, like she did once with my father, she was in full control. Even now, I'm amazed that she ever went out with me, let alone told me she loved me.

She and I got to be good friends with two other journalists—Ellen Powers, who was the new Channel 3 reporter, and Dan Ring, the new Nantucket bureau chief for the *Cape Cod Times*. The four of us hung out and bonded over the Boston Celtics, who were on their way to another championship. My apartment, where we consumed popcorn and Scotch and sodas with equal gusto, became the central location for watching the games. This was a great time.

As much fun as we were having, it was a moment that just couldn't last. We all had our real lives ahead of us, and as it turned out, all four of us would be back on the mainland within two years. I had been on Nantucket for four years and my parents, worried that I was getting too comfortable, started to push me to get off the island just like they had done 25 years earlier. I had too much potential to waste on a pile of sand in the middle of the Atlantic Ocean. I knew they were right. I was only getting paid $210 a week and there was no room for advancement at the paper. I didn't want to wake up one morning at age 35 and find myself unable to afford a house or support a family. Worse, I wasn't learning anything or growing professionally.

I started looking for newspaper jobs and got nowhere. The *Cape Cod Times* was the logical place for me and I got a respectful meeting with the managing editor, but he was raving about some kid who had been the editor of the University of Massachusetts campus newspaper and ended up hiring him instead of me. I had a perfunctory yawn-filled meeting at my hometown newspaper the *Brockton Enterprise*, which bugged me because I thought the *Enterprise* was beneath me and I wanted to be the one to blow them off instead of the other way around. I did get a job offer from the *Quincy-Patriot Ledger* to be the beat reporter for the Podunk town of Norwell. When I asked whether any of the local beat reporters, who worked alone out of tiny offices in those towns, ever made the leap to the main newsroom in *Quincy*, they said no. I said thanks but no thanks.

At this point, I was not only disheartened, but also questioning whether journalism was the right profession for me at all. I absolutely hated calling people on the phone if I thought I'd get a negative response. For example, for the Margaret Kilcoyne story, I never bothered to call Leo Kilcoyne, the people she had her last meal with, or her colleagues at Columbia Presbyterian, because I was afraid of rude hang-ups. And I could never force myself to call the families of people who had died or even been in accidents. What kind of reporter can't make phone calls? Worse, I never wanted to write stories that would make people mad and cause them to yell at me.

I was interested in politics but didn't know how to get started. My friend Kate Stout was from Kentucky and introduced me over the phone to a friend who was chief of staff to an ambitious County Judge/Chief Executive who needed a speechwriter. Move to Kentucky to work for a County Judge? No way. Which is how I ended up missing a chance to get in on the ground floor of Mitch McConnell's career.

My break, when it happened, came from my college friend Jim Robinson. He had left college intending to be an academic in American Studies but in a life-changing twist for both of us, had ended up at the University of Maryland instead of Brown, which wouldn't give him a scholarship. Maryland was just too close to Washington, D.C. for a political addict and after getting his Master's, he went to work for a political PR firm, where he helped write radio addresses for former governor Ronald Reagan. He then became press secretary for his hometown Congressman, Jerry Solomon. Now he was leaving the Congressional job to write speeches for the U.S. Chamber of Commerce. Would I be interested in replacing him in Solomon's office? Absolutely.

On the Friday before Memorial Day, I flew to Albany and Jim drove me up to Glens Falls, New York to meet Jerry Solomon in his small district office. When he called five days later to offer me the job, I accepted immediately. Although she knew this day was coming, Dale sobbed when I told her the news, but we agreed that after I got settled in my new job, she would quit hers and join me in Washington.

I wrote a farewell story in the paper saying that when I took the ferry that would lead me to my new life, I wouldn't just be throwing pennies overboard (which is the island's good luck charm to guarantee a return), I would be throwing a whole roll of pennies. Three people stopped by the paper to give me rolls of pennies. And then a woman I didn't even know wrote a letter to thank me for my personal essays in the paper; she said they had been the one thing to cheer her up the previous winter when her son had died. That rendered me speechless. And to top it all off, Dan Ring, the *Cape Cod Times* writer, did an interview with my most famous fan, Russell Baker, who asked him why I was leaving. When told that I was going to be a press secretary, he made a face and said I was too good a writer to do that. *Now* you tell me!

Ellen Powers from Channel 3 threw me a fun going-away party that was attended by Wayne and Lee, the selectmen, and other local big-wigs. By then, all my belongings were packed in my car. After the party, I spent the night at Dale's and woke up at 6:00am to take the 7:00am ferry to Hyannis. I drove straight through to Washington, arriving at 7:30pm to spend a few nights on Jim's living room couch. It had only been three weeks since my interview with Jerry Solomon and time seemed to be accelerating. That morning, I had woken up in one of the most charming and bucolic parts of Nantucket and looked out the window to see the Atlantic Ocean. Now, I was trying to sleep in a noisy, ten-story apartment building situated in a densely urban neighborhood. There were prostitutes and homeless people on the street, the sound of random car alarms shrieked in the background, and there was so much ambient light from the streetlights that the living room never got fully dark. And I was thrilled.

CHAPTER 19

Washington, D.C.

I arrived in Washington, D.C. on June 13th, 1981, as excited as an aspiring starlet stepping off the train in 1930's Hollywood. My hero Ronald Reagan was in the White House, almost completely recovered now from the bullet deposited in his chest by John Hinkley Jr. Every place I looked oozed with history. Why, there was Ford's Theatre! And jeepers, David Stockman, the head of the Office of Management and Budget, lived just a block away from my apartment, and I would occasionally see him and his briefcase climbing into a town car on his way to cutting more government waste. Every day I was encountering locations familiar to me as backdrops to the important events I'd read about in political novels and the many history books I'd read about the Civil War, New Deal, Cuban Missile Crisis, and Watergate. What could be more thrilling than that? I felt like I was living on the movie set of my dreams.

I can't remember a time when I wasn't interested in politics. One of my earliest memories was the bitter disappointment of learning that Richard Nixon wouldn't demand a recount of the two states that JFK had stolen from him in the 1960 presidential election. In other words, my very first political lesson, at age six, was that Democrats cheat and the media lets them get away with it.

My parents fueled this fascination with politics, especially my father, himself a frustrated politician. He was a natural glad hander, but in my overwhelmingly Democratic hometown, he had no chance. He did once actually get on the ballot as candidate for the Southeast Regional Technical Vocational High School Committee, which was the governing body of the area's public trade school. As expected, he got trounced by the Democrat. So, that was that.

In 1964, we had a bumper sticker on our car that said Au+H2O=64, which I thought was clever. At Ellis Brett, though, some of the more gullible kids spread the rumor that we'd have to go to school on Saturdays if Barry Goldwater was elected president. That's assuming we even had school, since the first item on Goldwater's purported agenda was to start a nuclear war. That was my introduction to fake news.

In 1966, my father became a Brockton volunteer for Edward Brooke's first race for the U.S. Senate. One fall morning, he roused my sister and me before dawn and drove us to the Brooke-For-Senate headquarters on lower Pleasant Street, where we met the great man himself. One of our proudest photos is a Polaroid snapshot of Brooke draping his arms around Thalia and me—we look sleepy and shy but Brooke is beaming. Brooke became the first Black man elected to the Senate since the 1870s and I took great satisfaction in the very small role that my father had played in making that happen.

As far as I knew, rooting for the Republicans was about the same as rooting for the Red Sox. The GOP was my team, just as it had been for my parents and grandparents. I watched political conventions like they were sports playoffs, and election night was as exciting as the World Series. But this was not an obsession. With no cable news or social media, politics was something you only thought about in the autumn of an even-numbered year. Otherwise, we had real lives to lead and more important things to think about. Republicanism was just one part of my identity, like being Protestant, one-quarter Swedish, Nantucket-born, or Ellis Brett Elementary-educated.

Since politics then concerned itself primarily with dividing up the financial spoils of society instead of establishing who was morally superior, it was less vicious. It was not a performative self-expression of morals, values, or self-worth. That was what church was for. The parties didn't disagree on hot button "identity" issues like patriotism, abortion, gay rights, or racial quotas, because no one even thought they *were* issues. Parents might not want their children to marry someone of a different race, ethnicity, or religion, but to object to a potential son- or-daughter-in-law because of party affiliation? Who would do that?

That began changing in the late 1960s, when people really started loathing each other over the basis of values—a phenomenon that metastasized during the Vietnam War. At a time when most 18-year-old guys had just started to enjoy adult freedoms, the war and the draft began running at full throttle. That was a bad combination. The most privileged members of the most privileged generation in world history threw a fit because they didn't want to fly halfway around the world to get shot at. It's hard not to sympathize with these kids, who were my older cousins' age. They were being asked to make very big sacrifices for—well, for what, exactly?

As a 15 year old, I was a hawk, but not a strong geopolitical thinker. I had completely bought into the premise that we needed to stop Communism. Whether the war itself was a mistake, wanting to stop Southeast Asia from being overrun by totalitarians didn't mean that America was an inherently bad country or rotten at the core. Millions died when the Communists took over in South Vietnam and Cambodia, just as had previously happened in China and Russia. Trying to prevent that terrible outcome may have been hubris, but it wasn't malign. Jane Fonda eventually apologized for posing with an anti-aircraft gun in Hanoi and laughingly pretending to shoot down American airplanes, but it is emblematic of the anti-war movement's world view that she ever imagined it was a good idea to be in Hanoi in the first place.

What was most shocking was how fast everything changed. Only four years separated LBJ's landslide victory in 1964 and the multiple catastrophes of 1968, when everything seemed to fall apart. And while it's obvious now that America was not paradise for Black people, gay people, or women, they weren't the ones raging against the idea of America. This was a revolt of white, affluent men. Almost overnight, millions of middle- and upper-middle class students and their media cheerleaders turned against the country itself, unleashing a cynicism that has still not abated—although, as I noted previously, even though the war continued through 1975, the huge anti-war demonstrations ceased when the drafted ended in 1972. When college students no longer had any skin in the game, their attention turned elsewhere.

Not only was I turned off by the hate-America attitudes of the left, but I was aesthetically repulsed as well. The dirty, matted hair, scraggly beards, and tattered clothing that they wore so proudly were just plain ugly to me. The rampant drug scene scared me also. As I look inside myself now, I think there's a component of political conservatism that's based on fear—a fear that civilization is only loosely held together and that once you start scraping away long-held customs, norms, and values, the beast inside all of us might emerge. Conservatives believe in original sin and scoff at abstract concepts like the perfectibility of humanity. To be frightened and disgusted by ratty hair and dirty clothes may seem silly now, but what they symbolized—the rejection of a way of life that had made my life possible—alarmed me.

Still, it wasn't until I got to college and found myself surrounded by aggressive, virtue-signaling activists that I started to wonder what it was I did believe. It was one thing to root for the GOP because my parents did, and another thing to be instinctively against the excesses of the '60s and '70s. But what was I *for*?

I started subscribing to *National Review*, the magazine founded by William F. Buckley Jr., who had such a zest for life that he made Conservatism seem fun. I also started reading books by Conservative authors—Milton Friedman, Irving Kristol, Russell Kirk, and Tom Wolfe—which helped crystallize intellectually what I was intuitively feeling.

I went all in on capitalism. I'd seen it at work in my own life. Out of nothing but his own hard work, my father had created a business that supported several employee families and helped dozens of guys pay for college. He'd been able to do this because of: 1) the discipline he'd learned in a stable, two-parent family; 2) a small business-friendly atmosphere with few regulatory roadblocks; 3) a good enough education; and 4) a booming economy. We needed more of that.

I also became a big believer in the traditional two-parent family; I thought the popular culture's celebration of "free love," divorce, and coarse language was just an excuse for selfishness and lack of self-discipline. As a hyped-up teen, I would certainly sneak a peek at a *Playboy* whenever I could, but it made me uncomfortable that the country's most sophisticated intellectuals hailed the porno *Deep Throat* as an avatar of sexual freedom. That trend could not end well.

I became more anti-Communist than ever. I read Solzhenitsyn and hung his picture on the door of my dorm room right next to one of Andrei Sakharov. It infuriated me that from the time I was in college until the fall of the Berlin Wall, there was an actual debate about whether the Soviet Union or the United States was a bigger force for evil in the world.

The free market, traditional family values, and anti-communism were the pillars of Reagan's presidency. I had been a late convert to his bandwagon, supporting Gerald Ford in 1976. In 1980, I originally favored Howard Baker, of all people. In other words, although I had seemed far right in college, I'd really been just a standard moderate Republican. Reagan changed that and I became a "movement conservative" who believed in the full package of conservative positions. And when I arrived in Washington, I considered myself a foot soldier in the campaign to restore the country's place in the world.

As excited as I was to be in the middle of the action though, I had a hard time letting go of Nantucket. I missed my friends and I really pined for my distant girlfriend. Dale and I exchanged letters and I called her frequently from work, sometimes going into the office on weekends just to use the phone. She visited me for a long weekend in July and we drove down to meet her parents in Virginia. The homestead was at the southernmost tip of the Eastern shore, in a small rural town at the very bottom of the Delmarva peninsula. Only ten miles of flat-as-a-pool-table farmland divided the Chesapeake Bay and the Atlantic Ocean where they lived.

It took us five hours to get there and when we arrived at 10:30pm, her parents took one look at me and thought: "Yankee." Dale had previously been married to another Northern guy whom they had liked, so it wasn't necessarily my birth geography that was the problem. This former husband had been a jovial, hard-drinking good-old-boy, and they seemed to sense I was the bad kind of Yankee—taciturn, flinty, soft-spoken, and let's face it, silently a little judgy about the whole slavery thing. Dale's father, a tall, erect, prosperous local farmer who could have stepped out of a Faulkner novel, offered me a drink before I even sat down, and he didn't seem to think that being tired an hour before midnight, even after a long drive, was a sufficient excuse not to enjoy a good Scotch and soda. I finally gave in just to be polite, but after this initial tug of war, he never did warm up to me.

I had another reunion with Dale a month later in early August, when I flew to Nantucket to retrieve my remaining clothes and household supplies. The visit was a bit frantic because I was trying to see everyone over two days. I was disappointed to learn she didn't want to move to Washington after all, but I assumed we'd try to keep a long-distance relationship alive to see where it was headed. I assumed wrong.

A few weeks after I was back in Washington, she broke up with me. The sobbing, can't-live-without-you passion of the spring hadn't even survived the summer. Apparently I had failed two important boyfriend tests: I hadn't sufficiently ingratiated myself with her parents, and when she saw me through their eyes, she realized I was out of place in her world; and I hadn't treated her special enough, as evidenced by my failure to whisk her away to a romantic (i.e., expensive) restaurant during my Nantucket visit, arranging instead for us to go out with the old gang and have fried clams at a downscale fish house—which I recognize now as a goof of epic proportions.

I was heartbroken because a very serious relationship had once again fallen apart after just a few months of separation. I somewhat pathetically tried to remain "friends" in the vain hope that she'd change her mind, but by the end of the year she vanished completely from my life, never to be heard from again. I took every one of my break-ups very hard and when I stopped being morose about this one half a year later, I realized that a woman who'd fume about not being treated to a fancy restaurant was probably not right for someone as callow and unworldly as I was then. She'd already lived the bohemian life in New York City and been married to a man who set her up in an affluent Connecticut suburb, and I was trying to woo her like I was still in college.

As I mentioned earlier, every community has its myth of unique hardship. In Nantucket, they believed the island had the highest rate of alcoholism in the country. Washington's myth was that for every "available" man there were two—or three or four—dateable women. It was said that the workforce consisted primarily of married men, ambitious single women, and a few single guys who presumably had a smorgasbord of eager women to choose from.

In fact, Washington was as close to a meat market as any place I've ever lived, with tons of singletons of both genders working cheek by jowl in cramped offices where waves of young eager newcomers continued to flow. And the married men were not exactly devoted to their marriage vows, so they weren't off the menu either. Almost everyone was on the prowl. Even today, there is probably no city less in need of Tinder.

I should have had a fun, varied, and memorable dating history. But inexplicably, from the time I broke up with Dale until I met my wife seven years later, I had no romantic entanglements. Despite being seriously infatuated a number of times, I never found the way to launch myself out of the starting gate without landing flat on my face. In the end, it all worked out and I eventually embarked on a great marriage, but boy, those seven lost years during the prime of my mating life felt like an eternity.

Compared to my difficulties in adapting to the world of Big Boy dating, getting used to living in Washington D.C. was easy.

The question of where to live was decided in exactly one day. Jim had already identified a couple of potential apartments to look at, and I selected a small studio with two walls of exposed brick in a building called the Cairo. At 12 stories, this was the tallest residential structure in Washington. My landlord, an indulgent father who had purchased a condominium for his daughter several years earlier and kept it as an investment property even after she absconded to Boston with a boyfriend, rented it to me for $390 a month.

The Cairo was faux exotic, with an Egyptian theme that included Moorish and Romanesque Revival touches like gargoyles, winged griffins, and a carved arched stone facade. Despite the Middle Eastern exterior, I turned my unit

During my first year in Washington, I lived in the Cairo,
the tallest non-government building in the District.

into a Swedish sanctuary. At Dale's urging, I had prowled Nordic furniture stores like Scan, Scandinavian Design, and the Door Store, and then outfitted my place with blonde wood, natural fabrics, teak, and severe straight lines.

Only 13 years earlier, Washington had been one of the many U.S. cities to go up in flames during the riots following the assassination of Martin Luther King Jr. 14th Street, in the Northwest quadrant of the District, once a major corridor of arson and looting, was considered a dividing line: danger and poverty lurked on one side of the street, with gentrification and relative safety on the other. The further west you went from this frontier, and the higher the street numbers, the swankier and more expensive it became. Not being an urban homesteader, I wanted to be on the right side of the line, but not so far away as to be suburban. The Cairo was on Q Street between 16th and 17th Street, which put me two blocks from 14th Street—upscale enough to be safe but gritty enough to feel adventurous.

My Dupont Circle neighborhood was young, diverse, and hip. There were a couple of gay bars around the corner on 16th street nestled among the sushi, Mexican, Spanish, Vietnamese, and Ethiopian restaurants. It was a short distance to Connecticut Avenue and DuPont Circle itself, with its cafés, rug stores, art-house movie theatres, boutiques, beauty shops, and the very cool KramerBooks, where you could buy a book or magazine and then have a quick meal or dessert. The Adams Morgan area, with an eclectic and inexpensive restaurant scene that reflected its immigrant population, was only slightly further away. And in a pinch, I could even walk to Georgetown, still the most upscale, trendy, and glamorous part of town.

Washington had its share of culture too—more than I expected. I loved the National Gallery of Art, the Corcoran Gallery of Art, and the National Portrait Gallery, not least because they were free. The Kennedy Center presented concerts (where I saw everything from George Winston to *Messiah*), the ballet (*Swan Lake*), and the opera (the first performances of *Nixon in China*). The Kennedy Center also housed the American Film Institute, which screened exquisitely restored prints of classic American movies. And the downtown area, as dowdy as it was, included a couple of decent old theatres, which is how I saw *Evita* and other Broadway shows. Life in Washington was good.

The city also offered the gentle tingling sensation of being adjacent to power. It was not unusual to run into Congressmen and Senators, and once, when I turned the corner in the Georgetown Safeway supermarket, I found myself face to face with Defense Secretary Caspar Weinberger. And I never stopped being excited at the approach of a motorcade, which meant I'd be able to wave at the president as he sped past.

My best friend from college and my best friend from high school both lived within half a mile of the Cairo, so I had a built-in social structure. Jim Robinson worked for the U.S. Chamber of Commerce and Philip Tasho had gotten an M.B.A from George Washington University and was investing money for First American Bank. Jim and I had a routine every Friday night, when I would go over to his apartment on New Hampshire Avenue, sometimes with pizza, sometimes after dinner to watch the TV show "Dallas," which was his then-obsession. And sometimes on a hot Sunday evening, Philip and I would hop in the car and drive with the windows down to Tower Records, where one of us would buy an LP we didn't really need in order to justify the excursion.

It wasn't that hard to make other friends either. The city was awash in people just like me—former little political nerds who had grown up reading *Advise and Consent* and *Seven Days in May*. Other 20-somethings constantly poured in to work for new members of Congress, fill internships, or get entry level jobs at think tanks or trade associations. I befriended a couple of colleagues in Jerry Solomon's office and they had roommates and friends of their own, so the network stretched even further. At a party, I'd meet all kinds of interesting characters, from a freelance writer for the *New Republic*, a research analyst for the State Department who had fascinating things to say about the change in leadership in the Kremlin, to a right-wing polemicist who had dedicated his entire life, except for serially dating one Asian woman after another, to cutting taxes.

I also found companionship with a couple of other Nantucket refugees. Mary Flannagan, who I'd met a few times on Nantucket because she was a friend of Kate Stout, popped her head into Jerry Solomon's office one day to tell me she was a legislative assistant for a blue collar Democrat from Pennsylvania. Along the way, she'd somehow met Larry Dunham, a scion of the Nantucket Dunhams, whose heritage went way, way back and who was now working in the Office of Protocol in the State Department. The three of us got together for dinner every couple of months, sharing Nantucket gossip, giving each other career advice, celebrating each other's successes, and going to each other's parties.

A lot of this freewheeling, easy-living casualness is no longer possible in Washington. As the size of the government grew, lobbying metastasized and Washington became the most affluent metro area in America. K Street, the center of federal lobbying, used to be a charming thoroughfare with early 20th century office buildings, most of which were knocked down to build glitzy, grand, and nearly identical monuments to special interest. Neighborhoods that were then shabby or even outright slums are now corporatized; marble and concrete have replaced brick and cast iron. The higher rent has pushed the young and eager newcomers further away from the central city. No more low-stress parking outside your apartment building. And the subway system, which was then brand new and the pride of urban planners everywhere, is now decrepit and falling apart.

An even bigger change is the way in which politics has evolved into a perpetual state of war. Plenty of humorless, die-hard partisans crossed my path during the 1980s but in general, Washington was more live-and-let-live than now. You could go to a party and not expect to be sneered at when another guest found out who you worked for—not even if your boss was a Far-Right, bomb-throwing troublemaker like Jerry Solomon. In the 1980s, my Washington friends spanned the political spectrum. I even MARRIED someone from the enemy side. I don't know if that would even be possible today. People in Washington have a lot more power now, more money, more influence, and they get more media attention. But I don't think they have more fun.

CHAPTER 20

The Wild World of Jerry Solomon

A s Representative Jerry Solomon's press secretary in the early 1980s, I thought I was at the ground floor of the Reagan Revolution. 40 years later, I realize I was actually on the cusp of a different, even more enduring movement.

The Reagan Revolution really gelled when Reagan and Congressman Jack Kemp teamed up to promote "supply side economics," which theorized that lower income tax rates would stimulate economic growth and job creation. Both Reagan and Kemp had a sunny, optimistic belief in freedom, entrepreneurialism, and the American spirit, and they believed that most of America's problems could be solved by unleashing the potential of the American people.

Jerry Solomon's politics were somewhat different. That's not to say he wasn't a very loyal Reagan lieutenant. As one of only nine Republican Congressmen to support Reagan ahead of the 1980 primaries, he never stopped wrapping himself in the Reagan mantle. But Solomon was a less intellectual and more confrontational conservative who intuited that the average American felt put upon by more than just high marginal taxes. He drew almost equal support from small business owners who liked his economic policies, and from the blue collar workers who admired his "give 'em hell" rhetoric. Apropos of nothing, he once accused his 1980 opponent—a Vietnam Vet, no less—of wearing "open-toed sandals." Were there any other kind of sandals? No matter. That was his way of signaling anti-elitism and demonstrating an affinity with ordinary folks. This put him in the vanguard of the populist movement that evolved into Newt Gingrich's Contract With America, later morphed into the Tea Party, and eventually culminated in "Make America Great Again."

If he'd lived long enough, I'm sure Solomon would have been a Trump supporter, but personally he was almost nothing like the insecure and self-pitying 45th President. He was remarkably kind to the staff, even if he didn't always know all our names. A couple times a year, when he heard it was someone's birthday, he'd order sub sandwiches and we'd all crowd into his office to eat lunch; him behind his giant desk shooting the breeze, even deigning to laugh when one of us attempted a joke. Once, he even came to my cramped apartment for a welcome party I was throwing for one of the workers in our Saratoga Springs office. He had no compunction about going to the House floor to yell loudly at a fellow congressman, but never raised his voice in the office or called us out for our mistakes. He survived on red meat, Scotch, and cigarettes, hung out with some of the wilder frat boy members of the New York delegation and exuded testosterone, but was no caveman. He was outright prudish in the office, where lewd jokes, flirting with younger staffers, or inter-office hanky panky were nonexistent.

(Having said that, Solomon's relative rectitude in the office did not prevent him from palling around with sleazebags like Congressman Ray McGrath, known in our office as "Mr. Ray" or "Blow Dry Ray" because he resembled a high-end hair stylist. One night, I attended after-hours drinks in his office with Solomon, a couple other New York Representatives, and some staff members. One of McGrath's legislative assistants made a reference to a pocket rocket and he lasciviously responded, "I've got a pocket rocket in my crotch." Nice. Unsurprisingly, after he left Congress, McGrath became president of the Beer Institute.)

But the biggest difference between Jerry Solomon and Donald Trump was their backgrounds. As a proud representative from the vast, faceless, patriotic middle class, born in Florida and reared in upstate New York, he enlisted in the Marines during the early 1950s. Injured during a state-side training exercise, he never deployed to Korea, which is why his carefully worded bio said he'd "served in the Marines during the Korean War." And if someone jumped to the conclusion that he'd seen combat (as his Wikipedia page does), well, that wasn't *our* fault.

Back from the military, he became a successful insurance and investment broker and was elected to the New York State Assembly in 1972 at age 42. Six years later, he challenged the sitting congressman, a Cornell-trained lawyer who'd been elected during the Watergate landslide of 1974. Jerry Solomon definitely didn't go to Cornell, but he was smart enough to know that it was a bad idea to tell *Playboy* magazine you'd smoked marijuana, which is what his opponent did in the October 1978 issue. Jerry rode the *Playboy* interview all the way to Washington, one of the few Republicans to defeat a sitting Democrat that year.

Solomon, who the staff called either "the boss" or "GBS" after his initials (Gerald B. Solomon) probably would have won that race anyway, even if the incumbent hadn't admitted in a porn magazine to being a dope fiend. Upstate New York was very rural and conservative. Bisected by over 100 miles of the Hudson River and bordering Connecticut, Massachusetts, and Vermont, the district had only one Democratic stronghold—Troy, New York. Its few small cities—Glens Falls, Saratoga Springs, and Hudson—leaned GOP, and its dozens and dozens of small towns were either enthusiastically Republican or implacably opposed to what the Democratic Party had come to stand for.

When the Founders fashioned the lower house of Congress as the *vox populi*, they had someone just like Jerry Solomon in mind. He was almost a perfect embodiment of the district, highly attuned to its political and cultural twitches. He wasn't necessarily smarter, more articulate, or charismatic than the average constituent; he was just more ambitious, energetic, and less afraid of being embarrassed. He was the common man writ large, with prematurely

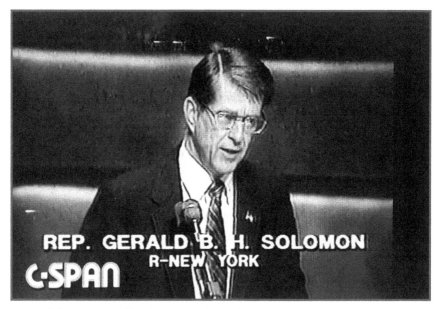

GBS spent a lot of his time on the House floor arguing with other members.

grizzled good looks. His day-to-day uniform was a blue blazer, gray pants, white dress shirt (short-sleeved in the summer so that his wrists hung nakedly out of the jacket), and a red, white, and blue tie, of which he had an endless supply. No expensive suits or Brooks Brothers ties for him.

GBS was so prone to outrageous statements that it was hard to tell where reality ended and performance art began. He once called an opponent a "pinko," which made me shake my head and laugh because it was such an anachronism—no one had used that as a serious epithet since the early 1960s, and by the 1980s, it carried no real sting. Unfortunately, it did not amuse a sensitive reporter from the Albany *Times Union*, who called me up and yelled at me, claiming my boss was a red-baiter. What could I say? That was Jerry Solomon.

With a district packed with hunters and other gun owners, Solomon was adamantly opposed to gun control. This led to the infamous day that he challenged Representative Patrick Kennedy, the nephew of one assassinated president and one assassinated Senator, to "step outside" and settle the issue after an acrimonious debate on the House floor. The colloquy also included this riposte: "My wife lives alone five days a week in a rural area in upstate New York. She has a right to defend herself when I'm not there, son. And don't you ever forget it." I laughed long and hard at the audaciousness of that too. To challenge a Kennedy on gun control and get away with it! Unbelievable. I'd been to Jerry Solomon's house in the upscale, extremely safe town of Queensbury, and the idea that his elegant wife Freda would ever be barricaded inside their stylish Colonial with a pearl-handled handgun strapped to her thigh to protect herself against crazed crack cocaine dealers was both so over-the-top and unanswerable that it was a work of political artistry.

He was a master of political theatre. An aggressive defender of General Electric (GE), a major employer in the district, he adamantly opposed state efforts to force the company to dig up PCBs that the company's Schenectady plastics plant had discharged into the Hudson River. When the New York State Department of Environmental Conservation held an anti-GE hearing in Albany, Solomon tried to crash it and when, as expected, he was not allowed to speak, held a rabble-rousing impromptu press conference in the hall for the TV and print media who had been tipped off that such a thing might happen.

A tough guy with political adversaries, he was surprisingly averse to confrontation with any voter. Even so, I was not prepared for the day we were in his Saratoga Springs office and a delegation of Jewish constituents suddenly appeared to discuss his support for Reagan's plan to sell the AWACS (Airborne Warning and Control System) system to Saudi Arabia. The Israeli government, bitterly opposed to the sale, had whipped up opponents in every Congressional district. There was no way that Solomon was going to vote against Reagan on a defense bill, but he didn't want to tell them that, especially in an unscheduled ambush meeting, so he instructed me to tell them he'd gone out. They didn't really believe me, but left politely. He was nowhere to be seen when I returned to his office to tell him it was safe to come out again. I finally heard a voice asking, "Are they gone?" He stuck his head up from behind the desk, where he was hiding on his hands and knees in case they rushed past me and pushed their way in. Again, unbelievable!

Despite these foibles, Jim Robinson and I had a great deal of affection for the boss. We collected and traded stories like they were baseball cards.

His "outrageousness" made our jobs more difficult but also vastly more interesting. I had lunch one day with the press secretary for the bland Minnesota Congressman Arlan Strangeland. He somewhat condescendingly asked me: "What's it like to flack for Jerry Solomon?" Hard stare from me. "He's very controversial, you know." "Maybe with the other Members," is the best comeback I had, although what I was thinking was, "What a dick."

But it was exactly this willingness to be controversial that Jim and I marveled at. Jerry Solomon was a bit of a troll before the term even existed. And thank God he didn't live long enough to deploy Twitter. He thrived on getting a rise out of people and making them sputter in exasperation. Obviously, Jim and I would have been unamused if we were not ideologically aligned with him; a troll is funny when he's saying things you secretly wished you could say yourself and maddening when he's not.

It might seem obvious that politics is "political," but I wasn't expecting that the hardest fought political battles would occur within Jerry Solomon's own domain. When during the interview process, Jim had arranged for me to meet Solomon in his Glens Falls office rather than in Washington, I didn't give it a second thought. But once I got the job, he explained the situation. His pending departure was top secret. No one was to know, including, or really, especially, GBS's own Administrative Assistant (i.e., Chief of Staff), Lorraine. GBS wanted to fill the position with someone loyal to him rather than to her.

It was only a coincidence that Lorraine was from his district, via the city of Troy, because she was really a creature of Washington. She had started out in Capitol Hill as a receptionist and risen through guile, ambition, and street smarts to become the Administrative Assistant of another Congressman. When GBS won his seat, he needed someone who knew how to navigate Washington, and this other Congressman needed to find another job for Lorraine, who was about to become Mrs. Congressman. So he did a favor for his new colleague and got an experienced operator in the bargain.

I didn't know her age but would have guessed late-30s. She was quite pretty, but had a brittle, defensive smile that she'd probably acquired from her years climbing the ladder in the aggressively male world of the House of Representatives.

Lorraine was undoubtedly capable, but she was steeped in the traditional way of doing things. To the extent that she had any ideology at all, it was the dogma of getting the Boss re-elected, and she was unsympathetic to GBS's theatrics. She had hired everyone in the Washington office except one Legislative Assistant, who had worked on GBS's first campaign in 1978. I think GBS might have been a little bit scared of her and worried he'd get talked into hiring a DC hack for press secretary if she had any say in the decision. He wanted to be sure that his spokesperson was a doctrinaire conservative.

In addition to being press secretary, I was to have the additional title of Legislative Director and oversee the legislative strategy. And it was important that I have the second largest salary in the office (after Lorraine's) to demonstrate my authority over the other staff. That meant I was to be paid $26,800 a year, quite a jump from the $12,500 I was making in Nantucket.

As expected, Lorraine was not happy when I was presented to her as a *fait accompli*. As Jim Robinson's best friend, she treated me warily until she realized I was not the threat that he had been (and she had reason to worry about him because when Jim resigned, GBS had offered him Lorraine's job if he would stay). After that, we got along fine and stayed out of each other's way. Her job was to run the office, make sure the mail got answered, plan fundraisers, cater to donors, deal with major political problems, and see how far she could push campaign finance laws without committing an actual, discoverable violation. She did not involve herself very much in press or legislative strategy.

After a while, she seemed to respect me, or maybe she was just trying to con me into being an ally. I couldn't really tell because even her compliments were often barbed. Once she told another woman in the office, in my presence, that she should date me: "He looks like Woody Allen on the outside but underneath he's Cary Grant." Huh? My only similarity to Woody Allen was that we both wore glasses and had receding hairlines, and I had zero in common with Cary Grant. A week later she explained that she only compared me to Woody Allen because he was so intelligent and I was too. Um, okay.

225

But if she actually did like me, she also let me know from time to time who was boss, like the day she grabbed my ass and squeezed hard in front of her assistant. She'd probably learned that move in other Congressional offices. Like millions of other subordinates (almost exclusively women) who had their asses grabbed in an office, I was too embarrassed to complain. I doubted GBS would have fired her even if I had gone to him. And she never did it again anyway. I guess one squeeze was enough.

Here's the thing about Congressional offices—all 435 of them. From the outside, they all look the same, with about a dozen people squeezed into the same three rooms. But at a closer glance, they are completely autonomous fiefdoms that reflect the boss's personality. And there's almost no interaction among them. I rarely met staffers in other offices. I did attend a few Republican press secretary events and was disillusioned to discover that my counterparts were not very conservative and not very interesting. So I never did find out whether our office was "typical." I do know that when the *Washington Monthly* and *Washingtonian* did their annual features on "Capitol Hill's Worst Bosses," we were never mentioned, so I assumed we fell midway between the rational, efficient offices and the outright dysfunctional ones.

Congress famously exempted itself from any of the workplace protections they imposed on the actual productive economy, so the staff are completely at the mercy of the elected members and their Administrative Assistants. Some are terrorized, others feel fulfilled, but almost all of them work in hothouse conditions.

And how could they not? The set-up of a typical congressional office is like this: You walk in the front door and are greeted by a receptionist and the Representative's personal assistant. Straight ahead, there will usually be a flimsy divider, on the other side of which is workspace for the Administrative Assistant, an office manager (who's really the AA's slave), and one or two other admin types. To the right, there's another room crammed with the legislative and press staff. To the left, there's the member's own enormous personal office, which includes a big, heavy wooden desk, two or three couches, a private bathroom, half a dozen chairs, and a long vanity wall of photos of the boss with famous people. If GBS was in that office when a constituent family walked through the door, they'd be rushed in for a handshake, a pat on the head for the kids, and a family photo.

Each Representative is allocated the same amount of money to hire staff. Some AAs hired long-time, no-drama Hill veterans. That was not our approach. Except for GBS's personal assistant, Skip Cook, who had started working in Congress when Sam Rayburn was speaker, all of us were under 30 and holding our first jobs in Congress. Lorraine never hired anyone from the district, which I assumed meant she didn't want anyone gossiping about office shenanigans back home. She favored non-ideological types like herself— nominal Republicans who didn't really care that much about policy.

And once she hired this staff, she pushed them hard. I'm sure she believed that a woman had to work twice as hard as a man to get ahead, but she'd have been more effective if she'd worked *half* as hard or had a better sense of what motivated people, especially such a young staff.

Our forced closeness, lack of privacy, and extreme youth led to a certain amount of immature behavior. Our two legislative assistants (LAs) were constantly at each other's throats. Theoretically, their job was to advise GBS on upcoming bills, keep track of his record, and help him draft bills. But GBS made up his own mind on how to vote and the two of them spent about 75 percent of their time answering constituent mail or drafting form letters to special interest groups. Consequently, they were frustrated with their jobs.

One of the LAs, Lawrence, had been with GBS since he was a state assemblyman running for Congress, and as the O.G. staffer, thought he had a proprietary relationship with the boss. Even though he didn't buy the outrageous behavior or right-wing rhetoric, he claimed to be the most loyal one of us. With his hangdog demeaner, he felt threatened by the other Legislative Assistant, Ed Gallion, who was his complete opposite: intensely smart, proudly gay, laceratingly witty, pencil-thin, charismatic, and rabidly conservative (he was the one right-winger that Lorraine had let slip through). Ed liked to quote classic female movie stars, especially Elizabeth Taylor in *Who's Afraid of Virginia Woolf*, which, when GBS and Lorraine were out of the country one summer, he screened numerous times on GBS' VCR, complete with popcorn and Bloody Marys. He also once composed this response to the thousands of seniors who were sending us postcards unnecessarily begging us not to cut Social Security: "Thank you for your letter on Social Security. I will personally set my Administrative Assistant (who hails from Troy) on fire on the Capitol steps and impale myself on a meat ax before I ever vote to stop your Social Security checks." Alas, cooler heads prevailed.

Each of them—Ed and Lawrence—always believed the other one was trying to upstage, undermine, and insidiously insult him, like the time Lawrence asserted that Ed was gaming the letter count system by using the memory typewriter for some of his letters, which made Ed go ballistic. Matters finally came to a head one day when Lawrence threatened to break Ed's arm if he didn't shut up. They were a little like Dwight and Jim on *The Office* without the practical jokes.

The one thing they agreed on is that they didn't like me—at least not at first. A month earlier, I'd been covering Planning Board meetings on Nantucket, and now I was not only earning more than they were, I was also technically their supervisor, just because I happened to be Jim Robinson's very good friend. It took a while, but Ed eventually recognized me as an ally since we were the only ones in the office who fully endorsed the Jerry Solomon legislative package. I don't think Lawrence ever did warm up to me.

Ed and Lawrence weren't the only source of tension in the office. Our Legislative Correspondent, Marjorie Thompson, whose job it was to respond to the mass mailings, was the daughter and sister of extremely conservative Republicans, but if she'd ever been a Republican herself, she wasn't much of one when she returned from the London School of Economics, where she'd picked up a Welsh fiancé, a slight British accent, and an aversion to right-wingers. She sat right next to Ed and whenever one of them voiced outrage over something stupid that had been said on the House floor, the other would respond with countervailing, loud sarcasm and they'd be off.

Marjorie and the receptionist, Susan Brewer, were the office feminists, but that didn't mean female solidarity. Marjorie took to calling her insufficiently committed female colleagues "tootsies," because they were allegedly just on the prowl for husbands. And far from seeing her female boss as a role model, she called Lorraine "Evita," and sometimes "Eva Braun." The latter

228

epithet was sometimes accompanied with a faux-Fascist salute. She really resented authority, especially if it was deployed in Lorraine's clipped tone and tight smile.

I report all this with fondness because Marjorie quickly became my best friend in the office, inviting me to her Fourth of July party the second weekend I was in Washington. Tall and willowy, she had a let-it-all-hang-out personality that reflected her West Coast origins. We attended receptions to eat the free food, shared a lot of wine at each other's apartments, and occasionally went to the movies, including the time we brought wire clothes hangers to a showing of *Mommie Dearest* to get half-priced tickets. Once, she drunk dialed me from a Colorado bar at 3:00am and when I picked up the phone shouted, "Nuclear War! Nuclear War! Nuclear War!" Another night, when she needed to go to the emergency room at 1:00am, I was the one she called. Even with all the office turmoil she created, I was sorry when she quit to get married and move to Wales.

There was one other real character in the office—GBS's personal assistant, Skip Cook, a former good-time professional gal who'd aged into a leathery, gravel-voiced troublemaker. Her favorite hobby, besides checking the House's quarterly report on office-by-office spending to see who earned what, was gossiping. She once speculated that Dan Amon, a former Glens Falls *Star* reporter who was helping out with GBS's campaign in the district, might take over my job. When I said I hoped not, she called GBS's wife and told her I was insecure about my employment status; next thing I knew I was in GBS's office with the door closed, listening in mortification as he reassured me that my job was safe.

Another time, Lorraine announced in a staff meeting that I would be in charge of the Washington office while she and GBS were away. Skip's response: "Everybody's got such confidence in Gary, it makes me sick. He's useless now because he can't call Jim Robinson to get instructions." I might have been hurt, but what she said to Lawrence was worse: "If you weren't so useless, you'd be comical." Afterwards, Ed told me to brush it off; Skip was just spewing venom because she was worried about an upcoming medical procedure. But to be honest, I was just flattered that she thought everyone had confidence in me.

Our office was plagued by turnover. Marjorie, Susan, and Lorraine's assistant Kim quit, to be replaced by Maria, Daisy, and Edie, all of whom also became good friends. Then Lorraine herself announced she was leaving for greener pastures, which eventually turned out to be head of the Washington office of a "Baby Bell" phone company. The stress of being a tough-as-nails boss was hurting her health and she was suffering from flare-ups of colitis. She almost certainly got a big raise and the fact that her husband was on the House Commerce Committee couldn't have hurt either.

When she came to say goodbye, several of us made legitimately affectionately fake weeping sounds and she grabbed me by the neck and said, "You should be crying because you didn't get my job. It wasn't my fault." Huh? She was advocating that I replace her? Why would I want that? In any event, we became much friendlier when we no longer worked in the same office. We'd have lunch about twice a year, and when her employer became a major sponsor of the PGA's Kemper Open at the Congressional Country Club in Bethesda, she invited me to watch the golf match from their tent on the 18th green.

Instead of doing something dumb like promoting me, GBS hired Art Jutton, the administrative assistant of Representative Gary Lee, a Congressman from western New York, who had just lost his re-election bid. Art was another creature of Congress. He went to mass every morning at 7:00am, then had breakfast at 7:30am with his other Administrative Assistant cronies. So he came into the office every morning full of the received wisdom from other long-time denizens of the House. I almost had a coronary one day when I went to leave a message on his desk and saw a constituent letter he was drafting that said higher taxes were inevitable, but that GBS would try to make sure any increases would be fair. What the hell? GBS would never send anything like that.

Art's contribution to the office wasn't his legislative or policy advice. It was getting it on an even keel. He was a sweet guy, practically a saint, who managed via positive reinforcement. Lorraine had a good heart, but she ran the place with so much urgency and insecurity that she almost gave the *rest* of us colitis. And why? GBS was immensely popular in the district and unless there was a major scandal, that seat was safe for as long as he wanted. Why were we killing ourselves?

These changes at the beginning of his third term in office signaled GBS's growing confidence in himself. He wasn't mellowing—not by a long shot—but he was coming to understand that all he needed from his staff was the basic blocking and tackling. He didn't need big personalities and drama; he just needed a modicum of low-key competence and that's pretty much what he got from then on, especially as the average age of the staff approached actual adulthood.

CHAPTER 21

Tales of a Congressional Press Secretary

Jerry Solomon might have been a minority-party, second-term representative with little institutional opportunity to stand out from the other backbenchers, but he wasn't going to sit around and wait his turn. Chronologically he was older than my father, but he acted more like a hell-raising, hard-partying younger uncle. Firebrand remarks were part of it: two months after I began, he said that members of Congress were like "pigs at the trough—they can never get enough," which caused a stink, but was replayed that evening on the *NBC Nightly News*. He also had an instinct for squeezing all the political juice out of a previously unrecognized issue. This made the media promotion part of my job easy. I hardly needed to do anything to get his name in the newspapers back home.

Talking to the press is only a small part of a press secretary's responsibilities, though. I spent about two-thirds of my time less glamorously wielding the written word. I churned out a weekly column under the Jerry Solomon byline that went to all the district media. The ten or so daily newspapers, three TV stations, and two dozen radio stations usually wouldn't use it, but each town had a weekly paper that would occasionally run it verbatim. I also wrote two or three press releases a week, prepared short remarks (called "one-minutes") that would be entered into the Congressional record and drafted the occasional proclamation. Having formerly been a reporter working against short, inflexible deadlines was a big help in training me to be a speedy propagandist.

This was not only before the internet, but before reliable Xerox machines. To make multiple copies of a press release, I had to bring a mimeograph sheet to our remote storage room on the top floor of the Cannon Office building, put on a white smock, ink up our mimeograph machine, and literally crank out the copies myself. We also had a memory typewriter called the MICOM that I could sometimes hijack to type multiple copies. If I urgently needed to promote a story, I would "telecopy" (aka, fax) the press release to a main newsroom, call up the targeted reporter, tell him (it was almost never a "her") to go find it, and hope he'd get off his rear end to track it down.

Once a quarter, Congress allowed members to mail eight-page newsletters to every District household. The justification for this taxpayer-funded, self-aggrandizing postal dump was that constituents needed to know how hard their Representatives were working on their behalf: the bills supported, key votes taken, grants obtained, important hands shaken. A yearly poll was standard. We'd ask constituents a dozen yes/no questions and they'd cut out the questionnaire and mail it back to us. The number of responses was overwhelming; in a way, it was inspiring that so many people cared enough to go to the effort of finding a stamp and envelope just to let us know what they thought. The office filled up with box after box of questionnaire responses. We couldn't tabulate them all, so we'd take a random sample—sometimes this system would be as crude as reaching deep in a box and grabbing a handful. If a constituent scrawled apocalyptic comments about Social Security in the margins, Ed would yell out, "Screw you, you old bat" or "Another one for the Home," before sarcastically reading the message aloud as we guffawed.

Except for GBS's secretary Skip, who resolutely refused to participate in any kind of team-building exercise that involved grunt work, everyone in the office, from the receptionist to the press secretary, would help with

With other GBS staffers Ed Gallion, Maria Horgan, and Daisy Drake.

the tallying. When we decided the sample was big enough, we'd find the office calculator to tabulate the result. The voters almost always backed GBS's positions—we wouldn't have asked the question if we thought they wouldn't. And if the margin of support wasn't sufficiently impressive, all it would take was a few marks of GBS's pencil to change, say, the 53 percent who said they were in favor of letting the PCBs lay undisturbed in the Hudson River, to 63 percent. These revised results were the ones we'd report to the media and post in the next newsletter. Appalling, right? Maybe, but not that much worse from political pollsters who manipulate the wording of their questions to get the answers they want.

Not in my job description, but something I did quite frequently was shuttling GBS back and forth to the airport, sometimes in his car and sometimes in my crappy 1977 Mustang (one of the perks of being a senior staffer is that I had an assigned parking space). Sometimes, I'd even have to pick up Mrs. Solomon at GBS's apartment and drive her to the airport. I probably should have resented this but was happy to curry favor with the boss and—especially—the boss's wife, who was so very nice.

Another unofficial part of the job was to keep an eye out for Jerry Solomon's antics on the House floor. The TV set in every member's office had a channel that carried the Senate floor debate and another that followed the House. That's how I happened to catch a fantastic, but immediately suppressed, Congressional faux pas. During the debate on the Budget Bill of 1982, there were five options being considered, including a Congressional Black Caucus proposal. This was a non-starter because of its drastic cuts in defense spending, but was supported by a handful of white liberals anyway. One of those endorsers was Ohio Representative John Seiberling, who'd made a name for himself on the Watergate impeachment committee. He rose to voice his support for the Black Caucus budget saying, "This is the only budget that is fair to all Americans. Let's call a spade a spade." Mouth agape for the next 12 hours, I eagerly checked the Congressional Record the next morning to confirm what my eyes and ears had recorded. Alas, some version of Seiberling's speech was there, but not that particular line. It had been stricken from the record by his staff. As far as anyone in those pre-Twitter, pre-VCR days was concerned, it never happened.

I'd occasionally help on fundraising, although that was really Lorraine's job. I didn't know if our activities were fully compliant with federal ethics rules, but I was assured this is what everyone else did. So, okay then! Ahead of the 1982 re-election campaign, Lorraine and her assistant Kim spent weeks planning a breakfast for lobbyists at the Capitol Hill Club, the private Republican hangout located in a five-story townhouse down the street from the Cannon House Office Building. For their $250 contributions, our guests were treated to scrambled eggs and the opportunity to mingle with significantly more influential GOP luminaries than Jerry Solomon. Lorraine's Congressman husband urbanely emceed the event and smoothly orchestrated a steady stream of New York Congressional big shots (Senator Al D'Amato and Representative Barber Conable) and Cabinet Secretaries (OMB Director David Stockman, HHS Secretary Richard Schweicker and Transportation Secretary Drew Lewis) on and off the dais. For our efforts, we netted $16,000, which was about 20 percent of total spending on the re-election campaign that year.

And if that fundraiser wasn't enough of a strain on office resources, on the Capitol lawn the very next morning, I helped manage a press conference for the New York delegation in support of tax credits for tuition paid to private and parochial schools. My role, besides getting reporters to attend and passing out GBS statements once they arrived, was to help unload a truckload of petitions to serve as a background prop. With half a million signatures, this took a while, but since the media swarmed us, the effort was worth it. The Democratic Party was not yet a wholly owned subsidiary of the teachers' unions, so no one thought it unusual that Democrats like Senator Daniel Patrick Moynihan or other New York City-based Representatives with heavily Catholic constituencies would join GBS and other Republican free-marketers to make rousing speeches in favor of these education tax breaks. It turned out to be mostly for show. Very few of these guys besides GBS cared enough to fight behind the scenes for this issue and there was never a chance of it passing.

Tuition tax credits was one of those issues that Jerry Solomon involved himself with because he cared about it ideologically, not because the district clamored for it. In fact, only a small percentage of his constituents sent their kids to private or parochial schools. Something else that the folks back home really didn't care that much about was the fate of Taiwan, but GBS decided to make it one of his signature issues anyway. He was already very active with other hardline anti-Communist issues and he came out strong for Taiwan's right to be recognized as a separate entity. The mainstream media was a lot more interested in foreign affairs than they are now, and they couldn't wait to talk to the red-hot quote machine that was my boss about the entity we called "Free China."

As great as it was to get GBS some national attention, my main priority was keeping him on the right side of the local media back home. Three or four times a year, I'd drive upstate and spend a week in the district to touch base. We had four district offices and almost as many staffers in New York as we had in D.C., all of whom tried to solve problems that constituents have with the government. At my hiring, Jim explained that Congress is essentially a self-perpetuation racket. It passes complicated bills that encroach on every facet of an ordinary person's life and then allocates funds to itself so that each Representative can hire a dozen local caseworkers to address the difficulties that its own legislation has created. The undying gratitude that this problem-solving generated is just another way that members curry favor with the voters.

Centrally located, Saratoga Springs was the mother office for our district. GBS shared this space with State Assemblyman Bobby D'Andrea, who, in addition to being one of 13 local siblings, was an indefatigable year-round campaigner and the only politician in the area who was as popular as GBS. Sharing space with Bobby was one way that GBS kept an eye on him. Another was to hire his brother, Joe D'Andrea, to be head of the office. Joe was a well-known local businessman and GBS's conduit to local political gossip. When I visited the district, I frequently stayed at Joe's house. His wife was a generous hostess and the D'Andreas had five good-natured kids, including an older daughter who was an Olympic-caliber speed skater, and a teenage son who rejected my suggestion that he might like The Pretenders, protesting they were "New York City trash." I don't remember much about the younger ones, except that I spent one laughter-filled evening with them watching the 1962 movie version of *The Prince and the Pauper*.

Joe kept his focus on the biggest of the big pictures, and the day-to-day work of solving constituent problems fell primarily to two people—Patty Raucci and Maryellen Tarantino—who were deeply devoted to GBS. Patty was a single mother with one son, Paul, and I stayed with them one week when the D'Andreas couldn't take me in. She was passionate and almost equally protective of her son and GBS. Maryellen, who lived in a beautifully decorated house, was cool and unflappable.

There was a great deal of affection and kidding around between the kids in Washington and the middle-aged ladies in Saratoga Springs. Maryellen, for example, was so proper that Ed Gallion loved to see if he could discombobulate her with dirty jokes. One week, he called her three or four times on the speaker and said "Maryellen—research says that everyone either sings or masturbates in the shower. What do they sing?" When she said "I don't know," we all laughed, especially since she just couldn't understand the joke. By the fourth time, she was legitimately angry that he kept calling with the same joke, so someone finally explained privately that if you didn't know what people sang, it was because you were one of the ones who masturbated. The next time Ed asked what people sang in the shower, she answered "My Funny Valentine," which convulsed the rest of us in laughter.

Jerry Solomon achieved his greatest media celebrity on an issue that no one could have anticipated—military draft registration. GBS was pro-military, pro-veteran, and pro-draft, and if ever there was an issue for him to exploit, this was it. His enthusiastic support for the lost cause of the compulsory draft was such a joke that even he was in on it. When he signed my birthday card one year he wrote, "You're still young enough to get drafted!!!"

Nixon had ended the draft a decade earlier, but in case there was a need to mobilize quickly in a national emergency, every 18-year-old male still had to register on his birthday. GBS was annoyed that compliance—especially among entitled, upper middle class guys—was not 100%, and that there was no strong enforcement mechanism. Then one day, Lawrence came back from a meeting at the Selective Service with an idea—how about if we deny federally funded student loans to college students who don't register for the draft? It took GBS less than a microsecond to agree. "Let's do it."

The result was "the Solomon Amendment," an add-on to the defense authorization bill of 1982. The logic of it was simple. Why should the government provide benefits (student loans) to citizens who refused a simple, non-invasive responsibility of citizenship (registering for the draft)? It was immediately embraced by a wide spectrum in the House, even most Democrats.

Passage of the Solomon Amendment created a media bonanza. Freighted with cultural symbolism that reporters could easily grasp, it received nationwide coverage. ABC flew GBS to New York City and put him up in a hotel so that he could appear on *Good Morning America*, which was a huge TV platform in those days before round-the-clock cable TV news (CNN had launched only two years earlier and was not a major player yet—the other cable networks were at least a decade in the future). Bob Simon of CBS came into the office to interview him for a segment on the *CBS Evening News* and was kind enough not to laugh out loud when GBS made the preposterous claim that he'd talked to two Supreme Court justices about the constitutionality of the Amendment. I wasn't sure that he even knew the names of two justices, never mind being in a position to chat with them about constitutional law. *MacNeil/Lehrer* also stopped by to see him for a respectful, earnest interview. George Will called and said, "Representative Solomon, you're a hero of mine," before getting a few quotes that he worked into both his nationally syndicated column and his talking points for the PBS political talk show, *Agronsky and Company*.

After the initial rush of excitement, we heard that a number of colleges either wouldn't enforce the law or would make up lost loans for students who refused to register. We came up with a second amendment that would cut off government grants and contracts with colleges that tried to subvert the first Solomon Amendment.

That made some of the more liberal colleges really squeal. Yale sent a very polite note inviting GBS to campus to discuss this proposal. Somehow a trip to New Haven never found its way onto his travel schedule, and the next thing I knew, the President of Yale, Bart Giamatti himself, was sitting in GBS's reception area waiting to see him. He was all alone so I went out, introduced myself, and sat next to him. He seemed surprised to receive such a friendly reception in the office of a right-wing nut, but I wanted to tell him how moved I'd been by his baseball essay that had appeared in the *Boston Globe* five years earlier at the end of the 1977 Red Sox season.

Giamatti's essay has one of the most famous openings in sports writing: "It breaks your heart. It is designed to break your heart. The game begins in the spring, when everything else begins again, and it blossoms in the summer, filling the afternoons and evenings, and then as soon as the chill rains come, it stops and leaves you to face the fall alone." I told him that I, too, was a long-suffering Red Sox fan and we chatted about the existential ennui of rooting for one lost cause after another.

When it was time for Giamatti's appointment, GBS's door opened and out walked retired Major General John Singlaub, the hard-right former commander of U.S. forces in Korea, who'd achieved notoriety a few years earlier when he caused himself to be fired by President Carter for publicly questioning Korean military strategy. Giamatti and Singlaub looked at each other like they were members of a different species. Because he didn't know his way around the halls of Congress, I walked Singlaub and his aide to his next appointment in the Longworth Building. The aide expressed disgust at having been forced to breathe the same air as the President of Yale and I explained, extremely irrelevantly, that he and I were both Red Sox fans. Needless to say, that explanation didn't cut it with the humorless aide, who only lived for politics. A week later I received a letter in the mail postmarked from New Haven, Connecticut, and inside was a photostat of Giamatti's baseball essay and a short, handwritten "Nice to meet you" note, which I still have. When Giamatti was later named Baseball Commissioner I thought, "That's my friend."

As for the Solomon Amendment, its scope expanded over the years to include a number of other punitive measures against colleges that disfavor the military. It's better known today as the federal law that withholds federal funding from colleges and universities that prohibit ROTC on campus. And yes, it did make its way to the Supreme Court, where it was upheld. I guess GBS's informal lobbying of those two Justices paid off, after all.

Handling the media for the Solomon Amendment was exciting, but again, my real job was to help re-elect my boss. With the country in a severe recession and the Democrats demagoguing hard about social security, 1982 was shaping up to be a bad year for Republicans. It got so bad that when I called my grandmother in Nantucket to wish her a happy birthday, she emotionally expressed her fear that Ronald Reagan was going to take away her social security check. *Et tu*, Grandma?

Re-election campaigns in the early 1980s were not the year-round extravaganzas that they are now, and ours didn't kick into high gear until Labor Day. There was considerable discussion among GBS, Lorraine, and me about my role. GBS decided that although I would remain on the Congressional payroll, I would move to Saratoga Springs for the final five weeks of the campaign and be his wingman at all events.

The campaign got off to a bad start, though. In mid-September, Lorraine summoned me to GBS's office, closed the door, and the two of us called the

Congressman in Saratoga Springs. He told us this story: for some reason (it was never explained to me why or how), he'd been helping a Long Island woman get child support payments from her estranged husband, a union organizer. In retaliation, the husband had filed a lawsuit claiming that GBS was the real father of his 14-year-old daughter; he was seeking restitution for the years of child support that he'd already paid. GBS swore up and down that the allegation was untrue, but after a year and a half of being the conduit for his deliberate evasions, I couldn't wholeheartedly believe anything he said. If this turned out to be true, his career would be over and probably mine too. Because there was no DNA testing back then, no one would really know for sure.

It's human nature to try to suppress news like this, but it's virtually impossible. Lorraine and I were sworn to secrecy, which was fine. But she marched out and told everyone in the office to direct ALL media calls to me IMMEDIATELY. This made the staff suspicious because—why would you need to emphasize that? And the next day, when GBS came into the office, he was in the worst mood that anyone could remember. When you've got a dozen people crammed into such a small space, any change in office vibrations is quickly detected, with Skip and Lawrence nearly out of their minds from curiosity and resentment at being out of the loop.

The first media call on the lawsuit came in from *Newsday* on Long Island. Since it was an unfamiliar reporter, GBS called the guy back himself pretending to be press secretary Gary Holmes. Whatever he said suppressed the story for a day or two. But then the Troy *Record* called, and then the Albany *Times Union*. When the Schenectady *Gazette* reporter tried to reach me, he outlined the allegations to our receptionist Connie who, rather than putting him on hold and locating me in the office, which let's face it, was not exactly as big as Grand Central Station, placed a detailed message about "the paternity suit" in the middle of my desk for everyone to see. Thanks for using the old noggin, Connie!

By positioning this as "obviously a cheap political hit job" and appealing to journalistic ethics and a sense of fair play, we managed to fend off the story for three days. Most of the reporters had reservations about printing sleazy, unsubstantiated personal allegations, a consideration that doesn't exist anymore. But all it would take was for one paper to go first and everyone else would hold their nose and jump in too.

GBS gave the news to Lorraine on a Monday afternoon. When I came in Friday morning, all three numbers on our phones were ringing continually. I'd answer one call and the reporters on the other two would insist on being put on hold, essentially shutting down any other incoming calls to the office. The Schenectady *Gazette*, which had told me the day before that it was their job to publish the news rather than try to distinguish between who was telling the truth, had put the story on page 23 of the paper. That was enough for AP to run it on the national news wire. The media hysteria was like the run on a Depression-era bank. All I could do for the entire morning was read GBS's denial to one reporter after another. The electronic media were particularly inflamed. Every TV and radio station in the district made it the lead news story hour after hour. Lorraine finally called an all-staff meeting in which she laid out the facts. Skip, a malicious gossip and the main reason GBS and Lorraine left the whole staff in the dark in the first place, bitterly protested that they hadn't been confided in, but Lorraine held her cool and didn't get rattled. At the end of the day, two-thirds of the staff went out for drinks at Bullfeathers, the most popular bar on the House side of Capitol Hill, and I quickly downed three gin and tonics.

By Monday, the story was already starting to die. The mother seeking child support denied the allegations completely, calling her husband "money hungry." The polls eventually showed that an overwhelming majority of the constituents either didn't think the story was true or didn't care if it was. A week later, no one mentioned the scandal except to joke about it. When I called my college roommate, Chris Ryer, who had grown up in Glens Falls and whose parents were still friends of the Solomons, he asked me, "What kind of constituent services are you providing in that office?"

In October, I moved up to Saratoga Springs for the rest of the campaign. It would be overly burdensome to stay with the D'Andreas for five weeks, so Maryellen found me a spare room in a widow's house for 50 bucks. At $10 a week, it was an unbelievable bargain even though she didn't provide any meals. I think she mostly wanted the company and I actually did spend several evenings watching the World Series with her. Both of us rooted for the Milwaukee Brewers and were disappointed when the St. Louis Cardinals won.

Campaigning was honestly a lot of fun. I took turns driving GBS to campaign events with Dan Amon, the guy I was supposed to worry about losing my job to, and we became friends. GBS joked that he couldn't decide who was the worse driver, which was just his way of showing affection. (Dan actually was pretty bad behind the wheel, but GBS pretended we were equally inept.) We took him to the Washington County Fair, where he hilariously and good-naturedly participated in a cow-milking contest. And to the Greene County apple picking parade. And to a pancake breakfast in Watervliet.

Not everything went smoothly, though. One Sunday, we showed up four hours before the start of an Athens volunteer fire department barbecue and found only a half-dozen volunteer firefighters smoking a whole pig. After 15 awkward minutes of standing around admiring their barbecue technique, GBS had me go to the van to get an American flag. I grabbed one of the blank forms that certified it had been flown over the Capitol, wrote in a date, and forged his signature. He then solemnly presented this sacred banner to them before we left. In almost every other job I ever had, a scheduling screw-up like that would have ended up with someone getting reamed out, but GBS just shrugged it off and made another joke about my lousy driving as we went to the next event.

The campaign had a distinct do-it-yourself feel. The real campaign was GBS riding around in that van. We didn't even have a PAC, and with a budget of only $75,000, we were only able to pay for a few TV ads, some radio ads, a handful of staff salaries, one poll, and the rent for an official campaign space down the hall from the Congressional office. There were no campaign consultants and as much as the Democratic establishment disliked GBS, they didn't send in any outside money to prop up his poor, beleaguered opponent. This was a super safe district.

The sacrificial lamb that the Democrats had chosen to run against GBS was Roy Esiason, a town supervisor from the little town of Granville. As a former social studies teacher, he probably thought it was his civic duty to make sure GBS didn't run unopposed. But he could never identify an issue or line of attack that would even raise our ire enough to really dislike him. For a

With the 1982 campaign staff in the Saratoga office.

while, his main criticism was that GBS hadn't voted for the big 1982 tax hike that President Reagan had foolishly been talked into signing. Only a run-of-the-mill liberal like Esiason would think this was a winning issue.

The bulk of the campaign consisted of a series of candidate forums sponsored by organizations like the League of Women's Voters. Every candidate on the ballot, including state senators, assemblymen, and local town supervisors, got a turn to speak at these events. At one "Meet the Candidates" event at a senior center in Hudson, about 200 elderly voters listened politely to nearly 20 different five-minute speeches, beginning with GBS and ending with the candidate for county coroner. What that guy had to say to a group of senior citizens, I will never know, because we left after an hour.

The beauty of the candidate forums was that the limited amount of time for each candidate prevented an unknown like Roy Esiason from gaining traction. Also, a skilled politician like GBS would know how to tailor his message. At the Clifton Park Rod and Gun Club, I saw more flannel shirts and jean jackets in one room than at any time since I'd graduated from college.

When Esiason started whining about corporate PAC money, GBS let loose, knowing that a room of gun-loving guys' guys would appreciate a little testosterone. "You're damn right I welcome their support," he nearly shouted, with practiced anger in his voice. "Ford, Bendix, International Paper employ a lot of people in the district and if you think I'm not going to accept contributions from them, you're crazy." He then tossed down a stack of receipts from people who had (supposedly!) contributed five and ten dollars to the campaign. "I've got a thousand of these. How many have you got? Ten?" It was brutal, but the flannel shirts seemed to enjoy it.

We did agree to a single one-on-one debate late in the campaign at a community college in Glens Falls. This was Esiason's turf, because the students were all for the Nuclear Freeze and defense cuts. GBS acted a lot more statesman-like than he had at the Rod and Gun Club, but he did unveil another prop. When bragging about everything he'd accomplished, he pulled out a scroll that (supposedly!) listed all the federal grants he'd won for the district. When he unfurled the scroll and it rolled across the stage, the Esiason team could only groan.

GBS visited every district newspaper for an editorial board meeting. The bigger the newspaper, the more liberal the editors and the more idiotic the questions seemed—the unexamined premises of these semi-antagonistic inquiries were born out of ideological "hive" thinking, where everyone at these big editorial boards thought alike and couldn't imagine that anyone other than a dolt would disagree with them. (Example: "given that we're no better than the Soviets, why should they believe our promises on arms control?") He also did a fair number of call-in radio shows, including one where four of the six questions were posed by the Congressional staff back in the office. I liked being on the road with GBS because when I wasn't running around in the van, I was either spending endless hours writing and rewriting a newspaper ad that would never run, or helping the volunteers stuff envelopes.

None of this mattered very much. All the activity was mostly for show, to demonstrate that GBS was not taking the voters for granted. As was typical with GBS though, the complications were self-induced. About a month before the election, he told us that he needed to have a heart operation that couldn't wait. So about ten days before the election, he flew down to

Washington for a top-secret procedure at the Walter Reed Naval Hospital. The media was not to know that he wasn't in the district, so when Esiason made some fresh attack about GBS and PACS while he was under anesthesia, Lorraine and I drafted a statement that we issued in his name.

Late in the morning, the word filtered back that there'd been a complication and he was still sedated. We never did hear anything else about it that day. At 7:30am the next morning though, my landlady knocked on the bathroom door as I was showering to say that Maryellen Tarantino was on the phone. My heart was pounding as hard as it ever did as I dried off and got dressed. What had happened to GBS during the night? As it turned out, Maryellen was calling about something completely different. The Glens Falls radio station was reporting that one of the Solomons' daughters had been arrested for a hit and run last night.

I rushed into the office, expecting another round of negative press while GBS was out of state in the hospital. And the boss's heart issues turned out to be a good news/bad news joke. The good news was that the angiogram showed he had no arterial blockages or heart damage. The bad news was that because he was allergic to the dye used in the angiogram, his heart had stopped during the procedure. It had taken three electroshocks (each of which lifted him "a foot off the operating table," he later said) to revive him. When he returned to the office two days later he showed us his chest, which now looked like it was branded with the Olympic symbol, except that instead of five interlocking circles, there were six.

There was surprisingly little news coverage about the hit and run. A few newspapers called to confirm that the driver was Jerry Solomon's daughter. After all the grief they gave him about his alleged love child six weeks earlier, the media mostly decided to give him a break on this one.

Still, a day later, one of GBS's personal friends called the office and said Roy Esiason was running a radio ad that said he'd be "a better father" than Jerry Solomon, clearly a cheap attack on GBS's daughter. This threw the office into an uproar. I called the friend back and questioned him closely. Absolutely, he insisted. The ad mentioned being a good father. Well, he amended it, maybe it was a good husband. He wasn't sure now. I called the radio station and they played me the ad—Esiason had pledged to "clean up the Hudson."

Apparently, "Hudson" sounded like "husband"? Unbelievable. But that was not the last time a spouse, friend, daughter, or parent got my principal meal ticket upset by something he or she had misread in an unremembered newspaper or misheard on an unidentified TV news program.

By this time, the campaign was essentially over. GBS was too weak for public appearances. Lorraine left the district early to spend the last week with her husband, who was also running for re-election. We wouldn't see her again until mid-November. I didn't even go into the office that last weekend.

On election night, we went through the motions of pretending to care, with a half-hearted celebration in the cramped campaign headquarters. The result was anticlimactic. Jerry Solomon received 74 percent of the vote. It was a grim night for the rest of the GOP, though. With unemployment running at over 10 percent and inflation still unsustainably high, the Republicans lost 26 House seats. I knew people who worked for those vanquished incumbents, which highlighted how insecure all our jobs were. If those electroshocks hadn't restarted GBS's heart, I would have counted myself among the jobless too.

I didn't intend to become a Congressional lifer, and wasn't exactly looking for a job, either, but when Jim Robinson said that one of his White House friends was trying to fill an analyst job, I jumped at the chance. It took a long time—until March 1983—for the offer to come through, but when it did, I accepted it on the spot. I'd be working in the White House!!!!!!

I felt legitimately bad telling GBS I was leaving, and I think he was a bit sad to see me go, but he was also pleased to think of his office as a launching pad for the White House. I gave him two weeks notice and wrote four extra weekly columns for the office to send out after I left. He had no obligation to do this, but he gave me two extra weeks of vacation time as a bonus. When I went to say goodbye on my last day, he stood up, shook my hand, punched me in the shoulder and said, "Take care, my friend."

After I left, our new Administrative Assistant, Art Jutton, wanted to replace me with Congressman Larry Craig's former press secretary, but GBS fell back into his old tricks and hired a guy from the district, John Kostas, with no input from Art. John and I became friends, bonding over the vicissitudes of working for Jerry Solomon. And I kept in close touch with my other friends in the office too. When I went to the White House, they'd often ask for information about Administration policies. I picked up the phone once and it was Ed Gallion: "GBS asked me to call you to get some data about Reagan and women's issues. He needs it for his own background but he told me to tell you it's for a debate." We both laughed sardonically that GBS felt the need to burnish even a simple information request to make it sound more important than it was—it was as if he didn't remember that the two of us had seen him pull this same move on scores of others and wouldn't immediately recognize the exaggeration for what it was. He was literally incorrigible.

As the years rolled on, GBS never truly mellowed, but as he built seniority, he became more establishment. He got himself placed on what was always called the "powerful Rules Committee," and eventually became Chair when the Republicans gained control of the House. This put him in a position to do an unfathomable number of favors for the Republican colleagues, which translated into hundreds of millions worth of pork projects back in his district—everything from bridges, skating rinks, roads, courthouses, and even the federal cemetery that was both named after him and became his final resting place.

Ed Gallion and I remained friends. With his sharp sense of humor and conservative ideology, I think he might have been GBS's favorite employee of all time. He went to law school at night for several years and when he graduated, GBS helped him get a clerkship with a Federal Appeals Court judge that he knew from New York. Ed then parlayed that judgeship into a job at Sullivan and Cromwell, which was one of the most prestigious law firms on Wall Street. We kept in touch for years both in Washington, D.C. and New York City, and would have hilarious friends-and-family dinners at my house in Connecticut until his health deteriorated and he stopped returning my phone calls. In 2010, I sent him a Facebook friend request and two years later, I was thrilled to see he'd accepted it, until I looked at his page and saw that he'd just died. His sister had gained access to the account and accepted all the requests so his friends would know he was gone.

In a few years, everyone I knew in GBS's office left, except for Lawrence, who had been promoted to Administrative Assistant and stayed until the end, thus serving the boss from start to finish. We'd parted on good terms—on the day I left, he gave me a funny fake note from GBS to President Reagan warning him about the "Holmes Defense Budget." For some reason, Lawrence was under the impression that he was stronger on defense than I was. Okay, whatever. I appreciated the effort, but not enough to call up randomly and ask him how GBS was doing, so I lost touch with the office.

GBS retired in 1999. At that time, I was working for a public relations firm in New York City and GE was one of my clients. In a meeting about how to deal with the PCBs in the Hudson River (yes, that issue was still alive 20 years later), someone in the company's government relations office mentioned dismissively that Jerry Solomon, who now had his own small lobbying firm, was pushing hard for a retainer. But after fighting their battles in Congress for two decades, he wasn't much use to them anymore. Although they eventually did retain him, I doubt it was for a lot of money.

He died of congestive heart failure two years later. I couldn't get away for the funeral because of some now-long-forgotten announcement that another one of my clients was on the verge of making any day. Not going to that funeral remains one of my biggest regrets. If he hadn't taken a chance on me, I can't even imagine how I would have ever made it to Washington, met my wife, or had a career in corporate public relations. I really owed him.

CHAPTER 22

The White House, Part One

W orking in the Reagan White House should have been a dream come true, but it taught me a valuable lesson: sometimes the thing you want more than anything else in the world can make you miserable. Even so, I'd do it again in a second if I was given the option. This frustrating year was one of five or six key inflection points I needed to pass through to achieve my ultimate career.

My connection to the White House was again through my loyal friend, Jim Robinson. While working for the political PR firm owned by Reagan's former California advisors, Mike Deaver and Peter Hannaford, he'd flown to Detroit in July 1980 to work at the GOP national convention. Finding himself in one of the boiler rooms responsible for drafting the Republican platform, he ingratiated himself with a coterie of mid-20s libertarian policy nerds and Ayn Rand acolytes. These included Brian, who later became his partner in a small debate prep business.

Brian eventually became head of a micro-group called The Office of Policy Communication (OPC), which languished near the bottom of the White House ecosystem. The would-be propaganda wing of the Office of Policy Development (OPD) (and by the way, sorry for the acronyms, which are necessary when discussing anything to do with the government), it was primarily the regurgitator of slightly behind-the-curve policy reports.

OPD theoretically set domestic policy in the same way that the National Security Council ran foreign policy. But it reported to Special Counselor Ed Meese—the quintessential decent guy, who was constantly being outmaneuvered by the President's more Machiavellian Chief of Staff, Jim Baker—and was in the political equivalent of Siberia. In other words, my White House fate was to work in one of the least consequential parts of a larger group that was, itself, generally inconsequential. This point was driven home in my second week there, when I introduced myself to Misty Church, a fact-checker in the speechwriter's office who disdained Brian but just LOVED Jim Robinson. She bluntly told me: "No one ever uses OPC stuff. I can't understand how anyone can spend time writing reports that no one ever reads."

Brian's problem wasn't a lack of smarts. In his Kansas City high school, he'd been a debate team champion and the winner of a state-wide science fair. At his small Baptist college in Missouri, he'd gotten a math degree by taking a year of courses and testing out of the rest. Because of his work in the 1980 Reagan campaign, he had an encyclopedic knowledge of Reagan's policy positions. He was a fast, strong writer and occasionally a good editor.

Unfortunately, he struggled to oversee and inspire a small group of writers hired to provide timely position papers for administration spokespeople. Besides me, there were two other writers on staff. Steve was a tightly wound lawyer whose most important responsibility was writing Meese's speeches, and Rob was a charming fraternity brother from the University of North Carolina and one of the few Black staffers in the White House. At one point, Steve tried to organize a coup in which the three of us would go to Meese and expose how mismanaged the office was. I absolutely refused, not only because I couldn't bear to perpetrate such a personal stab in the back, but because there was no chance we'd win a showdown, anyway. Meese might like Steve's speeches, but he was still close enough to our boss to affectionately call him "Bri."

All dressed up and ready to work in the White House.

Brian's main problem was that he couldn't sign off on anything without completely revising it again and again, no matter how urgent the deadline. Finding myself rewritten, and then rewritten, and rewritten a fourth, fifth, or sixth time was a shock because I was so accustomed at my previous jobs to having a free hand. At both the *Inquirer and Mirror*, as well as in Jerry Solomon's office, my first drafts had sailed through with only minor changes. Now almost every paragraph came back scrawled with red ink. According to the diary I had started keeping, when I turned in a draft of one speech, he said it was "too upbeat," "too downbeat," "too strong," "too weak," "it doesn't flow," "it needs transitions." Two weeks later, the third draft of a paper on regulatory reform was "too bureaucratic," "lacked parallelism," had "too many non sequiturs," "doesn't flow well," "is imprecise." A fourth draft of an op-ed on welfare was "too defensive," "too demagogic," "too unfocused," "too disorganized." You get the picture.

It's not like I was too proud to have my writing improved upon, but I couldn't wrap my head around why, after the first round or two of revisions, these drafts never seemed to be getting better. One op-ed on tuition tax credits went through 15(!!!) sets of edits before we finally circulated it for approval to the other White House departments. Another time, when everyone in the White House was upset about a David Broder column in the *Washington Post*, White House Communications Director David Gergen asked us to write a letter to the editor for him to sign. As a former press secretary, I knew the letter had to be hand-delivered to the *Post* THAT AFTERNOON to have any chance of getting into print. Instead, it took us nine laborious drafts over six days to come up with a five-paragraph response. Of course, this never got submitted to the *Post*, never mind published; by the time we were done, no one could even remember what the fuss had been about.

The Sisyphean experience of handing in a draft that finally seemed very solid after nine rounds of edits, only to get it back covered with dozens of additional changes, literally depressed me. I was on a treadmill of uselessness, rushing harder and harder to get nowhere for nothing important. I started to get headaches and had trouble sleeping.

If I'd had enough confidence to laugh this away and simply enjoy the perks of working in the White House, I'd have been better off. But I had a puritanical phobia of being unproductive; I hated to waste time, which I considered to be life's most limited resource. I desperately wanted to both make a difference and believe that I was at least competent.

Brian was able to demand so many drafts because we were using something called word processors. I had previously written on electric typewriters, so if someone revised my first drafts, they had to be typed anew; this cut down the editing-for-editing's-sake nonsense. At the White House, I had a MICOM desktop which stored my work on a collection of loose floppy disks—this was way before Microsoft Word or hard drives. God forbid that you lost a disk, because there was no backup. There was no internet or LAN either, so instead of emailing my drafts to Brian for his review, I had to print them out and physically place pieces of paper on his desk.

Possibly sensing how demoralized I had become, Brian tried to praise me. Once, after finishing a particularly painful editing process on an energy policy paper he said, "Great job. I just hope Ben Elliott [the head of the White House Speechwriters Office] doesn't find out what a terrific writer you are and try to hire you away." I smiled thinly, but when I got home, I raged in my diary, "Does he think I'm an idiot?" Not one sentence from my original draft had made it through his meat grinder. 90 percent of the words were his; I had merely typed them in. By ostensibly praising me, he was really just praising himself.

He was inconsiderate of our time too. More than once, he'd sit on a draft I'd handed in Friday morning, only to return it covered with edits that had to be made that night as he walked out the door at 6:00 pm. So much for my Friday night plans. This lack of consideration is how I ended up working in the office on Easter Sunday 1983. I had to rewrite a paper on "comparable worth" that needed to be handed in first thing Monday morning. That was the year I had Easter dinner at the McDonald's at 16th Street and Pennsylvania Avenue.

That paper on "comparable worth"—the idea that the government should set salaries so that jobs dominated by women (e.g., nursing, teaching, secretarial work, domestic work) would receive comparable pay to those dominated by men (e.g., trucking, construction, firefighting, etc.)—illustrates the evanescence of so many of the issues we fought so bitterly over in the 1980s. Many of the strongly argued pieces I wrote—on the line item veto, school prayer, term limits, enterprise zones, and the Equal Rights Amendment—now seem as musty and antique as William Jennings Bryan's "Free Silver" crusade.

One issue that we addressed constantly—women—remains politically divisive, even today. (And, yes, I do see the irony in me becoming the group's point person on this issue because we didn't have any female analysts.) The early 1980s saw the rise of the "gender gap." A then-new phenomenon, the parties divided along gender lines and the GOP had a lower approval rating among women than men. It never occurred to the media to ask why the Democrats had a problem with men. Instead, for most of 1983, the media rode this hobby horse with story after story about how women hated Reagan. And none of White House Chief of Staff Jim Baker's transparently cynical ideas—like appointing more women to the Cabinet or issuing proclamations—improved matters.

The media hysteria about the gender gap finally came to a head that August. A woman named Diane, a good friend of Brian's from the 1980 campaign who had been farmed out to the Justice Department to work on a task force on women's issues, published a long essay in the *Washington Post* claiming that her task force was a "sham" because the administration was dragging its heels on its recommendations. She cited Brian by name, saying that during the 1980 convention, the two of them had, as an alternative to the ERA, dreamed up something called the "50 States Project" to identify and repeal discriminatory laws and regulations. This idea had made its way into both the party platform and Reagan's acceptance speech, but Diane claimed that not one law had been repealed in three years, an explosive charge that the media magnified with relish.

As she made the rounds of all the TV networks, Diane temporarily became one of the most famous women in America. But the people who knew her personally said she was kooky. According to Jim Robinson, she had been particularly obsessed with parading around the GOP convention floor in a head-to-toe Easter Bunny costume carrying a sign that said "Wabbits for Weagan." Now, I am well aware of the long history of men referring to difficult women as "crazy," but in this case, the women who knew her, including Brian's own secretary, unanimously agreed she had a screw loose. Brian himself was in a bit of a bind. Up to the day the piece dropped, he'd been trying to get her a job back in the White House. Now he'd been fingered as her collaborator. He responded by writing a very good op-ed of his own in just an hour and a half, showing that he could focus when he wanted to. That piece never got published, but President Reagan used some of the language in a statement that afternoon, which I thought was pretty cool.

The Justice Department furiously denounced Diane as a self-aggrandizing attention-seeker but made a serious PR blunder by referring to her demeaningly as a "low level Munchkin." That was an accurate description, but still. She produced a photo of herself and Reagan from the 1980 campaign and declared, "If I'm a Munchkin, then this is the Wizard of Oz." I'll give her credit for a clever line. Fortunately for Reagan, and to the complete dismay of her feminist allies who were calling her a heroic whistleblower, she quickly outed herself as an unsmiling, unblinking conspiracy theorist, most memorably on *Nightline*, when she described the "voices" that were advising her, and grandiosely claimed that only she understood what was happening in the Reagan Administration. The feminists dropped her fast but by then, the damage to her cause was done. The fever broke on the women's issue. The gap between how men and women perceive the two political parties remains, but the day-to-day media moved on to other obsessions.

This fiasco raised the visibility of a 15-page paper on women's issues that I'd been writing—something I'd started more than a month earlier and which was, as usual, hung up in Editing Hell. Suddenly, there was an urgent need to get it out, and people in the various White House offices (OMB, Cabinet Affairs, the Council on Economic Advisors, Personnel) were now calling to give me changes. I needed to get it to the White House printer by 4:30pm on the Friday after Diane's *Nightline* appearance, because the Office of Public Liaison wanted to distribute it first thing Monday morning. After not paying attention all week, Brian called me at home Thursday night and unsurprisingly informed me that he had quite a few more changes. I needed to be in the office at 6:30am the next day so I could revise the draft and bring it to Ed Meese's office before his morning staff meeting. I grudgingly got up at 5:00am, wearily popped my floppy disk in my computer at 6:15am, and managed to walk a revised draft to the West Wing by Brian's deadline. Naturally, that wasn't the end. Brian had more changes at noon and then tacked on even more at 3:00pm, just 90 minutes before it absolutely, positively had to be at the printer. I barely made it, and as it was, I had to beg the printers to make 1,000 copies over the weekend.

The paper was a huge hit and I felt great that it was distributed throughout the administration. All day Monday, people called for extra copies. Even Misty Church, the naysayer, wanted one. But on Tuesday, someone identified a few typos in the changes I'd made late Friday afternoon and we had to reprint it. Brian was furious and I was deflated. Those typos were entirely my responsibility, but I also resented that Brian's "wait and hurry up" management style had put me in a nearly impossible position, dramatically increasing the likelihood that I'd make mistakes under the pressure of rushing.

In all honesty, I can't blame the low-grade depression of my White House year entirely on Brian. My once-promising social life had suddenly collapsed.

When I first moved to Washington, my two best friends had lived close by, but Jim had gone west to be the Communications Director for California Governor George Deukmajian and Philip had decamped for a different financial job in Richmond, Virginia. Further, the convenience of making face-to-face plans with my pals in Jerry Solomon's office ended when I left. This forced me to work harder to remain socially active. And it really was work.

People in the 21st century complain about how the internet has made social planning difficult, but the habit of holding out for a better weekend deal was widely practiced in the 1980s too. To find company for a Saturday night movie, I needed to make several telephone calls just to get someone on the line; if I was lucky, there'd be a tentative acceptance, followed by several days of waiting for a confirmation. This was even before answering machines, so all the abortive calls back and forth could be frustrating. And my would-be companions always seemed to have an out of town friend who might be visiting, so the last-minute cancellation was quite common and an outright no-show without a courtesy call was not unheard of.

Because of my parents' hyperactive social life, I'd been raised to believe I had an obligation to get out there and enjoy myself every single Saturday night. Sitting home and reading a book was more than a sad social failure; it was a form of pathology if it happened too often. It didn't help that they started quizzing me on how I was spending my weekends, clearly worried that I was turning into a hermit. So I became the one who was worried, because I was worrying them. Plus, there was the persistent issue I didn't like being reminded of—why didn't I have a girlfriend? It was a legitimate question, but I couldn't explain it to myself, never mind to them.

I don't know how much diet contributes to mood, but looking back 35 years later, I have to admit, my nutrition was atrocious. On Saturday mornings, I'd go out and buy two bagels and two croissants, and because you can never have too much fat or too many carbs for breakfast, I'd eat one of each that day and the rest on Sunday. Dinner wasn't much better. When I left Jerry Solomon's office, the staff had given me a classic 1980s gift—a wok—and I used it on Sunday nights to prepare quasi-Chinese meals that at least had both vegetables and protein. The rest of the week, I ate crap. Nachos at after-work drinks, popcorn and a peanut butter sandwich for a quick dinner, Domino's pizza when I was even lazier, and raisin bran cereal—for dinner!—when I was trying to be healthy. The nutrition was bad but at least there wasn't much of it. I didn't have a scale at home, but when I went for my annual physical, I weighed 153 pounds—only ten pounds more than high school.

My unexpected isolation within the White House added to my loneliness. Back in Jerry Solomon's office, a dozen of us had been crammed into a couple of rooms with constant physical contact, joking around and blowing off steam. Now I had my own office in the Old Executive Office Building, an enormous wedding cake structure next to the West Wing. Built during the Gilded Age after the Civil War, the OEOB had once been the largest office building in the world, housing the State, War, and Navy departments. Even with those departments dispersed to the Pentagon and the new State Department building, it was still a daunting structure, with tall, wide corridors and spacious distant offices. Walking down those empty halls with just my echoing footsteps was like being in a mausoleum.

Joking around or blowing off steam in the OEOB? That didn't happen—at least not in OPC.

In my tiny office in the OEOB.

We hardly ever interacted with each other and my personal contact became so infrequent that on a sleepy afternoon, I could lay my head on the desk for a 15-minute nap, pretty confident that I wouldn't be interrupted.

This lack of human contact became painfully apparent on October 25th, 1983, when my childhood friend Rich Martel, the only one besides me who had cared about politics back at Ellis Brett, called at lunch to complain that the U.S. had invaded the tiny island of Grenada to free American medical students who were being held hostage by the country's Communist government. "What are you talking about?" I said. "We're still looking at our options." That's what I'd read in the *Washington Post* that morning. Rich was incredulous, saying that Reagan had announced it four hours ago, to which I replied, "That can't be true; I'm working in the White House; I would know." I hung up and walked down the hall, peeked in an office that had a television, and saw Secretary of State George Schultz giving a briefing. Oh shit. Rushing back to my office, I called Ed Gallion in Jerry Solomon's office, who filled me in on the details. I then sheepishly called Rich to concede he was right about the invasion at least, if not about his opposition to it.

Rich thought my lack of awareness was hilarious and attributed it to the Administration's internal communications incompetence. That wasn't really fair. It wasn't my job to know about invasions or to be officially notified of them. The real takeaway was that I was so far out of the loop, I couldn't even see the loop. I had no buddies who would poke their heads in my door to say, "Hey, what about that rescue mission?" In the cafeteria at lunch, no one had high-fived me about President Reagan standing tall. If Rich hadn't called, I might have gone home without hearing a thing and only learned about it the next morning when I picked up my newspaper outside my door.

As isolated as I was, I did make one new friend (sort of) in the White House: Brian himself. He quickly came to see me as an ally, which is why I feel somewhat morally compromised now in laying out my complaints. It feels like a betrayal of that relationship, even if it was so unbalanced.

I knew he thought of me as a friend and confidante after a particularly volatile staff meeting during which Steve and Rob pushed back against his edict that we all be in the office at 8:30am. He came into my office, closed the door, and said plaintively, "Do you see what I'm dealing with?" Thinking we were buddies, he started confiding in me about his dreams and aspirations. More than anything else in life, he wanted to be a novelist. In fact, he'd already written one novel that he wanted me to read. He brought in the three-inch high manuscript and told me I could spend two hours per day reading it in the office, which I dutifully did, grateful that he hadn't assigned it for weekend homework.

Even with an overly didactic theme about the need for a free market in energy policy, it wasn't awful, and I read it through. The story climaxed with the main villain, a power-hungry command-and-control regulator who wants the government to take over energy production, ironically freezing to death after accidentally locking himself in the stairwell of a building that had been forced to turn off the heat over the weekend. Still, I was impressed that he'd even managed to finish the thing. Two years later, I picked up the *Washington Post* and read that he'd won a $2,500 prize in a novel-writing competition for newcomers. He got an agent out of that but never managed to find a publisher.

Later, learning that I was also a fan of the first two *Star Wars* movies, he asked me to join him, his wife, and his best friend at the first night's screening of *Return of the Jedi*. The catch was that I had to leave work early and wait for three hours at the Uptown theatre to buy the tickets and save them a place in line for the 9:30pm show. Was this an abuse of the employer/employee relationship? I don't know. I definitely did want to see the movie and was glad to get out of work early, but I wouldn't have waited in line that long for the convenience of any of my real friends.

He started asking me to play racquetball—that quintessential 1980s sports fad. This I enjoyed, although we always played it on his terms—at times that were convenient for him and at the court that was closest to him. I didn't mind this too much because, well, what else was I doing? If he called me at 9:00am on Sunday morning and said he wanted to play at 2:00pm, I could usually make it. One Saturday he called at 5:00pm to play at 10:00pm, so

I ate dinner, watched a movie on my VCR, and drove out into the darkness at a time that I now view as my bedtime, not the time to be starting the night.

He lived in Springfield, Virginia, which was a 40-minute ride from my apartment, and he'd have us meet at his house so he could drive us both to a court about two miles away. I once suggested that we meet at a place that was somewhat closer to my apartment, which he rejected, supposedly because it would cost two dollars more.

When we finally got around to playing, I usually ended up enjoying myself. At least I was getting some exercise, although he often had us return to his house without showering, so I'd end up sitting on his couch caked in dried sweat as I downed a can of Coke. Sometimes we'd meet his wife at a pizza place near his house. On those occasions, we'd usually hang out and talk, but once in a while, he'd be agitated and want to go home as soon as we gulped down the meal—one night because he'd only written 12 pages on his novel that day and needed to get back to it. Only 12 pages! I was trying to write a novel too, but the most I'd ever churned out in a single day was one really terrible page.

I shouldn't imply that ours was a purely transactional relationship. Once, I was standing in the anteroom of his office suite when he called in from the road and asked his secretary to put me on the line. She handed me the phone and I stood there talking to him, passing along a story about his boss, Ed Harper, and adding a few acerbic observations of my own. When we hung up, his secretary looked at me with amazement—she'd never heard Brian laugh before. His default mode was super-serious with a slight scowl.

Because I never pushed back or said no to any of his requests, he began to think of me as a loyal appendage—the guy who would help him fulfill his dreams of getting out of the White House, which he increasingly hated. Every month he had a new scheme. He once proposed writing a "humorous book on welfare," going so far as to write an outline of the 28 amusing chapters that would be included. He also proposed a serious book on welfare with Bob Carlson, one of Reagan's policy advisors. Bob would supply the ideas, I'd write the book, Brian would edit it, and we'd split the proceeds. That sounded like as much fun as a root canal. Later, he suggested that we co-write a book on jobs programs, which hardly sounded like a bestseller. He even had a plan to go into the speechwriting business with Jim, in which I would play some supporting part. To that end, he encouraged me to buy my own home computer—an IBM that cost $2,000 in 1983, which was about a month's take-home pay.

None of these ideas were going to happen, and I just nodded when he proposed them. It's hard to tease out now whether he was using me or I was using him. Probably a little bit of both. But I felt trapped. I hadn't cultivated enough relationships in the White House to find a new job and I didn't want to remain in my increasingly frustrating position. How was I going to extricate myself from this mess?

CHAPTER 23

The White House, Part Two

M y year in the White House might have been professionally frustrating, but it was still a thrill every day to walk up to the security desk in the Old Executive Office Building (now called the Eisenhower Executive Office Building, by the way), flash my ID badge, and enter the inner sanctum of the government. In my very corny way, I gaped like Dorothy when they threw open the doors of Oz. Remember, just three years earlier, I'd been stranded on Nantucket, fielding rejection letters from the *Cape Cod Times* and *Brockton Enterprise*.

And okay, so maybe where I was working was in the very outer orbit of this inner sanctum. The words "working in the White House" have a fairly elastic meaning. Several decades of TV shows have made the West Wing synonymous with the White House, but that building is so small that most of the White House staff works in the OEOB and tells everyone they know that yes, they work in the White House.

My badge did not give me immediate access to the West Wing, but at least I didn't need to go through the laborious security rigmarole required of outside visitors. I'd just go out the back exit of the OEOB, cross a narrow driveway, and present myself 20 feet away to an entrance guard, who'd admit me after either confirming that my name was on a guest list or calling up to the office I was visiting.

I definitely wasn't a VIP, but I had errands that took me into the West Wing once or twice a week and eventually the guards got to know me well enough to wave me through. One of my jobs was to assemble a weekly compilation of the President's key quotes, which we'd circulate to the staff. This was another of my work products that people would usually throw straight into the trash as soon as it hit their inboxes, but because Brian had finally come up against someone he couldn't edit—the President—it was the least painful of my pointless responsibilities. To identify these quotes, I'd first go to the White House Press office and grab a week's worth of presidential speeches, prepared statements, and transcripts. Not to beat a dead horse, but this was before the internet or email, and the only way to track down documents from the press office or anywhere else was to get someone to put them in internal mail or walk over to get them myself. Fine with me. This gave me an excuse to visit the West Wing and pretend for even 15 minutes that I was a person of importance: yeah, this is me; no big deal; I'm just strolling around in the West Wing like it's the most ordinary thing in the world.

The West Wing is just a small, square, cramped, three-story structure with room for maybe 30 offices. I'd usually enter into the ground floor, home to just a handful of offices and the White House Mess, where I ate lunch exactly twice. Also on that floor is the Situation Room, which is about the least impressive famous room in America; it's a medium-size conference room with about six or seven screens on the wall. I had to go into it once, and it was so far removed from what I'd seen in the movies that I first thought it must be the anteroom to the *real* Situation Room hidden away in a secret bunker.

The Oval Office, the press office, the Cabinet Room, and fewer than ten small offices make up the West Wing's first floor. I couldn't wander around because the Secret Service was especially touchy about access. A secretary in the press office once asked me to deliver an envelope to Jim Baker on my way back to the OEOB. Sure! The problem was that to get to Baker's place, I had to walk past the Oval Office. The Secret Service agent at the head of the corridor allowed me to pass, but the agent stationed outside the door of "The Oval" stopped me cold even though the President wasn't there. So I had to retreat, walk down the stairs to the ground floor, cross over to the other side of the building, climb back to the first floor, and arrive at Baker's office from the opposite direction.

The Executive Office Building isn't as famous as the West Wing, but it's still plenty historic. Home to the State, War, and Navy Departments for nearly 75 years, many famous Cabinet secretaries had worked there. Brian and Bob Carlson shared a suite of two enormous and elegant adjoining rooms that had previously been the War Department's headquarters. Bob could point to a photo of former Secretary of War Howard Taft standing on the balcony outside his office acknowledging the crowds gathered on 17th Street moments after he won the Republican presidential nomination in 1908. He also told me that during the "Bonus March" of 1932—when the army had to disperse World War I veterans seeking Depression-related bonuses—his office had been used by General Douglas MacArthur and Brian's by his aide, Dwight Eisenhower. I really lapped up that kind of history trivia.

I was interested in more recent history too. President Nixon liked to escape the fishbowl of the West Wing by walking over to a so-called "hide-away" office in room 175 in the OEOB, a space that was now used by the head of the White House Office of Political Affairs. I thought that was cool whenever I walked by. Misty Church told me that her group occupied offices once used by the White House's lawyers, and that one of the speechwriters had the former office of White House Counsel John Dean, who had helped bring Nixon down. As a former Watergate junkie, I thought that was SUPER cool. The Vice President's staff also worked in the OEOB and on my fourth day on the job, I glanced in and glimpsed the Veep himself, confiding to my diary that night: "Saw George Bush in his office. Was standing there tall as can be, holding a briefcase. Gosh he looks preppy."

My own office was not very impressive: long and very narrow with remarkably tall ceilings. Given that it had a rear door into Steve's much nicer office, it had obviously served for much of its history as the waiting room for the more important executives next door. Yet, I couldn't complain—it was the first time I'd ever had an office. And as small as it was, it could attract a little attention. One day, two secret service agents came in with beeping and flashing detectors. They claimed they'd identified radio signals emitting from my office. Maybe my office was bugged by the KGB? Me? That would be completely ridiculous. They never found anything, but the incident didn't give me a lot of confidence in our counterintelligence operations.

There were several nice benefits of working on the White House payroll. My favorite was sitting in the Presidential Box at the Kennedy Center. Brian wasn't a skilled bureaucratic infighter, but one thing he was smart about was staying on the good side of the White House Social Secretary, who controlled a number of good perks, including tickets to the Presidential Box. Access to the Box was highly coveted and deployed strategically by senior administration leaders in order to curry favor with Congress, political allies, donors, and other key constituencies. But sometimes there were last-minute cancellations or even nights when no one wanted to go. In those cases, someone had to take the tickets.

Brian was on the list of people she'd call if she had a last-minute opening and he'd always accept the tickets when offered; if you declined them, you might not get asked again. If he invited me to join him, I always accepted too, for the same reason. He'd bring his wife and I'd scramble to find a female friend to be my "date," because this was definitely a couples kind of outing. And once there, we all tried to act like we really belonged.

The first time I sat in the Presidential Box was for the play *Noises Off*, a British farce staged in the Eisenhower Theatre. (FYI, there are actually three Presidential Boxes—in the Eisenhower Theatre for stage plays, the Opera House, and the Concert Hall.) You'd present yourself at the entrance to the Box and be ushered into a plush red foyer. To the left was a small room with food and drinks. As a gawking goober, I grabbed a small bottle of Presidential champagne to give to my mother later. Across the hall from the snacks room was a bathroom with the quietest toilet I've ever experienced before or since.

Moving out of that little welcome room, you'd step out into the Box itself, just underneath the first tier of the balcony. There'd be eight chairs to arrange as you saw fit and you'd have the best view in the house—not just of the stage, but of all the schmoes who had to sit down there in the orchestra.

Brian took me to the Kennedy Center two more times. Once again at the Eisenhower Theatre, we saw *Death of a Salesman*, starring Dustin Hoffman and John Malkovich, and another time, we attended a performance by the American Ballet Theatre in the Opera House. The women in our group were electrified when the lights went down and Mikhail Baryshnikov, then the Artistic Director of the ABT, slipped into the box next to us. I kept an eye on him during the performance and noticed his frequent and angry gesticulations at apparent ballerina mistakes that were completely indiscernible to me. During the intermission, Baryshnikov fled the box for some privacy and the rest of us popped another bottle of champagne and laughed and gossiped about the great dancer and his beautiful but slightly plump girlfriend. All of us except Brian, who wouldn't permit himself to enjoy anything so frivolous. He wanted to talk to me about work—did I think the Immigration section in our "President Reagan's First Three Years" report should come before or after the Welfare section? What? Are you kidding me? You want to talk about this now? I would have suggested that he have a glass of bubbly, but he didn't drink.

Holidays were another good source of perks. On the Fourth of July, I brought my Nantucket friend Mary Flannagan to the annual picnic on the South Lawn. We listened to B.J. Thomas perform "Raindrops Keep Fallin' On My Head," ate free hamburgers, hot dogs, and ice cream, and took photos of each other as we roamed the grounds. Somehow in our explorations, we unknowingly ended up sitting on the lawn furniture of the Oval Office patio before the Secret Service gently told us to hit the road.

At Christmas, I received a deluxe Christmas card from the President and First Lady, which I gave to my mother to frame and display in the house back home. White House staff were invited to attend the White House Christmas reception from 5:00 to 6:00pm on the last Sunday before Christmas. Jostling with each other to get a cup of eggnog and a piece of fruitcake or take a photo of the exquisitely tasteful decorations in the Red, Yellow, Blue, East, and State

With Mary Flanagan at the Fourth of July picnic.

With my parents at the White House Christmas party.

Dining Rooms was like being in the Louvre gallery where the Mona Lisa hangs. But when our hour was up, I felt like I'd seen it all, which was fine because leaving was one of the highlights—we exited onto the Pennsylvania Avenue side of the building, with spotlights illuminating us as we walked down the driveway. You really felt like a VIP all lit up in front of the most famous house in America.

An unofficial perk of working in the White House was being able to take a guest on a West Wing tour. If you had open access to the West Wing or knew someone who did, you could show friends and relatives around offices once the workday was over. My cultivation of Misty Church paid off during a visit from my mother and her friend. I cleared them into the OEOB at 7:00pm and Misty brought us over to the West Wing to peer into the Oval Office, the Cabinet Room, the Roosevelt Room, and the press briefing room. My mother got a kick out of being able to stand behind the podium where Larry Speakes gave his daily briefing and an even bigger kick when people in the press office said hi to me. You're never too old to want to make your mother proud.

Even though I didn't work in the West Wing, I did occasionally get to see the President—something that never failed to excite me. Occasionally, we'd get summoned to witness him signing a bill in the Rose Garden, boarding a helicopter, or welcoming a head of state. The closest I came to him physically was the going-away party for Brian's boss, Ed Harper, which took place in the Roosevelt Room, just across the hall from the Oval Office. About half-way through the party, Reagan stuck his head in the door with an impish twinkle, and entered to make a few nice farewell remarks about Harper. As he made his way towards me, I idiotically shrunk back, afraid he might talk to me and transform me into a stammering fool. But he did get close enough to convince me that either he didn't dye his hair or had an amazing colorist: some of the individual strands were white, others were brown, and a few were black. I also noticed something I'd first observed when Nixon showed up on Nantucket—people attain a heightened sense of reality when they are around a mega-celebrity like the President. When Reagan made a few mild jokes, the crowd just laughed and laughed.

If I didn't feel very important in my day-to-day job, there was the psychic perk of casually mentioning where I worked and hearing that sweet, sweet,

"Oh, really!" My dentist told me he was proud to have a White House staffer as a patient, adding that he was even bragging to his friends about it. He'd come in and start talking to me while the hygienist cleaned my teeth, confiding that we shared "the same political persuasion." He was very pro-Reagan, remarking that too many people had forgotten how terrible the Carter years had been. With my wide open mouth, I could only nod along, glad that we'd wrapped up the dental vote. I had to see a lawyer a couple of times and every time I was there, he'd quiz me extensively about the inner workings of the White House. How did the "Big Three" (Meese, Baker, and Deaver) work together? What was Ed Meese really like? Would Reagan run for re-election? "Even though my office is less than half a mile away from the White House," he explained, "people like me don't really know what's going on inside." Later, when I was ghostwriting a letter to the editor of the New York *Daily News*, I called the head of the New York State Catholic School Superintendent's Association to get some information about Latino education in New York City. I'd known him from working on tuition tax credits in Jerry Solomon's office, and he told me that I was the "most important person" he knew in Washington. All this was a reminder that as much as I complained about my day-to-day job, I was lucky to have the experience.

Being a White House staffer allowed me to rub shoulders from time to time with former, current, and future "Washington famous" personalities. Ed Meese was the highest ranking White House official that I most frequently ran into. Jim Baker derisively referred to him as the Pillsbury Dough Boy, and true, his friendly face did shine out from a pudgy head, but he was genuinely nice. He was the only top-ranking staffer I ever knew to visit the OEOB—he came over from the West Wing to attend Bob Carlson's birthday party and went around the room introducing himself to everyone there.

Then there were the two future cabinet members that I interacted with. Bill Barr, who later became Attorney General twice, worked on legal policy just across the hall from me. Although much, much skinnier in his mid-30s than he later became, he already had that perpetually unamused look he displayed as Donald Trump's Attorney General. I can't say he was very happy whenever I asked him to review a draft of a judicially focused "Issues Alert" or "Issues Update." He'd usually sit on them for a week, and when I bugged him for a response, he'd tell me to send them over to the Justice Department for their approval. Elaine Chao, who later became the second Mrs. Mitch McConnell, and even later, the Secretary of Labor, and finally, Secretary of Transportation, worked on industrial issues for OPD. I occasionally supplied her with information and even did a little writing work when she needed it, so she was much friendlier to me than Barr was.

Does being privy to White House gossip count as a perk? The juiciest concerned a high-ranking senior staffer who was rumored to be having an affair with a top aide, a woman who had moved up fast in the White House hierarchy. I first dismissed the story as straightforward maliciousness, but when I became friends with Ed Harper's secretaries, they swore it was true. In an institution that was dominated by men, the women's network was strong and the girlfriend in question was heard lamenting to the other women at lunch and in the ladies room that he wouldn't leave his wife. Janice Farrell—one of the secretaries and my best source in the West Wing—quoted her mother as saying, "In my day, the men would just give their mistresses fur coats and jewelry. Now they give them jobs."

I always worked hard to be on good terms with the secretaries where I worked. I usually got along better with them than with their hard-charging bosses. I also knew that if they liked me, they'd give me the straight story on what was happening behind the scenes. But for months, I had a hard time charming Brian's secretary, Maggie. I was replacing her fiancé, Bruce, who, as Brian's deputy, had gotten himself fired. It takes a lot to get fired in the government, but apparently Brian had given him a lot of authority and he'd messed up in a very public way, including writing over-the-top memos that got leaked to the media. Mind you, there were only five people in OPC, including Brian, Maggie, and Bruce, so why Brian needed to delegate anything to a deputy is a good question. In any event, Maggie resented me for being the beneficiary of her fiancé's bad fortune.

When Maggie quit after the wedding and Brian asked if I knew anyone who could replace her, I suggested Maria Horgan, a bright, young former colleague from Jerry Solomon's office. She didn't want to be a secretary, but Brian promised he'd upgrade the job to include professional work besides typing.

Maria was wary of any job that involved sitting outside an executive's office and answering phones, but, like me, she reasoned that being in the White House would be an adventure and maybe a good chance to meet influential people. This turned out to be a good bet: she eventually worked three years in the West Wing and another three as head of public liaison in a federal agency. But I still felt guilty when, about a month into the job, she told me fiercely, "He treats me like a dog. He just walks by my desk, throws a paper on my desk and doesn't even tell me what he wants me to do with it." Nevertheless, as bad as I felt for convincing her to take what turned out to be a lousy job, I was still glad she was there. Finally, I had a normal person to confide in—someone who could grasp just how crazy the whole place was. And she looked out for my interests too, trying to fix me up with some of the other secretaries and planning my semi-surprise 30th birthday party in the office. For about two years, until she got married and had new priorities, she was practically my best friend.

As 1984 approached, the President's re-election campaign committee, known as Reagan-Bush '84, seemed like a possible avenue of escape. Lawrence had met Jim Pinkerton, who later became a well-known policy analyst and political columnist; in 1984, he was an all-purpose assistant to Deputy Campaign Director Lee Atwater. Lawrence arranged for us to chat, after which I sent Jim some writing samples. We hit it off but nothing came of it.

An even better contact fell into my lap when John Kostas, my replacement in Jerry Solomon's office, asked if I knew of an open apartment that was available to rent. His former colleague in the Lew Lehrman for New York Governor campaign had been hired as the deputy press secretary for Reagan-Bush '84 and needed a place to live. As a matter of fact, I did. A year earlier, I had moved out of the Cairo apartment building into Jim Robinson's condo complex at New Hampshire Avenue and R Street, and because he had subsequently taken off for California, I had become the de facto property manager of his condo—a unit that happened to be empty at that very moment.

Jim's new tenant turned out to be John Buckley, a nephew of both *National Review* founder William F. Buckley and former New York Senator

James Buckley. He was by far the coolest friend I ever had and his stories were vicarious glimpses into a more exalted Washington existence than mine. Not only was he a member of conservatism's royal family, he was a former punk rock critic for the *Village Voice* and an aspiring novelist who got up every morning at 5:00am to write. He'd already completed SIX unpublished novels. He owned a first edition of James Joyce's *Ulysses*, which I gazed upon in awe, as if it were the finger bone of a medieval saint. He discoursed knowledgeably about Proust's *In Search of Lost Time* being the greatest novel ever written, which would have seemed pretentious coming from anyone else. He could talk about these things without rubbing you the wrong way because he was modest about his personal advantages and self-aware enough to pass along information without sounding boastful.

John lived two floors above me and was new to the city, so I knew him before he became well-known enough to be profiled in the *New York Times* and *New Yorker* as the GOP's hot young press secretary. I'd lend him my vacuum cleaner, he'd pick up my *Washington Post*'s when I was away for the weekend, we'd go out for pizza every once in a while, and when I wanted to see a foreign or indie movie like the French film *Danton* or the Talking Heads' concert movie *Stop Making Sense*, he'd sometimes accompany me.

On the night Reagan officially announced he was running for re-election, John got me in by giving me a pair of press passes for the gala party at the Mayflower Hotel. I took Daisy Drake, another friend from Jerry Solomon's office, and we explored the room looking for political VIPs, listened to the jazz musician Lionel Hampton and his band, and waited until 11:00pm, when Reagan appeared to say the magic words. I ran into one of the women that Maria was trying to fix me up with and she introduced me to her very proprietary date, Marlon Fitz-something, a dumpy, overweight guy who didn't want to waste an unnecessary minute talking to us. The next day, I looked him up in the White House directory and saw that it was Marlon Fitzwater, Larry Speakes' deputy press secretary. There was no way I was going to compete with that.

John Buckley also took my resume over to the campaign and advocated for me, but in the end, it was Brian who got me out of the White House, after all. Sometime around November, he'd reconnected with Ken Khachigian, who had run the speechwriting office when Reagan first became president in 1981, writing the first Inaugural Address. Wanting to return to his lucrative legal/communications practice, he'd left the White House after a year or two, but now Reagan wanted him back for the campaign. Ken, in turn, wanted Brian to join him.

For months, I heard about this arrangement—first it was on, then it was off because of the usual bureaucratic resistance within the White House to ceding any important communications functions to the campaign. Ken was particularly at odds with Reagan's pollster, Richard Wirthlin, over who was going to control the messaging. After some pushing and pulling, Brian told me that it was finally on for real. He was leaving the White House to work with Ken at the campaign and I was going to be his first recruit.

I wasn't sure I wanted to go. After all, if he was the main reason I was unhappy at the White House, would it really make sense to go someplace else with him? But what would my future be like if I stayed? I wasn't sure that OPC would survive without him since Ed Meese was leaving to become Attorney General.

In mid-March, Ken came to the White House to finalize the last details of his job and, wanting to be sure I'd fit on his team, asked to see me. He didn't know anything about me but I knew all about him. Still less than 40 years old, he'd already worked in Nixon's press office and along with Diane Sawyer, been among the small handful of White House aides who'd boarded the plane with the disgraced ex-president as he flew into exile in San Clemente. He'd ghost-written Nixon's memoirs and still lived in San Clemente, where he'd built a successful consultancy business among the palm trees and ocean mist. I'd first heard his name a few years earlier, when he'd interviewed Jim Robinson for a White House speechwriter job. He'd hired Ben Elliott instead, but had subsequently recommended Jim, the runner-up, to his fellow Armenian-American, Governor George Deukmajian, which is how Jim ended up in California.

Ken later told me I'd seemed surprisingly diffident during our interview, which was true because of my reluctance to be Brian's slave-boy at another job. When Brian slipped out of the room for a minute, I asked, "Will I be able to work directly with you?" "Absolutely," he said, clinching the deal. The job, he explained, was to prepare opposition research and issues papers about the Democratic candidate. "I think this will be the most important job in the campaign and we're already far behind where we should be." "Far behind" I could believe—the election was just seven months away. The "most important job in the campaign" was more of a stretch, but I admired his enthusiasm.

I never did make an affirmative decision to leave—Brian was telling so many people I was going with him that it became a fait accompli. My friends in the West Wing heard about my pending departure when Brain's wife called and asked for a meeting with Jack Svahn, the new head of OPD, because she wanted to interview for "Gary Holmes' job." I'd never heard her venture a political opinion and when I asked Brian about this very strange request, he said he'd had no idea she was going to do that—an assertion that, as I wrote in my diary, was "pure horseshit."

The next day, Brian went over to the campaign for an organizational meeting. He called me at home that night to say that Lee Atwater had commented that, "Everyone seems to like Gary Holmes." It was hard to believe he knew my name and I assumed that it had been Jim Pinkerton and John Buckley who had put in the good word for me. By now, there was no chance of me backing out.

Maria was pretty mad that I was abandoning her but she still helped plan a nice farewell party for Brian and me, where various OPD staff said nice things to me. Better late than never, I guess.

My last official day as a White House employee was Sunday, April 1st, 1984. I woke up with a bad stomach flu. But I'd agreed to meet Brian in the OEOB at 10:30am to help him clean out his office. I went in, as promised, and packed what I could, but after being there alone for two hours, I called him at home to find out where he was. Oh, he wouldn't be there for ANOTHER two hours. Thoroughly pissed off by this last act of passive aggressive inconsideration, I retired to his couch, shivering under my winter coat to take a nap. At this point, it hurt to even move. When he arrived, he didn't acknowledge that I was sick and didn't exactly rush as I watched him sort through what he wanted to take or leave behind. Finally, at 5:30pm, we packed everything into our two cars and drove to the campaign headquarters, which was empty except for Jim Pinkerton. We dumped the boxes in Brian's new offices and I raced home, where I ate a bagel for dinner and went to bed at 7:30pm.

The next day, I had to return to the OEOB to pick up some additional papers from Maria. Just like that, I was a nobody again. The guard was unsmiling and my ID no longer worked. She had to sign me in like I was any stranger off the street. My White House days were over.

CHAPTER 24

Reagan-Bush '84

f I was looking for the typical presidential campaign experience, complete with a frantic cheek-to-jowl, roll-up-the-sleeves, shoestring-budget workplace, Reagan-Bush '84 was not the place to find it. Blessed with an uncontested path to the nomination, a booming economy, and a big lead in the polls, the organization that I joined in early March 1984 lacked urgency. The headquarters could have easily been mistaken for the head office of a mid-size insurance agency. When Brian and I arrived just seven months before election day, the staff was still only half fleshed out. The building had plenty of empty offices and many of those who did claim a desk didn't seem to be over-exerting themselves. John Buckley confirmed what my eyes told me: "There's a lot of dead wood," including more than a few big names with big titles who didn't contribute much.

The vibe itself was weirdly, soullessly corporate. Located on Capitol Hill, across the street from a Hyatt and around the corner from the famous Irish pub, the Dubliner, we found ourselves in a quasi-luxurious but extremely generic office building owned by the National Association of Counties (NACo), a quintessential low-key trade organization that lobbies for God knows what. Instead of the crammed, cluttered, and chaotic atmosphere I'd expected, I found it sleek, serene, and civilized.

Even in 1984, "opposition research" had a bad reputation for dirty tricks, and our boss Ken Khachigian told us to avoid the phrase—we were the Issues and Research team. We wouldn't be doing original research, though. The Republican National Committee (RNC) would pull together a team led by Mike Bayer, a gung-ho retired army colonel, to identify and catalog 75,000 "quotes and votes" by the likely Democratic nominee, Walter Mondale. We'd exploit that information to expose Mondale as a far-left prisoner of special interests and muddled academics.

We'd sometimes received support from a hardcore political research group that reported up to Lee Atwater. This team was headed by Gary Maloney, a political junkie and arguably the hardest working person at the campaign, who nevertheless found time to proselytize for Bruce Springsteen, going so far as to record, unprompted by me, the "Born in the USA" album onto a cassette tape so I could learn to appreciate its greatness. Which I did. And ironically, to Springsteen's lasting annoyance, the album's title track, a protest song about the despair of a Vietnam veteran, would become an unofficial anthem for Reagan-era defiance, optimism, and triumphalism.

Brian and I quickly jumped into things. The first order of business was to join the daily "Attack Meeting" chaired by Lyn Nofziger, who had been with Reagan from the very beginning in 1966. He sported a goatee and a Mickey Mouse tie to show he didn't take anything too seriously. I was impressed to be in the presence of such a politics-famous person. His co-chair was the lean and hungry looking Vic Gold, who, despite being a speechwriter for the moderate George H.W. Bush, brandished an equally impressive conservative pedigree stretching back to 1964, when he served as the presidential campaign press secretary for Barry Goldwater. In contrast to Nofiziger's disheveled lethargy, I came to prefer Gold's approach, if only because his increasingly vehement and white-hot diatribes against the biased media were so entertaining. In one epic rant, he bitterly complained that the *Washington Post* was so populated with left-wing ideologues that no section of the paper was free from cant, not even the weather page! We all laughed because it was so true.

The "Attack Meeting" started every morning at 7:30am with about a dozen youngish, aggressive white guys and a handful of less caffeinated white women sitting around a conference table, spit balling ways to hit the Democrats and their plans to subvert the American way of life. This was better than morning yoga at centering us and discharging our collective bile, but I quickly came to see why Nofziger had not been named White House press secretary—he hardly ever followed through on our ideas and even Gold eventually labeled him "incompetent."

Someone who was *not* incompetent was our boss, who quickly earned our team's complete and undying loyalty. With a Groucho Marx moustache and gray-flecked black hair, Ken was a decade older than us, funny and acerbic, finely attuned to our emotional needs. Because he had the President's ear, we knew he was truly important, not self-important like so many others at the campaign. Unfortunately, he was splitting his time between Washington and his home in San Clemente. When he was in the office, it was a demanding but normal work environment. He'd hand out assignments that made sense, review our work quickly, and make changes that improved it. But once he got back on the plane to California, we were vulnerable to make-work assignments.

My first real assignment was a crucial one—to fact-check the first round of 18 television ads from the campaign's advertising team led by Doug Watts, a friend of Ken's from California politics. This group was called the Tuesday Team because they met on Tuesdays, and it included some of the most successful advertising executives in the country, including BBDO's Phil Dusenberry, who, back in New York, was coincidentally my elementary school friend Rich Martel's boss.

Because of my experience in the White House, I knew where to find the information they needed. These ads, including the famous "It's morning again in America" spot, were some of the most successful political commercials ever produced, and I had to either confirm or fill in the data points ("With interest rates at about half the record highs of 1980, nearly 2,000 today will buy new homes, more than at any time in the past four years. This afternoon, 6,500 young men and women will be married...") This was grunt work, but I was thrilled to do it. But even as I was doing this real work, Brian insisted that we write a dozen of our own competing ads; he then directed me to fact-check our copy too. For some reason, he thought that we could dream up better TV commercials than the ones produced by the decade's leading ad agencies. It was madness.

Yet I have to give Brian credit for one immensely important thing—he recruited an unusually talented and diverse research team. At no time in my entire career have I ever felt as sympatico and close to a group of colleagues as I did to these folks. It helped that we knew we'd only be there for seven months and wouldn't be competing for promotions, praise, and perks. It was like being in a limited-run theatrical production—we were involved in an intense, exhausting shared experience that had a firm end date, after which we would all move on.

Our team was anchored by a pair of well-connected, smart, and down-to-earth women—Sheila Dixon and Linda Holwick—who also happened to be blonde and beautiful. In an organization as alpha-male as Reagan-Bush '84, their glamour and intelligence added immensely to the credibility of our group. If women like that took us seriously, we must be okay.

Sheila was only a couple of years older than I was but much more sophisticated, and the erect, purposeful way she strode down the hall captured everyone's attention. Even Lee Atwater, who already had a wife at home and a girlfriend at the campaign—and who, in an organization that also employed Roger Stone and Paul Manafort, still managed to be the chief sleaze—came sniffing around. He tried to impress her with a birthday gift of Gore Vidal's *Lincoln*, which came inscribed with the prediction that they'd both make a lot of money after the campaign. She'd previously worked in the White House press operation and had seen enough of this behavior to be unimpressed. She eventually became Ken's de facto deputy and confidante and was given the job of managing editor for our "Attack Book" of damaging Mondale quotes.

For her part, Linda had an uncanny strategic intelligence for someone in her late 20s. Brian had recruited her from the press office in the Office of Management and Budget, an unlikely launching pad for someone as wired-in as she was. Ken Adelman, the chief U.S. arms control negotiator, was a good friend and she arranged for him to brief a few members of our team. On another occasion, I asked her why supply-siders believed that inflation caused unemployment, and she immediately telephoned her other good friend, Jude Wanniski, the popularizer of the phrase "supply-side economics," who gave me a ten-minute lecture on the subject. She was unflappable where I was excitable. Whenever I barged into Sheila and Linda's office outraged by something that Mondale said, they'd laugh at my high dudgeon and Linda would calmly elaborate on why Mondale's comment was even more offensive than I'd realized.

Brian had also recruited two other guys besides me. Arnold Tompkins, one of the few Black Republicans on the campaign, was a Vietnam Vet who told us harrowing stories about his experience in the war. A pragmatic Republican and a small-time entrepreneur who sold political pins on the side, he joined us from the Department of Health and Human Services policy office. Our final policy analyst was Spencer Warren, a frank elitist from the Upper East Side of Manhattan, who seemingly had stepped out of a time machine from another decade. He favored opera, classical music, 1940s Hollywood movies, and the 1950s New York Yankees, opposed many of the GOP's déclassé issues, like its support for guns, and was even more prone to launching into rants about the perfidies of the Democrats than I was.

"Ken's Angles." Ken Khachigian with Sally, Sheila, and Linda.

Our initial team was rounded out by our secretary Sally Campbell, a no-nonsense 24 year old from South Carolina with White House experience, who quickly learned to delight Ken with her sass and hard work.

Ken made sure we got settled into prime real estate on the same floor as the campaign leadership, in modernist two-person glassed-in offices. Linda and Arnold were put in charge of assembling the most devastating quotes by and about Mondale into a book that would be distributed to the campaign's attack dog surrogates. Spencer and I were to write a series of 6–8 page research papers that hit Mondale and the Democrats on specific policy issues such as education, agriculture, and the budget deficit. We were to stress the dangers of big government, the "Nanny State," over-regulation, and special interests. According to Ken, these would form the intellectual foundation of the campaign.

Writing the papers was hard enough, but fact-checking was almost harder. Every fact, vote, and quote we received from the RNC needed to be backed up with xeroxes of the news articles where the quotes had appeared. When the RNC delayed in providing the hard copies, several of us went over there to find out why. It turned out that, while the quotes themselves were computerized, the original sources were filed away in rows of filing cabinets. What a mess. It took us days to find and recopy every story for our files. It seems quaint now that we were so meticulous about fact-checking campaign claims, but we all believed it was essential to be accurate. (Not that it did us any good. When Reagan unloaded some of our research during campaign speeches—such as Mondale's claim that he was "proud" to raise taxes on his own constituents—the media denounced him for making this up, never caring that I had a file in my office that proved he really said it.)

We finally finished these papers in early July. They had to be delivered to the campaign leadership on the Monday that the Democratic National Convention started. Knowing they were in good shape, Ken gave them his final approval and left to return to California. As soon as he landed on the West Coast, Brian emerged from his office with extensive changes for every paper. I was fuming, having gone through this now for two years. Not only was he making the prose more turgid, he was also adding quotes that we wouldn't be able to fact-check before the book was due Monday morning.

I was even more furious when I returned that Monday and discovered that Sheila had been forced to work on this until 11:00pm Saturday night. I was ashamed of myself for not hanging around to help and astounded that Brian had made her stay so late. Ken had explicitly said that she should take it easy that weekend because she was both recovering from an illness and scheduled for the grueling job of monitoring the Democratic Convention proceedings next week and writing a nightly summary to deliver to Ed Rollins every morning.

I never complained directly to Ken, but I think he knew we were frustrated. One day, I came home late from the office and found a handwritten letter from him in my mail. Out of the blue, on his flight back to California, he'd written: "Dear Gary, I'm sorry that these last trips have not allowed me more time to spend with you, but I wanted to know how much I appreciate the energy—and long hours you are putting in the campaign. You clearly exhibit the discipline and capacity for clear-sighted research and crisp writing. Thanks for all the effort. It's going to pay off." I assumed that Sheila, knowing how annoyed I was about non-essential make-work projects in the office, had put him up to this. It was an obvious ploy to raise my morale—and it worked! He'd guessed correctly that my emotions and sense of loyalty could easily be bought with a little flattery.

By the time summer rolled around, we were working much harder. I arrived at the office every day at 7:00am and didn't leave for 12 hours, when our daily 6:30pm staff meeting concluded. And it wasn't unusual to work until 10:00 or 11:00pm. Some nights, I'd drive John Buckley home and he'd tell me office gossip, more than once expressing his admiration for Ken, who, he said, had a soothing, calming presence in senior staff meetings.

Getting up so early sometimes left me sleepy after lunch and I'd take a quick nap, turning my chair to face the outside window so my back was to the glass wall. This supposedly would make people think I was reading or contemplating, which worked fine until the day Jim Pinkerton showed up in my office with a delegation from the Canadian Conservative Party who wanted to know about opposition research. I tried to fake it but I'm sure they knew they'd discovered me conked out.

In addition to the 12-hour days, I worked every Saturday. I even came in on the Fourth of July, our one day off that summer. I woke up feeling patriotic and decided that the most important thing I could do for my country was to go into the office and work. Spencer and I were the only ones in the building, but I was happy to be there. I left mid-afternoon for a barbeque in Virginia with my old friends in Congressman Jerry Solomon's office, who roasted me for what they perceived as the defensiveness of the Reagan campaign and our willingness to let Mondale set the agenda.

They were right. We were defensive and the White House leadership was the problem. The campaign, and our group in particular, was much more aggressive and ideological than they were. We wanted to fight hard on the issues to achieve a mandate for a conservative second term. But White House Chief of Staff Jim Baker and his gnomish, power-mad deputy Dick Darman who we called "Darman Vader," disdained right-wing ideologues and pushed for a bland, don't-make-waves strategy.

This came to a head in early August when the White House and campaign agreed that Vice President Bush would hold a press conference to denounce Mondale as a tax addict. It's hard now to remember how significantly the budget deficit loomed over policy discussions for nearly 40 years. Citing the deficit at his convention in San Francisco, Mondale had promised to raise taxes to close the budget gap, claiming that Reagan would do the same but just wouldn't admit it. So seriously was the deficit taken as a looming financial catastrophe that Mondale somehow believed a pledge to reduce it via higher taxes was a political plus.

This press conference was the opportunity we'd been looking for. Based on Mondale's extensive record as a Big Government junkie, we drafted a tough statement for the Veep and looked forward to the thrashing Bush would give him. But at 2:00pm, Jim Pinkerton came by and showed us the statement that Darman had substituted for ours. We all hit the roof when we saw how mushy and vague it was. And as if the statement itself wasn't bad enough, Bush's performance in the press conference was even worse. When asked how Reagan would reduce the budget deficit without raising taxes, he said the

286

administration would consider some sort of "revenue increases." Huh? "Any President would keep options open," he said. "Conditions can dramatically change one way or the other." Democrats had a field day, given that earlier that very morning, the President himself had promised not to raise taxes. Mondale now said that there should be a debate between Reagan and Bush, adding, "And I'll pay for the microphone." Great line, damn it.

The next day, Ken came back from the White House and said Bush was "chagrined" at the episode. But Bush really did believe that Reagan practiced "voodoo economics" and never did learn his lesson. When he got his own chance to be the decider, he first promised, "Read my lips. No new taxes," but then signed a bill to raise them, thereby sinking his one-term presidency. And who convinced him to renege on his pledge? His Budget Director, who, lo and behold, happened to be none other than Dick Darman.

After Bush's debacle of a press conference, Ed Rollins asked us to prepare a document on Mondale's spending promises to quantify how they would result in higher taxes. Brian took control of the process, basing his analysis on a detailed story in the *Wall Street Journal* about a theoretical Mondale budget. Then he added spending projections that seemed dubious even to me, especially when I had to fact-check them. From my perspective, he was using the wrong baseline—a 1985 projected budget, but projecting it out to 1988. I argued unsuccessfully against using these numbers and they stayed in.

I was surprised that the campaign, the White House, and the whole Administration would base its entire budget-busting, big-spending attack on an analysis that Brian had assembled in one morning. We labored over that document for almost a month, trying desperately to find the backup to justify the projections. One thing we never did was run it by a think tank, economist, anti-tax lobbying organization, or any other kind of expert to make sure we were in the ballpark. Nope, Brian and his calculator were all we needed.

I was afraid we'd be exposed as shallow thinkers and my anxiety went up a notch when, after sitting on it for a week, the White House panicked over Labor Day weekend, suddenly nervous that we were losing on this issue, and decided that Treasury Secretary Don Regan should use Brian's analysis to blast Mondale. This resulted in a huge scramble to find Regan; apparently the United States Secretary of the Treasury was unreachable most of the weekend, or maybe he was just not answering his phone. In any event, when he did resurface and saw the statement, neither he nor his staff ever asked to see the supporting assumptions.

Regan held his press conference the day after Labor Day and charged that by 1988, Mondale would raise the average tax bill by $3,300, more than twice as high as we'd been claiming before then. This was Brian's greatest triumph in the campaign, and you know what? I'd been naïve about the whole thing. No one in the media, the Mondale campaign, the pundit community, or anyone else of importance ever asked how we derived that $3,300 projection. Apparently in a presidential campaign, no one takes any issues attack very seriously.

By early July, we'd completed our core assignments—the anti-Mondale "quote and vote" book for surrogates and the book of anti-Mondale issues papers for the speechwriters—but the pace only picked up. Mondale was so far behind in the polls that he resorted to the then-high-stakes gamble of selecting a woman, any woman, to be his running mate. After a drawn-out search, he settled on Geraldine Ferraro, an obscure three-term New York Representative. Her resume was about as short as Sarah Palin's when John McCain attempted a similar "Hail Mary" 24 years later, but unlike the media scorn heaped on Palin, the media fell in love with Ferraro, even though she was a party hack at best.

We immediately set out to write an anti-Ferraro briefing book using the public sources, but there wasn't much to pull from. She had a particularly undistinguished record in Congress and there weren't many news stories with the kind of embarrassing quotes that politicians usually make when they don't think they'll be running for Vice President one day. We cobbled together the standard high-tax-and-big-spending arguments that would apply to any liberal Representative from New York City and waited for someone that inexperienced to self-destruct. Which is exactly what she did. It eventually became known that her parents had been connected to organized crime. The media also realized that she and her real estate developer husband were rich, lived in a mansion, and had vacation homes in the Hamptons and St. Croix; they were even richer than George and Barbara Bush, who the media lampooned as out of touch elitists. Then, it turned out that her husband was a landlord to the mob, which was, among other things, running a porn distribution center in one of his buildings. And she made some bad rookie mistakes too, such as saying that Reagan was a "bad Christian," which went down poorly among people who thought religion should be out of bounds in a presidential campaign.

These revelations had a lot more impact on her reputation than our dry policy analyses. Most of this information had been dug up by the super-secret detective work of Ed Rollins' aide, John Roberts (definitely not the future Chief Justice). I did make an extremely minor contribution, however, when he came to me one day and asked for information about her husband's company and his related dummy corporations. I looked through our clips and identified about ten of them. I hope that helped!

By this time, our team had become an all-purpose repository for information on Mondale, Ferraro, and public policy. After every Mondale or Ferraro speech, we'd write surrogate responses, and if a member of the campaign was appearing on one of the Sunday shows, we'd produce talking points. The surrogates almost always failed to make the attacks land as effectively as they could have. It took me a long time to understand our problem: we assumed they understood and cared about policy as much as we did—or at all. I guess it was asking a lot to expect them to read even a one-page memo so they could educate themselves on an issue. We'd have been better off if we'd just sent them one or two sentences with a note that said, "Just say this and keep your mouth shut after that."

In the end, for all the reports, statements, and analyses we wrote, our most important job was to provide Ken with moral support and fact-checking. He was the President's speechwriter and the words that came out of Reagan's mouth were far and away the most important part of the campaign. In the month leading up to the GOP convention, he was writing Reagan's acceptance speech, making it ideological and focused on issues, not platitudes. We were feeding him ideas, facts, and quotes, which he smiled at benignly and even occasionally included.

The biggest perk of the campaign is that we'd all get to go to Dallas for the convention, which took place the third week of August. On the plane ride down, Sheila, Linda, and I made ourselves a tiny bit obnoxious when we sat together and sang the theme songs of old TV shows. We then continued this display on the bus ride to the hotel, switching over to show tunes. Oh, those wild Issues and Research analysts!

Dallas was a blast for everyone except Brian, who pitched a FIT when he learned that Roger Bolton's team, who had the actual responsibility of writing and coordinating the statements for our surrogate spokespeople, would be vetting and revising the speeches from the other convention speakers. (By the way, although I didn't know it at the time, Roger would eventually shape my career as profoundly as Jim Robinson did.) I suppose I should have felt worse about being unproductive in Dallas, but I'd never been to a presidential convention and was glad that Roger's guys were stuck with that unrewarding job. I didn't want to be in a boiler room for 14 hours a day, fighting with egomaniac speechwriters about every edit being made to the beautiful prose they'd ghostwritten for their principals. We eventually did get an assignment—to monitor the news coverage throughout the day and produce frequent updates to let the top brass know how the convention was playing on TV. This seemed kind of pointless, but at least it justified us being there. And unless you had the 6:00am shift, it wasn't so bad.

We had plenty of time to have fun. Sunday morning we all ended up in the swimming pool, which introduced me to a way of living that included having a deck bar to swim to, order a pina colada from, and charge it to your room. Later that day, Spencer made reservations at the swanky Mansion on Turtle Creek, where we had a blow-out brunch with Linda, Sheila, a new member of our team named Bill Huroda, my old White House friend Misty Church, who had just escaped a short, unhappy stint as Maureen Reagan's advance person, and a guy who worked for Reagan's favorite pollster, Dick Wirthlin. I don't remember who invited him, but the two of us got into an argument when he said that my favorite Congressman, Jack Kemp, needed to "moderate his views" if he wanted to succeed in 1988. No, no, no, I argued— you've got to shape public opinion, not follow it.

And then, fresh off of gorging ourselves at that extravagant $30-a-head brunch, Linda announced that she'd been invited to the Black Republicans party at South Fork, which was the real-life external set for the TV show

Dallas. So off we headed with Arnold, Sally, and Misty. After ribs and pulled pork, Misty and I took a cab to the Dallas World Trade Center for a reception for foreign diplomats, which was as boring as it sounds. I didn't get back to the hotel room I was sharing with Spencer until after midnight. I was dead tired, but in true Spencer form, he wanted to ruminate about an interesting but esoteric subject in political history; that night it was the weird co-dependent relationship between Richard Nixon and J. Edgar Hoover. We didn't turn the lights out until 1:30am. It was like an eighth grade sleepover, but with Scotch and presidential trivia.

The whole week went like that—racing around from party to party and eating meals at a famous rib joint one day and a famous chili house the next. To make it even more fun, Jim Robinson was there. He'd written the speech that his boss, California governor George Deukmajian, was delivering to re-nominate George Bush as Vice President. He didn't have much more to do than I did, so one afternoon, he commandeered the huge van that the state was renting for the governor and the two of us drove downtown to Dealey Plaza to see where JFK had been shot. This was a surprisingly emotional

At the entrance to Southfork in Dallas.

experience, especially when we turned around and looked back at the Book Depository. Switching from hyper-reality to fantasy, we then drove back to South Fork and walked around like tourists. This was a half ironic/half serious pop culture pilgrimage. Jim had turned me on to *Dallas* way back when I lived on Nantucket, and after each episode, we always called each other to discuss the amusingly ridiculous plot twists.

The highlight of the week was Reagan's Thursday night acceptance speech. Spencer and I went together to the convention center, which, when we arrived at 8:45pm, was throbbing with anticipation. We didn't have passes for the convention floor, and there were no seats anyway, so we stood on a wide runway in front of the glassed-in CNN booth. Noticing Diane Sawyer, Ken's old colleague from the Nixon years and now an ABC correspondent, standing about ten feet away from us, Spencer ambled over to talk to her and drop Ken's name. I was too shy to join him but was amazed at how tall, railthin, and movie star-glamorous she looked in her dazzling white pantsuit. When Spencer returned, he said she'd confirmed that Ken was "lovely" and "one of [her] favorite people."

As much as I looked forward to Reagan's speech, I was even more excited about the introduction. The Tuesday Team had produced an 18-minute video that drew heavily on their "Morning in America" theme. Video introductions are now standard at political conventions, but this was a startling innovation in 1984. I'd previously watched it in the press relations boiler room two days earlier when John Buckley had screened it for *New York* magazine's Michael Kramer, while a dozen of us crowded to watch it over his shoulder. The climax of this introduction was Reagan speaking in Normandy on the 40th anniversary of D-Day: "These are the boys of Pointe du Hoc. These are the men who took the cliffs. These are the champions who helped free a continent. These are the heroes who helped end a war." Most of us in the press room had cried when we first saw it and the impact was almost as significant in the convention center. I was staring in at the CNN correspondents and producers and even those cynics were spellbound.

And then out came Reagan to an explosion of applause and cheers, delivering Ken's speech, with its soaring rhetoric, jabs at an unnamed "my opponent," vivid word pictures, and anecdotes of the American dream come to life. It also put a stake in the ground on a wide range of issues. On taxes, for example, he said, "Our opponents are openly committed to increasing your tax burden. We are committed to stopping them and we will. Our tax policies are and will remain pro-work, pro-growth, and pro-family." I was glad to have that on the record.

I was thrilled with the whole speech but noticed one rhetorical miscalculation. The remarks built to an extended climactic image of the 1984 Olympic torch being carried across the vast expanse of the United States in one long relay. On paper, the text was extraordinarily beautiful as it evoked, by name and image, the small towns, big cities, and natural beauties through which the torch had been carried. Unfortunately, as each location was mentioned, its state delegation would cheer—something that no one had anticipated—which threw off Reagan's rhythm and spoiled the effect. Huh. The law of unintended consequences even applies to oratory.

But this was a minor complaint. The speech was well received and sent the euphoric delegates home with their blood pulsing. From my perspective, its real strength was that it grappled with the issues and framed the election as a contest between two different political philosophies.

Not everyone agreed this was a good thing. Three days later on Sunday morning, Ken called me at home to get Sally's number and lament a Marty Schram piece in the *Washington Post* that said senior White House aides were concerned about the "harsh partisan tone" of the convention speeches. Schram claimed, without even checking with Ken, that he had supervised the rewriting of all the speeches at the campaign to make them more hard hitting and partisan. "I can't believe my Svengali-like reputation," he marveled. This was ridiculous. As I'd seen with my own eyes, Roger Bolton's team had reviewed all the speeches; Ken had his hands full just shepherding the President's speech through the approval process and was in no position to worry about anyone else.

Remarkably, this drumbeat kept up. David Broder, the *Post*'s top political reporter, produced a couple of follow-up stories about White House aides objecting to Reagan's partisan rhetoric. We assumed that Dick Darman and Richard Wirthlin were the source of these complaints, especially after one of the reporters on *Washington Week in Review* said Wirthlin had told him the speeches were too harsh. Why Jim Baker would allow this to continue I never could understand because it made the President himself look bad. It also started a narrative, picked up by the *New York Times* and other mainstream newspapers, that Reagan's increasingly "mean" tone would tarnish his nice guy image. I'm pretty sure the real goal of these stories was to catch the eye of Nancy Reagan, who was fiercely protective of her husband's image and was known to squash staff that didn't serve him well. If so, it didn't work; Ken was solid with the First Lady because she knew he was unstintingly loyal to the Reagans and not a careerist like Darman.

What helped the most was that Reagan got a solid "bounce" out of the convention, and that, over the course of the last month, his lead over Mondale in the polls had increased from eight to 21 percentage points. The messaging was finally working just fine, thank you. Why mess with success?

CHAPTER 25

Fritzbusters

When we returned from a successful convention in Dallas, the reward for the entire 200-person, Reagan-Bush headquarters staff was a trip to the White House. I'd been there before for the annual Christmas party, but this was better—not as crowded and less frenetic. We had the run of the first floor and were treated to a nice spread of high-end appetizers and good liquor, which really set the tone.

We milled around for an hour with most of us pinching ourselves that we were really there before we congregated in the East Room so the President, Vice President Bush, and the First Lady could enter to our sustained and enthusiastic applause. Reagan, looking waxy from all the makeup, vocalized a canned speech containing some of the same old jokes I'd heard before. Then we all lined up to shake hands and have our pictures taken with all three.

"I work for Ken Khachigian," I said when I came face-to-face with the President, hoping it would be a good conversation starter. "Hey," he replied, meaning, I think, "good for you." Well, I mused, that's probably the lamest exchange anyone's ever had within these walls. But for what it's worth, when our group compared notes later, everyone else admitted to being similarly flummoxed when they met him. All except for Spencer, who conversed without inhibitions about classic Hollywood movie composers and handed the President an LP of the Max Steiner-composed soundtrack to his 1941 movie *Dark Victory*. (Reagan later sent Spencer a one-page handwritten thank you letter reminiscing about the making of the movie. He might as well have just mailed a $10,000 check because that's what the letter turned out to be worth.)

I didn't mind the stepped-up pace and intensity that accompanied our return from Dallas because I was having so much fun at work. Earlier that spring, Linda had come across the song "I'm Proud to be An American," which was not yet the ubiquitous go-to anthem for Republicans that it has

Meeting the President and First Lady at our White House reception.

since become, and whenever we needed a boost, we'd play it and kiddingly—but not really—stand up and salute during the chorus.

Mondale's nickname was Fritz, so we started calling ourselves the "Fritzbusters." An enterprising t-shirt entrepreneur had appropriated the *Ghostbusters* logo from the movie poster and substituted a Mondale caricature where the ghost's head should be, thus creating the perfect team-bonding uniform. All of us except the humorless Brian bought them and would occasionally wear them in the office when things got too serious.

Ken's 40th birthday arrived that fall and we celebrated it with a team party at Linda's apartment in Virginia. We made Mexican food and whoever mixed the margaritas had a heavy hand, because we all lost our inhibitions very fast. We gave Ken a bottle of expensive Scotch and his own Fritzbusters t-shirt. Then we all donned ours and Linda and I handed out parody lyrics we'd written that morning for a song that would anoint Ken as the leading

I still have my Fritzbusters t-shirt.

Fritzbuster. This was the key refrain, sung to the tune of "There's No Business Like Show Business":

There's no busters like Fritz Busters, There's no Busters we know
Everything about Fritz is obnoxious, Everything he says just
makes us sick
He tries to scare our mothers and our fathers, and our
grandmothers too.

There's no Buster like our Buster, Ken smacks liberals around
Even though he's virtually over the hill, he still likes to kill,
can't get his fill
He'll kick him, stomp him, chew him, spit him out on the grass
His job is to kick ass.

And okay, so neither Linda nor I went on to a career writing song parodies for *Mad* magazine, but it was hilarious at the time, especially by about the third time we sang it and finally got it right.

As if that wasn't enough, we proceeded to boisterously belt out "I'm Proud To Be An American." When we came to the line, "And I'd proudly stand up next to her and defend her still today," we all leapt to our feet and sang even more vehemently. Jim Strock, a recent addition to our team, had innocently brought a date with no previous exposure to any of us, and I'm sure she thought she'd stumbled into a secret cell of neo-Nazis. But for once, I didn't care what a stranger thought, because I was as intoxicated by the camaraderie as I was by the tequila.

You wouldn't have guessed it at first sight, but the serious and intense Ken Khachigian—advisor to presidents, defender of traditional values, buttoned-up corporate consultant—was actually a bit of a party boy. He wasn't the gross, girl-chasing frat type I'd found on Capitol Hill, but he did like to have fun, tell a few stories, laugh at our jokes, have a drink or two, and profanely play the part of a good-natured macho man in front of his male peers. In late October, I invited him, Sheila, and Sally for dinner at my apartment, where, among other mid-'80s treats, I boldly served hummus, a new appetizer

I'd learned about. After we finished the first two bottles of wine and I put the *American Graffiti* soundtrack on the stereo, Ken got up and demonstrated how to do both the "Shag" and the "Shimmy," two early boomer dance fads that Sally had never heard of.

Since a lot of my need for personal interaction and validation was being met at work, I didn't care as much as I had the year before that my real life socializing was still close to moribund. I was still spending a lot of time on the phone talking to old friends from previous periods of my life. I was still going to the movies by myself, reading at least two books a month, and eating cereal for dinner. My parents were still inquiring, bluntly and consistently, why I didn't have a girlfriend. But aside from the ongoing famine that was my romantic life, I was happy enough getting my socialization from work.

Not that there weren't the occasional fun outings. One Friday morning in September, Susan Bricker from the Tuesday team stopped by my office and let me know that in gratitude for all the hard work I'd done fact-checking their ads, they were giving me two tickets to the Michael Jackson concert that weekend. When I called to invite my West Wing friend, Janice Farrell, she said her boss, Jack Svahn, had coincidentally just given her his tickets to the same concert and suggested we use those instead. Since her offer also involved a VIP package, I handed my tickets to Sally.

The event turned out to be a classic lobbying boondoggle for White House officials and Republican lawmakers. Thrown by Pepsi, which was the major sponsor of the Michael Jackson tour, the night began at the Capitol Hill Club, which I knew well from attending GOP fundraisers and receptions when I worked for Jerry Solomon. Since corporate giants like to play both sides of the fence, I wondered whether there was a similar party happening for Democrats someplace else. Janice's boss wasn't the only high ranking Republican who'd bailed on the concert. As I scanned the room for VIPs, I saw mostly lower-ranking staff like myself, although the always-egalitarian Ed Meese was there, along with the occasional senior staffer like Roger Porter who brought his young son, Rob (who, unrelated to this story, would grow up to work in the Trump White House, date Hope Hicks, and be forced to resign following domestic abuse allegations from his former wife).

After we had our fill of fried food, soda, and desultory conversation, we boarded a bus for RFK stadium, where our seats were in the top tier and about halfway back from the stage—good but not great. Michael Jackson was then at the very peak of his popularity and this was the tour when, as a favor to his brothers, he opened the show with the Jackson Five. Hearing those old songs ("ABC," "I Want You Back") was a lot of fun but the audience really wanted Michael's new material from the "Thriller" album. When he closed the concert with "Billy Jean" and "Beat It," the crowd approached near-ecstasy. In Dallas, I had thought the reception for Reagan was rapturous, but this concert was a good reminder that even the most popular American politician couldn't (at least not then) arouse crowds to the same level of frenzy as a pop star—and a good thing too.

The campaign was cruising by the time we got to October. Reagan still enjoyed a 20-point lead in the polls and now that Mondale's I'll-nominate-a-woman gambit had backfired, only a disaster could prevent the President's re-election.

The upcoming Presidential debate was Mondale's last chance to dent Reagan's lead. Our team didn't have a big role in the debate preparation, which was being run out of the White House by our nemesis, Dick Darman. Even so, I helped prepare a summary of Mondale's top vulnerabilities, which Ken forwarded to Michael Baroody, the organizer of the debate briefing book.

About two weeks before the debate, we got our first look at the briefing materials. They stunk. Out loud. Defensive, disorganized, and heavily dependent on statistic after statistic, the briefing book had obviously been prepared by policy nerds, not writers or True Believers. The anti-Mondale sections were bland and bloodless, and contained none of our content. We tried a second time to insert some harder-hitting language, but Darman and Baroody rejected this as well and the briefing book continued to reek of governmentese.

The only saving grace was that Ken was participating in the debate prep at the White House in the week leading up to the big day. He came back after the first session and said it had gone poorly. OMB Director David Stockman had played Mondale and stunned Reagan with his relentless slashing attacks. And everyone at the briefing had agreed that the debate book didn't cut it and that our team had to provide new content. Linda, Sheila, Arnold, and I were assigned to write "one-liners," which were anti-Mondale jokes, and "zingers," or oddball facts about Mondale's record. We piled into Sheila and Linda's office and treated it like the writer's room of a sitcom, spitting out joke after joke. We amused ourselves at least.

When Ken came back from the White house after the second day of debate prep, he said Reagan was getting better and that some of the material we'd produced earlier was now in front of him. He looked at our one-liners and zingers and made a few edits. I typed in the revisions to the one-liners and Sheila took the zingers. Even though it was past 8:30pm on a Friday night when we finished, the rest of the group crowded around in back of us until the end, suggesting rephrasings to make them even sharper and funnier. No one wanted to leave until what seemed like an important team project was done.

On the night of the debate, Sunday, October 7th, there was nothing for us to do, but most of us came into the office by mid-afternoon anyway. We weren't alone. Gary Maloney's team was also there in full, blasting old Beatles and Rolling Stones songs when they weren't watching football games in the conference room. It was one big, swaggering geek party. As day turned to night, we ordered Chinese food for dinner, broke out the Scotch, and crowded into Ken's office to watch the big showdown on his television.

I had a particular interest in the outcome. Earlier in the week, Ken had said that if we wanted to submit proposed closing statements, he would pass them along to the White House. A few days later, he told Jim Strock and me that Jim Baker liked our submissions and that the final closing statement would contain language from both. Wow. I had dreams of becoming a White House speechwriter after that.

As I anxiously awaited the closing minutes, I thought Reagan's performance was mildly disappointing compared to what he was capable of. He'd stumbled a bit and was obviously annoyed by Mondale's attacks, but Mondale hadn't been that great either. Then it was finally time for the candidates to sum up. I leaned forward eagerly. Here's what I had written in my draft:

> "Four years ago, I asked all of you if you were better off than you had been when Jimmy Carter and Walter Mondale entered the White House. Most of you decided that the answer was 'no,' and we had a change of leadership."

So I was pleased when Reagan's actual first sentence was "Four years ago, in similar circumstances to this, I asked you, the American people, a question. I asked: 'Are you better off than you were four years before?' The answer to that obviously was no, and as a result, I was elected to this office and promised a new beginning."

So far, so good. It was a great start and I was pretty pleased with the rest of my statement too, which had read like this:

> "I believe that if I asked the same question now, most of you would say that you ARE better off than you were four years ago, and that it IS easier for you to buy things and plan for the future.
>
> But tonight I'd like to ask a slightly different question. Is your COUNTRY better off now than it was four years ago? Are you prouder to be an American? Are we headed in the right direction as a nation? Do you think America will continue to be the best country in the world? These questions are really what this election is all about."

But instead of that beautifully crafted prose, this is what ultimately came out of Reagan's mouth:

> "Now, maybe I'm expected to ask that same question again. I'm not going to, because I think that all of you—or not everyone, those people that are in those pockets of poverty and haven't caught up, they couldn't answer the way I would want them

to—but I think that most of the people in this country would say, yes, they are better off than they were four years ago.

The question, I think, should be enlarged. Is America better off than it was four years ago? And I believe the answer to that has to also be 'yes.' I promised a new beginning. So far, it is only a beginning. If the job were finished, I might have thought twice about seeking re-election for this job. But we now have an economy that, for the first time—well, let's put it this way: In the first half of 1980, gross national product was down a minus 3.7 percent. The first half of '84, it's up 8.5 percent. Productivity in the first half of 1980 was down a minus 2 percent. Today, it is up a plus 4 percent. Personal earnings after taxes per capita have gone up almost $3,000 in these four years. In 1980—or 1979, a person with a fixed income of $8,000 was $500 above the poverty line, and this maybe explains why there are the numbers still in poverty. By 1980, that same person was $500 below the poverty line."

Huh? What was that? Man, what a downer. The statistics that Darman had crammed into Reagan's head came out as mumbo jumbo. My career as a White House speechwriter had just vanished in front of my eyes. To make matters worse, I found myself in heated disagreement with my colleagues, who thought the whole performance had been a disaster.

Maybe I was delusional, but I fiercely maintained that, except for the closing statement, Reagan had been fine, or at least as good as Mondale. Most of my true-believing friends—Jim Robinson, Ed Gallion, John Buckley, and even Ken when he returned the next day—also agreed that it had been a draw except for the closing statement. In a poll taken the night of the debate, 38 percent said Reagan had "won" the debate and 39 percent said Mondale. In other words, what is now considered by conventional wisdom to have been a Reagan disaster was seen by viewers at the time as a tie.

I was especially aggravated to turn on the CBS news the next night and hear unnamed White House sources—probably the same ones who'd run the debate prep—opining Reagan had looked old during the debate and that they needed to heroically engage in "damage control." I lost my temper after this and stormed out of the office yelling that we should be defending Reagan, not hanging our heads and feeding the media's narrative. I felt somewhat vindicated when, for all the handwringing, we only lost three percentage points in the polls and were still ahead by 15 percent.

The media's nonstop diagnosis that Reagan should be raced immediately to a nursing home was relentless after this. But three things helped turn it around. First, the Vice Presidential debate between Bush and Ferraro was a wipeout. I doubt the conversion was real, but somehow the Vice President preached supply-side religion and demolished Ferraro. Unsurprisingly, the media refused to admit it, claiming that he'd patronized her by treating her in the same rough-and-tumble way he'd treat any other debate opponent.

Second, the campaign sent Reagan out on an old-fashioned whistle-stop train ride throughout the Midwest. Ken had written a tough speech and before it went to the President, I took a copy to the White House, where I walked the fact-checkers through the anti-Mondale claims by showing them the hard copy backup for every quote or vote. These whistle-stop speeches and the acclaim of the small town crowds reinvigorated the President and restored his self confidence.

Most importantly, Dick Darman's oversight for the second debate was reduced considerably and hardliners like Ken and Roger Ailes were given more say. The messaging became simpler, with fewer facts and figures. And this time, Ken himself wrote the closing statement. He deliberately didn't try to overthink it, repurposing familiar language that Reagan had used many times before, including a cornball anecdote about an imaginary letter he'd put in a time capsule to be opened 100 years in the future. Through pre-arrangement with deputy chief of staff Mike Deaver, when the debate team met in the Roosevelt Room, Deaver handed Reagan the closing statement to read out loud, rather than distributing the draft to everyone else to react to first. After the read-through, Reagan pronounced himself happy with Ken's draft and no one contradicted him, thus avoiding the prose-deadening practice of writing-by-committee.

On the day of the second debate, Philip Tasho was visiting from Richmond and I took him to the White House so we could watch Reagan take off in the

Marine One helicopter. The President emerged from the residence, waved at the crowd, and clasped both hands above his head in the classic I'm-the-champion pose. Following this, I took Philip to the train station and drove to the office. The atmosphere at the headquarters was definitely not party-hearty this time around. Spencer and I watched a little football and ordered pizza around 6:00pm, and the rest of the team slowly wandered in after that. We were all in this together, sinking or swimming as a team. Once again, we all crowded into Ken's office, but this time we were barely able to breathe as 9:00pm approached.

From the first minute, it was clear that Reagan had rebounded, showing confidence, determination, and good cheer. Maybe he'd taken a couple of naps on the plane and woken up feeling frisky. As usual, the media had overreached. Since they'd spent the previous two weeks portraying Reagan as a doddering old fool, Reagan could beat expectations simply by not drooling. When Henry Trewhitt, the foreign affairs editor of the *Baltimore Sun*, asked him if he was too old to be president, he responded with one of the most famous lines in debate history: "Not at all, Mr. Trewhitt, and I want you to know that also I will not make age an issue of this campaign. I am not going to exploit, for political purposes, my opponent's youth and inexperience."

And with that, the campaign was over.

The day after the second Presidential debate, the media opined that it had been "a draw" between Reagan and Mondale.

Hahahahahahahahahahahahahahahahahahahahahahahahahahahahahaha hahahahahahaha!

It was around this time that I began to wonder if I should stick with politics because I was

so sensitive about the blatantly biased reporting of CBS, the *New York Times* and the rest of the news media. After all, who really cares when Dan Rather determines the "winner" of a debate according to some invisible metric that's comprehensible only to him? Yet, although I could rationally try not to be bothered, I never really hardened my emotional shell against media bias.

With the conclusion of the debates, the only remaining question was whether Reagan would carry all 50 states or let Mondale win his home state of Minnesota. The work of our group was essentially done. Over the next two weeks, I had a few mop-up tasks to complete, but my attention turned to how I could support myself after the election.

Given that we'd all left good jobs to work for the campaign, Ken promised to help us land on our feet when the paychecks stopped coming in the middle of November. I told him that I eventually wanted to be a White House speechwriter and he nodded politely, acting like that wasn't the most outlandish suggestion he'd heard that day. He said the best way to accomplish that would be to write first for a Cabinet Secretary, and he subsequently followed through on his promise to make introductions around the agencies.

On Ken's last day in the office before the election, we had a very early meeting in his office at which he told us we'd done a great job and promised to return on November 12th for a farewell dinner. He also reaffirmed his earlier promise that he'd help us find jobs. Then he left to return to California. Linda, Spencer, Sally, and I hung out the windows until he emerged on the street below us and we yelled good luck and waved signs that said "Armenians kick ass" and "You ain't seen nothing yet," the famous Al Jolson line that he had repurposed to close out each campaign speech.

I started job hunting later that day. My first interview was at the Treasury Department, where I met with Don Regan's chief speechwriter, Terry Bresnihan, who wanted to hire me because he admired Ken so much. But I also had to meet with his boss, Jim Smith, the deputy for public affairs. Jim and I got along fine until he let me know he was leaving that job in a week, something that not even Terry knew. He thought that Roger Bolton would replace him, but that the final decision was still up in the air. So any movement on new personnel was on hold.

Ken also asked if I'd be interested in writing for Margaret Heckler, the Secretary of Health and Human Services. This was a quandary. I was interested in the issues that HHS oversaw, but Heckler herself had a terrible reputation. A former U.S. Representative who'd been defeated for re-election in 1982, she'd been named Secretary during the White House panic over the gender gap. Now, she was reportedly driving the White House crazy with her lack of management experience. I went for an interview and her head of Public Affairs offered me the job on the spot. But he was honest enough to admit that Heckler was hard on her speechwriters. She was never happy with their drafts but couldn't explain what she did want: "If you need the personal satisfaction of hearing the Secretary say the words you've written, this is not the place for you." I'd already had one boss who made me feel like I was doing a lousy job and didn't need another, so I passed. Nine months later when she was ousted as Secretary, I reflected that I'd made the right decision.

Ken also set me up for an interview at the Transportation Department, writing for Elizabeth Dole. This seemed like my best shot because the head of Public Affairs was his former protégé. I had a good interview with her deputy, but she later told Ken she wouldn't hire me because I didn't have any experience as a speechwriter.

Not knowing what the future held didn't spoil those last days at the campaign. The final poll from Richard Wirthlin said Reagan was ahead 57 percent to 35 percent, so there was no anxiety about the result. I'd like to think our extraordinary campaign efforts had made the difference, but there was no way Reagan could lose in 1984. For the first time since the 1960s, the economy was healthy. It had taken a severe recession in 1982 for the Federal Reserve to bring inflation under control, but now jobs were booming and prices were stable. It really was "morning in America" again. And if incumbency and a feel-good economy wasn't enough, Reagan himself was much more charismatic than the gray, dull, monotoned Mondale, who, in 1984, ended up being little more than a ritual sacrifice by the Democrats to the two-party system.

When I heard the poll results from Wirthlin, I called Jerry Solomon in the Saratoga Springs campaign office (where I'd been working two years earlier) to wish him good luck and give him a heads-up on the coming landslide. He seemed grateful for the inside information and lamented that he had a tough race this year because his opponent had raised $75,000 to run against him. Huh, I thought. That's funny. Both Ed Gallion and John Kostas had previously told me the real number was $60,000. I'd have been disappointed, though, if my old boss hadn't used the occasion to try to sneak one more needless white lie by me.

Election Day itself had a dreamlike quality. The frenzy of the last seven months was over and all we could do was sit quietly and wait. The TV showed long lines of people all over the country waiting to vote, which I always find very moving. Linda brought in bagels, croissants, orange juice, and champagne and we toasted each other and played Lee Greenwood's "I'm Proud To Be An American" three times, this time completely unironically.

All morning long, my phone rang: my grandmother from Nantucket, Maryellen Tarantino from Jerry Solomon's office, my college roommate Chris Ryer, Maria Horgan from the White House, and half a dozen others from all periods of my life. A surprising number of them confided they were so nervous they couldn't sit still, and I reassured them it would turn out fine.

I was the last one to leave the office that day because I literally had no place to go. Finally, at 4:00pm, I drove to the Shoreham hotel for the victory celebration. The ballroom was virtually empty, so I went upstairs where the political team had a suite of rooms set up to monitor the results. Gary Maloney told me the exit polls looked great and I called Jerry Solomon again—he'd asked me to fill him in on any scrap of information I had and I was happy to oblige.

I wandered around a couple of hours, hanging out with people I knew from the White House (including future cabinet secretary Elaine Chao). The ballroom quickly became mobbed and there were private parties going on in rooms all throughout the hotel. I eventually ended up back at the political suite where I could follow the results on TV. CBS called the election for Reagan at 8:00pm and NBC at 8:30pm based on exit polls alone. And just like that, it was over, before there was even a hint of suspense. The only state that was close was Minnesota, which, along with the District of Columbia, eventually did go for Mondale after all. It was anticlimactic, to be honest.

A half hour later, our team decamped to the nearby home of our volunteer, Lenni, who had made a delicious curry that I hoped would offset some of the alcohol we were guzzling. Finally, I was able to get everyone together for a group photo that we'd sign and give to Ken. By 10:00pm, we already had 400 electoral votes. Mondale conceded graciously at 11:30pm, then Reagan came out at midnight and delivered the election night speech that Ken had

Our Fritzbusters team on election night.

written the week before. As always, and for the final time, it concluded with Ken's favorite line: "You ain't seen nothin' yet."

I woke up at 8:00am the next morning, wondering what I was going to do with the rest of my life. Before going to work, I went to the grocery store and noticed scores of Black fathers walking hand-in-hand with their daughters and sons, escorting them someplace. That's when I noticed, 18 months after moving in, an elementary school around the corner on R Street. Since I'd never been home during the workday, I'd never before seen kids in the neighborhood. It was a sweet vision of domestic reality performed by people who could not care less if Mondale said some stupid thing as a senator in 1973.

Arriving at the office at 9:30am, I picked up the phone to call Philip in Richmond and found myself so overcome with emotion that I had to hang up and compose myself. The reality was finally hitting me. The ride was over.

I'd probably never work with these people again; probably never have this much fun at a job again.

Ken returned from California the next Monday and finished wrapping things up. He gave each of us personal letters that he'd written on Air Force One stationary during his last flight with the president. I brought in my camera and we took photos of each other. Then Ken looked around his office and remarked wistfully, "We had a lot of good meetings in here." He was even more sentimental than I was.

Our last time together was at a farewell dinner at a dive pizza joint on Capitol Hill called A.V.'s. Ken stood up and handed out presents—Presidential cufflinks for the men and pins for the women, and inscribed photos for everyone. He then went around the table making little speeches about us individually. It was all over-the-top flattery—he cited my dedication to the job and my "cultural knowledge," so I guess that American Studies major in college paid off after all. He made each of us offer one sentence about our experience on the campaign, and I said, "I've never had so much fun with my clothes on," the kind of bawdy joke that I knew he liked. The team had delegated me as their spokesman, so then I stood up and gave him our presents, including the group photo we'd taken at Lenni's house on election night. I made some brief remarks about how this had been a memorable experience for all of us, etc., etc., but I was cut short by the waiter who came over and said it was 11:00pm and they were shutting the lights off. Like the campaign itself, the night ended too soon.

When I got home, I looked at the photo Ken had given me. It was a pensive picture of the President sitting on the Truman balcony with Ken standing behind him, chin in hand, leaning over his right shoulder as the two of them reviewed a speech. This was the inscription: "To Gary: Our Fitzbuster Extraordinaire—whose dedication to the cause and determination to bury the bad guys made him an invaluable member of our team. Bravo to your strength of conviction—Always keep at it! Warm regards, Ken."

CHAPTER 26

On the Job Hunt Again

I left Reagan-Bush '84 with no solid job prospects but lots of confidence. My plan to become a speechwriter to a Cabinet Secretary seemed plausible, especially with the backing of Ken Khachigian, not only the President's best-known speechwriter, but a "player" who was wired in across the government.

It turns out, I was naïve about the speechwriting cartel's barriers to entry. An actor trying to get into Actors' Equity would recognize the experience. Without the union card, I couldn't work, but I couldn't work without the union card. In the end, it would take nine months and two visits to purgatory before landing what turned out to be a dream job in a small agency I'd never even heard of.

Coming out of the gate, I aimed high: the Treasury Department, which would be leading the charge on a complete rewrite of the tax code in the second term. And it seemed on the verge of happening after my encouraging initial interview with Terry Bresnihan and his follow-up calls to me in Brockton, where I was spending Thanksgiving with my parents.

When I returned to Washington, John Buckley reported that Roger Bolton, Terry's new boss, was leaning towards hiring Bob Maistros, one of the writers who had worked for him at Reagan-Bush. Oh. Maistros and I would become on-and-off colleagues over the next 35 years, but all I knew then was that he was an ardent and outspoken conservative, a whirlwind of energy, a boundlessly self-confident talker, and a speedy writer with the inside track for most of the jobs I wanted.

While I waited for the Treasury Department to sort itself out, I needed a paycheck, so Ken called his former White House protégé Sharon, the Assistant Secretary for Communications at the Department of Transportation. She told Ken that as a big favor to him, she'd give me a 90-day temporary appointment. I hated to be anyone's "big favor," but I couldn't be fussy.

The Department of Transportation (DOT) was my introduction to the federal bureaucracy. It's hard to comprehend how huge these government departments really are. With about 55,000 employees, DOT then consisted of eight major agencies, referred to internally as "modes," as in modes of transportation. These modes, which were themselves huge, included the Coast Guard, the Federal Aviation Administration, the Urban Mass Transit Administration, the National Highway Safety Administration, the Federal Railroad Administration, and the St. Lawrence Seaway. In other words, DOT had its fingers in anything that carried people or products by planes, trains, or automobiles.

Sitting atop this bureaucracy in an office larger than my apartment, in a part of the building called the "Gold Carpet Area" because it had a yellow rug, sat Secretary Elizabeth Dole and "Leader." Leader was half canine and half PR prop, a gift she'd received when her husband, Senator Bob Dole, had become Senate Majority Leader. I've never understood how a consensus forms that someone should become a member of the Cabinet, and Elizabeth Dole was Exhibit A. She'd previously led the White House Office of Public Liaison, which arranges meetings with the various political interest groups that are always demanding something from the government. She apparently impressed someone, and maybe this "someone" also wanted to curry favor with Majority Leader Dole, because she ended up running one of the biggest federal organizations in the country. The media loved to promote the Doles as a "power couple," then a new phenomenon, and she developed an aggressively-nurtured reputation in the outside world as savvy, charming, and highly intelligent. Within the agency though, she was surrounded by sycophants who ardently believed they were toiling for the first female president-to-be, and she was reputed to be ambitious, indecisive, image-conscious, and insecure.

I suspect Dole took out her insecurities on the political team, because an avalanche of anxiety flowed down to the communications department. When I saw that the public relations staff lived in perpetual terror of Sharon's tirades, I quickly realized she had done me a great favor by not hiring me. "You've ruined the reputation of this department," she once yelled about a misplaced memo that clearly did not ruin the reputation of the department. When I heard that story I thought: I'm glad that's not me.

Sharon was intimidatingly tall, relentlessly all-business, and obviously very bright. We were the same age—30—but she was on a much faster track to success, eventually becoming the second wife of a prominent conservative columnist. Since she did me the huge favor of giving me a temporary landing spot when I needed one and then practiced benign neglect, I can't complain about the way she treated me. I mostly tried to stay out of her line of sight.

"Ken talks about you like you walk on water," she said, sizing me up when we finally met, and not in a particularly warm way. She then gave me a real assignment so I'd have something productive to do while I was looking for permanent work: create a monthly transportation-related consumer column under the Secretary's byline and arrange to mail it to weekly newspapers across the country. I had to contact the PR people at the various "modes" and get them to give me useful ideas for transporting the public. This meant suggestions like "how to save energy by taking the train" or "tips on boating safety from the Coast Guard." (Did you know that a surprising number of recreational fishermen drown when they have too many beers and tumble into the water while trying to urinate over the side of the boat? Unfortunately I couldn't use that useful warning in my column.)

I named the column "America On the Move" and drafted a memo outlining the distribution strategy, which turned out to be remarkably complicated. Even though the department had an actual mailing list just for this kind of thing, no one could figure out how to print and mail several thousand monthly copies. I even wrote six columns to give the project a running start. The actual work took about a month to complete and—typical bureaucracy—two months to get approved.

I assumed Sharon didn't berate me like she did everyone else because she didn't want me to complain to Ken. Or maybe she just had more important things to worry about. Either way, she rarely laid eyes on me. I wasn't working in the main communications department area—I was one floor lower, in an annex suite of offices that housed the people who handled the Freedom of Information Act (FOIA) requests and other department functionaries removed from the upstairs drama. Sitting on that floor gave me a sense of what working in the bureaucracy was like. Everyone cleared out at 5:00pm and even when they were in the office, they didn't exactly break a sweat.

I came to understand that within every agency there is a definitive line between its few political appointees—called "Schedule Cs"—and its many, many permanent bureaucrats. There are only about 1,500 Schedule C positions in the entire government and they have zero job security. When your boss leaves, you're usually next to go, because each political appointee wants a team that is loyal to him or her. The permanent bureaucrats who staff most of the government jobs take a jaundiced view of the Schedule Cs, who wash in and out with the tide and have varying levels of competency. Nevertheless, these jobs are highly coveted and closely hoarded within each agency, which is why I had trouble landing one.

All the aggravation brought Sharon's direct reports closer together. I became good friends with some of them, including Cathy Barr and Betsy White, who somehow survived despite being on the firing line. For years afterward, they told stories that suggested they had PTSD. We became lunch buddies with enough ironic detachment to joke about Dole's ego, Sharon's temper, and little Leader's "accidents" in the Gold Carpet Area. What I learned from them is that sometimes laughing about a semi-dysfunctional workplace is the best coping mechanism.

I was not the only one having trouble finding a permanent job. Most of my friends at Reagan-Bush '84 were similarly adrift, although it took a while to figure that out. We didn't have email, text messaging, cell phones, or social media, which meant no easy mechanism for reconnecting after we'd scattered at the end of the campaign. When I returned from my two-week unpaid Thanksgiving break, I didn't even have my former colleagues' phone numbers and didn't know who was hanging out where. Somehow, Sharon's Deputy, Fred Quinn, knew how to reach Linda Holwick who was dating his former boss, Gene Pell, the head of the Voice of America. I called her new number and she gave me Arnold Tompkins' contact, and he gave me Spencer's and so on. By mid-December, we were finally all reconnected, and were talking frequently on the phone or having lunch to exchange gossip, compare notes, or buck each other up.

Someone who wasn't having trouble finding a job was John Buckley. Both George Bush and Jack Kemp wanted to hire him as their press secretary and he eventually decided to go with Kemp, the more ideologically compatible choice. John and I had dinner so I could give him a few modest tips about being a press secretary for a congressman, because even though Kemp was a

Despite the frustrations of job hunting I was happy to have the support of my Brockton friends, Jane Prince, Rich Martel and Philip Tasho, shown here at Christmas.

national figure on the verge of announcing for President, he still needed to represent his district in upstate New York. Kemp, he told me, was a tough boss, completely impervious to charm, and much smarter and more intellectual than anyone guessed.

But John's experience was decidedly not the norm. Even if you had a job lined up, it could fall apart at the last minute. One morning, Maria Horgan called from the White House and said, "I bet you're glad you didn't go to Treasury." I thought she was talking about a negative story about Tax Reform in that morning's *Washington Post*, but no. Treasury Secretary Don Regan and White House Chief of Staff Jim Baker had decided to switch jobs. Jim Baker would be bringing in his own team of faithful acolytes, including the especially loyal Margaret Tutweiler as Head of Communications. This meant that Roger Bolton would be pushed out as Communications Director after only a few weeks on the job. So that door, only slightly ajar for me in the first place, was definitely slammed shut.

The job search quickly became an ego-deflating experience. The White House Office of Personnel was ostensibly the clearing house for political jobs in the administration, but when I went in to see the woman who was responsible for finding me something, she looked at my resume and asked the same three questions for each of the six positions I'd held since college: How much were you paid, what did you do, and why did you leave the job? She then pulled out a folder of unfilled job positions that no one else wanted, the best of which was speechwriter to the Assistant Secretary for Special Education, and none of which appealed to me.

The White House was no help but Ken was still in my corner. Thanks to him, I had a shot as a speechwriter for Ed Meese, the new Attorney General. I met with Terry Eastland, Meese's Head of Communications, in his elegant paneled office. We sat facing each other in two very comfortable leather wingback chairs and hit it off fine. We were ideologically aligned on a range of hot-button cultural issues and when he asked what I read for pleasure, he seemed impressed that I was a fan of Victorian novels (Trollope, Thackeray, Dickens) since his favorite novel was *Anna Karenina*, which was from the same century. But he threw me for a loop when he asked what Supreme Court decisions I disagreed with. This should have been a layup for me, but I had a brain freeze and couldn't think of a single one. I don't know how badly that detail hurt my chances, but nonetheless, I received a letter a few weeks later saying they'd hired someone else.

I was a candidate for position after position but could never get across the finish line. Ken had also recommended me to Senator John Heinz, then chair of the Republican Senate Campaign Committee, because the Committee needed a head of research. As heir to the Heinz Ketchup family fortune, he had a gorgeous mansion in Georgetown, where we met one Saturday morning. (He also had a house on Nantucket that would later become famous when his widow's second husband, presidential candidate John Kerry, was photographed windsurfing in front of it during the 2004 campaign.)

Heinz was good-looking and confident, though I noticed he had small clumps of dark hair growing out of his ears. After serving tea from a silver tea set, he started the conversation by complaining that Elizabeth Dole wasn't taking his bill to privatize ConRail seriously enough. After detailing the benefits of his bill, he aggressively asked, "What's the matter with that?" as if I spent my days in the Gold Carpet Area whispering advice to the Secretary. He then chatted about his house on Nantucket, telling me, apropos of nothing, that his caretaker (a guy named Buzz and an acquaintance of my mother, as it turned out) was a reformed alcoholic. We finally discussed various ideas on how to use research to buttress the fortunes of weak Senate incumbents and he said he liked me and would get back to me soon.

I had another job possibility that sounded promising. Jim had recommended me for his old position as chief speechwriter at the U.S. Chamber of Commerce. They'd become disenchanted with his replacement, Grover Norquist, who would eventually become a powerful anti-tax lobbyist in the 21st century, but was then just a run-of-the-mill pain in the ass to his employer for too zealously pushing his own hard-line agenda instead of providing the more accommodating rhetoric his bosses favored.

My first two interviews at the Chamber went well. Jim's reputation within the organization was still high, which gave me an advantage. But when I went to see CEO Richard Lesher, the ultimate decider, he took one look at my resume and said, "Why can't you keep a job?" He then asked me if I'd be willing to write speeches selling razor blades for $100,000 a year at Gillette. Um, yeah. How about working for Philip Morris for $125,000 a year? God, no. How important to you is a sense of mission in your career? Oh, very important, sir—nothing could be more important than advocating for the nation's free enterprise system, which has created so much wealth and prosperity.

A couple of days later, I learned that Lesher had hired Bob Maistros instead of me. I didn't get the job at the Republican Senate Campaign Committee either. Heinz had picked someone I didn't know—a guy named Stu. Arnold Tompkins scoffed at the choice, saying he was incompetent. John Buckley tried to assuage my disappointment with the opposite approach, telling me not to feel bad because Stu was such a talented rising star that there was no shame in losing to him. I don't know what it says about me, but I was more comforted thinking they'd hired someone totally incompetent. There was not much solace in knowing I was still jobless because my more talented peers were getting the jobs I wanted.

In any event, this turned out to be another one of my lucky breaks. The GOP lost a net total of eight Senate seats in the 1986 election, and thankfully I avoided being associated with THAT debacle.

I did take one break from job hunting during Inauguration weekend. As a former campaign staffer, I had access to Inauguration Ball tickets. My mother wanted to go to the ball, and because that was not exactly my father's thing, she invited my Aunt Lee to be her date. I bought a tuxedo for $250 and asked Misty Church to join us. Lee and my mother slept in the double bed in my bedroom and I camped out on the living room couch. The weather was bitterly cold and windy—so windy that the snow blew in under the door from the balcony to my bedroom, and so cold that they cancelled the outdoor swearing-in and parade.

The ball itself was a dud. Spread across the city were nine different balls to accommodate all the Republican office holders and party functionaries from

With my mother before the 1985 Inaugural Ball.

the 50 states who wanted to celebrate in Washington. With tickets assigned by state, I, with other Massachusetts Republicans, attended the event at the Convention Center, a cavernous space that had all the glamour of a high school gym. My mother, aunt, and I knew hardly any of these people, so it felt like being at someone else's low-rent prom. The evening's only excitement was the arrival of the President and First Lady at 9:30pm, after which they made a few remarks, danced one number, and then headed off to one of the other balls.

Upon exiting at 11:00pm, we encountered a near riot at the coat check. The coat retrieval system had broken down completely and hordes of angry people in black tie and ball gowns were yelling that they wanted their coats back. With thousands of expensive fur coats lost in the bowels of the Convention Center, the frustration eventually approached hysteria. The police arrived to sort things out but were not very helpful—they further infuriated the crowd by holding up a mink coat at random and calling out to the crowd to see if it belonged to anyone there. Finally at about midnight, they completely gave up trying to sort things out and let ball-goers into the back rooms to find their own wraps. When it was my turn, I had to go through three different rooms to locate ours. I was glad to be home safe and sound at 1:30am that night.

And how fitting, I thought. The Inaugural Ball symbolized how my post-Campaign experience was going—eager anticipation that landed with a thud when faced with reality. The frigid temperatures of Inauguration Day were nothing compared to the reception I was getting in the job market.

CHAPTER 27

Landing a Job

T he only good thing about my protracted job search was that it gave my parents a break from their weekly interrogation about why I didn't have a girlfriend. Instead it was: What had I done to find a job that week, how many interviews did I have lined up, how many calls had I made, was everyone else having the same problem? At my age, my father had taken substantial risks, leaving a steady job to create his own business, but when it came to my career, he wanted job security for me. I appreciated the concern, but their anxiety only increased my own. And I was already plenty anxious.

By the end of February, my temporary job assignment at DOT was ending. Then Sharon surprised everyone by resigning to become Vice President for Corporate Communications at a Chicago-based conglomerate. About a week later, I walked into the communications suite to gossip with Betsy and Cathy, and there sat Roger Bolton waiting to talk to Sharon about high-level communications jobs, including potentially hers. I sat down to commiserate with him about the randomness of political musical chairs, and asked him to keep me in mind if he heard of anything.

Along the way, Arnold Tompkins mentioned that a guy who'd held a position of indeterminate responsibility at Reagan-Bush, someone we'd always joked about as a cipher, had landed a big job at the Department of Energy (DOE). After I got through exclaiming "What??? HIM?? How'd *he* get that?!?" I immediately called him to ask about positions there. Ten days later, I had an offer to be special assistant to the new head of Congressional Affairs. Just in time, too, because I had stopped getting a DOT paycheck a week earlier. Technically I shouldn't have even been in the building, but I was still going into the office so I'd have a place of business to answer phone calls.

After months of getting the runaround at nearly a dozen other organizations, I was amazed at how fast the bureaucracy could move when it wanted to. I had my interview at DOE on March 15th, got the offer two days later, and started the job within the next three days. And that is how I ended up with one of the longest titles in the government: "Special Assistant to the Assistant Secretary of Energy for Public, Congressional, and Intergovernmental Affairs."

Well aware that being someone's assistant, no matter how special, was not my long-term avocation, my new boss, Bob, still urged me to come aboard to see if I liked it. If not, no hard feelings. Bob was in his early 40s and already an experienced and extremely competent operator who knew the ins and outs of the Department. As head of Congressional Affairs, he was in charge of everything related to developing energy policy and getting those policies through Congress, and from him, I learned how the government really worked.

Before accepting the job at DOE, my contact in White House personnel had described Bob as a "womanizer with a yacht—a Nixon-Ford type." All true, although "womanizer with a yacht" had nothing to do with being a "Nixon-Ford type." An often-told story concerned the Sunday he'd toppled overboard into the Chesapeake Bay when none of his hard-partying, far-from-sober friends could operate the boat, leaving him to tread water helplessly as it sailed away. Eventually they managed to rescue him and he subsequently claimed that the near-death experience had changed his life. If so, I can't imagine what he'd been like *before* being chastened, because he was still a remarkably high-living good-time boy on the prowl who occasionally came back from a successful conquest at lunch with a huge grin on his face.

I admired the relish with which he approached life and work—he seemed to love energy policy as much as he loved the female form.

On my first day at DOE, Bob took me to a meeting with John Harrington, the new Secretary of Energy, to prepare for a White House meeting on the Energy Policy Conservation Act. Our bureaucrats were worried that Don Hodel, the more experienced Interior Secretary, would do a better job representing Interior's conflicting position on some now-forgotten point. They had good reason to worry. Harrington was another Elizabeth Dole—a former White House functionary (head of the White House Personnel) who had inexplicably been named to the Cabinet. I was surprised at how little he knew about energy issues or even how Congress worked.

My opinion about Harrington wasn't enhanced when I was later commissioned to write a speech for him on nuclear power. I prepared the draft, subsequently massaged by Bob, other department experts, and the Public Affairs office. Harrington himself approved it and then the day before the event, threw the whole thing out. He wanted to recycle remarks he'd delivered a month earlier, with the addition of three plagiarized pages from a speech he'd heard Senator Bennett Johnson give. It was a mad scramble to pull everything together at the very last minute, with people literally standing over me as I merged text from four discs into one coherent document, changed everything into upper case letters, and made sure the pagination and line spacing were perfect on every page. What a waste of time and energy—not just for me but for everyone who had helped revise the draft.

Harrington's dithering over the speech was nothing compared to his approach to major decisions. A month later, he had to pick a nuclear laboratory to close. He finally made a choice and we drafted 26 individual letters that were to be sent to the relevant members of Congress. The day before the announcement, he changed his mind, which meant another fire drill to draft new letters announcing the closure of an entirely different facility. This process turned into near chaos when his office sent back the letters to be redone three hours before delivery because I had written that the materials explaining the decision were "attached" instead of "enclosed."

My reservations about John Harrington aside, I knew almost immediately that this was not the job for me. For starters, Bob was a yeller. He'd yell if: a) he didn't like the font on a letter; b) someone in the building disagreed with his point of view; c) the Office of Management and Budget removed his favorite sentence from a report; d) the pace of answering Congressional mail was too slow; or, e) you name it.

The yelling I might have been able to take, since he was yelling *through* me, not *at* me. The real problem was that I was spending at least 75 percent of my time shepherding Congressional letters through a sluggish bureaucracy. DOE was another massive federal department with its fingers in every aspect of people's lives. I'd previously thought its main responsibility was to manage the country's use of fossil fuels; nope, the most important thing it did was manufacture nuclear weapons and conduct nuclear research at "laboratories" all over the country. Congress was intensely interested in these programs, or rather, lobbyists were interested in these programs, which resulted in members of Congress sending the Secretary a steady stream of letters advocating for one thing or another.

Soon after I started my new job, Bob had a meeting where he yelled at his staff (loudly and at length) because at least 75 Congressional letters that we'd been sitting on for more than a month had not yet been answered. My assignment was to clear up the backlog. This was not easy because, reasonably enough, Bob also wanted the answers to be legible and in plain English. Bureaucrats, of course, prefer opaque, difficult-to-understand prose that doesn't fully answer the question or commit them to a particular position. I endured one contentious battle after another on English composition and sentence construction. I could usually resolve these conflicts myself, but there was one letter that the Industrial Energy department decided to go to the mat over. I had edited their version to take out the passive voice and clarify a few points, but the original author rejected all the changes and demanded a sit-down meeting at which he argued that since his version was factually correct, I had no business revising it. Bob yelled about that too. Eventually, we had to get the Deputy Secretary of Energy to referee, convening a meeting where we presented him dueling versions of the same letter. He agreed to send my draft, a very minor victory for clarity of communication, but sheesh, what a load of drama for such a low-stakes controversy.

Although I'd started my D.C. career working for a trouble-making Congressman, I came to loathe the way some members abused their oversight powers. The worst was Representative John Dingell of Michigan, the Chair of the House Energy and Commerce Committee. He was generally lionized in Washington as a "fighter," but sometimes that's just code for "bully." The media delighted in his so-called "Dingell-grams," each of which had at least a dozen accusatory questions. And they weren't politely worded, either. Fed by leaks and grievances from disgruntled DOE employees, he was always on the lookout for a high-profile scandal to turn into a PR bonanza. Because he sent so many nasty, contentious letters with similar questions, it's not surprising they got mixed up in our tracking systems.

Trying to answer Dingell's letters created a lot of stress. At one weekly staff meeting, Bob irritably asked why a particular letter about the Defense Production (DP) division (i.e., the bomb-making part of DOE) had not been answered. About five minutes later, after we'd moved on to two other topics, the staffer responsible for tracking DP correspondence burst out: "I never saw that sucker before." All heads swiveled in his direction. "I didn't spend two years in Vietnam and not learn how to avoid land mines." Fueled by resentment, he then proceeded to rant on, telling Bob that, "I'm the only one at DP looking out for your interests and I always get cut down." As someone prone to outbursts himself, Bob let it slide, but became legitimately angry when Anne Sheehan, who actually had to deal with those assholes day-to-day, then reported that when she called Dingell's committee the night before to tell them it was still delayed, the staffer had said, "Fuck her!" to a colleague before slamming the phone down. Bob was so outraged that he said he was going to ask Secretary Harrington to call Dingell to complain. Maybe that happened? Probably not.

By June 1985, I was at my wit's end. My first three and a half years in Washington had been everything I could have dreamed of—Congress, the White House, a presidential re-election campaign. But now, eight months later, I was stuck. In interview after interview, I'd failed to impress the decision-makers and was now languishing in a job that was not for me.

For some time, Jim Robinson had been asking me to join him in California as Governor George Deukmejian's speechwriter. The prospect of spending three more years arguing about the passive tense filled me with dread, so I finally said I'd consider it. I flew to Sacramento and met Deukmejian's chief of staff, Steve Merksamer. Going into the meeting, Jim said he was a nice guy, but this interview was no idle chit-chat. He grilled me on my writing ("You haven't really been a full-time speechwriter before, have you?") and dissected me at length on "what kind of conservative" I was. I was most interested in economic issues but, yes, I also supported Reagan on social issues. That set him off and he drilled down on school prayer. I'm not sure what this had to do with anything since I'd be articulating the Governor's views, not the other way around, but Jim later told me that Merksamer was Jewish and had a "thing" about Jerry Falwell.

After that meeting, Jim drove me around Sacramento and we swam in the pool at his apartment complex, which was the life. Later, we drove up to Reno to visit some low-rent casinos, stopping to gaze at the lovely Lake Tahoe. The West was like a dream, with steady, bright, arid days and none of Washington's fetid humidity. Beautiful in an entirely different way from the East, it was weirdly familiar because all my life I'd been vicariously experiencing California through the lens of television and movies and now here it was for real.

I didn't really want to move away and uproot my life, but I was tired of the rejection in Washington and this seemed like the way to make a fresh start. If I'd been offered the job on the spot, I would have said yes. But I didn't get an offer right away. Nor the next week, the week after that, or even the month after that. Jim told me not to worry, but it was clear I hadn't really impressed Merksamer, who was sitting on the decision.

Coincidentally, the day after I returned to Washington, I received a call out of the blue from Roger Bolton asking if I'd be interested in working at a small agency called the Office of the U.S. Trade Representative (USTR). I'd made peace with the idea of moving to California and was initially dismayed by the overture. I didn't want to deal with all the extended psychological turmoil and inner conflict that re-opening this decision would entail. But without a firm job offer in hand from California, I agreed to consider it.

Even though Margaret Tutweiler had taken over all his responsibilities as head of communications, Roger was still on the payroll at the department of Treasury, so we met there. At Reagan-Bush '84, he and I had worked in slightly competitive areas and not been personally close, but now that we sat down to talk one on one, we hit it off. I appreciated his frank and open no-B.S. approach, without posturing and preening. I'd never heard of USTR but now learned that it was the arm of the White House that coordinated trade negotiations. Now *that* sounded interesting. Free trade was a key component of conservative economic philosophy and I could become part of a national discussion around this issue, which was becoming highly contentious as the U.S. trade deficit soared.

Roger made it clear that he wanted to hire me, but there were still a couple of obstacles. First, Clayton Yeutter, the nominee to head the agency, needed to be confirmed. Then, Roger's own position as Head of Communications needed to be finalized. And lastly, they needed to find the money to fund my position.

The decision on whether to move to California or stay in Washington became another great inflection point of my life. Taking the USTR job meant I'd remain on the path I'd set myself on four years earlier—involved in national politics on the East Coast, close to my family and friends and work connections. On the other hand, a move to California would have dramatically changed everything. I'd have become, if not exactly a big shot, then a prominent person in the capital city of the largest state in the country. I'd have developed a whole new social circle, almost certainly met and married a California girl, and probably gone on to work in corporate communications for one of the state's Fortune 500 companies.

I'd resolved to accept the first firm offer I received, so my fate was out of my hands. My two potential futures were in a race against time with each other. The longer it took for the Governor's office to reach a decision, the more excited I became about USTR.

In mid-July, six weeks after my interview in Sacramento, Jim called and said the job was mine. The very next day, I heard the same thing from Roger. The race turned out to be a tie.

Jim offered me a salary that was 25 percent higher than I was making in Washington. I could live pretty luxuriously on that in Sacramento. Despite the lower salary at USTR, I decided to take it anyway. Part of it was laziness. The very idea of having to sell my apartment, pack, and move across the country exhausted me. But the real reason for staying in Washington was because it was where the action was. I loved Ronald Reagan and wanted to do my small part to make his administration a success. I also thought becoming an expert in trade policy would look great on my post-Reagan resume. The calculus about the resume turned out to be off-base, but going to work at USTR turned out to be one of the best decisions I ever made.

My new job wouldn't start for another month, which was fine because the delay gave me time to take my first overseas trip. Except for the high school trip to Antigua and a weekend in Montreal with my parents, I had never been outside the United States. My family traveled more than most others from my hometown, but going to Europe was still too exotic for us—like table wine or Chinese food.

As it happened, I had two separate invitations to go abroad. I was then closer to my former high school girlfriend, Pat, than we'd been at any time since the summer before college. She was working for the National Marine Fisheries Service and when she came down to Washington for meetings with her bosses, she usually stayed in my apartment. She, Philip, and I would go out on the town and it was almost like high school again except now we had a little bit of money. She'd never been to Europe either and proposed that the two of us visit London.

My other invitation came from Jim, who held no hard feelings that I'd stayed in Washington. If anything, he was relieved, because now he wouldn't be in the position of feeling guilty if it didn't work out. He suggested two weeks in Japan and Thailand. I decided to accept his offer, reasoning, correctly as it turned out, that I'd have plenty of other chances to see London but might never get back to Asia.

And what a trip for a yokel from Brockton. In 1985, Japan was just on the verge of becoming an industrial colossus. After being carpet bombed in World War II, Tokyo had emerged four decades later as the world's most modern city, with more neon than Times Square and newer skyscrapers than midtown. Yet we rarely saw other Americans or even Europeans and when we did encounter Europeans, they were usually in large, noisy tour groups.

Even in modern Tokyo, once you ventured beyond the main business districts, it was easy to get lost in warrens of narrow alleys crammed with noodle shops, tiny clothing stores, and other businesses whose purposes we couldn't decipher. Our experience with "foreignness" was even more acute in the smaller towns. Hardly anyone outside the obvious tourist spots spoke English. Today, you can go to any city in Kazakhstan and find an English speaker, but in 1980s Japan, the only way to order lunch was to look at the menu and point at the picture of what you wanted (restaurants also had display cases that featured plastic replicas of their meals, which was also helpful). Even then, half the time we either ended up with either too little food or too much.

We spent one afternoon dressed in suits because Jim wanted to add a business element to the trip. One of his responsibilities for the Governor was keeping an eye on the programs that promoted California's foreign exports, and of course I was just about to start work for the Office of the U.S. Trade Representative. He arranged for us to meet a couple of mid-level functionaries at the Japanese trade ministry and two executives at Mitsubishi. We were all deferential to each other and I learned a little, mostly about Japanese discipline, unity, and hard work.

But what was the point of all that industriousness? All the consumer goods I saw in the store—the TVs, record players, and cameras—cost more in Japan than in the States. Once during a rainstorm, I bought an umbrella from a street vendor for ten dollars. For ten dollars in the U.S., you could get a nice, sleek, pop-up umbrella that would be reasonably sturdy. But the Japanese equivalent was awkwardly designed and hard to use. Why did the

Japanese tolerate such shoddy and expensive products for themselves, knowing full well that Americans would never stand for such junk?

After the relative modernity of Japan, Thailand was a bit of a shock. The low-slung buildings, lack of infrastructure, and crowded, chaotic, beggar-filled streets of Bangkok reminded me of the newsreels I'd seen from Saigon during the Vietnam War. Nothing was new, well-organized, or particularly clean, but I delighted in being so far from the mundane, antiseptic world back home.

Through mutual friends, Jim knew a guy named Choom, a college-educated native Thai who was working as a bellboy at the Indra Hotel. Like many of his generation, he couldn't find a professional job and was hustling to make ends meet. After meeting us at the airport, he breezed past the line of official cabs to find a gypsy driver, with whom he engaged in a loud and rancorous argument over the fare. He told us he'd bargained the driver down from 300 baht to 100 baht, about four dollars. This was my first introduction to the principle that everything in Thailand is up for negotiation.

Choom had arranged for us to stay in a very acceptable double occupancy room for a discounted rate of $40 per night. As a token of our appreciation, Jim had, during our airport layover in Taiwan, bought two bottles of Johnny Walker Black, considered the most prestigious alcohol brand

In Thailand with Jim and his Thai friends Choom and Tom.

in Thailand. One bottle he gave to Choom, and the other one we presented with great ceremony and many obsequious remarks to the Indra Hotel's dour, unsmiling hotel manager.

I was glad to know a native resident like Choom because, in addition to being a guide and an advisor, he gave us a peek into what local life was like. One night, his friend Danny drove us to his house for dinner—a 90-minute ride into the boondocks. The women and children had already eaten by the time we arrived, so now it was time for the men. We ate in a furniture-free living room, loomed over by a huge wall poster of the Alps, which Choom dreamed of seeing some day. Six or seven of us men sat cross legged on a newspaper-covered floor and ate dinner from serving dishes that the wives placed in the middle of our circle. The food was delicious but extra spicy, and everyone amused themselves by watching me and my WASP palate trying to choke it down. By the end of the night, that bottle of Johnny Walker Black, standing sentinel in the middle of the food, was empty.

Thailand, then as now, is famous for its sex tourism. The ever-helpful Choom, who was used to every single guy arriving in Thailand looking for a sexual escapade, said he'd be happy to arrange a prostitute for me. The hotel had a guard on each floor and the only way to have a Thai woman visit my room was for a member of the hotel staff to escort her in. Just name the price, he said eagerly. He knew women who charged $20, $50, even $100. I never did get a full explanation about what I'd get for my extra 50 bucks, but one thing I *didn't* want to get was a venereal disease, so I politely declined the kind offer, to Choom's uncomprehending disappointment.

But I couldn't extricate myself from the sex show he'd arranged for us to attend the very night we arrived. He was so proud that he'd procured front row seats that it seemed ungrateful to turn him down. Besides, I was curious, and how bad could it be?

Really, really bad. We entered a smallish half-circle auditorium that seated a couple hundred people, mostly European and Indian men who had been deposited there by their tour buses. The admission was 250 baht (about nine dollars) and for that you got one beverage—in my case, a Coke that I soon lost a taste for. Alcoholic drinks cost more, visits to your seat by the female performers cost more than that, and short visits with the women to a row of curtained side cubicles cost the most. Meanwhile, on stage, only about ten feet from where I sat, about a dozen remarkably flexible naked women paraded in and performed bizarre anatomical and physical gymnastics involving horns, liquids, ribbons and projectile bananas. My curiosity was sated after ten minutes but we were stuck there for another hour and a half. I never thought I could get bored watching people have sex but I somehow did. Needless to say, given my deep puritanical streak, this was one story I related very infrequently when I got back to Washington, D.C.

I had been nervous to tell Bob I was leaving after only four months at DOE, but he was true to his word. No hard feelings. "I knew we wouldn't be able to keep you," he said graciously.

I worked hard up to the end, clearing letters until about 3:00pm on that last Friday when Cappy Alverson, one of my best friends in the department, said I was wanted in the conference room. I was legitimately surprised by the surprise party. And touched too, since I didn't think I'd made much of an impression there. Cappy had bought a cake, which was hard to eat after the long lunch I'd just had with Bob and his secretary, Gwenda. Then at 5:00pm, about ten of us ferried over to the National Press Club for a couple hours of drinks. I was so impaired from gin and jet lag when I got home that I ate another slice of cake and passed out. My long search for the right job was finally over.

CHAPTER 28

USTR

After months of frustration and wheel-spinning at other agencies, I finally hit pay dirt during my three and a half years at the Office of the U.S. Trade Representative. It was both a marathon and a sprint. It provided everything you'd want in a job: meaning, professional growth, ego gratification, intellectual stimulation, camaraderie, and a wife.

Trade had been, at best, a third-tier issue during Reagan's first term. Even the Law of the Sea Treaty had a higher profile. I'd written hundreds of policy statements in the previous four years, none of them about trade. But while no one had been paying attention, and without any real debate or planning, America had transformed itself from a manufacturing powerhouse to an information and services-based economy and the imports were just pouring in. The wake-up call came two weeks before I joined USTR, when a trade-bashing Democrat unexpectedly won a special Congressional election in rural Texas and the Democrats smelled a winning issue. That Texas election was the beginning of the populist backlash against trade that would make Ross Perot famous and Donald Trump president.

Arriving at USTR at the end of August 1985, I found myself in a political and policy maelstrom. On my first day, Roger handed me some background material and said: go write a speech for the President. A few days later, after some late nights and considerable editing, we sent a draft to the White House. I knew Ronald Reagan wouldn't read my words verbatim and was happy that his speechwriters returned a more eloquent version that included even a few of my paragraphs. That didn't last long. Nothing from my word processor remained after a hard-fought battle with White House Chief of Staff Don Regan and his deputy Al Kingon, who threw out that second draft, which celebrated free trade, and substituted one more focused on "fair trade." Thus, I was introduced to the cumbersome and contentious process of clearing presidential remarks through a dozen agencies and White House offices.

Since I had been a Congressional press secretary, Roger also decided I'd be the back-up press spokesman, which meant immediately getting up to speed on a request from the shoe industry to keep their factories open through dramatically higher tariffs. Coming from the former Shoe City of Brockton, my ears perked up at that one. The very Southern states that had stolen the factories from my hometown were now complaining that foreign countries were doing the same to them. When USTR rejected the request and Missouri Senator John Danforth thundered that we were destroying the U.S. shoe industry, I felt a little bit of sympathy, but in a now-you-know-how-it-feels way.

Counterintuitively, our small size was what made it such a wild ride at USTR. We were officially part of the White House staff, and the U.S. Trade Representative himself, Ambassador Clayton Yeutter, was a member of the President's cabinet. So even though the agency was relatively tiny, we had clout without any cumbersome bureaucracy. Our nimble communications staff, with only two and a half people, could accomplish far more than the massive Cabinet Departments because we weren't getting in each other's way.

I knew I was in a completely different environment on my second day, when Yeutter appeared in the office I shared with Desiree Tucker, the USTR press secretary, and handed her his handwritten changes to the upcoming statement on the shoe decision. I can promise you that Clayton Yeutter was the only member of the President's Cabinet who'd mark up a press release and walk it down to the press office himself. The idea that Elizabeth Dole would ever spontaneously show her face in the communications department without an advance team to plan the visit and then write talking points to handle the encounter was inconceivable. But that's what USTR was like—informal, non-hierarchical, and fast-moving.

USTR then had a staff of about 150, the perfect size, anthropologists say, for a tribe. Anything smaller and you lose diversity of talent and opinion; anything larger and you lose social cohesion. And it was true. Everyone knew everyone else.

Better still, USTR was not the place for your typical government drone. Hardly any staffers expected to spend their entire careers there. Our negotiators, recruited from other departments where they'd already excelled, were the cream of the crop in the government. The typical USTR employee would spend five to ten years coordinating and leading trade negotiations before moving on to a more lucrative position in the private sector, creating ongoing opportunities for new blood.

In the late 1980s, USTR employed a remarkable number of young, hard-working, hard-partying singletons. This meant a lot of blowing off steam, interoffice romances, and outright fun. The USTR Christmas parties, which featured sweaty dancing on the second floor's executive corridor, were easily the most buoyant ones I ever attended. One of my most patriotic experiences occurred at one of these parties. Just as the Christmas punch was working its magic, I noticed six or seven identically dressed members of a Chinese trade delegation peering quizzically out of a negotiating room and imagined what we must look like from their perspective: people of different races dancing with each other; support staff getting down with supervisors; government workers just having FUN. China was then a colorless, authoritarian state, and I fantasized that they envied our free-wheeling approach to life. I might have been delusional thinking that an office Christmas party represented all that was great about the American way of life, but when I left for the night, I noticed that some of our female staff had coaxed a handful of the Chinese to dance with them in the corridor and they seemed to be enjoying themselves.

Partying or working, we were all crammed into the Winder Building, a small but elegant 1840s office building on 17th Street facing the Old Executive Office Building. It was built entirely of iron and masonry, with no wood at all. Even the floors were brick, and the corridors were like interior echoing sidewalks. It served as the U.S. Army headquarters during the Civil War, and President Lincoln had routinely come to the building to read telegram reports from major battles. I always fantasized that the telegraph had been in my office, right off the first floor entrance, and that I was sitting in the exact spot where Lincoln had once absorbed the news from the front.

Yeutter, a corn-bred son of the Nebraska plains and the spitting image of Mikhail Gorbachev, was an even-tempered, kind-hearted, hard-working, slightly egotistical former CEO of the Chicago Mercantile Exchange. He knew the issues and could explain them clearly and effectively. But Roger was also right when he shook his head and said, "Clayton is a goober." Somewhat unworldly, completely uncynical, and impervious to irony, he lacked the filter that cautioned most politicians to practice false humility. Early in his tenure, during a "Who is Clayton Yeutter" interview with AP, he blithely said that he'd made a "huge financial sacrifice" to join the government, couldn't think of any mistake or setback he'd ever experienced, and was blessed with good genes that enabled him to work harder than anyone else. He called the resulting story "weird" and was irritated that what to him had been innocent and honest observations made him look conceited. No more profile pieces, he decreed!

He also had a loose-lips problem, saying things that were easily misinterpreted, especially when it came to the dollar. Instead of answering "no comment" on whether the dollar was too strong or too weak, he would try to analyze the issue and invariably a foreign wire service reporter would write that Yeutter was signaling a change in U.S. policy. This would result in big fluctuations in the currency and stock markets, followed immediately by an irate call from the Treasury Department demanding that we get our boss under control. Once, he mused that maybe we'd address a drought out west by withholding wheat exports and saving them for American consumers. This sent commodities markets gyrating, to the annoyance of the Agriculture Department.

The atmosphere he created was professional but casual. One day, I was having lunch on the building's back steps with Roger's secretary when Yeutter stopped to chat on his way to the stationary store. He was going to buy a 70th birthday card for Agriculture Secretary Dick Lyng (again, something that Cabinet Secretaries rarely did for themselves). Apropos of nothing, he told us he'd recently attended an American Enterprise Institute conference in Colorado where there'd been a magician walking from table to table doing tricks! Imagine that. There was literally no one at USTR, from the secretaries to his deputies, who was too intimidated to talk to him.

Despite being a goober, Yeutter knew how to make a speech. I'd been hired as his speechwriter, but since he delivered every speech extemporaneously, this turned out to be one of the most superfluous jobs in the government. He literally could not read a script without going off on tangents. Our solution? For major addresses, I would prepare an "official" speech that we would distribute at the event and share with media that had not attended. If we were lucky, Yeutter would occasionally stick to a few of its main themes.

U.S. Trade Representative Clayton Yeutter briefing President Reagan.

In other words, after all my efforts to snag a speechwriter's job, I was still in a position where no one—except, occasionally, the President of the United States—verbalized my words. But I didn't really care because I had plenty else to write: op-eds, articles for specialty magazines, position papers, press releases, Presidential veto messages, press statements for the White House, and letters to Congress. I never before or since churned out so many high-impact documents on such tight deadlines.

And yet I was once again bedeviled by constant computer failures. Just like at the Old.

Executive Office Building and Reagan-Bush '84, my desktop would routinely crash and I'd either lose documents or be prevented from accessing them for hours. And this wasn't just a USTR phenomenon. One morning, Deputy White House press secretary Rusty Brashear had me pulled out of a meeting; he needed to edit an upcoming announcement about sanctions against Taiwan and had lost the disk it was on. But both White House internal email and USTR computers had crashed and I couldn't help him; one of his assistants ended up retyping the paragraph in question, printing it out, and literally cutting and pasting it over the old one (as in, with actual scissors and paste) and xeroxing copies of that version. So the White House was no freer from screw-ups than any other press office.

We worked closely with the White House press office and participated in a weekly call they hosted with the economic-based departments (Treasury, Commerce, Labor, Agriculture, etc.) This was like any other weekly call I've had the misfortune to be associated with, with people taking turns giving their own brief reports and then tuning out when someone else was talking. Roger usually handled it, but when he wasn't available, I'd go into his office and report for USTR. I got so nonchalant about them that one time, when I was leaning too far back in Roger's chair with my feet on his desk, I flipped backward and landed on the floor with the phone dangling. "What's that?" Rusty asked. "Everything okay?" I never fessed up that it was me.

Because of our high profile, the White House had to approve almost everything we announced, in case they wanted to make it a Presidential announcement. This occasionally became a source of frustration if they took too long to decide. My ire boiled over one night in October 1986 when we were imposing sanctions against Japan on their tobacco quotas.

As I wrote in my diary: "Was furious with the WH about Japan Tobacco. They didn't even put out a press release. They just released a memo from Reagan to Yeutter. Idiots. No quotes, no nothing. They can't think about anything but Iceland and that stupid summit." Imagine the nerve of the White House, at the height of the Cold War, being more concerned about the imminent meeting between Reagan and Gorbachev in Reykjavík than they were about cigarette exports to Japan? Hard to fathom.

Even though my title was USTR speechwriter, dealing with the media became a bigger and more satisfying part of my job. It was also a high-stress responsibility because we were fighting to advance free trade across so many fronts, each of which had its own media strategy. There were at least a dozen reporters on the trade "beat," and because I talked to each of them at least two to three times a week, they became friends. Roger, I, and whoever was the press secretary at the time gossiped with them, proposed feature stories, provided access to whatever they wanted, and took them to lunch. The relationship between the trade media and the USTR press office was cozy enough that, several years later, our single-most influential beat reporter, the *Washington Post*'s Stu Auerbach, married Roger's secretary, Lena Lee. When I left USTR at the end of the Reagan Administration, the *Wall Street Journal*'s Art Pine told me that our office was the most informed and most helpful one in the government.

Occasionally, they'd cut us a break in return. For example, our swashbuckling Deputy USTR, Mike Smith, was a bit of a loose cannon. Despite being a career foreign service officer technically on loan from the State Department, he was far more blunt and outspoken than the traditional milquetoast diplomat. He was the kind of guy who, when a Japanese trade delegation showed up at USTR and felt dishonored because no one besides our security guard was there to greet them, got so annoyed at their prolonged threats to file a diplomatic protest with the State Department that he finally started shouting at them, "Okay, we screwed up. What do you want us to do about it now?!"

Unfortunately, on another occasion, while informally briefing a dozen reporters on the status of our semiconductor negotiations with Japan, he jocularly referred to the Japanese as "Nippers." This outraged the guy from the San Jose *Mercury News*, who decided to make a stink about it. In trying to wave the problem away, Smith somewhat unhelpfully explained that it was standard practice for American negotiators to have pet names for their foreign counterparts. The Koreans, for example, were called the ROKs (for the Republic Of Korea).

The rest of the media ignored the resulting story in the *Mercury News*. They liked Smith and knew he was just being, well, idiosyncratic. Frustrated, the reporter attended the next day's White House daily press briefing and asked Larry Speakes if President Reagan approved of his trade negotiators referring to the Japanese with racist slurs. That finally generated some attention for his scooplet. We had to get various Japanese and Japanese-American officials to affirm to the White House press that no, Mike Smith was not a racist. That helped, but if our beat reporters hadn't assured their White House counterparts that he was a good guy, he might have lost his job.

A few months later, Smith had his revenge, unknowingly. When we made a deal with Japan that gave the U.S. semiconductor industry enough time to get its act together to compete internationally, Smith called in the *New York Times*, *Washington Post* and *Wall Street Journal* for a full victory lap briefing. No one consciously said, "Let's screw that guy at the San Jose *Mercury News*," but since Silicon Valley wasn't really a phenomenon yet, he simply wasn't on our radar. When the reporter called to complain about being left out, I tried to commiserate with him about the drawbacks of working for a smaller regional paper, which offended him even more. They'd won a Pulitzer Prize last year and the *Washington Post* hadn't, he said. They had a larger circulation than the *Post* too. Geez, sorry, but call me when one of your stories has an impact in Congress.

We worked hard to raise USTR's profile and explain our trade policy, which had three main prongs: 1) negotiate to lower trade barriers in other countries either through multinational agreements, one-on-one free trade zones, or industry specific deals; 2) retaliate against unfair practices from our trading partners; 3) fight against protectionism in the U.S. To that end, Yeutter was very available to the media. He'd go on virtually any TV program that asked him. One night, when he was on the *Larry King Show* at 11:00pm, Mrs. Yeutter and I were in the control room, and she pulled me aside and told me not to schedule him again for broadcast appearances that were so late. Good luck with that. Yeutter loved the camera.

We also instituted bi-weekly press breakfasts. The format involved six different reporters for a background conversation over bagels and coffee. These ranged from White House correspondents who didn't know much, to international media who only cared about issues related to their country, to our regular beat reporters.

And yet as high-profile as trade was in the U.S., that was nothing compared to what it was like for other countries. America was far and away the biggest export market for many of them, and they cared deeply about every twist and turn in U.S. trade policy. Take Canada, which most Americans don't even think of as a foreign country. We were negotiating a "free trade area" that would increase the amount of trade between our two nations. This was a huge issue in Canada (it wouldn't gain attention in the U.S. until Mexico joined the free trade area, creating NAFTA). Their chief negotiator, Simon Reisman, was a well-known éminent grise. When we announced that our negotiator would be 35-year-old Peter Murphy, a nobody from their perspective, the people of Canada got their noses out of joint, claiming that we weren't taking them seriously (cue our eye-rolling within USTR). Whenever Reisman came to Washington to negotiate, there would be a gang of 30 or more Canadian journalists, photographers, and camera crews congregating on the sidewalk outside USTR so they could capture his comings and goings like a movie star.

The way the Canadians treated trade was most vividly illustrated when their Prime Minister Brian Mulroney came for a State visit. Bill Merkin, the U.S. deputy negotiator for the Canada talks, attended a reception for him at the State Department. Going through the receiving line, he politely shook hands with Secretary of State George Schultz, who didn't recognize the name until Mulroney grabbed his hand enthusiastically and said, "Bill Merkin! Just the man I wanted to meet." Merkin was famous in Canada and virtually unknown in our own State Department.

There's an old saying that the best way to get a job is to have a job. Almost as soon as I had the title of speechwriter for a Cabinet member, the offers came rolling in. Clark Judge, the Vice President's chief speechwriter, tried to recruit me. He was honest about what a sweatshop it was over there, with the VP making eight or nine appearances a week and the speechwriters constantly on the road. I didn't mind the work or the traveling. My concern was policy. He wasn't conservative enough for my taste and I didn't want him to be the GOP nominee in 1988. John Buckley's advice was clear—stay away from the "snake pit" that surrounded Bush. Also, he warned, if I took this job, he'd make sure I was blackballed in the upcoming Jack Kemp administration. Ha, ha. Maria Horgan had the most sensible advice: If I worked for Bush now, I'd be so burned out doing VP speeches that I'd be in no shape to write speeches for him if he became President. So, when I formally received the offer, I turned it down. (And as it turned out, Clark soon thereafter became a Reagan speech-writer and he never wrote for Bush when he was President either.)

Fresh off the plane in Punta del Este, Uruguay.

Somehow, my name also got thrown into the mix as Head of Communications for the Export-Import Bank, which loans money to major exporting corporations. That would have meant a 50 percent raise. I went for the interview but decided, again on philosophical grounds, that I didn't think the government should be in the business of lending money to anyone, least of all conglomerates, so I turned that down too.

And then Terry Eastland, Ed Meese's Head of Communications at Justice, who had sent me a rejection letter after our chatty interview a year earlier, called again after talking to Ken Khachigian, and this time said wanted to hire me. I had no animosity towards him, and I definitely didn't have a problem writing for Meese, but I didn't even go in for an interview. I was happy where I was. He did charm me though by asking "Are you sure?" and then, when I paused, humming the *Jeopardy!* theme song ("da da da da, da da da da.") "Yeah, I'm sure," I said, laughing.

Looking back on these job opportunities makes me shiver because any of them would have diverted me from my ultimate life path. Fortunately, despite sometimes being so stressed and busy I could almost cry, I really did feel fulfilled. I was on speed dial with the White House press and speechwriting offices. I had a great relationship with the media. I was respected within the agency, had a lot of personal friends, and got to go on some interesting trips.

I'm quite sure, for example, I never would have made it to Uruguay if I hadn't worked for USTR and been part of a delegation that traveled to Punta Del Este, a resort town that reminded me of 1950s Cape Cod, to launch a global round of trade talks under the auspices of the GATT, the acronym for the General Agreement of Tariffs and Trade, which we sometimes joked should have been named the General Agreement to Talk and Talk. (This organization was later rebranded as the World Trade Organization, or WTO, which became famous during the anti-trade riots that exploded when it convened in Seattle for a trade ministers meeting.)

Strengthening GATT was a major component of our trade strategy. GATT set the trade rules among all the non-communist countries, and liberalized trade would presumably make it easier to export American products. The point of this particularly unwieldy meeting, which included trade and economic ministers from about 75 countries, wasn't to negotiate new rules on the spot, but to set the framework for future negotiations, which would take place over the next two years.

My job in Uruguay was to babysit the American press corps, which included a handful of our most dedicated beat reporters. We'd reserved the cozy Hotel Milano for the media and I stayed there as well to keep an eye on them and arrange media briefings to keep them occupied. We also went shopping together and bought so many cheap sweaters that we joked that the next round of trade talks should be called the "Sweater Round."

Almost every night, I ate Argentinian beef and spent a few minutes at the nightly parties in the room of Rich Meier, who, as the coordinator of all the comings and goings of the American delegation, had a huge executive suite. These parties included staff from the Commerce, State, Treasury, Agriculture, and Labor departments. They were there most nights drinking, dancing, and fraternizing while their bosses were off negotiating the arcana of intellectual property protection, trade in services, or agricultural quotas. In the spirit of inter-agency cooperation, not everyone ended up in their assigned rooms when the lights went out.

It's hard to get 75 countries with economies as different as the US, France, Japan, Brazil, and India to agree on anything. On the last day, the talks lasted until 3:00am, after which we announced a deal to negotiate new rules in 17 different areas. The "Uruguay Round," when completed in 1994, became the last successful "round" of multilateral trade talks. The proposed "Doha Round" of 2001 crashed and burned when the Europeans wouldn't give up their agricultural subsidies, and given the populist backlash against any trade liberalization, there may never again be another effort like this.

A few months after returning from Uruguay, where I'd seen first-hand how hard it was for any country, never mind a single person, to make the global economy bend to its will, I got a glimpse inside the Trilateral Commission, believed then by right-wing conspiracy nuts to be controlling the world. I accompanied Yeutter to an appearance before the group at the old money River Club in New York City, and I can assure you that if these stuffed shirts were really calling the shots, it must have been at another secret lair.

The hundred or so business and government leaders in attendance were not very impressive political strategists and couldn't have conspired to fix a cock-fight, never mind the global economy.

Only one executive lived up to her reputation—Katharine Graham, the publisher of the *Washington Post*. I had been assigned to her table and wit-nessed for the first time what it's like to be royalty. Everyone else at the table (all men) treated her like the queen, asking fawning questions when they weren't outright kissing her ass. Far from being the figurehead I suspected, she was completely on top of the operations at the paper. When the other CEOs complimented her on the *Post*'s coverage of the Iran-Contra scan-dal, she agreeably conceded that her paper was "cleaning the clock" of the *New York Times* on that story. When the CEO of Mack Truck timidly tried to play pundit and said he was high on John Glenn for president in 1988, she regally dismissed his chances saying he didn't "have the candle power." She also opined that White House Chief of Staff Don Regan was a disaster and had to go. (When I later told this to Yeutter, he agreed.)

I was the only one at the table who pushed back even a fraction on anything she said, and that was because she annoyed me by dismissing the *Washington Times* as "VERY conservative" and thus not a legitimate news organization. Well, I observed, they were two days ahead of the *Post* on the story about Frank Carlucci being named Defense Secretary. She graciously conceded the point. In fact, she was gracious all evening. I sat next to "Jack" Heinz, the former CEO of the H.J. Heinz company, who, at 78 years old, was really out of it. He couldn't understand who I was or why I was sitting at the table. Mrs. Graham kindly explained my role and didn't treat me like the nobody I was. Later, Heinz ruminated out loud that his son, John Heinz (the same guy who had failed to hire me two years before), was a bit of a disappointment. "But Jack," Mrs. Heinz reassured him, "he's doing VERY WELL in the Senate." Imagine living in a world where being a U.S. Senator isn't enough to satisfy your dad.

My final clue that the Trilateral Commission didn't rule the world came at the end of the evening when I saw the group's co-founder, David Rockefeller, standing outside, waiting for Yeutter so he could drive him to the Waldorf

(I was staying at the Comfort Inn, by the way). Oops, Yeutter hadn't gotten the memo and just hopped in his own car, leaving this mogul of all moguls cooling his heels at the curb.

That trip also gave me an insight into fame's transience. The next morning, Yeutter spoke at a conference arranged by the financial consultants Smick-Medley. As we left for the airport, reporters swarmed, asking him questions about trade. Watching him vanish into this scrum, I glanced across the lobby and noticed our old nemesis from the 1984 campaign, would-be-Veep Geraldine Ferarro, standing quietly alone, obviously waiting for someone. Two years earlier, the roles would have been reversed. She'd have been the one who couldn't cross a hotel lobby without being mobbed and Yeutter would have been invisible.

As if to emphasize the point, when we got back to Washington, we had to sneak in the back entrance of the Winder Building; with a Japanese trade delegation inside the building, there were so many reporters outside the front door that we were afraid Yeutter's very presence would cause a riot. So yes, for a few years, Yeutter was the man of the moment. But once he left the government, he too fell back into relative obscurity. Celebrity, indeed, is fleeting.

The last week of 1986, which featured potential trade wars with both Canada and Europe, and an announcement of new import quotas for impoverished countries, left me gasping for breath. But it also pointed me to my future, even though I didn't know it at the time.

The Canadian dispute was particularly high-strung. The Canadians, who always acted like teenagers who bristled whenever Mom or Dad looked at them sideways, were furious that we might penalize them for subsidizing lumber exports. Almost as emotional were the American lumber executives who'd brought the complaint. The total dollar amounts were small, but it was such a sensitive issue north of the border that it could have single-handedly derailed our "Free Trade Area" talks. To avoid launching a New Year's Eve trade war, the U.S. and Canada embarked on a marathon negotiating session in the Winder Building the Monday after Christmas. This meant government officials arguing with each other in one room, the American lumber companies second-guessing our negotiators in another room, and the usual assortment of Canadian camera crews and reporters either hanging around our front door or calling repeatedly to find out when the talks would end.

An even bigger unfolding issue involved the European Commission (which is what the European Union was called at the time.) They had raised tariffs on American corn imports to Spain and Portugal, and we were preparing to retaliate with increased tariffs of our own on European food and alcohol imports. The plan was for Yeutter to brief President Reagan in Palm Springs on Tuesday, and then announce the news to the White House press out there. The fact that sanctions were coming was well-known, and an entirely different set of reporters (i.e., journalists who couldn't have cared less about Canada) were calling our office to find out how and when the news would be announced.

That Monday, I stayed in the office until 10:00pm, when our chief negotiator for the Canada talks, Alan Woods, finally told us to go home. This was another evening when I had popcorn for dinner. But I was in much better shape than my colleague, Debra Busker, then seven months into a difficult pregnancy. The way she coped with not being in control of her body was to assert control at work. Even though I begged her to take it easy, she refused, saying I had covered for her too many times and that she would hang in there.

Almost immediately after arriving home that night, I got a call from a *New York Times* reporter complaining that Lou Cannon of the *Washington Post* had a big page one story about the European sanctions that he'd missed. Apparently someone at the White House had planted old news with Cannon and packaged it as a scoop. In fact, there was not much in that story that the *Post*'s trade reporter, Stu Auerbach, hadn't reported two weeks earlier. But Auerbach wrote for the business section and Cannon covered the White House, so because someone in the West Wing had whispered into Cannon's ear, this regurgitated report got the front-page treatment. What do you want me to do? I asked the guy from the *Times*. I couldn't control leaks that were coming straight out of the White House.

When I got to work on Tuesday morning, the phone rang constantly about both the E.C. and Canada. I ran up the stairs to see where Canada stood. Alan Woods, who looked like he'd been run over by a lumber truck, told me they'd been up all night talking, and since the deadline for sanctions wasn't until midnight they'd probably be at it again until then.

That was fine with me—there was no time to deal with Canada because Yeutter was planning to brief the White House press about the E.C. sanctions at 2:00pm and every European newspaper, magazine, news agency, or radio network needed to know the background of the issue and the details about the briefing. Yeutter was good, but the reporters in the briefing got weirdly obsessed with what a fifth of gin would cost when the sanctions went into effect. There were at least ten questions about that. When it was over, Roger, Debra, and I spent the rest of the afternoon trying to explain to the media what this issue was all about. I even gave a recorded radio interview to the BBC.

We were able to focus again on Canada at about 6:00pm. The talks had once again dragged on all day and as a midnight deadline approached, negotiators finally made a deal. But the leaders of the U.S. lumber companies weren't happy with it and Alan Woods had to yell at them to get on board, which they eventually did. To save face, they agreed to be the ones to announce the news. Six of them trudged down to our office for a chaotic press conference among our desks, with camera crews climbing on our furniture to get a better vantage point, until Roger yelled at them to get off the couch. We then organized an official photo op of U.S. and Canadian officials shaking hands back upstairs in the rather fragrant negotiating room, another unruly affair, and everyone rushed into the cold night as fast as they could.

Meanwhile, as if the European and Canadian disputes weren't bad enough, I was dealing with a third trade issue that was ridiculously esoteric. In a normal year, it would have passed without notice. The U.S. has a little-known trade program called the Generalized System of Preferences (GSP), which makes it easier for the world's poorest countries to export to the U.S. Every year, we'd announce the countries and products that would be included in the GSP. In a normal year, we'd be able to get away with a simple press statement, but in 1986, every trade decision seemed important. Before Christmas, we had even thought the White House itself would announce it, but with so much else going on, they punted it back to us and we ended up staging a big press conference that Friday in the amphitheater at the neighboring Federal Home Loan Bank Building.

During the preparation for the press conference, Yeutter confided that Don Regan had berated him in Palm Springs about the GSP program because some of the recipient countries like Taiwan had big trade surpluses. Regan had also chastised him for the big Canadian surplus and said we didn't have any ideas on how to bring the trade deficit down. "I told him he was more protectionist than the Democrats," Yeutter claimed. Since the Treasury Department was the most influential voice on economic issues, including trade, I did wonder what would have happened if Regan and James Baker hadn't switched jobs as Chief of Staff and Treasury Secretary at the beginning of the second term. I had my problems with Baker's moderation and so-called pragmatism, but at least he was an internationalist and not a reflexive protectionist like Regan.

In any event, the press conference was another mob—with over 50 U.S. and foreign reporters and about ten camera crews lined up in the back, all for an announcement on GSP! It was crazy.

I spent the rest of the day trying to decompress, while simultaneously handling mop-up questions from reporters about Canada, the EC, and GSP. Yeutter came downstairs later that afternoon to find me because the White House had called looking for Roger, who'd gone home a little early on the Friday after New Year's Day. Again, Yeutter was probably the only member of the Cabinet hand-delivering telephone messages to the press office.

By 6:30pm that Friday night, only a handful of us remained in the building. It was the last day for a woman who worked in the European office; someone bought a couple of bottles of champagne and we went into the building's main negotiating room, sat around the table and shot the breeze. Yeutter sauntered in, too, and this motley collection of secretaries, junior staffers, and mid-level negotiators lobbed questions at him and joked about the foibles of our negotiating partners.

Here's how I describe it in my diary: "I hung around reading clips until 6:30, then went to a going away party in room 203. Wendy Paquin is leaving. About ten people were still hanging out—Karen Porter, Dave Shark, Jim Gradoville, Meg Ricci, Catherine Curtis—a diverse group. The most eye-opening thing is Meg Ricci carrying on. She's really pretty funny, almost wild."

And that, Dear Reader, is the first mention in my diary of my future wife.

CHAPTER 29

USTR, Part Two

As a Congressional press secretary, I'd been thrilled by the handful of times I got my boss into the national media and starstruck whenever I found myself on the phone with a TV reporter or national columnist who wanted to learn more about the most recent controversy that Jerry Solomon had embroiled himself in.

But at USTR, I took it for granted that I was in daily contact with White House correspondents, TV bookers, and reporters from the country's most prominent newspapers. NBC's White House reporter, Andrea Mitchell, and her fellow correspondent, Irving R. Levine, came to our USTR press Christmas party. ABC's White House reporters, Sheliah Kast and Steve Aug, regularly attended our press breakfasts. The *Washington Post, New York Times,* and wire services quoted me frequently. I usually tried to say the most innocuous things possible—as in, "no decision has been made yet." The one exception to this code of blandness was the *Boston Globe.* I deliberately tried to be quotable enough to get my name in that paper so my parents (and, just as importantly, their friends!) would be impressed.

The nonstop pace energized me at first, but it just never let up. The number of trade disputes kept growing, as industry after industry complained about: subsidies that made foreign goods cheaper; foreign import quotas that kept our goods out of international markets; overly cautious health regulations that provided ridiculous excuses for keeping our food out of other countries; lax intellectual property protections, and much more. We were in a mini-trade war with almost every one of our major trading partners: Airbus aircraft from Europe; information products from Brazil; almonds from India; rice, fish, and oilseed exports to Japan. Each of these disputes required White House coordination, press releases, talking points, and a blizzard of media inquiries. And as the agency's speechwriter, I still needed to churn out the speeches, op-eds, and reports I'd been hired to do. With no such thing as "remote work" or even home computers, this meant coming into the office on the weekends so I could concentrate on writing without the phone ringing.

Working the media in a small, high-profile agency was time-consuming. Without the internet, there were no email blasts, so whenever we had a press conference, we had to pick up the phone and personally invite 50 or more reporters, each of whom wanted to know whether it was worth their while to come over. During the periods when we didn't have interns, it could take us two hours to make all these notifications. Press releases were also a problem. For the most urgent ones, we would call our A-list reporters and dictate the text over the phone and ask the rest to send over messengers to pick it up. I know. The Dark Ages, right?

We weren't just in a trade war with foreigners—we were also fighting a rear-guard action with Congress, trying to fend off two major protectionist trade bills. One would have limited imports of textiles and apparel, thereby raising the cost of clothing. I wrote an op-ed outlining the bill's various horrors and placed it in the *Washington Post* under Yeutter's name. The next day, South Carolina Senator Fritz Hollings denounced it as a "pack of lies." I doubt the op-ed changed many minds, because the bill passed both Houses of Congress, but not by enough to sustain the subsequent veto. I wrote the President's veto message too, so take that, Fritz!

The other trade bill was a monster hodgepodge of ideas and pet projects from both Democrats and Republicans—some good, most bad.

The Democrats who controlled Congress passed a protectionist version, which Reagan vetoed. We then worked on a compromise bill—these were the days when Members would actually make deals along the lines of "you give me this and I'll give you that." The Administration obtained the authority it needed to negotiate the "Uruguay Round" of world-wide trade talks. The Democrats got laws that would make it easier to retaliate against "unfair" trade practices. You might as well have called it the "Trade Lawyers Enrichment Act," because any time you increase regulations, it's always the lawyers and lobbyists who get rich.

The most bitterly contested part of the trade bill had nothing to do with trade. The Democrats demanded a new law requiring companies to give factory workers a two-month warning before closing a facility with over 500 workers. Reagan had vetoed the first trade bill precisely because of this provision, but as the 1988 election approached, the Bush campaign got cold feet and convinced Reagan not to veto it when it passed as a separate bill. I was absolutely furious that George Bush's ongoing backsliding led to this betrayal of everything we'd fought for over the past nine months—I'd written countless op-eds and letters to Congress about this and believed deeply in the righteousness of the cause. In the end, though, the plant closings bill, like so many other issues that seemed so important at the time, turned out to be far less consequential than either its supporters or detractors claimed. It certainly didn't arrest the slowdown of factory closings. What had all that wasted energy and emotion been about anyway?

As usual, I would have been happier if I'd found a way to take my job a little less seriously, because, really, did it matter in the long run if we sent out another press release about corn exports to Spain? But I couldn't turn off the intensity and found myself aggravated half the time.

And it wasn't just our trading partners, the media, and the Democrats who gave me heartburn. Sometimes it was the other agencies, too. The only Cabinet Department that never created any problems was the Agriculture Department, whose leader, Secretary Dick Lyng, was one of Yeutter's good friends. To make it even cozier, Lyng's chief of communications was Lynne Melillo, who was first Roger's girlfriend, then his fiancé, and eventually his wife. So yeah, the communications between USTR and Agriculture were very smoothly coordinated.

Everyone else drove me nuts. The State Department cared a lot more about the feelings about our trading partners than they did about our exporters. When we decided to retaliate against Brazil, State insisted on a six-hour lid on the news, thereby pushing the announcement out to 8:00pm so they could inform the Brazilian Government and give them time to prepare their statements denouncing us. "They have an election coming up," the Brazilian desk officer lamely explained to me, as if we didn't have elections of our own in the U.S. Another time, when we successfully resolved a dispute with Canada, they delayed the press release to give a Michigan Congressman—a Democrat!—the chance to announce it first. This gave me a stomachache because this asshole was one of our biggest critics. Why reward him?

Then there was the Commerce Department, which included the International Trade Administration (ITA), an agency that seemed to be in the pocket of the country's most protectionist businesses. USTR was supposed to take the lead in setting and implementing trade policy, but we always found ourselves in a struggle with Commerce Secretary Malcolm Baldridge over press strategy, meaning he wanted a more visible role with the press. The White House tried to referee, but the first time both Yeutter and Baldridge did a joint briefing in the White House press room, they practically wrestled for the podium. The interagency tension was eased somewhat when Desiree Tucker, the USTR press spokesperson when I arrived, left to become Communications Director at the ITA. Roger, Desiree, and I all got along great, but there were still days when she'd call up and say, "Don't kill me, I'm only the messenger, but can you mention the Commerce Department in the first paragraph of the press release you're putting out today?"

What made my job particularly hard was that for a couple years after Desiree left, the position of USTR press secretary became a revolving door. For long stretches, it was just Roger and me handling all of this. And although he did pick up some of the slack by taking media calls and writing a couple of speeches, he had plenty else on his plate besides that.

It took four months to find Desiree's successor—Debra Busker, a tall, intense, goal-oriented spokesperson from the U.S. Chamber of Commerce. But soon after she started, she found herself in a tough pregnancy that required a lot of time off even before she went on maternity leave. Once Debra gave birth, we temporarily hired Cathy Barr, my good friend from the Department of Transportation, as a stand-in. That turned out to be very temporary indeed, because she almost immediately found a job with Pfizer in New York City. Rather than hire another short-time replacement, we decided to wait for Debra's return. Unfortunately, her infant son needed around-the-clock attention and when her maternity leave ended, she called tearfully to say she couldn't return.

Eventually we hired Kelly Winkler, an ebullient and energetic spokesperson from the agriculture department. She became a close partner, but the seven months between Diane's departure and Kelly's arrival had really worn me out. I was further put out when I learned that Debra, Cathy, and Kelly were all paid at the *GS-14* pay level while I was still languishing as a *GS-13*. (I also discovered while writing this memoir that my future wife, who worked in USTR's computer group, was also a *GS-14*, so apparently EVERYONE out-earned me.)

It seems petty to whine about salary when you're a single guy living pretty comfortably, and I'd have preferred not to think about any of it because I hadn't come to Washington to get rich. Most political appointees hadn't. But in the government, everyone seems to know everyone else's salary and they talk about it. A lot. The career staff, in particular, spend a lot of energy pursuing "step" and "grade" increases. My good friend Christina Lund, a career person who handled negotiations with Brazil, was aghast that I was only a *GS-13* and implied it was a character flaw not to fight harder for a promotion. Another career person said she'd seen a salary breakdown and that within USTR, there were 19 *GS-15s*, 17 *GS-14s*, and only 5 *GS-13s*. What the heck?

Other jobs started looking enticing. Cathy Barr recommended me for the position of Pfizer spokesperson and I traveled to New York City for a series of interviews with her bosses. I thought I did great and was perfect for the job. Apparently I didn't impress them because I never got a call-back,

something I still don't understand. (For the next year, whenever Cathy men-
tioned her boss's name I responded, "You mean the man who ruined my life?"
Later, when I met my wife, which wouldn't have been possible if I'd moved to
New York, I started calling him "The man who saved my life.")

I also made a semi-serious run at becoming a Presidential speechwriter.
One Wednesday morning, the White House speechwriters' office called to
say the President's radio address that Saturday would be about the evils of
the Democrats' trade bill. Since they were swamped, could we do a first
draft? I went into Roger's empty office, banged something out in a couple
of hours, got it cleared, and sent it over later that afternoon. When they
circulated it for Cabinet-wide approval, the speechwriters had hardly made
any changes.

As it happened, my cousin's 12-year-old son Ryan, a kid like me who
obsessed over Washington as a tween, was visiting that weekend. Since I'd
written the radio address, I cleared the two of us into the White House press
room to listen to Reagan's piped-in delivery from Camp David. This was a

*With my USTR friends Karen Porter, Kelly Winkler, Caroyl Miller,
and Lena Lee at Roger's wedding.*

cool experience for both of us. I introduced him to ABC's Sheliah Kast and a couple of other reporters I knew, took a photo of him standing behind the press secretary's briefing podium, basked in compliments from members of the press office for a good speech, and even got one of them to give Ryan and me a tour of the West Wing, complete with a peek at the Rose Garden and Oval Office. All this scored major points with the extended family back in Brockton.

The next Monday, Tony Dolan, one of the President's main speechwriters, got in touch to find out who I was. How come he'd never heard of me before? Going back to the days of Misty Church, I'd been good friends with the fact-checkers but had done a lousy job of marketing myself to the actual speechwriters, who tended to be self-important guys that fancied themselves the true keepers of the Reagan flame. More than once, I ranted in my diary that they were "arrogant pricks" because they wrote speeches advocating for the ideologically pure free market trade policy they wanted instead of the actual policy we'd hammered out. "Pricks" or not, I was eager to join them for the honor of writing for the President full-time. I told Dolan my background and convinced him that I was almost as much of a True Believer as he was. When he asked if I wanted to be considered for a position as a Reagan speechwriter, I leapt at the chance and said of course.

Later that week, the woman who coordinated agency-wide clearances of Presidential speeches told me she was pushing for them to hire me. "We already have six speechwriters, but [NAME REDACTED BY AUTHOR] and [NAME REDACTED BY AUTHOR] spend half their time writing Hollywood screenplays, so we could use some more help."

Dolan asked if I'd submit to a try-out by writing a Reagan speech about something other than trade. He had a specific event in mind scheduled two weeks later, but then called back to say they were going to do it themselves. Then he called back *again* four days before it was due to say they wanted me to write it after all. By that time, it was nearly impossible for me to carve out the time because I was so busy. I said I'd be willing to try again if I had more advance warning, but my reluctance to drop everything to do their bidding was basically the end of my burgeoning career as a White House speech-writer. I suppose if I'd been more ambitious, I would have done my usual work during the day and then stayed until midnight to grind it out over a few nights. Three years earlier, I would have done that in a second. By 1988, a more jaded me could only handle so much bullshit.

In any event, Roger eventually pushed through a raise for me in mid-1988. He tried to get me a two-grade jump from a *GS-13* to a *GS-15*, but that didn't fly and I ended up as *GS-14*. In compensation, he gave me a new title—Director of Communications, which sounded a lot better than Chief Speechwriter. This would help a bit when the time came to look for post-Reagan employment. In fact, it's still the title I use on my LinkedIn page when describing my experience at USTR.

One of the perks of the job was travelling with Yeutter and his deputies. Ostensibly, I was along for the ride to handle local media, but I functioned mostly as an advance man, companion, and gofer on their business trips. I was more than happy to play these roles for the chance to see different parts of the world.

On one trip to New York City with Deputy USTR Alan Woods, I found myself 49 floors above the Museum of Modern Art in the penthouse apart-ment of American Express CEO Jim Robinson (definitely not the same Jim Robinson who was my college friend). He was the chair of USTR's private sector advisory committee on financial services, the group we consulted with to help us develop our trade policy for banks, credit card companies, and insurance companies. We wanted his support in lobbying Capitol Hill against the Democrats' trade bill.

Robinson then loomed large in the business press as a Wall Street titan. In addition to its core credit card business, American Express also owned an investment bank (Lehman Brothers), two retail brokerage firms (Shearson Loeb and EF Hutton), and God knows what else. He was as polished as a crystal decanter and exuded a soft-spoken patrician calm. His trade policy aide, Joan Spero, joined us and we sat facing each other in a small circle in his gorgeous, antiques-packed living room. An elegantly attired butler silently served the most delicious Scotch and soda I ever consumed, to complement a steadily replenished stream of shrimp and tiny ham and cheese sandwiches that only I seemed to be eating.

I was amazed at how well-briefed Robinson was about the trade bill—he even rattled off the names of the key House and Senate staffers who were drafting it. What I couldn't anticipate at the time though, was that within a year and a half, I'd be working for his wife's PR company, thus almost certainly becoming the only member of Linda Robinson's firm to ever penetrate the inner sanctum of that fantastical apartment, which was truly everything you'd expect from a master of the universe.

The next day, we visited an entirely different corporate mogul—Ed Pratt, the CEO of Pfizer. As chairman of the President's Advisory Committee for Trade Negotiations (ACTN), he lobbied hard for stronger intellectual property protection for American-made drugs. We arrived at Pfizer's headquarters on 34th Street at 5:30pm to find the whole corporate floor deserted with no one to greet us. Apparently the quitting time whistle had sounded at 5:00pm and the staff had fled the premises. We wandered around in the eeriness for ten minutes until we finally stumbled onto the one room on the floor that still had lights on—a remarkably modest chamber for such a powerful CEO.

Where Robinson had been elegant and serene, Pratt was down-to-earth and blunt—so unconcerned with putting on airs that he seemed indifferent to the hole in the sole of his shoe (although, to be fair, Alan also had a hole in *his* shoe. What was it with these guys?) Halfway through Alan's standard pitch about why we needed to defeat the Democrats' Trade Bill, Pratt interrupted with a long speech of his own to complain that we hadn't done enough to reduce the trade deficit. Thrown off stride, Alan mentioned his disappointment that the American car companies had chosen to raise prices rather than try to build market share in the face of Japanese competition. Oops. Pratt also served on the Board of General Motors and cogently explained how there was no Japanese competition in the large vehicle sector, where GM had raised prices. As the meeting ended and he walked us to the door, he stopped at a closet to retrieve some parting gifts—bottles of Stetson aftershave and Coty perfume. In addition to its main pharmaceutical business, it turned out that Pfizer had a small fragrance business too.

You never knew what these CEOs would be like. On a trip to meet with corporate bigwigs in Pittsburgh, Yeutter and I first drove to National Airport where we boarded the Alcoa corporate jet. We discovered that the aircraft's only two other passengers were the company's CEO Paul O'Neill and its tax attorney. That was definitely the way to travel, since we were back on the ground in Pennsylvania just half an hour after takeoff.

Even though he didn't mind deploying a corporate jet when it suited him, O'Neill was an egalitarian corporate executive, almost to a fault. At the Pittsburgh airport, he took the wheel of his own small Toyota and proceeded to ferry Yeutter and me to the company's headquarters. This included a drive through the most monstrous hailstorm I ever experienced. I sat in the back seat wondering if we'd end up in a ditch as O'Neill and Yeutter blithely chatted about trade policy and gossiped about figures in Washington that they both knew. After Yeutter's public speech at the swanky Duquesne Club, O'Neill whisked him to a very private dinner with the city's top CEOs—so private that I was excluded. Instead, I had dinner with Alcoa's VP for Public Affairs, who confessed her frustration with O'Neill: he was too determined to do eccentric things like playing chauffeur to visiting dignitaries and he disregarded the staff's recommendations on how a CEO should conduct himself. Eccentric or not, O'Neill was a remarkably successful corporate leader. Less successfully, he later became the first Treasury Secretary of George W. Bush (i.e., "43"), where his I'll-do-it-my-way approach eventually led to his firing.

The U.S. trips were fun diversions, but international travel really exposed me to a different way of living. I made a couple of trips for some dull multinational trade meetings in Geneva, Brussels, and Paris. And who cared if the meetings were as boring as a George H.W. Bush (i.e., "41") press conference? Just being in a foreign city where I could go to fancy restaurants and drink unfamiliar wine with my colleagues made me feel sophisticated.

The best international trips, though, were with Yeutter himself. In November 1987, he scheduled a five-day trip to Geneva, London, and Dublin and I went along to help coordinate the speeches and media interviews. I called Roger and Kelly in Washington several times a day to hear what was happening in the office and to report on how Yeutter was being received in Europe. Good thing, because the foreign media so frequently misinterpreted Yeutter.

To be fair, he gave such overly nuanced and easy-to-misunderstand answers to audiences without a great grasp of English that a financial crisis was always one mistranslated remark away. Sure enough, when we landed in London, Roger told us that a Japanese wire service reporter had quoted Yeutter as saying the dollar was too high, which as usual, was disrupting currency markets and once again raising the ire of the Treasury Department. Thankfully, I had the tape from the speech and could prove this had never happened, enabling us to immediately issue a denial.

The advantage of traveling with a member of the Cabinet is being able to go behind the scenes. In London, Yeutter, Jim Murphy, our USTR coordinator for Europe, and I met with British Trade Minister Kenneth Clarke in his office in Parliament. The meeting lasted about 15 minutes, which Yeutter later declared a "waste of time" because Clarke was uninterested and unknowledgeable about the issue at hand—European subsidies for Airbus jetliners (an issue that was STILL not resolved more than 35 years later, by the way). I didn't care as much about the meeting as the surroundings. Despite being both a member of the British Cabinet and a member of Parliament, Clarke inhabited a small, cramped office staffed by only a handful of Parliamentary aides. This was nothing like the U.S. Congress, where each Representative, no matter how lowly, had an office big enough for the CEO of a Fortune 500 company and a staff to match. Yet somehow the British MPs managed to do their jobs. Imagine that.

The Parliament building itself turned out to be a labyrinth. After the meeting, Clarke walked us down to the House of Commons so we could see some of the debate. From the outside, the building, officially known as the Palace of Westminster, is majestically imposing, but inside, it's a warren of narrow staircases, uneven door jambs, and long twisting halls that could well be haunted.

Yeutter made three speeches on this trip, each one in a setting more historic and overpowering than the next, culminating at the Middle Temple Hall, a magnificent building with an ornate English Gothic Ceiling dating back to the reign of Queen Elizabeth I. This had been the setting for the premiere of Shakespeare's *Twelfth Night* and the hang-out for generations of prestigious British barristers. Just like at Hogwarts, we all sat at a handful

361

of parallel 100-foot-long tables beneath the elevated platform from which Yeutter delivered his speech. If you squinted, it could have been the year 1587 instead of 1987.

When Yeutter returned to Washington, I remained for a week-long vacation in London. One of Spencer Warren's London friends arranged for me to stay at the Reform Club, which was everything you'd want from a Victorian-era, uber-stuffy, exclusive men's club. Modeled after an Italian palace, it had a big, hushed court area called "The Saloon" where Members of Parliament, political writers, business leaders, and various Lords languidly sat in armchairs reading newspapers, chatting softly or dozing silently with their chins on their chests, but definitely *not* conducting business, which was officially verboten. Alas, the downstairs grandeur was not reflected upstairs in the overnight guest quarters, where I stayed in a small room more spartan than any freshman dorm in America, furnished only with a narrow bed, a chest of drawers, a metal cabinet with six clothes hangers, a boarded up fireplace, a chair, and a sink where I washed my hair in tepid water the next morning.

I normally don't enjoy traveling by myself, but this trip was an exception because I had so many friends, or friends of friends, in London. Cathy Barr, as enthusiastic an Anglophile as anyone I knew, was also there for a few days, and she introduced me to her British friends and favorite haunts. We went to plays (*Kiss Me, Kate* at the Old Vic), other famous private clubs (The Garrick, which was crammed with memorabilia from centuries of stage productions), and popular pubs (where I was flummoxed when I ordered a pint of ale and the bartender asked for a brand. I stood there, mouth agape with no clue).

She knew the man-about-town conservative journalist John O'Sullivan, who later succeeded William F. Buckley as editor of the *National Review* back in the U.S. We met him and his friends in the Cork and Bottle, my first introduction to something I'd never heard of before—a wine bar. Six of us lunched underground in a crypt-like converted wine cellar where O'Sullivan held court and discussed politics, art, theatre, and film. I was led to believe this is how he and his friends spent every Saturday afternoon, and they were settling in for a long program of conversation when Cathy and I, after a glass of champagne and a lamb stew, left to visit the National Gallery.

When Cathy returned to the United States, I stayed for five nights with Marjorie Thompson, my old friend from Jerry Solomon's office. She had moved to the U.K. five years earlier to marry a young Welsh student, but she'd divorced that guy and was now living with a different Welshman. Her new partner was an up-and-coming Member of Parliament—Dafydd Elis-Thomas, who is now a Baron and a member of the House of Lords, a role I never would have guessed for him at the time since he seemed to be a Welsh nationalist and anti-monarchist.

I slept on their living room couch, which was a considerable upgrade in comfort from my two nights at the Reform Club. Marjorie, who had been a liberal Republican back in Jerry Solomon's office, was now even further left. In fact, while I was visiting, she became vice chair of the Campaign for Nuclear Disarmament, a pacifist organization trying to get nukes out of the U.K. The next morning, there were articles about her in the *Times* of London and the *Guardian* pushing the same line: "Former 'Goldwater Girl' [a political phenomenon when the right-wing Barry Goldwater ran for President in 1964] Named to Lead the British Peace Movement."

Life seemed a lot more interesting in London than in Washington D.C. It was not only the political capital of the U.K., but also the media, financial, art, and news capital. And it was so damn historic. This neighborhood looked like Dickens had invented it; that neighborhood looked like the Duke of Wellington had lived there. And everywhere you looked, there were Indian, Pakistani, Jamaican, or Singaporean restaurants. Marjorie got me tickets to the Prime Minister's question time where I saw Margaret Thatcher beat down the Labor Party leader. I saw a play starring Maggie Smith at the Globe Theatre. I went to a reception at the South African embassy. When I couldn't get into Marjorie's apartment because she wasn't home yet, I waited with her downstairs neighbors, who, despite having a living room of cheap Jesus iconography and crucifixes, never missed an afternoon rebroadcast of *The Golden Girls*. I had lunch at the Beefsteak Club, yet another exclusive club, where they called all the waiters "Charles" because no one could be expected to remember the names of all the servants, and I embarrassed myself in front of the waiter by ordering tea instead of coffee at lunch (a major faux pas in itself) and then pouring salt instead of sugar into it when it arrived. I stayed overnight at the house of a woman who'd gone to college with my Brockton friend Rich Martel, and she and her husband took me to see *The Barber of Seville* and then hosted a small dinner with their friends, one a big shot at the BBC and the other an investment banker in "the city." And to get around, I became an expert at navigating the "Tube" to avoid spending money on taxis.

It was a letdown of epic proportions to leave London and travel straight home to Brockton for Thanksgiving. The only ones who seemed genuinely excited about my trip were Rich Martel and his mother. When I called to talk to Rich, Mrs. Martel answered the phone and said she was so impressed to hear that I'd been traveling in Europe with George Shultz! That would have impressed me too.

Rich and I were extreme nostalgists, so we attended our 15th high school reunion two days later. Walking into the function room of Christo's, our favorite pizza and Greek salad joint, we quickly realized that none of our friends were there. Being distant acquaintances didn't stop some of the women from commenting on my receding hairline though. During dinner, we sat with two women who'd been in Rich's advanced classes and their extraordinarily dull husbands. A few days earlier, I'd been debating nuclear disarmament, the novels of Anthony Trollope, and French New Wave cinema in a Sri Lankan restaurant in London. Rich had just finished filming a Diet Pepsi ad with Michael C. Fox. Yet neither of us could think of a thing to say because these women—both teachers at the high school and dressed like they were attending the Inaugural Ball—only wanted to discuss their jobs and the pools they planned to install next summer.

Rich and I got out of there as soon as the dessert arrived. Back at his house, Mrs. Martel sympathized with us, saying she had a feeling we wouldn't enjoy ourselves. She then stroked my ego, opining that out of all Rich's friends, I had the best chance of being famous. "You should write a book," she said. I didn't become famous, but I did write the book. It took me 35 years and to my real regret, neither Rich nor his mother are alive to read it.

CHAPTER 30

Leaving Washington

A s the end of the Reagan Administration approached, I felt the same helplessness that I'd had at the end of college. My future hurtled towards me but I had no plan for taking control of it.

On January 20th, 1989, there would be a new President and my position as a Reagan appointee would end. It looked like George Bush would replace Reagan, and as a loyal, experienced Republican, I could probably find another job in the government. But after eight years of griping about that squish, Bush, what kind of hypocrite would that make me?

I could try to attach myself to the vast and enormously lucrative lobbying industry that was transforming Washington into the richest metropolitan area in the country, but I didn't really want to get into a "say for pay" situation, advocating for political causes I didn't really support. A nice conservative think tank would have been ideal, but I didn't have any contacts, having played the schmoozing game very poorly. If I'd been more gregarious or less hung up on my self-image as a "movement" conservative, I could have very easily settled into a comfortable existence in D.C.

Still, even as I waited for my future to sort itself out, my day-to-day existence had never been better. USTR might be exhausting, but I had an active
social life as fulfilling as anything I'd ever experienced before. So many single
people working so closely together resulted in a lot of well-lubricated bonding.
If I'd been so inclined, I could have gone out for drinks almost every night.
And if I didn't get an actual invitation, I could have found myself welcomed
after work by walking across the small plaza in back of the Winder Building
to Maison Blanche, a swanky expense account restaurant with a fun bar scene.

I joined the softball team—"The Free Traders"—and was a decent enough
player to be invited for aftergame drinks at the 21st Amendment bar. Every
couple of weeks, I played racquetball or tennis with my former intern, Mark
Dow. For a while, a group of us spent lunch breaks playing Trivial Pursuit
in one of the negotiating rooms. That same gang ventured up to California
Avenue in the Adams Morgan neighborhood for dance outings at Kiliman-
jaro, an African social club. A couple times a year, someone at USTR would
organize a bus to attend a Baltimore Orioles game.

Roger asked me to be a groomsman in his wedding, which took place in
Lynne's hometown of Louisville. He, too, had built a large group of USTR
friends, so almost a dozen of us, including Clayton Yeutter himself, flew
out to Kentucky to help him celebrate. Even weddings were occasions for
USTR parties.

And at least once a month, I attended or hosted one of a steady stream
of rotating dinner parties, brunches, or pre-dinner cocktail get-togethers that
tilted heavily to my USTR friends. My apartment was just the right size for
small parties and I took full advantage of it. My eighth-floor balcony, which
faced a gently sloping hill of rooftops leading up to Adams Morgan, was perfect for pre-dinner cocktails. My living room featured a small, cloth-covered
futon couch, a teak stereo stand for my turntable, tuner, and LPs, and a
built-in liquor cabinet, complete with a mirror and glass shelves for my
stemware. I kept a bottle of syrupy Stolichnaya vodka in the freezer, but for
brunches, I preferred to serve white sangria made with Chablis, Cointreau,
fruit, and a splash of Perrier. At one party I served the Australian food spread
"vegemite," which featured so prominently in the music of "Men at Work,"
but none of us could choke down more than one bite of the stuff. I proudly

spun my George Winston, Marvin Gaye, Roxy Music, and Sade LPs, demonstrating to discerning visitors that I was one with the '80s zeitgeist.

Surprisingly, my best friends at USTR were not my fellow political appointees but the career staff, most of whom, as Democrats, were secretly looking forward to having Republicans ejected from government. My closest friend at work was Roger's no-nonsense, over-qualified secretary, Lena Lee, who lived with her mother, a Chinese-speaking immigrant. She became my "work wife" (i.e., a person of the opposite sex who platonically has your full confidence in the office). We had lunch together more often than not and she watched my back. She was wired in with the other secretaries, including the ones in the administrative office who she called the "old biddies," and kept me abreast of office gossip, which helped me navigate agency politics. I also listened to her romantic problems and once, when she was having a particularly difficult time, she slept at my apartment while I crashed on the living room couch.

I had another close friendship that mystified the rest of USTR because we seemed like such an unmatched pair. Christina Lund, our negotiator for Brazilian issues, stood out at USTR for her beauty and acerbic tongue. Once, complaining about not knowing where the Cabinet stood on the question of retaliating against an unfair trade practice, she told me, "I'm like a mushroom.

With Yeutter at the Acropolis in Athens, with USTR and Embassy staff.

Kept in the dark and fed shit." Like the rest of the USTR negotiators, she was a thousand times more famous overseas than in the U.S. and was once described in the Brazilian press as a "bitter old hag." A hag she was not. I'm pretty sure she was the only woman who ever dated both Oliver North and Pelé. She and Victor, her former long-term boyfriend from the Peace Corps, but now her long-time platonic gay roommate, lived within walking distance of my apartment and we saw each other a lot. At one of my brunches, she contributed the immortal conversation-starter: "What's the most embarrassing thing you ever did with food?" I thought she was worldly, amusing, and plugged in. I'm not sure what she saw in me, except that I was probably one of the few men at USTR who listened to her ruminations without hitting on her.

Rounding out this trio of three close USTR friends was Caroyl Miller, a junior negotiator, first for GATT talks and then for textile imports. I met her through Desiree Tucker when I first arrived, and she quickly became a pal and part of the dinner/dance party gang. She was always up for a movie, after-work drinks, or any other casual good time. She and my Reagan-Bush '84 friend, Spenser Warren, were in my apartment on one of the worst days of my life—the night Bill Buckner allowed Mookie Wilson's ground ball to dribble between his legs during the 1986 World Series.

My life-long Brockton friend Philip Tasho was back living in Washington less than a ten-minute walk away, and I integrated him into my USTR group of friends, and he introduced me to his work friends too. We saw more of each other during these years than at any time since high school. I still had buddies from my previous jobs on Capitol Hill, Reagan-Bush '84, and the Transportation and Energy Departments, but I was gradually discovering that Washington was hard on long-term friendships because people kept moving away. Almost everyone I'd hung around with in Jerry Solomon's office had left Washington by now and, even at USTR, some of the greatest sources of social entertainment were farewell parties.

And yet, still no girlfriend. I had plenty of female companionship, but ever since my Nantucket girlfriend Dale had broken up with me seven years earlier, there'd been no romantic relationships. It was inexplicable at the time, given how many women circulated through my life and the number of infatuations I experienced.

Pop psychology has dreamed up a male baby boomer condition called "Peter Pan Syndrome," which posited that men of my generation didn't want to grow up and therefore skipped noncommittally from one short-term relationship after another. I had the reverse of that. Subconsciously, I must have known that if I engaged in a noncommittal, theoretically casual relationship, I'd have trouble extricating myself without a lot of disagreeableness; consequently, before I did anything romantic, I needed to be sure.

So when my dental hygienist, an actress on the side, invited me to see her perform in *Hamlet*, I attended, complimented her backstage, but didn't suggest after-show drinks, which might have led to God knows what. Of course, it didn't help that she told me about a patient who'd dated a fellow hygienist and then done her wrong: "The next time he came in, I made sure that his three-millimeter gum gap became ten millimeters."

My female friends couldn't understand why I wasn't dating and kept suggesting matches. Desiree set me up with one of her deputies at the Department of Commerce—an attractive fellow Republican—and we went out for a five-hour tea at a fancy hotel. It was very pleasant but halfway through she announced that she had a boyfriend who made $250,000 a year. I should have been insulted by the transparent implausibility of the brush off, but I was more amused than anything that she thought she needed to head me off before I started to make assumptions. Did she think I was going to suggest that we get a room upstairs? I was way too cheap for that.

I only had three criteria for a dating partner: a personality to keep me interested; to be a nonsmoker; and to have the ability to make me feel like I could be myself when we were together. You wouldn't have thought that was a tough combination, but it was.

And then on Monday, May 23rd, 1988, Meg Ricci from the computer group called me to see if I wanted to go bike riding with her and some other USTR people that weekend.

Years after we were married, Meg and I compared notes and neither of us remembered meeting the other. USTR was just one of those places where literally everyone knew everyone else eventually. We didn't run into each other much because her fifth floor office was as far away from mine as was physically possible. Still, we were acquainted enough that when Debra went on maternity leave, I had suggested to Roger that we detail her down to our office for a couple of months to help out with the press calls.

Outspoken, opinionated, and interested in a range of topics, she had caught my eye, but I had assumed she was involved with the married, smart, cynical guy also on the fifth floor with whom she was inseparable. Untrue, I later learned. He was her "office husband" just like Lena was my "office wife."

One day when we were casually bantering in the hall, I'd hinted at a cycling interest, so it wasn't a complete shock when she invited me to join the bike party she was putting together over Memorial Day weekend. We ended up being a group of five: Meg, me, Maryanne Beatty, a secretary for the agriculture negotiator's office, Jackie Koltz, who worked with Meg in the computer group, and Warren Lavorel, our chief negotiator in the Uruguay Round of global trade talks, with the title of Ambassador. Warren was a strong, silent, guys' guy from my father's generation and a serious biker. How he and Meg developed their long-standing biking relationship was another of those USTR platonic couples mysteries.

On a beautiful Sunday in May, we all ferried to Calverton, Virginia and biked for two hours through the gorgeous, gently rolling Virginia countryside to Warrenton. After lunch, during which I drank about five ice teas, we biked back to Jackie's house where everyone except Meg hopped into the hot tub. After a backyard barbeque, Meg and Maryanne wanted to go to the movies, so we attended a 9:30pm screening of *Moonstruck*. And after *that*, we had a couple of drinks at Timberlake's, a casual restaurant in Dupont circle, where Meg, who was woke before woke was a thing, provoked a huge argument by claiming that the Boston Celtics were a racist basketball team because they had more white players than any other NBA club ("yeah, it's really racist to have Larry Bird, Kevin McHale, and Danny Ainge on your team!") When the day was over, we'd spent 16 hours together.

So began a slow, tentative courtship. Since I was still riding my clunky college bicycle and she was the expert, I asked her for help in buying a new bike. Then she invited me to go riding with her and Warren again in the Virginia countryside.

The next weekend, I flew to Atlanta to spend the weekend with Cliff and Marilyn Lorick. Cliff had been one of my best friends at Reagan-Bush '84 and his wife had worked as Alan Woods' secretary at USTR, so we'd hung out a lot before they'd moved back to Georgia. After I returned, Marilyn called to report that Maryanne Beatty had been in touch to find out what I'd said about Meg, because she really liked me. (When, much later, I told Meg this story, she said that Maryanne had done that on her own because she hadn't been thinking of me romantically then.) "You'd better be careful if you're not interested in her," Marilyn warned. It seems I had a bad reputation among the secretaries because I hadn't adequately discouraged one of their friends who had aggressively sought a relationship with me before being transferred to Geneva. That was the only time that I was aware of being desirable enough to be considered a cad.

One of the reasons that things didn't move faster between us was that in early July, I went on another long European trip with Yeutter, this time to Geneva, Brussels, Rome, and Athens. This was almost as much fun as London and Dublin, although scarier. Because terrorists had threatened Americans in Europe, the Italian security forces transported our small USTR team from meeting to meeting in a screaming, lights-blaring motorcade that raced through the Roman streets, throwing us from side to side inside the vehicles as we lurched from lane to lane. In between harrowing motorcade rides, I saw the Colosseum and the Spanish Steps and attended dinners with leading members of the Italian government, one of whom confided in me how proud he was that the American Secretary of Defense was Italian. Huh? What? Is Frank Carlucci Italian? It had never occurred to me.

In Athens, the Greek security forces took an entirely different approach to our terrorism-threatened transportation. They moved us from place to place in small nondescript vehicles, trying to make our tiny motorcade as inconspicuous as possible. Our formal meetings didn't make much of an impact— Greece was a small player in the European Community—but I loved being in Athens, which was sultry, earthy, and almost pre-modern, with street after street of small shops and cafés and almost no tall buildings. One afternoon,

Yeutter, the rest of the team, and I took a guided tour of the Acropolis and the remnants of the ancient agora that had been unearthed right under it. This is where Socrates, Plato, Pericles, and others from the classical Greek world had invented the West and I was astonished to find myself standing there.

When I returned to Washington, Meg and I resumed our relationship, which wavered between companionate friendship and burgeoning romance. One Sunday, driving her home after an afternoon of swimming at a public pool in Bethesda, the muffler fell off my car. Normally I would have been mortified by something like this, especially by the subsequent loud roaring drive to the nearest Sears auto repair shop. And yet something about being with Meg made me feel okay. She took it in stride, acted like it was no big thing, and seemed happy just to be along for the ride. If there was a pivotal moment in our relationship, this was it—even during a potentially embarrassing experience, I felt relaxed and fully able to be myself when I was with her.

The next Saturday she asked me to go with her to a farewell party for Chris Marcich, a European negotiator who was being posted to our Brussels office. Chris and his wife lived in a townhouse in Springfield, Virginia, and the guest list was an assortment of hardcore USTR staff from the Winder Building fifth floor, many of whom probably wondered what I was doing there.

We left the party at midnight, ended up in her apartment, and over the course of the next 12 hours, through a lot of verbal and some non-verbal communication, transformed our relationship into something other than platonic companionship. In an organization that produced its fair share of intra-agency romances, ours was the most improbable. I was the most adamantly conservative among all of the USTR political appointees and she was definitely not that. She'd worked at USTR since college, and was an outspoken person of the left, one of a handful of career staff who had sued the Reagan administration for requiring drug testing for all the White House employees, something else we argued about more than once.

I didn't deliberately set out to find a political sparring partner, but I got one and was impressed that she could give as good as she got. She didn't wilt or get offended when I challenged her assumptions. And unlike a lot of folks in today's Fox News/MSNBC world, we were able to look past our political differences to appreciate what we had in common, the most important of which was our shared values (which included family, generosity, honesty, humility) and interests (books, movies, politics, art, theatre, stand-up comedy). I found her terrifically funny and sometimes I made her laugh too.

Having been companions first made for an easy transition to dating. We already knew that we liked each other, so we didn't have to worry about whether this was more than a physical attraction. And it was understood almost from the beginning that this was an extremely serious thing. I can't remember when exactly she first mentioned marriage, but I had to put a six-month moratorium on that talk because I wanted to make sure there weren't any hidden incompatibilities that hadn't surfaced in the first blush of new love.

So here I was in August 1988. Life was finally great. I had it all—a good job, a great girlfriend, a nice apartment, lots of friends. Naturally, that couldn't last.

*With Meg at one last White House Christmas party
as we begin to face the future together.*

In mid-September, I heard from Jim Lake, who'd been in charge of media relations for Reagan-Bush '84, but who now ran the Washington office for a New York-based public relations company. His partner, Ken Lerer, was looking for a writer in New York. Roger and John Buckley, who'd worked for Lake during the campaign, both spoke highly of me. I knew of him not only from 1984, but because he was one of Yeutter's very good friends, and someone frequently seen squiring clients around USTR. More to the point, I'd made a mental note a year earlier when Lake's company had hired Bob Maistros—the guy who had beat me out for the speechwriting job at the Chamber of Commerce—for what was reported to be very lucrative pay.

Meg cried when I called and told her about this potential new job, claiming she hated New York. I mulled this over for a while, because I'd lost every other girlfriend I'd ever had when I moved out of their daily lives, but then she called back to say she wouldn't stand in my way if I wanted to change cities. I got Maistros on the phone in New York to get his take, which was surprisingly downbeat. "They make you write and rewrite and they never know what they want." Moreover, he was quitting the very next day. He also lobbied me to live in Jersey City if I took the job. Huh? Why would I do *that*?

I flew up to LaGuardia Airport the next Sunday and spent the day with Rich Martel who aggressively urged me to move to New York. He took me down to Greenwich Village while we window-shopped for antiques, dropped into art galleries, and generally soaked up the cool vibe. Later, he took me to dinner at Café Luxembourg, his favorite place on the West Side, to pay off the bet I'd won about the presidential primaries.

I met Ken Lerer for half an hour the next morning. He was about my age but had great, luxuriant hair. He presented as extremely unassuming, verging on being rumpled, while also exuding a low-key self-confidence that put him completely in control. His office, on the sixth floor of 90 Rockefeller Plaza, an art deco building facing Rockefeller Center, had an aquarium in the shape of an MTV logo. MTV had been a major client, my first clue that he was wired into the cutting-edge of the late 1980s business world. My second clue was learning that his biggest client was

Michael Milken, the junk bond king (er, make that the "high yield bond innovator"). Milken had recently been indicted for insider trading by Rudy Giuliani, the then-showboating U.S. Attorney, and three or four staffers worked full time on the account.

He wanted to know if I was a fast writer and seemed impressed that I had written a Presidential radio address in two hours. He didn't say so, but from the lack of probing questions, it seemed clear that he'd decided to hire me even before meeting me if I was presentable. Apparently, if Jim Lake said I was okay, then that was good enough.

Listening to him talk about his clients, I was slowly coming to grasp that, although what we did in Washington was important, New York was really driving the transformation of the country. In D.C. we could fight abstractly over plant-closing legislation all we wanted, but the actual decisions to close plants, invest in new industries, or make the economy more efficient were made in the private sector. And Ken was at the center of all that as a quiet, nearly invisible, CEO-whisperer.

His partner Linda Robinson made even less of an effort to find out if I were qualified. More intense than Ken, she didn't bother questioning me when we met. Instead, I was to ask her anything I wanted to know. "Be as blunt as you want." I had half-toyed with the idea of confessing that two years earlier I'd spent an hour with her husband, Mr. American Express, eating shrimp in her living room, but quickly abandoned any thoughts of banter as her eyes bored in on me. I could barely think of anything to ask and the meeting ended quickly. This was probably just as well with her because she was deeply involved in the most high-profile business story of the time—the battle to take over RJR Nabisco (later immortalized in the book and HBO movie *Barbarians at the Gate*, where she was portrayed by the actress Joanna Cassidy)—and had other things on her mind.

Ken told me to think about whether I wanted to work for them, and when I left New York, I knew that the company then known as Robinson, Lake, Lerer & Montgomery was my future. Roger had made an interesting point even before I went for the interview: "The idea of working for a PR company seems boring after working here at USTR, but when I open the newspaper,

I see their clients everywhere." If I took the job, I'd have a ring-side seat for many of the profound changes taking place in the American economy.

Nevertheless, it took a month to iron everything out. When Maistros landed there two years earlier, I had been led to believe through word of mouth that the salaries were more generous than they actually were. Perhaps sensing my disappointment over pay, Ken had me return for a second interview in October before raising the offer by $5,000 a year, which probably, to be honest, came out of my bonus.

These delays were fine with me because it gave me extra time to wrap my head around my new fate. Perhaps even more important, it gave Meg a chance to reconcile herself to the idea that I'd be living in Manhattan and that this might be her future too.

Rich Martel, thrilled that we'd be living in the same city again for the first time since we were teenagers, scouted apartments for me, and Meg and I drove up to check them out one rainy Friday. We looked at three places. Two were terrible and one was acceptable: a one bedroom with a private backyard on West 80th Street, around the corner from the Natural History Museum. The rent was $1,200 a month and I snapped it up.

That last month in Washington seemed like a blur. Work never let up a bit, although I had to formally recuse myself from anything to do with Jim Lake's clients, which wasn't all that easy. I needed to pack, put my apartment on the market, and clean up loose ends at the office. Somehow, Roger had already found my replacement—Cary Walker, who coincidentally, had also worked for Jim Robinson in California. I had to train him and hand off my portfolio of projects.

Every departing USTR employee eventually goes through the ritual of a farewell party and I was no exception. I was touched that both my former officemates, Desiree and Debra, returned to say goodbye, as did several former interns and all five fact-checkers from the White House speechwriters office. There were quite a few reporters too, ranging from a guy from the Japanese wire service Jiji Press, who arrived uninvited with five boxes of chicken McNuggets, to the *Wall Street Journal*'s Walt Mossberg, who semi-ironically gave me a set of Red Sox pens, since we'd bonded over our shared pain of being long-suffering fans.

With Yeutter and Roger at my farewell party.

Roger delivered some generous remarks and Kelly read two parody press releases written by Chip Roh, a USTR lawyer who worked on Canadian issues. I tried to be both heartfelt and amusing in my own response without being maudlin or corny. (Sample joke: "If Chip Roh spent less time working on joke press releases and more time on the U.S.-Canada Free Trade Area, the Mulroney government might not be in danger of falling right now.")

I did manage to get off one legitimately funny line. I pulled out my prepared remarks and said, "I actually wrote a little speech, but I don't think I'll give it now." When everyone said, "No read it, read it," I shot back, "I've been writing speeches here for three and a half years and no one has ever delivered anything I've written. So why start now." Even Yeutter laughed at that one.

Two days later, Friday, November 4th, 1988 was my last day at the office. Roger took me to lunch at the White House Mess and we were sentimental for a few minutes, but only a few. And then true to form, I went back to my office and let myself get seriously annoyed one last time by a botched media announcement. At Yeutter's request, I had written a strong statement protesting European subsidies of the Airbus jetliners. USTR's Airbus point person had shared it with the State Department and they got the White House and Treasury Department involved. Over the course of the day, it got progressively watered down and didn't go out until 6:00pm—so late that no one in the media was interested in it. You'd have thought I would have gained some perspective about these things, but I was aggravated up until the very last minute.

The next week, Meg helped me move to New York. Before he would give me the keys to the apartment, the owner told me I now had to work through a hitherto unmentioned real estate agent, who would help me with all the details of moving in. Oh, and the standard fee for a real estate agent, even one who had done nothing to help me find the apartment, was one month's rent. Welcome to New York.

After all the excitement of deciding whether to uproot my life, I was depressed at the actuality of it. The apartment was smaller than I remembered. You could hear people talking in the adjoining unit. The phone jack was broken, there was no mailbox key or gas for the stove, and every little fix that the owner had promised to do—such as painting the heater cover—remained undone.

But at 5:30pm, Rich showed up with a huge welcome-to-New-York basket, filled with books and magazines about New York, a subway map, and breakfast for the next morning. He helped me assemble my Ikea wardrobe and generally raised my level of excitement about living in the best city in the world.

The next day was Philip's 34th birthday, so he came up to spend the weekend with us. We walked over to Zabar's, the famous West Side deli emporium, to buy several containers of semi-exotic food which we ate with a bottle of champagne when Rich arrived later that night. So there I was with my two best friends from elementary school and my future wife, celebrating my new life, laughing about the pitfalls of renting apartments, listening to Rich's stories about filming a Pepsi ad in the USSR, and wishing that Miss Bond, that scourge of third grade, could see us now, all grown up and well on our way to conquering the world.

I'd fulfilled my childhood dream of working in Washington. But as usual, I had no idea what was to come next. I was too self-absorbed then to realize that I'd been fortunate every step of the way on the journey that had led me to this night with three of the people I was closest to in the world. None of us even thought of this as a special evening—the next day would arrive soon and I had more unpacking to do and a job to start. It was only in hindsight that I was able to see that on this weekend, one door closed and another opened. I was ready for the second half of my life to begin.

CPSIA information can be obtained
at www.ICGtesting.com
Printed in the USA
BVHW041501161021
618999BV00004B/13